D0075080

SANITATION, LATRINES AND INTESTINAL PARASITES IN PAST POPULATIONS

Sanitation, Latrines and Intestinal Parasites in Past Populations

Edited by

PIERS D. MITCHELL
University of Cambridge, UK

ASHGATE

Published by
Ashgate Publishing Limited
Wey Court East
Union Road
Farnham
Surrey, GU9 7PT
England

Ashgate Publishing Company
110 Cherry Street
Suite 3-1
Burlington, VT 05401-3818
USA

www.ashgate.com

British Library Cataloguing in Publication Data
A catalogue record for this book is available from the British Library

The Library of Congress has cataloged the printed edition as follows:
Sanitation, Latrines and Intestinal Parasites in Past Populations /
    edited by Piers D. Mitchell.
        p. ;   cm.
    Includes bibliographical references and index.
    I. Mitchell, Piers D. [DNLM: 1. Intestinal Diseases, Parasitic – prevention & control.
    2. Sanitation – history. 3. Toilet Facilities – history. WA 11.1]
    RA607
    363.72'94–dc23   2014029258

ISBN   9781472449078 (hbk)
ISBN   9781472449085 (ebk-PDF)
ISBN   9781472449092 (ebk-ePUB)

Printed in the United Kingdom by Henry Ling Limited,
at the Dorset Press, Dorchester, DT1 1HD

Contents

List of Figures

List of Tables

List of Contributors

Evilena Anastasiou, Department of Archaeology and Anthropology, University of Cambridge, UK.

Andreas Angelakis, Institute of Iraklion, National Foundation for Agricultural Research (NAGREF), 71307 Iraklion, Greece.

Georgios Antoniou, Deinokratous 73, 11521 Athens, Greece.

Adauto Araújo, Fundação Oswaldo Cruz, Escola Nacional de Saúde Pública Sergio Arouca, Rio de Janeiro, Brazil.

Françoise Bouchet, Faculty of Pharmacy, University of Reims Champagne-Ardenne, EA 3795 GEGENA, Reims, France.

Sheila Maria Mendonça de Souza, Fundação Oswaldo Cruz, Escola Nacional de Saúde Pública Sergio Arouca, Rio de Janeiro, Brazil.

Juliana Dutra, Fundação Oswaldo Cruz, Escola Nacional de Saúde Pública Sergio Arouca, Rio de Janeiro, Brazil.

Luiz Fernando Ferreira, Fundação Oswaldo Cruz, Escola Nacional de Saúde Pública Sergio Arouca, Rio de Janeiro, Brazil.

Martin Fugassa, CONICET, Universidad Nacional de Mar del Plata, Argentina.

Allan Hall, Department of Archaeology, University of York, UK.

Alena Iñiguez, Instituto Oswaldo Cruz, Rio de Janeiro, Brazil.

Harry Kenward, Department of Archaeology, University of York, UK.

Matthieu Le Bailly, CNRS UMR Chrono-environment, Faculty of Sciences and Techniques, University of Franche-Comté, Besançon, France.

Daniela Leles, Universidade Federal Fluminense, MIP-UFF, Departamento de Microbiologia e Parasitologia, Instituto Biomédico, Niterói, Rio de Janeiro, Brasil .

Augusta McMahon, Department of Archaeology and Anthropology, University of Cambridge, UK.

Piers Mitchell, Department of Archaeology and Anthropology, University of Cambridge, UK.

Karl Reinhard, School of Natural Resources, University of Nebraska, Lincoln, USA.

Min Seo, Department of Parasitology, Dankook University College of Medicine, South Korea.

Dong Hoon Shin, Institute of Forensic Science, Seoul National University College of Medicine, South Korea.

Luciana Sianto, Fundação Oswaldo Cruz, Escola Nacional de Saúde Pública Sergio Arouca, Rio de Janeiro, Brazil.

Craig Taylor, Department of Humanities, MacEwan University, Edmonton, Canada.

Chapter 1

Why We Need to Know About Sanitation in the Past

Piers D. Mitchell

Sanitation describes the disposal of human faeces and urine, wastewater and rubbish in order to maintain hygienic conditions. This is known to be a key factor in optimising health in poorly developed parts of the world today.[1] Millions of children die every year from diarrhoeal illness and many adults suffer malnutrition and chronic ill health from parasites caught due to poor sanitation.[2] Latrines are one of the cornerstones of effective sanitation, as they help to physically separate people from their urine and faecal waste. They also provide a place for such waste to decompose, which tends to kill off those viral, bacterial and parasitic diseases that can be spread by urine and faeces. Those of us interested in how our ancestors lived, and what their lives were like, quite reasonably assume that similar diseases may have afflicted people living long ago. However, surprisingly little research has been undertaken to investigate the big questions such as how did sanitation change as early populations changed their lifestyles from hunter-gatherers to city dwellers, and what impact did those sanitation technologies have upon their health?

This book aims for the first time to tackle the issue by bringing together research from archaeologists, historians and paleoparasitologists. It does so by focusing on three key areas through which past hygiene can be evaluated, namely evidence for sanitation and waste disposal, the technologies such as latrines that were developed to facilitate sanitation, and the diseases such as intestinal parasites that can be spread by poor sanitation. The manner in which these three areas are interlinked is the cornerstone for the book, and explains why it is so important that

---

[1]   Kariuki, J.G., Magambo, K.J., Njeruh, M.F., Muchiri, E.M., Nzioka, S.M., Kariuki, S., 'Effects of hygiene and sanitation interventions on reducing diarrhoea prevalence among children in resource constrained communities: case study of Turkana District, Kenya', *Journal of Community Health* 37 (2012): 1178–84; Kumar, S., Vollmer, S., 'Does access to improved sanitation reduce childhood diarrhoea in rural India?', *Health Economics* 22 (2013): 410–27.

[2]   Halpenny, C.M., Kosi, K.G., Valdés, V.E., Scott, M.E., 'Prediction of child health by household density and asset-based indices in impoverished indigenous villages in rural Panama', *American Journal of Tropical Medicine and Hygiene* 86 (2012): 280–91; Ngui, R., Lim, Y.A., Chong Kin, L., Sek Chuen, C., Jaffar, S., 'Association between anaemia, iron deficiency anaemia, neglected parasitic infections and socioeconomic factors in rural children of West Malaysia', *PLoS Neglected Tropical Diseases* 6 (2012): e1550.

they are considered in one place. We cannot hope to understand intestinal diseases in past populations if we do not also investigate their approaches to sanitation. Changes in waste disposal technologies such as cesspools, flushing latrines, drains and hand washing have limited meaning without our interpreting the consequences for the lives of those who developed those technologies.

However, the reason that this has not been done before is that certain elements in this process are extremely hard to evaluate. While past public health can be studied using written sources from suitable populations,[3] this is clearly not possible for prehistoric populations who lived before the invention of writing. For example, in these populations we cannot know why a sanitation technology such as the latrine was first developed, we can only note the date the first toilets appear and how they were built. In consequence, we can only speculate as to whether latrines were first developed to reduce smells in the home, cut down on flies, remove the need to walk to the town rubbish tip with a pot of faeces each day, or prevent diseases that could be spread by living with faeces around the living space. Another challenge faces those studying past health from human remains, as analysing the skeletons of those who died in the past cannot reliably tell us much about how sanitation affected health. However, by using modern clinical research on sanitation from the developing world we can employ theoretical modelling to estimate how different lifestyles (such as hunter-gathering, farming crops, herding animals and living in early cities) and the invention of sanitation technologies may have resulted in changes to health.[4]

Some of those sanitation technologies are then discussed with articles on toilets and waste management in early Mesopotamia,[5] and latrines in the classical Greek and Roman world.[6] Complementing a recent volume on Roman toilets,[7] the manner in which large cities such as ancient Rome and medieval London dealt with sanitation is explored.[8] The systematic study of sanitation in York over nearly two thousand years spanning Romans, Vikings, and medieval and Victorian inhabitants is a classic example of what such analysis can tell us about changing sanitation in past population centres.[9] These studies bring together considerable evidence for sanitation in different past civilisations, and help to demonstrate how they have evolved over time. The contrasting geographic, social and cultural environments of the ancient Near East, the classical Greek and Roman worlds, and medieval Britain can show how people facing the same challenges regarding

---

[3]   Rawcliffe, C., *Urban Bodies: Communal Health in Late Medieval English Towns and Cities* (Woodbridge: Boydell & Brewer, 2013).

[4]   Mitchell, this volume, Ch. 2, pp. 5–17.

[5]   McMahon, this volume, Ch. 3, pp. 19–39.

[6]   Antoniou and Angelaki, this volume, Ch. 4, pp. 41–67.

[7]   Jansen, G.C.M., Koloski-Ostrow, A.O., Moormann, E.M. (eds), *Roman Toilets: Their Archaeology and Cultural History* (Leuven: Peeters, 2011).

[8]   Taylor, this volume, Ch. 5, pp. 69–97.

[9]   Hall and Kenward, this volume, Ch. 6, pp. 99–119.

sanitation may respond in quite different ways, and accept varying degrees of technology to attain a level of hygiene which they presumably found acceptable.

Parasites can be described as infectious diseases that live on or in another species (their host) while contributing nothing to the survival of that host. Viruses, bacteria and prions are generally not classed as parasites although they do also meet this description. Parasites may be single-celled organisms (such as those that cause malaria or amoebic dysentery) or large multicellular intestinal worms many feet long. A number of intestinal parasites are spread as a direct consequence of suboptimal sanitation, so the surviving eggs of these parasites can act as an indicator of sanitation. Ancient parasites can be detected in latrines, coprolites (preserved faeces) and soil taken at excavation from the pelvic area of burials, where the intestines would have been located during life. One very useful edited book in Portuguese that complements this volume includes papers on infectious disease and parasites in the past.[10] However, the coverage of ancient parasite research today is not perfect as certain parts of the world have never undergone study (including much of Africa, Australasia and Oceania) and early time periods are less well understood due to the difficulty obtaining samples. Nevertheless, overviews of the parasites found in Africa and the Middle East,[11] Asia[12] the Americas,[13] and Europe,[14] provide a fascinating picture of how parasites came to infect humans, how certain parasites are only found in certain regions of the world, and how different parasites may have become more or less common over time. The analysis of the evidence for Entamoeba dysentery in the past[15] shows how considering all the evidence for one species can allow the construction of a hypothesis as to where the disease originated.

This book does not aim to provide all the evidence for sanitation in different regions of the world, nor can it cover all time periods. While the parasite papers do cover large geographic areas, the archaeological and text based articles on sanitation and latrines will by definition focus on a particular region, culture, or group writing in the same language. Nevertheless, these studies do help to show the variety in sanitation practices in different regions, highlighting that we have to be very cautious when trying to extrapolate findings from one area of the world to another until local evidence is identified. It will be many decades before such a comprehensive knowledge base is formed, from the study of ancient manuscripts in libraries, excavation of sewers and latrines, and the application of paleoparasitological analysis at new excavation sites.

---

[10] Ferreira, L.F., Reinhard, K.J., Araújo, A. (eds), *Fundamentos da Paleoparasitologia* (Rio de Janeiro: Editora Fiocruz, 2011).

[11] Anastasiou and Mitchell, this volume, Ch. 7, pp. 121–41.

[12] Seo and Shin, this volume, Ch. 8, pp. 149–64.

[13] Araujo et al., this volume, Ch. 9, pp. 165–202.

[14] Anastasiou, this volume, Ch. 10, pp. 203–217.

[15] Le Bailly and Bouchet, this volume, Ch. 11, pp. 219–228.

In the meantime, this volume does advance the field considerably as the first book to investigate the topic of past sanitation and health using examples from around the world, from a broad range of time periods, taking the perspective of the archaeologist, historian and parasitologist. Within it can be found a number of fascinating hypotheses that lay the foundation for that further work. The key questions we would all like to have answered are how did sanitation change as early populations changed their lifestyles from hunter-gatherers to city dwellers, and what impact did their sanitation technologies have upon their health? Those reading this book will know the latest evidence available, which will help them to make up their own mind.

Chapter 2

Assessing the Impact of Sanitation upon Health in Early Human Populations from Hunter-gatherers to Ancient Civilisations, Using Theoretical Modelling

Piers D. Mitchell

Introduction

The quest to understand the health of our ancestors fascinates many of us. We can only wonder what it might really have been like to live as an early human who hunted and gathered for their food, or a prehistoric farmer who scattered the remains of last year's grains upon the ground in the spring. It might seem obvious that life was precarious and disease might cause serious illness or death at any time. However, recent investigation of past health is starting to enable us to bring some scientific evidence to bear upon what diseases affected past populations, and what they may have done to avoid becoming ill. One of the key areas that seems to have impacted upon health in the past is sanitation, or the lack of it.

A number of key steps have been noted in the cultural evolution of anatomically modern humans.[1] It would be of great interest if we could determine what role the major steps in human evolution may have had upon health. There is likely to have been a clear advantage to those who chose to change their lifestyle, or they would not have done it. Human population size certainly seems to have increased significantly with these steps, so from a Darwinian perspective, the steps seem to have been effective for our species.[2]

The earliest anatomically modern humans appear to have been hunter-gatherers who evolved from earlier hominins living in Africa somewhere around 150–100,000 years before present (BP). Some groups then left Africa and migrated to the Middle East around 60,000 BP. They seem to have reached Asia by 50–60,000 BP, Australasia 40–50,000 BP, Europe 30–40,000 BP, and the

---

[1] Boyd, R., Silk, J.B., *How Humans Evolved*, 3rd edition, (New York: W.W. Norton, 2003); Pasternak, C. (ed.), *What Makes Us Human?* (Oxford: Oneworld, 2007); Holmes, T., *Early Humans: the Pleistocene and Holocene Epochs* (New York: Chelsea House, 2009).

[2] Darwin, C., *On the Origin of Species by Means of Natural Selection, or the Preservation of Favoured Races in the Struggle for Life* (London: John Murray, 1859).

Americas by 15–35,000 BP.[3] Agriculture seems to have developed spontaneously among populations in different parts of the world. In the Middle East wheat was cultivated from 12,000 BP, in China rice was cultivated by 10,000 BP, and in central America maize was in cultivation by 6,000 BP.[4] Cattle were domesticated in the Middle East by 7,500 BP.[5] With the need to look after crops came the need to settle in the same location, at least until the crops could be harvested. This must have necessitated more permanent structures in which to live, and so settlements appeared. Being able to grow crops was a more efficient use of land and of effort than hunting, so the populations in these settlements could grow.

In time we see the introduction in these towns of basic technology for water collection and storage, and sanitation. In an archaeological setting we may well be missing the earliest examples of sanitation technology if they were made of perishable materials. However, the presence of stone built water tanks, irrigation channels and latrine seats several thousand years ago strongly suggests that people of the time perceived water and sanitation to have been important.[6]

However, we remain ignorant as to what impact sanitation might have had upon the health of past populations. It is possible that they developed water storage facilities to prevent thirst, irrigation to improve crop yield, and latrines to improve smells, without having any concept that it might improve their health. In cultures before the development of writing, we can never really know of attitudes to health in such populations. Once writing was commonplace, written texts can be used to assess attitudes to sanitation and estimate how widespread it may have been.[7] We must always bear in mind that the use of ancient written sources to compile epidemiological data in order to assess past health is a complex process that can often be unrepresentative and so not truly reflect the past environment.[8]

The aim of this paper is to investigate to what degree these technological developments in sanitation and latrines may have had an impact upon the health of early human populations. We will compare what differences there may have been between mobile hunter-gatherers, sedentary agricultural farmers, pastoralists herding animals, and the later city dwellers of ancient civilisations. The topic will

---

[3]   Stone, L., Lurquin, P.F. (eds), *Genes, Culture and Human Evolution: a Synthesis* (Oxford: Blackwell, 2007); Pasternak 2007; Holmes 2009.

[4]   Harris, D.R. (ed.), *The Origins and Spread of Agriculture and Pastoralism in Eurasia: Crops, Fields, Flocks and Herds* (London: UCL Press, 1996); Johannessen, S., Hastorf, C.A. (eds), *Corn and Culture in the Prehistoric New World* (Boulder, Colorado: Westview Press, 1994).

[5]   Taylor, T., *The Artificial Ape: How Technology Changed the Course of Human Evolution* (New York: Palgrave Macmillan, 2010).

[6]   Rodda, J.C., Ubertinin, L. (eds), *The Basis of Civilization: Water Science?* (Wallingford: International Association of Hydrological Science, 2004).

[7]   Scobie, A., 'Slums, Sanitation and Mortality', *Klio* 68 (1986): 399–433.

[8]   Mitchell, P.D., 'Retrospective diagnosis, and the use of historical texts for investigating disease in the past', *International Journal of Paleopathology* 1 (2011): 81–88.

be investigated from a number of different approaches in order to determine which may be the most reliable for estimating past health.

Archaeological Evidence for Health in Past Populations

So long as we are studying a time period from which human skeletal remains survive well, it can be relatively easy to look at the skeleton of someone who died in the past and find evidence for diseases that affect bone (paleopathology). This allows us to determine whether those conditions were present in a past population. In this way a paleopathologist can identify congenital malformations, fractures, arthritis, and infections involving bone such as osteomyelitis, leprosy, tuberculosis, and treponemal diseases such as syphilis.[9] However, this can be a much more challenging process for people who died many thousands of years ago, whose bones may be highly fragmentary and poorly preserved. It can also be quite difficult to estimate how common certain infectious diseases were in these populations as only a proportion of those with leprosy, TB or syphilis ever develop any bone changes.

It is not easy to detect diseases that do not affect bones and just affect the soft tissues, as these generally decompose in the ground after death. Sometimes we are lucky enough to have mummies with soft tissues preserved which allow evaluation of the whole body for disease. Mummies may be artificially preserved as part of burial ritual (such as in ancient Egypt), or naturally dried, frozen or pickled in an acid peat bog.[10] When mummies are not available we may be able to extract the biomolecules (such as DNA) of infectious diseases from the teeth or bone of ancient skeletons and this can start to tell us how many individuals may have contracted a particular infectious disease, although not necessarily how many actually died from it.[11] However, DNA degrades over time so it may appear that

---

[9]   Roberts, C., Manchester, K., *The Archaeology of Disease* (Stroud: Sutton Publishing, 2005); Waldron, T., *Palaeopathology* (Cambridge: Cambridge University Press, 2009); Grauer, A. (ed.), *A Companion to Paleopathology* (Chichester: Wiley-Blackwell, 2012).

[10]   Cockburn, A., Cockburn, E., Reyman, T.A., *Mummies, Disease and Ancient Cultures*, 2nd edition, (Cambridge: Cambridge University Press, 1998); Aufderheide, A.C., *The Scientific Study of Mummies* (Cambridge: Cambridge University Press, 2003); Taylor, J.H., *Egyptian Mummies* (London: British Museum, 2010).

[11]   Fletcher, H.A., Donoghue, H.D., Holton, J., Pap, I., Spigelman, M., 'Widespread occurrence of Mycobacterium tuberculosis DNA from 18th–19th century Hungarians', *American Journal of Physical Anthropology* 201 (2003): 144–52; Zink, A.R., Grabner, W., Reischl, U., Wolf, H., Nerlich, A.G., 'Molecular study on human tuberculosis in three geographically distinct and time delineated populations from ancient Egypt', *Epidemiology and Infection* 130 (2003): 239–49.

fewer people suffered with an infectious disease in early populations just because the DNA has not survived as well as if they were from a more recent population.[12]

The remains of human faecal material can provide evidence for gastrointestinal diseases. In early time periods we have to rely upon coprolites (dried or mineralised faeces) or soil samples taken from the pelvic area of burials, where the intestines would have been as they decomposed.[13] Once sanitation technologies such as cesspools and latrines had been invented, soil from these facilities can also be analysed.[14] Microscopy can demonstrate the eggs of intestinal parasitic worms as they are fairly resistant to the process of decomposition that originally skeletonised the burial. Biomolecular techniques such as enzyme-linked immunosorbent assay (ELISA) can be helpful in detecting the organisms that cause dysentery.[15] Such parasite analysis does provide evidence for changes in gastrointestinal disease over the same time periods when population density and sanitation appear to have changed. For example, the eggs of intestinal parasites such as pinworm (*Enterobius vermicularis*) were less frequently found in the coprolites of hunter-gatherers living in small groups than was the case in later herders and farmers growing maize in both North and South America.[16] However, there are no comparable

---

[12]   Pääbo, S., Poinar, H., Serre, D., Jaenicke-Després,V., Hebler, J., Rohland, N., Kuch, M., Krause, J., Vigilant, L., Hofreiter, M., 'Genetic analyses from ancient DNA', *Annual Review of Genetics* 38 (2004): 645–79; Anastasiou, E., Mitchell, P.D., 'Paleopathology and genes: investigating the genetics of infectious diseases in excavated human skeletal remains and mummies from past populations', *Gene* 828 (2013): 33–40.

[13]   Araújo, A., Reinhard, K., Ferreira, L.F., 'Parasite findings in archaeological remains: diagnosis and interpretation', *Quaternary International* 180 (2008): 1–4; Bouchet, F., Harter, S., Le Bailly, M., 'The state of the art of paleoparasitological research in the Old World', *Memórias do Instituto Oswaldo Cruz* 98 (Suppl. 1) (2003): 95–101; Reinhard, K.J., 'Archaeoparasitology in North America', *American Journal of Physical Anthropology* 82 (1990): 145–63.

[14]   Mitchell, P.D., Tepper, Y., 'Intestinal parasitic worm eggs from a crusader period cesspool in the city of Acre (Israel)', *Levant* 39 (2007): 91–5; Mitchell, P.D., Huntley, J., Sterns, E., 'Bioarchaeological analysis of the 13th century latrines of the crusader hospital of St. John at Acre, Israel', in V. Mallia-Milanes (ed.), *The Military Orders: volume 3. Their History and Heritage* (Aldershot: Ashgate, 2008), p.213–23; Mitchell, P.D., Anastasiou, E., Syon, D., 'Human intestinal parasites in crusader Acre: evidence for migration with disease in the medieval period', *International Journal of Paleopathology* 1 (2011): 132–137.

[15]   Gonçalves, M.L., da Silva, V.L., de Andrade, C.M., Reinhard, K., da Rocha, G.C., Le Bailly, M., Bouchet, F., Ferreira, L.F., Araújo, A., 'Amoebiasis distribution in the past: first steps using an immunoassay technique', *Transactions of the Royal Society of Tropical Medicine and Hygiene* 98 (2004): 88–91; Le Bailly, M., Bouchet, F., 'Paléoparasitologie et immunologie : l'exemple d'*Entamoeba histolytica*', *Archéosciences* 30 (2006): 129–135; Mitchell, P.D., Stern, E., Tepper, Y., 'Dysentery in the crusader kingdom of Jerusalem: an ELISA analysis of two medieval latrines in the city of Acre (Israel)', *Journal of Archaeological Science* 35 (2008): 1849–53.

[16]   Reinhard, K.J., 'Cultural ecology of prehistoric parasitism on the Colorado Plateau as evidenced by coprology', *American Journal of Physical Anthropology* 77 (1988):

studies that have investigated changes in parasite prevalence in populations before and after the introduction of latrines.

What is perhaps most challenging is to determine the standard of health of a past population and to compare health in different populations. Ironically, this is what many people are most interested in, and many papers have been published attempting to make such comparisons.[17] We will only need to mention a few of the key difficulties here. One key challenge is that it can be very hard to determine life expectancy in past populations based upon human skeletal remains. While it is relatively easy to determine age from the bones of children as they are still growing, in adulthood growth stops and age estimation is much less accurate.[18] If we cannot determine the age at death in adults very accurately from human skeletal remains, we cannot reliably use apparent differences in life expectancy to argue that one population may have been healthier than another.

A further challenge is that the number and severity of pathological lesions on excavated bone does not equate in a simple manner to the health of an individual during their life either. It might seem logical that skeletons with lots of pathological lesions indicate more illness during life than skeletons with no such lesions, but this is not the case. This concept is known as the osteological paradox.[19] For example, if a frail individual dies quickly from a disease they will have no lesions from that disease on their bones. They die young with a pristine skeleton. A stronger individual who becomes ill but survives the same illness and dies some years later from something else may well have lesions from the earlier illness on their bones. In this example, the individual with the lesions on their skeleton was actually the healthier one during their lifetime. The healthiest individual is the one who never becomes sick from the original illness and dies old, again without any pathological lesions. However, since we cannot determine the age at death in adults very accurately, we often cannot distinguish the two groups (very frail

---

355–66; Ferreira, L.F., Araújo, A., Confalonieri, U., Nuñez, L., 'Infecção por *Enterobius vermicularis* em populações agro-pastoris pré-colombianas de San Pedro de Atacama, Chile', *Memórias do Instituto Oswaldo Cruz* 84 (suppl. 4) (1989): 197–99.

[17] Steckel, R.H., Rose, J.C., Larsen, C.S., Walker, P.L., 'Skeletal health in the western hemisphere from 4000 B.C. to the present', *Evolutionary Anthropology* 11(4) (2002): 142–55; Eshed, V., Gopher, A., Gage, T.B., Hershkovitz, I., 'Has the transition to agriculture reshaped the demographic structure of prehistoric populations? New evidence from the Levant', *American Journal of Physical Anthropology* 124 (2004): 315–29; Slaus, M., 'Osteological and dental markers of health in the transition from the Late Antique to the early medieval period in Croatia', *American Journal of Physical Anthropology* 136 (2008): 455–69.

[18] Milner, G.R., Boldsen, J.L., 'Estimating age and sex from a skeleton, a paleopathological perspective', in A. Grauer (ed.), *A Companion to Paleopathology* (Chichester: Wiley-Blackwell, 2012), pp. 268–84.

[19] Wood, J.W., Milner, G.R., Harpending, H.C., Weiss, K.M., 'The osteological paradox: problems of inferring prehistoric health from skeletal samples', *Current Anthropology* 33 (1992): 343–58.

and very robust) that had no skeletal lesions. When we factor in other challenges such as not knowing if migration into and out of the group is occurring, and what the fertility rate is (as this affects the statistics further) we can see that attempting to compare general standard of health in two populations from human skeletal remains alone is really difficult.[20]

We have seen that archaeology can tell us when sanitation technology was developed, and coprolites can show how the prevalence and type of certain intestinal parasites may vary in different populations. However, we can also see that it is not so easy to tell using archaeological methods whether the overall standard of health of a population was altered as a result of the development of sanitation technology. Perhaps we need to look at this in another way. If, in modern clinical studies, we could determine the effect of different aspects of sanitation upon human health, we could use theoretical modelling to estimate potential impact in the past.

Modern Clinical Evidence for the Effects of Sanitation upon Health

A large number of studies have been undertaken in order to investigate the effects of sanitation upon health. The principal diseases that are associated with poor sanitation are those of the gastrointestinal tract. These range from acute bacterial and viral infections that cause diarrhoea and/or vomiting, to chronic parasitic illness with worms that may live in the intestines for many years. What all these diseases share in common is that they impair the ability of the intestines to function normally. Acute diarrhoea and vomiting kills large numbers of young children each year in the developing world due to loss of water and salts from the body.[21] In contrast, infestation with parasitic intestinal worms causes chronic malnutrition in those children with poor diet, as the worms get to absorb the nutrients before the child can. This leads to anaemia, stunted growth, impaired intelligence and developmental delay in children.[22] Clinical research has highlighted a number of important factors that influence human health, and I have grouped them into seven areas.

---

[20]   Wood et al. 1992.

[21]   Kariuki, J.G., Magambo, K.J., Njeruh, M.F., Muchiri, E.M., Nzioka, S.M., Kariuki, S., 'Effects of hygiene and sanitation interventions on reducing diarrhoea prevalence among children in resource constrained communities: case study of Turkana District, Kenya', *Journal of Community Health* 37 (2012): 1178–84; Kumar, S., Vollmer, S., 'Does access to improved sanitation reduce childhood diarrhoea in rural India?', *Health Economics* 22 (2013): 410–27.

[22]   Halpenny, C.M., Kosi, K.G., Valdés, V.E., Scott, M.E., 'Prediction of child health by household density and asset-based indices in impoverished indigenous villages in rural Panama', *American Journal of Tropical Medicine and Hygiene* 86 (2012): 280–91; Ngui, R., Lim, Y.A., Chong Kin, L., Sek Chuen, C., Jaffar, S., 'Association between anaemia, iron deficiency anaemia, neglected parasitic infections and socioeconomic factors in rural children of West Malaysia', *PLoS Neglected Tropical Diseases* 6 (2012): e1550.

Clean Drinking Water

Piped water free from contamination has been shown to reduce the incidence of diarrhoea in young children.[23] People who do not have clean drinking water supplies have been shown to have a higher risk of intestinal parasites than those with access to clean water.[24] In tropical countries domestic rainwater collection and storage results in significantly less diarrhoea than if communal water supplies are used for drinking.[25] People who have clean water piped to their homes, so that they do not have to wade into the communal fresh water supply to obtain drinking water or to wash, are much less likely to contract the parasitic worms that cause schistosomiasis and dracunculiasis than those who do enter the water.[26]

Clean Hands

Hand washing with soap has been shown to significantly reduce the risk of contracting infections that cause diarrhoea and vomiting, as well as faecal oral parasitic worms such as roundworm and whipworm.[27]

Latrines

The safe disposal of human faeces and urine in toilets has been shown to significantly reduce the risk of contracting both diarrhoea and soil-transmitted helminths. Diarrhoea in young children is more common in families without a latrine than in those who did use one, and death in young children from diarrhoea is

---

[23]   Capuno, J.J., Tan, C.A., Fabella, V.M., 'Do piped water and flush toilets prevent child diarrhoea in rural Philippines?', *Asia Pacific Journal of Public Health* 11 (2011): doi: 10.1177/1010539511430996; Thiem, V.D., Schmidt, W.P., Suziki, M., Tho, L.H., Yanai, H., Ariyoshi, K., Anh, D.D., Yoshida, L.M., 'Animal livestock and the risk of hospitalised diarrhoea in children under 5 years in Vietnam', *Tropical Medicine and International Health* 17 (2012): 613–21.

[24]   Esry, S.A., Potash, J.B., Roberts, L., Shiff, C., 'Effects of improved water supply and sanitation on ascariasis, diarrhoea, dracunculiasis, hookworm infection, schistosomiasis, and trachoma', *Bulletin of the World Health Organisation* 69 (1991): 609–21; Ngui, R., Ishak, S., Chuen, C.S., Mahmud, R., Lim, Y.A., 'Prevalence and risk factors of intestinal parasitism in rural and remote West Malaysia', *PLoS Neglected Tropical Diseases* 5 (2011): e974.

[25]   Fry, L.M., Cowden, J.R., Watkins, D.W., Clasen, T., Mihelcic, J.R., 'Quantifying health improvements from water quantity enhancement: an engineering perspective applied to rainwater harvesting in West Africa', *Environmental Science and Technology* 44 (2010): 9535–41.

[26]   Esry et al. 1991.

[27]   Cairncross, S., Hunt, C., Boisson, S., Bostoen, K., Curtis, V., Fung, I.C., Schmidt, W.P., 'Water, sanitation and hygiene for the prevention of diarrhoea', *International Journal of Epidemiology* 39 Suppl. 1 (2010): i193–205; Halpenny et al. 2012.

lower in families with a latrine than those without.[28] Hookworm (*Ankylostoma sp.* and *Necator sp.*) is transmitted by its larval form burrowing through the skin of the foot as someone squats to defecate on an area of soil previously used for defecation by others. If faeces are deposited deep in a latrine and not onto the ground, then parasite larvae and feet are kept separate. Roundworm (*Ascaris lumbricoides*) and whipworm (*Trichuris trichiura*) are spread by the faecal contamination of food, drinking water, or hands used to prepare or consume food. The prevalence of these species has also been shown to be significantly reduced when toilets are introduced.[29] For similar reasons, it has been shown that families in houses with sewers have a significantly reduced risk of diarrhoea compared with families in houses without sewers.[30] Adequate sanitation and clean water has been shown to significantly improve growth in young children compared with those with poor sanitation and contaminated water, where stunted growth is common.[31]

Human Faeces as Fertiliser

Faecal material is a very effective fertiliser that improves crop yields.[32] However, using fresh human faeces as fertiliser does lead to contamination of those crops with human intestinal diseases when they are present in a population.[33] If human faeces are composted for six months before their application on the fields the risk of such contamination with live parasite eggs is significantly reduced, as the vast majority of parasite eggs are no longer viable. However, if people are unaware of the need to compost the faeces for a long period, re-infection remains high.[34]

---

[28]   Semba, R.D., Kraema, K., Sun, K., de Pee, S., Akhter, N., Moench-Pfanner, R., Rah, J.H., Campbell, A.A., Badham, J., Bloem, M.W., 'Relationship of the presence of a household improved latrine with diarrhea and under-five child mortality in Indonesia', *American Journal of Tropical Medicine and Hygiene* 84 (2011): 443–50; Capuno et al. 2011.

[29]   Zeigelbauer, K., Speich, B., Mäusezahl, D., Bos, R., Keiser, J., Utzinger, J., 'Effect of sanitation on soil-transmitting helminth infection: systematic review and meta-analysis', *PLoS Medicine* 9 (2012): e1001162.

[30]   Norman, G., Pedley, S., Takkouche, B., 'Effects of sewerage on diarrhoea and enteric infections: a systematic review and meta-analysis', *Lancet Infectious Diseases* 10 (2010): 536–44.

[31]   Fink, G., Günther, I., Hill, K., 'The effect of water and sanitation on child health: evidence from the demographic and health surveys 1986–2007', *International Journal of Epidemiology* 40 (2011): 1196–204.

[32]   Heinonen-Tanski, H., van Wijk-Sibesma, C., 'Human excreta for plant production', *Bioresource Technology* 96 (2005): 403–11.

[33]   Uga, S., Hoa, N.T., Noda, S., Moji, K., Cong, L., Aoki, Y., Rai, S.K., Fujimaki, Y., 'Parasite egg contamination of vegetables from a suburban market in Hanoi, Vietnam', *Nepal Medical College Journal* 11 (2009): 75–8.

[34]   Phuc, P.D., Konradsen, F., Phuong, P.T., Cam, P.D., Dalsgaard, A., 'Practice of using human excreta as fertilizer and implications for health in Nghean Province, Vietnam',

Role of Insect Vectors

Flies are a common vector for the transmission of the organisms that cause diarrhoea, dysentery and cholera when they land on faeces and then on food.[35] Reduction in the number of domestic flies with improved sanitation and other controls has been shown to decrease the incidence of these diseases.[36]

Education / Health Awareness

Teaching people the causes of gastrointestinal illness and how to prevent it makes a significant difference to the likelihood that such diseases will be common in their households. Families where the mother has a low level of education have consistently been found to have higher prevalence of diarrhoea and of intestinal parasites.[37]

Keeping Livestock

It might seem logical to suppose that a family keeping livestock would be at higher risk of diarrhoea and other gastrointestinal diseases than those not exposed to animal faeces. However, modern research in the developing world suggests that there is no higher incidence of diarrhoea and other gastrointestinal diseases in children with environmental exposure to livestock when compared with those

---

Southeast Asian Journal of Tropical Medicine and Public Health 37 (2006): 222–9; Jensen, P.K., Phuc, P.D., Knudsen, L.G., Dalsgaard, A., Konradsen, F., 'Hygiene versus fertiliser: the use of human excreta in agriculture – a Vietnamese example', *International Journal of Hygiene and Environmental Health* 211 (2008): 432–9.

[35] Levine, O.S., Levine, M.M., 'Houseflies (*Musca domestica*) as mechanical vectors of shigellosis', *Reviews of Infectious Diseases* 13 (1991): 688–96; Fotedar, R., 'Vector potential of houseflies (*Musca domestica*) in the transmission of *Vibrio cholerae* in India', *Acta Tropica* 78 (2001): 31–4.

[36] Chavasse, D.C., Shier, R.P., Murphy, O.A., Huttly, S.R., Cousens, S.N., Akhtar, T., 'Impact of fly control on childhood diarrhoea in Pakistan: community-randomised trial', *Lancet* 353/9146 (1999): 22–5; Cohen, D., Green, M., Block, C., Slepon, R., Ambar, R., Wasserman, S.S., Levine, M.M., 'Reduction of transmission of shigellosis by control of houseflies (*Musca domestica*)', *Lancet* 337/8748 (1991): 993–7; Emerson, P.M., Lindsay, S.W., Walraven, G.E., Faal, H., Bøgh, C., Lowe, K., Bailey, R.L., 'Effect of fly control on trachoma and diarrhoea', *Lancet* 353/9162 (1999): 1401–3.

[37] U, K.M., Khin, M., Wai, N.N., Hman, N.W., Myint, T.T., Butler, T., 'Risk factors for the development of persistent diarrhoea and malnutrition in Burmese children', *International Journal of Epidemiology* 21 (1992): 1021–9; Ngui, R., Lim, Y.A., Chong Kin, L., Sek Chuen, C., Jaffar, S., 'Association between anaemia, iron deficiency anaemia, neglected parasitic infections and socioeconomic factors in rural children of West Malaysia', *PLoS Neglected Tropical Diseases* 6 (2012): e1550.

who do not keep animals.[38] It seems that exposure to other humans with disease is a much greater risk than exposure to animals.

Theoretical Modelling for Past Populations

We would expect the water drunk by early hunter-gatherers to have been relatively clean and free of disease. This is because group sizes were small and the lifestyle necessitated moving on to new areas on a regular basis. With the dawn of agriculture, the need to settle and the increasing population size could have predisposed populations to drinking water contaminated by the excrement of others living at the same site. As technology advanced and civilisations developed, the introduction of aqueducts and other methods of piping clean water from the countryside to ancient cities may have led to a relative improvement in the quality of drinking water once again.

The date when the washing of hands and the rest of the body became common will most likely have varied markedly between cultures. It is also unclear whether such activities were undertaken for perceived health benefits, rather than as religious rituals. It has already been shown that hand washing with soap and clean water should have reduced the risk of both diarrhoea and intestinal parasites in the past. We must also factor in the social attitudes of different cultures to washing. Wealthier Romans went to the bathhouse on a regular basis, but in medieval England bathhouses were often associated with prostitution and so were linked with stigma.[39] Since the use of hand washing with soap and water seems to have been variable over time and between cultures, it is hard to quantify what impact this may have had on sanitation in past populations.

Latrines would not have existed for hunter-gatherers, who would have urinated and defecated where they chose. If they moved on every few days then the likelihood of contracting intestinal parasites from soil contaminated by the faeces of others should have been low, as species of hookworm and most faeco-orally transmitted parasites required a period of a week or two to mature on the ground before they become infective.[40] However, if the hunter-gatherer group were to stay in the same location for long, such parasites as roundworm, whipworm and hookworm could re-infect members of the group. With the development of agriculture, sedentary living, and higher population density before the invention of the latrine should in theory have increased the likelihood of contracting acute diarrhoea and vomiting spread by flies, and chronic intestinal parasites such as hookworm, roundworm

---

[38]   Thiem et al. 2012.

[39]   Yegül, F., *Bathing in the Roman World* (Cambridge: Cambridge University Press, 2010); Barron, C.M., *London in the Later Middle Ages: Government and People, 1200–1500* (Oxford: Oxford University Press, 2004), p. 259.

[40]   Garcia, L.S., *Practical Guide to Diagnostic Parasitology*, 2nd edition. (Washington: ASM Press, 2009), p. 330.

and whipworm. With more advanced civilisation and the introduction of latrines, we would expect less contact with faecally contaminated soil and so a reduction in hookworm. In consequence, we would expect the introduction of latrines and cesspools to have a positive impact upon health so long as the cesspools did not contaminate the drinking water supply.

The use of human faeces as fertiliser is something we would not expect to have taken place in hunter-gatherer populations. It may well have become used by early agriculturalists, but the first proof we have of its use in this way is following the development of writing. For example, we know that human faeces was taken outside towns to fertilise crops in ancient Rome, Medieval Europe, and the Arab world.[41] We would suspect that if human faeces was spread on agricultural land by early farmers then this would have impacted adversely upon the health of those eating that food, especially if the food was uncooked. This practice seems to have continued through history and as discussed earlier is still employed in certain regions of the world today. All the indications are that it would have been a health hazard to past societies who undertook this practice, even those with otherwise well-developed sanitation technology.

The role of insect vectors such as flies in transmitting gastrointestinal diseases might have been low in hunter-gatherer groups due to their small group size and mobile way of life. However, flies are fairly ubiquitous in warm countries, so they may have nevertheless been in a position to spread disease-causing bacteria from faeces to food, carried on their feet. We would expect the risk of disease spread by flies to have increased significantly with the development of towns and the farming of animals that produced dung. In civilisations that then developed enclosed toilets and covered sewers, the risk of disease spread by flies should in theory have reduced. However, in cultures using open latrines and uncovered sewers and drainage channels, the potential for the spread of disease by flies may have been as high as in civilisations who had not yet developed even basic sanitation technology. It is unclear to what degree prehistoric populations may have found flies annoying just from their noise and presence, or if they realised the link with disease as well.

Health education remains an unknown in populations prior to the introduction of writing. Once writing is used, early medical practitioners do show that they were aware some environments seemed to predispose to illness more than others.

---

[41]   Dodge, H., 'Greater than the pyramids: the water supply of Ancient Rome', in J. Coulston and H. Dodge (eds), *Ancient Rome: The Archaeology of the Eternal City* (Oxford: Oxford University School of Archaeology, 2000) p. 192; Morrison, S.S., *Excrement in the Late Middle Ages: Sacred Filth and Chaucer's Fecopoetics* (New York: Palgrave Macmillan, 2008); Jones, R., 'Why manure matters', in R. Jones (ed.), *Manure Matters: Historical, Archaeological and Ethnographic Perspectives* (Farnham: Ashgate, 2012), pp. 1–11; Varisco, D., 'Zibl and Zira'a: coming to terms with manure in Arab agriculture' in R. Jones (ed.), *Manure Matters: Historical, Archaeological and Ethnographic Perspectives* (Ashgate: Farnham, 2012), pp. 129–43.

The ancient Greek physician Hippocrates wrote such a text around 500 BC, entitled Airs, Waters and Places.[42] He stressed the importance of a healthy natural environment in order to avoid disease, and noted how air that smelled bad, dirty water, and unhealthy places often lead to illness. In the medieval period (14th century AD) the Spanish physician Arnald of Villanova wrote a text on how to maintain the health of an army on campaign. He included basic sanitation advice such as digging pits at the edge of the army camp to use as latrines and for dead bodies, and not to drink water from a pond before dipping in a white cloth and ensuring it remained unstained when it dried, so confirming it was fairly clean.[43] Medical texts such as these do suggest that there was at least some level of health education available to the learned that would help to improve sanitation and hygiene. However, it remains unclear what knowledge of basic sanitation and hygiene was held by typical members of these populations, as opposed to the learned doctors writing these medical texts.

Conclusion

Modern clinical research clearly shows that clean drinking water, washing hands, use of hygienic latrines, keeping flies off food, not fertilising crops with fresh human faeces, and educating children how to reduce health risks all reduce risk of diarrhoea, malnutrition, intestinal parasites, stunted growth, developmental delay, and infant mortality. While hunter-gathering is thought to have been a lifestyle associated with many risks including starvation during drought, injury from hunting prey, and limited technology to protect against inclement weather conditions, theoretical modelling suggests that disease from poor sanitation is unlikely to have been a major health risk.

We might infer that hunter-gatherers suffered sanitation-related diseases least, and these diseases may have become worse in agriculturalists prior to the invention of sanitation technology. Then certain aspects of gastrointestinal health may have improved with sanitation technology before the introduction of education and health awareness, when finally all aspects of sanitation-related health could improve.

However, it is extremely challenging to prove whether such modelling is correct. The osteological paradox shows the paleoepidemiology of human skeletal remains is very hard to interpret if the research question is to determine or compare the standard of health of a population. The logical alternative is to look directly for evidence of those intestinal diseases in coprolites, pelvic soil or cesspool soil, and this may well be the best way forward to infer the efficacy of sanitation systems

---

[42]   Hippocrates 'Περί αέρων ύδάτων τοπων (On airs, waters, places)', in T.E. Page (ed.) and W.H.S. Jones (trans.), *The Loeb Classical Library* 147, vol. 1, (London, 1962).

[43]   McVaugh, M.R., 'Arnald of Villanova's Regimen Almarie (Regimen Castra Sequentium) and medieval military medicine', *Viator* 23 (1992): 201–13.

in past populations. Changes in the prevalence of human burials positive for intestinal worm eggs, changes in the number of species of parasites in communal latrines and cesspools, changes in the concentration of worm eggs in individual coprolites, and the introduction of new species of parasitic worms to a region may all indicate changes in levels of sanitation.

Nevertheless, even these methods have their limitations. Earlier populations may appear to have had fewer parasites merely because their remains are older, and so there has been more time for the evidence to have been broken down by soil organisms or washed away as rainwater percolates through the soil. Environmental conditions may suit the survival of the eggs of some species of parasite better than others, which might make us suggest that those fragile species were not present in certain parts of the world. Hookworm is a good example of this, where the cold and arid conditions in mountainous areas of South America can desiccate the eggs before the larvae can hatch. The rarity of hookworm eggs in excavations in Europe, Africa and Asia may indicate that the parasites were rare, or that they just do not survive well in warmer, moister climates. The presence of dysentery in past populations is also a challenging topic to address. In time periods where coprolites are the principal source of faecal material, we might expect dysentery to be missed as dysentery causes diarrhoea. Only well-formed stools, not diarrhoea, result in coprolites that become preserved and identified at excavation. Similarly, the biomolecular ELISA test with which we can detect dysentery may not work on older strains if the species have evolved and the surface proteins under test have changed.

Research on modern populations suggests that the sanitary environment is very likely to have had a profound impact upon the health of past populations. Paleoparasitological analyses have already shown widespread evidence for different intestinal infectious diseases in the past. More focused research on certain under-researched regions of the world coupled with a more global interpretation of the current evidence should help us put together the bigger picture. In that way we can move beyond theoretical modelling to clearly demonstrate how health and disease in the past was affected by the environment, lifestyle and sanitation technologies.

Chapter 3

Waste Management in Early Urban Southern Mesopotamia

Augusta McMahon

Introduction

Mesopotamia is the locus of the world's earliest cities, and the early inhabitants of Mesopotamia were the first to face many problems of urban sustainability and challenges to individual and community health. The earliest cities in this region (Iraq, NE Syria, SE Turkey, SW Iran; see Figure 3.1) belong to the mid-4th millennium BC, when settlements grew to more than 50 hectares, urban populations reached the thousands, and socio-economic and political arrangements attained high levels of complexity. Agriculture was intensive, and the regional population density was high. Within cities, residents faced housing overcrowding, difficult access to water, and problems creating adequate space for manufacturing. Larger and denser populations would have increased the transmission of air-borne infectious diseases. And rapidly accumulating and unwieldy quantities of rubbish and human waste, with associated faecal-orally transmitted diseases, would have been an ongoing and long-term problem.

Writing appeared at the end of the 4th millennium BC in the form of economic records. By the mid-3rd millennium BC, we have adequate royal documents to assess Mesopotamian leaders' engagement with urban problems. However, these leaders' civic projects consisted of rebuilding or refurbishing religious complexes, building city walls, and creating or extending irrigation canals. In other words, government projects aimed at enabling general economic gain or at presenting and reiterating power through high-visibility public monuments. There were no civic projects that made daily life easier for Mesopotamia's urban inhabitants: paving of streets, supplying of clean water or provision of sewers or public latrines were never recorded as notable events of kings' reigns, nor are such projects present in the archaeological record. Irrigation canals were sources of drinking water, as well as providing water for fields and acting as transport routes. However, they were often at a significant distance from houses. It appears that the challenges of acquiring drinking water and disposing of human (and animal) waste were left to urban dwellers to solve at the level of the household. However, there are indications that rubbish in some cities may have been managed at the communal level and even, on occasion, with administrative intervention.

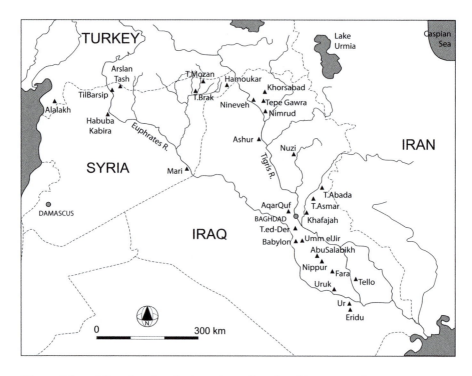

Figure 3.1   Map showing the key sites of ancient Mesopotamia

Texts about Toilets, Rubbish, and Disease

Ancient texts occasionally supply glimpses into Mesopotamian sewage, toilets, and rubbish, but such mentions are usually oblique references within documents on other subjects. For instance, a curse formula in the literary text *Descent of Ishtar* refers to a city sewer pipe or gutter from which the accursed should eat bread (Akkadian *habannat ali*). No details of this pipe or gutter are described, and there are no archaeologically known built features in appropriate locations or at a large enough scale to match our assumptions of a city sewerage system. It may be that this term simply referred to a shallow and informal open channel in the street that was created through erosion by rain and discard of waste water.

The Akkadian term for lavatory, *bīt musâti*, is well known, especially in the 1st millennium BC, but again the room and its features are never described in any detail. There are two types of lavatory/toilet rooms represented in the archaeological record (see below); it is not even certain that the same term applies to both. Several texts refer to the toilet/bathroom demon Shulak, a lurker in the *bīt musâti*.[1] This demon is one of many low-ranking, hybrid creatures in the Mesopotamian belief system who could act on behalf of more important deities or independently; they were responsible for illness, injury, or bad luck. Although the lavatory/bathroom should have the positive aspect of isolating and removing waste and/or dirty water, it is easy to see how a dark, miasmic hole into the earth within a small, windowless space may have engendered association with a demon. Such an association may also have led to a percentage of the population engaging in open-air defecation by preference. Rubbish heaps (Akkadian *tubkinnu* and *kiqillutu*) were also associated with demons. Curse formulae condemned transgressors of social norms to scavenging from or sleeping on such dumps; additionally, if a rubbish dump grew too high, this was a bad omen and the city would be abandoned.[2] Rubbish dumps could even catch fire – also a bad omen.

Mesopotamia did not have a written philosophy of medicine, per se, but numerous texts describing illness and the professional treatments for diseases exist, beginning from the late 3rd millennium BC. These medical texts are generally vague in describing symptoms (e.g., 'if her feet are cold') and often too obscure in vocabulary for scholars to match descriptions to specific diseases. Knowledge of disease acquisition was limited; throughout most of Mesopotamian history, there was strong adherence to the idea that illness was rooted in displeasure of the gods or trouble from deceased relatives. However, medical texts of the 2nd millennium BC indicate that a few Mesopotamians were aware of something like contagion theory. A text from the palace archive at the city of Mari exhorts others to limit contact with a sick woman, lest drinking from her cup make others ill.[3] A medical text warns against touching the eyes with unclean hands, lest the eyes become sore.[4] But while person-to-person transmission might have been occasionally acknowledged, and rubbish piles and toilets were generally negative places to avoid, rubbish-to-person contact was not explicitly viewed as a vector of disease transmission. And the association of disease with contamination of food or water or contact with insect or animal vectors was not made.

---

[1]   Kinnier-Wilson, J., Reynolds, E., 'On Stroke and Facial Palsy in Babylonian Texts', in I. Finkel and M. Geller (eds), *Disease in Babylonia* (Leiden: Brill, 2007), pp. 67–99; Scurlock, J., 'Ancient Mesopotamian house gods', *Journal of Ancient Near Eastern Religions* 3 (2003): 99–106; Scurlock, J., Andersen, B., *Diagnoses in Assyrian and Babylonian Medicine* (Urbana: University of Illinois, 2005).

[2]   Biggs, R., Brinkman, J., Civil, M., Farber, W., Gelb, I., Oppenheim, A.L., Reiner, E., Roth, M., Stolper, M. (eds), *The Assyrian Dictionary, Volume 18, T* (Chicago: Oriental Institute, 2006).

[3]   Biggs, R., 'Medicine, surgery, and public health in ancient Mesopotamia', *Journal of Assyrian Academic Studies* 19 (2005): 1–19.

[4]   Scurlock and Andersen 2005, p. 16, and further texts pp. 16–20.

Archaeology of Mesopotamian Toilets

The toilet, which contained human waste and separated it from other household activities of eating and sleeping, was a ground-breaking innovation. The cover of *The Economist* for 10 January 2013 asks, with regard to the modern flush toilet, 'Will we ever invent anything this useful again?' But one could argue that the modern flush toilet is merely a superficial adjustment to the deep pit and sloped-drain toilets first known from Mesopotamia in the late 4th to 3rd millennia BC. The earliest currently known possible toilet, comprising a deep cylindrical pit in a small room, was excavated in a building in the religious complex at the city of Uruk, dating to *c.* 3200 BC (see Figure 3.1 for location of all sites referred to in the text).[5] This deep drain is in the so-called Badehaus, a small building that may have served as both bathroom and lavatory. The associated room had bitumen and brick paving that implies high water use. The deep pit toilet remained popular through at least the 1st millennium BC and was joined by the invention of the less efficient sloped-drain toilet during the 3rd millennium BC. But although these innovations were widespread, they remained a minority solution throughout Mesopotamian history.

Deep Pit Toilets

The earliest pit toilets, known from the late 4th millennium BC, appear to have been relatively rare; but excavated examples increase during the 3rd millennium BC. The palace at Eridu had several deep pit toilets in small rooms, of which the best preserved is a cylindrical pit about 4.5 m deep with a drainage tube of at least 16 stacked and interlocking perforated ceramic rings inside it. These toilets are dated to *c.* 2750–2500 BC, the Early Dynastic II Period.[6] At the same time and slightly later, houses at Fara, Tello and Tell Asmar have the first known deep pit toilets in domestic contexts.

These deep pit toilets are remarkably consistent in form through the centuries and across southern Mesopotamia in all types of buildings. Once established, the cylindrical drainage system appears to have worked well and the tradition was widespread. The basic form was a regular, vertical, cylindrical pit (Figure 3.2). The purpose-made interlocking ceramic rings used for the internal tube structure were usually about 60 cm to 1 m in diameter and 60 cm to 1.1 m high; the sides of each ring were perforated with up to several dozen holes 2–3 cm in diameter; sherd packing was placed between the pit and rings to support the tube and to allow seepage. The soil in and around these drains is often stained a distinctive

---

    [5]   Lenzen, H., *XXI Vorläufiger Bericht über die von dem Deutschen Archäologischen Institut und der Deutschen Orient-Gesellschaft aus Mitteln der Deutschen Forschungsgemeinschaft Unternommenen Ausgrabungen in Uruk-Warka, Winter 1962/63* (Berlin: Gebr. Mann, 1965), 18–19, Taf. 8b, 9a, 32.

    [6]   Safar, F., Mustafa, M.A., Lloyd, S., *Eridu* (Baghdad: State Organization of Antiquities and Heritage, 1981), pp. 280–286, figs. 144, 145, 147, 157b.

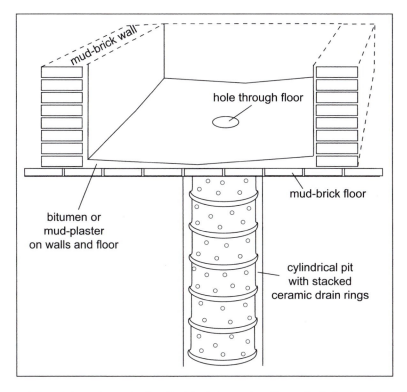

Figure 3.2   Plan of a typical cylindrical deep pit toilet as built in the 4th and 3rd millennium BC

rusty red and pale green that reflects its high organic content and implies that these structures were not wells.

The final upper ring of the drains was usually surmounted by a funnel or other domed form that linked to the floor or surface feature(s). Usually this final ring was bell- or dome-shaped, for instance, at early 3rd millennium BC Tello[7] and at early 2nd millennium BC Tell ed-Der.[8] Sometimes the upper unit was a long funnel-shaped segment, such as at mid-3rd millennium BC Tello[9] and mid-3rd

---

[7] Hemker, C., *Altorientalische Kanalisation; Untersuchungen zu Be- und Entwässerungsanlagen im Mesopotamisch, Syrisch, Anatolischen Raum*. Abhandlung der Deutschen Orient-Gesellschaft 22 (Munster: Agenda, 1993), p. 132, Nr. 260. Abb. 434a.

[8] De Meyer, L. (ed.), *Tell ed-Der IV, Progress Reports (First Series)* (Leuven: Peeters, 1978), Pls. 8:1, 25: 1; De Meyer, L. (ed.), *Tell ed-Der II, Progress Reports (Second Series)* (Leuven: Peeters, 1984), Pls. 7:2, 18: 1; Plan 7: Profil C.

[9] Hemker 1993, p. 92, Nr. 186, Abb. 311, 312; = Cros et al. 1910: 246.

millennium BC Ur.[10] Occasionally, a broken and inverted storage jar was used instead of a purpose-made final ring (e.g., 2nd millennium BC Nippur).[11] Whatever its form, this final upper element lay just below the lavatory floor, which may have been mud-plastered or baked-brick paved; most often, a simple hole in that floor allowed access to the drain. Above-floor features ranged from nothing more than a plastered surface to extended areas of paving or elaborate baked-brick foot-stands and seats.[12]

At times, adaptations were made to this basic format, usually involving shallower pits and recycled interior structural elements. For instance, a toilet was recovered in a small room in Area WF at Nippur in the Akkadian Period (*c.* 2200 BC).[13] The floor level features had a typical arrangement: a small plastered hole with a baked-brick plug. But the relatively short cylindrical pit below this hole had two large storage vats within it, rather than the purpose-made ceramic rings. These jars were fitted together rim-to-rim, and their bases were deliberately broken to allow liquid movement.

The combination of frequent house rebuilding and remodeling in the past and site erosion in the present has meant that many deep pit toilet drains have been recovered in south Mesopotamia without their associated ground-level features preserved. Examples are known from Abu Salabikh (*c.* 2300–2000 BC),[14] from Fara,[15] from Ur (*c.* 2500–2000 BC; Pit F, Area EH),[16] and from Umm el-Jir (*c.* 2100–1750 BC; Area D, Phase VI).[17] From contents of these drains, it is clear that they often had secondary re-use for rubbish discard: large quantities of sherds, animal bones and even obsolete cuneiform tablets have been recovered. It is rare that the full depth of any drain is preserved or excavated; however, depths between 2 and 12 metres have been recorded for deep pit toilets. Although the maximum depth can be quite significant, there was usually little threat of such toilets contaminating groundwater, since they are often found on deeply-stratified tell sites where floor levels were artificially raised. Even the deepest drains often

---

[10]   Woolley, C.L., *The Early Periods: Ur Excavations 4* (London: British Museum, 1956), Area EH; Pl. 45m; Hemker 1993, pp. 92–93, Abb. 314, 315.

[11]   McCown, D., Haines. R., *Nippur I: Temple of Enlil, Scribal Quarter, and Soundings*, Oriental Institute Publications 78 (Chicago: Oriental Institute, 1967), Pl. 69B; Area TB Level I, 2, room 31.

[12]   Hemker 1993, p. 132–3, nr. 261–262, Abb. 435–438.

[13]   McMahon, A., *Nippur V: The Early Dynastic to Akkadian Transition; The WF Sounding at Nippur*. Oriental Institute Publications 129 (Chicago: Oriental Institute, 2006), p. 22, Pls. 27, 28.

[14]   Postgate, J.N., 'How many Sumerians per Hectare? – Probing the anatomy of an early city', *Cambridge Archaeological Journal* 4 (1994): 47–65, see p. 49–50.

[15]   Martin, H., *Fara: A Reconstruction of the Ancient Mesopotamian City of Shuruppak* (Birmingham: Chris Martin, 1988), p. 31, Figs. 8, 11.

[16]   Woolley 1956, pp. 3, 57.

[17]   Gibson, M., 'Umm el-Jir, A Town in Akkad', *Journal of Near Eastern Studies* 31 (1972): 237–294, see p. 262.

cut mainly through earlier occupations and rarely reached virgin soil or the water table below. The same deep tell stratigraphy meant that intra-settlement wells were rare and cross-contamination would not have occurred.

Such deep pit toilets, no matter what their original depth, would have eventually filled if used by a household over some years. The excavator of Ur, Leonard Woolley, offered the possibility that they were periodically emptied.[18] Although this would have been a difficult operation given the depth and narrowness of the drain, if the pit could be dug, it could also be cleaned. An alternative exists, that these deep pit toilets were primarily used for liquid waste, which would have seeped through the drainage holes in the ceramic rings and through the sherd packing into the surrounding earth; a liquid-restricted use would have meant the toilet could be used for longer. Solid human waste might have had a different trajectory of disposal into smaller, periodically emptied, containers (see below).

Modern studies indicate that limited access to sanitation has an unsurprising damaging effect on individual health. But there is also a wider effect at the community level, with estimates that 75% of a community must have access to good sanitation before there is a group-related health impact.[19] Individuals with sanitation access will generally be healthier and taller than those without any sanitation facilities at all, but such individuals will still suffer relatively poor health until the great majority of their neighbours have similar access.

It might be assumed that, once invented, the toilet was widespread in Mesopotamian urban settlements. The technology was not particularly difficult and the materials needed were not expensive. However, permanent toilets seem to have been limited in number; where large horizontal extents of urban neighbourhoods have been exposed, for instance at Ur for the early 2nd millennium BC, there is by no means a toilet in every house. It must be admitted that the number of toilets in past Mesopotamian neighbourhoods at any moment can be difficult to quantify due to the lack of precise stratigraphic connections from house to house and the frequent rebuilding and repairs performed within any house. But even a generous assumption of contemporaneity leaves many houses without toilet facilities.

---

[18]   Woolley, C.L., Mallowan, M., *The Old Babylonian Period: Ur Excavations 7* (London: British Museum, 1976), p. 23.

[19]   Hogrewe, W., Joyce, S., Perez, E., *The Unique Challenges of Improving Peri-Urban Sanitation*. WASH Technical Report 86 (Washington, DC: US Agency for International Development, 1993), p. 30; Bateman, O. M., Smith, S., *A Comparison of the Health Effects of Water Supply and Sanitation in Urban and Rural Guatemala*. WASH Field Report 352 (Washington, DC: US Agency for International Development, 1991); Bateman, O. M., Smith, S., Roark, P., *A Comparison of the Health Effects of Water Supply and Sanitation in Urban and Rural Areas of Five African Countries*. Report No. 398 (Washington, DC: US Agency for International Development, 1993); Heller, L., 'Who really benefits from environmental sanitation services in the cities? An intra-urban analysis in Betim, Brazil', *Environment and Urbanization* 11 (1999): 133–144.

A great many deep pit toilet drains were noted in all excavation areas at Ur,[20] and this city provides a wealth of information about house size, urban living and space use. The density of data from Ur thus presents a useful case study for quantifying toilet frequency. In Area AH, where extensive excavations exposed a large part of a tightly packed neighbourhood of the early 2nd millennium BC, 34 houses were completely revealed; the nearby contemporary neighbourhood in Area EM had 11 exposed houses.[21] Some rooms in both areas can be clearly identified as toilets, since they are small rooms with vertical deep drains (16 in AH, three in EM). However, three houses in AH have two toilets each, so the percentage of houses with toilets there is only 38%; the smaller sample in EM indicated 27% had toilets. In many of these houses, the toilet was a small room attached to the largest room of the house; other toilets were located under stairs that led to the roof or upper storey.[22] If one adds those rooms that might be toilets because of their similarity in size and location to proven toilets (although lacking preserved or excavated drains), there would be 26 in Area AH (but only 68%, since three houses had more than one toilet) and four in EM (36%). Although the estimated number of toilet rooms in AH approaches the 75% level at which community health is positively affected, it still lies below it. There are additional drains in Area AH for which the main purpose was to remove rainwater from courtyards, and it is possible that other toilets could have connected to these courtyard drains. But overall, the Ur neighbourhoods together fall short of recommended densities of sanitation facilities for a positive impact on community health. It is tempting to assume that toilets would be associated with larger houses of wealthy and high status occupants; however, the houses in Area AH with toilets show the full range of possible sizes, and there does not seem to be a strong relationship between toilets and wealth.

Other sites show similar low densities of sanitation facilities, although sample sizes are smaller. In a neighbourhood partially excavated at Tell ed-Der, consisting of parts of seven houses of the early 2nd millennium BC, there were more bread ovens (five) exposed than toilet drains (two) in the best preserved phase (Phase Ii).[23] Both of these toilets were within the main central house, leaving the six other houses unprovisioned (14% coverage). One toilet was a deep vertical drain in a small, secluded room (Rm. 9), with a patch of brick paving preserved. The second was also in a small room (Rm. 2) but it had a sloped clay pipe drain below the floor that led from the access hole into the courtyard, where it joined a deep vertical drain that mainly removed rainwater from the courtyard (a similar courtyard drain

---

[20]   Woolley 1956.

[21]   Battini-Villard, L., *L'Espace Domestique en Mésopotamie de la IIIe Dynastie d'Ur à l'Époque Paléo-Babylonienne*. BAR International Series 767 (Oxford: Archaeopress, 1999); Woolley and Mallowan 1976.

[22]   Battini-Villard 1999, pp. 198, 204–7.

[23]   De Meyer 1978, Plan 2, Pls. 8, 25.

was present in an adjacent house). This merging of wastewater and rainwater would have been efficient and is also seen in bathrooms (see below).

Nippur in the early 2nd millennium BC offers a comparable situation to that of Isin and Ur. In Area TB at this city, for the most extensive exposure in Phase I/1, parts of seven houses were exposed.[24] Stacks of drain rings are recorded in two houses, in Rooms 58 and 3, although their tops were destroyed. The room 58 drain is appropriately located near the centre of a small room; the Room 3 drain is also appropriately located although it is in a rather larger room than seems warranted for a toilet. If the drains in Rooms 3 and 58 are both assumed to be toilets and were roughly contemporary, the percentage of houses with in-house toilet drains for this limited sample is less than 30%.

Monumental administrative buildings, such as palaces and priestly residences, could have multiple toilets, perhaps reflecting the large numbers of people working in such buildings. As for multiple toilet drains in any house, it can be difficult to prove contemporaneity of toilets in a large multi-roomed building with complex internal stratigraphy. Uruk's early 2nd millennium BC Sinkashid Palace had at least four deep pit toilets in two distinct quadrants (Room 76a in the NW quadrant and Rooms 54, 56 and 58 in the SW quadrant).[25] It is not certain that these four toilets would have been in use simultaneously, but in a building about 110 x 145 m, with at least 115 rooms and presumably a large staff of daily users, one can see the need for a proliferation of toilet facilities. Similarly, the late 3rd millennium BC E-Hursag residence within the Moon God Temple complex at Ur had at least two probably contemporary deep pit toilets.[26]

Sloped Drains: Toilets, Bathrooms, and Altars

Deep pit toilets were supplemented by systems of gently sloped drains or channels, constructed of interlocking ceramic pipes or plastered, roughly worked stones or baked bricks. Channel systems are known from as early as the 6th millennium BC (Tell Abada)[27] and 5th millennium BC (Tepe Gawra),[28] but their initial purpose appears to be to bring water to settlements (Abada) or to remove rain water. They

---

[24]   McCown and Haines 1967.

[25]   Lenzen, H., *XXII Vorläufiger Bericht über die von dem Deutschen Archäologischen Institut und der Deutschen Orient-Gesellschaft aus Mitteln der Deutschen Forschungsgemeinschaft Unternommenen Ausgrabungen in Uruk-Warka, Winter 1963/64* (Berlin: Gebr. Mann., 1966), Taf. 31, 33, 35.

[26]   Hall, H.R., *A Season's Work at Ur, al-Ubaid, Abu Shahrain (Eridu) and Elsewhere, Being an Official Account of the British Archaeological Mission to Babylonia 1919* (London: Methuen, 1930), pp. 163–65, Figs. 108, 111, 112.

[27]   Jasim, S.A., 'Structure and Function in an Ubaid Village', in E. Henrickson and I. Thuesen (eds), *Upon This Foundation – The Ubaid Reconsidered* (Copenhagen: Carsten Niehbuhr Institute, 1989), pp. 79–88.

[28]   Tobler, A., *Excavations at Tepe Gawra II* (Philadelphia: University Museum, 1950), Pl. XIV.

are increasingly common as elements of toilet drainage from the 3rd millennium BC and thereafter across northern and southern Mesopotamia[29] in houses, temples and palaces.

The rooms to which these sloped drains connect are usually referred to as 'bathrooms'; but in some cases, excavators have identified the rooms as mixed use, bathrooms and lavatories.[30] Such rooms are usually fairly small and paved with stones or baked bricks and/or plastered with bitumen (Figure 3.3). The waterproofing suggests that bathroom use may have been primary. Late-3rd millennium BC Tell Asmar has perhaps the best examples of baked-brick paved rooms with sloped drains in domestic contexts.[31] Some horizontal drains in temples, identical in all respects to those associated with bathroom-lavatories in houses, were attached to basins, altars, or ablution areas (e.g., mid-3rd millennium BC examples at Khafajah).[32] The multiple uses of such sloping channels and the ambiguity about the range of associated room functions make their sanitation impact difficult to qualify or quantify.

Careful planning during construction for effective sloped-drain placement would have been necessary;[33] toilets should be located near an outside wall to keep the drain length short, land slope and soil conditions should be assessed, and care is needed with waterproofing of adjacent walls. Although sloped channels would have been technically trickier to make than a deep pit toilet, the work effort to make such a channel is less than that invested in the excavation of a deep pit. The materials needed for deep pits and sloped channels are approximately comparable in expense and availability. Sloped drains have both disadvantages and advantages; inclines were minimal, pipe bores were narrow, and blockages by solid waste were likely to have been frequent. But the probable mixed use for rainwater, washing water and waste would have helped relieve these blockages. Such combined systems have also been noted for palaces in Minoan Crete.[34] But what happened in the summers when no rain fell in south Mesopotamia? Blockages probably would have increased during such seasons, but at least the shallow depth of channel

---

[29]   Hemker 1993.

[30]   Delougaz, P.P., Hall, H., Lloyd, S., *Private Houses and Graves in the Diyala Region*. Oriental Institute Publications 88 (Chicago: Oriental Institute, 1967), pp. 150–3.

[31]   Delougaz et al. 1967, pp. 150–3; Pls. 28, 29, 33, 67B, 68D, 70A and C.

[32]   Delougaz, P.P., *The Temple Oval at Khafajah*. Oriental Institute Publications 53 (Chicago: Oriental Institute, 1940), Figs. 56, 57; Delougaz, P.P., Lloyd, S., *Pre-Sargonid Temples in the Diyala Region*. Oriental Institute Publications 58 (Chicago: Oriental Institute, 1942), Figs. 57, 58.

[33]   Fink, A., 'Levantine standardized luxury in the late Bronze Age: waste management at Tell Atchana (Alalakh)', in A. Fantalkin and A. Yasur-Landau (eds), *Bene Israel: Studies in the Archaeology of Israel and the Levant during the Bronze and Iron Ages in Honour of Israel Finkelstein*. Culture and History of the Ancient Near East 31 (Leiden: Brill, 2008), pp. 165–96, see p.167.

[34]   Angelakis, A., Koutsoyiannis, D., Tchobanoglous, G., 'Urban wastewater and stormwater technologies in ancient Greece', *Water Research* 39 (2005): 210–220.

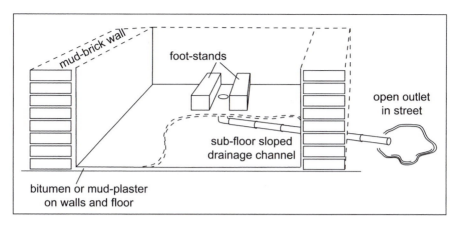

Figure 3.3   Plan of a typical sloped-drain toilet as built in the 3rd
                millennium BC

burial meant that any severe blockages could be reached and removed. The main
disadvantage of these drains seems to be the eventual outlet, which in most cases
appears to simply flow into adjacent streets. Waste would have been shifted, but
not very far, rather than eliminated or hidden. Some toilet and rainwater drainage
systems combined short runs of horizontal pipework with outlets into vertical pit
drains with the usual pierced stacked rings, for example in 2nd millennium BC
Tell ed-Der, Neo-Babylonian Babylon Haus IV.[35] At Habuba Kabira, a planned
town of the late 4th millennium BC, a drainage system of clay pipes in ditches
along streets was created,[36] but this was unusual. The addition of rainwater or
washing water would have helped flush waste through the system but would have
enlarged any puddles of standing water at the outlet and expanded the potential for
faecal-oral transmission of disease when compared to deep pit toilets.

There is a certain degree of association of paved rooms and sloped channel
drainage with larger buildings of elite residents. These buildings often incorporated
extended multi-channel connected systems that merged and removed water from
courtyards and several rooms (e.g., a Neo-Assyrian house at Ashur).[37] Particularly
in the 2nd and 1st millennia BC, paved rooms with sloped drains are associated
with palaces, such as the mid-2nd millennium BC palaces at Nuzi[38] and Aqar

[35]   Reuther, O., *Die Innenstadt von Babylon (Merkes).* Wissenschaftliche
Veröffentlichung der Deutschen Orient-Gesellschaft 47 (Leipzig: Hinrichs, 1926), pp. 95,
105f, Abb. 67, 71–72, Taf. 17, 26c.

[36]   Strommenger, E., *Habuba Kabira, Eine Stadt vor 5000 Jahren,* (Mainz: von
Zabern, 1980).

[37]   Preusser, C., *Die Wohnhäuser in Assur.* Wissenschaftliche Veröffentlichung der
Deutschen Orient-Gesellschaft 64 (Berlin: Gebr. Mann, 1954), Taf. 17, 27b; Room 26.

[38]   Starr, R., *Nuzi, Report on the Excavations at Yorgan Tepa Near Kirkuk, Iraq*
(Cambridge MA: Harvard University Press, 1939).

Quf.[39] Neo-Assyrian palaces at the 1st millennium BC imperial and provincial capital cities of Nimrud, Khorsabad, Nineveh, Arslan Tash and Til Barsip all featured small paved rooms adjacent to the throne rooms. Although not all had preserved – or excavated – drainage, these are generally assumed to be bathrooms with supplemental possible toilet functions.[40]

At their most elaborate, sloped drainage systems could be incredibly complex and interconnected. Tell Asmar's late 3rd millennium BC 'Northern Palace'[41] had a connected drain system that moved both rainwater and toilet water as much as 50 metres. The six toilets in this building consisted of long narrow rooms with baked-brick paving, two of which were placed back-to-back in order to share a drain. At least four sub-systems of channels in the mid-2nd millennium BC palace at Nuzi collected water from toilets, kitchens and courtyards.[42] The connected drains of the 1st millennium BC Assyrian provincial palace of Til Barsip[43] served variously to drain rainwater from courtyards (Court A), water from two bathrooms (Room XXVII) and waste from nine separate toilets (e.g., XIV). The distance the waste and water needed to travel in the latter building was upwards of 80 metres, and one wonders whether the water pressure would have been great enough to prevent blockages. The outlet of this large drainage system was not recovered but the final section left the building directly below the main entrance (Room I). If the outlet was nearby into a street or open area, as seems likely, this would have been extremely unwelcoming and at odds with the highly-decorated power statement of the palace. The longest horizontal drain known from southern Mesopotamia may be that in the Moon God complex at Ur in the Neo-Babylonian 1st millennium BC, probably dedicated to rainwater removal; this was over 200 m long, originating from the main courtyard southeast of the ziggurat temple tower and ultimately leaving the complex below the floor of the main gate.[44] Despite the sophisticated hydraulic knowledge such an extended system implies, the outlet was remarkably underdeveloped here, as elsewhere.

In summary, sloping drains supplemented deep pit toilets in Mesopotamia from the 3rd millennium BC. They may have had the advantage of filling up less quickly than a pit toilet, but their method of removing waste laterally would have presented a different set of problems. The outlet of such drains is usually simply into a nearby street. Although any waste would have been literally watered down by combination with rainwater and washing water, such mixing may have

---

[39]   Baqir, T., 'Iraq Government Excavations at 'Aqar Quf Third Interim Report, 1944–5', *Iraq* 8 (1946): 73–93, see p. 84.

[40]   Turner, G., 'The state apartments of late Assyrian palaces', *Iraq* 32 (1970): 177–213, see pp. 190–94.

[41]   Delougaz et al. 1967, Pl. 36, 37.

[42]   Starr 1939, Plan 13.

[43]   Thureau-Dangin, F., *Til Barsip* (Paris: Geuthner, 1936), Pl. B.

[44]   Woolley, C.L., *The Neo-Babylonian and Persian Periods: Ur Excavations 9* (London: British Museum, 1962), Pl. 60.

exacerbated health problems by adding volume and spreading waste further. Standing wastewater in streets carries a high health risk[45] to which house occupants and all neighbours would have been exposed.

Toilet Seats

As mentioned above, the most basic built toilet in Mesopotamia comprised a hole in a plastered floor. A slightly safer version, still with minimal construction demands, had a baked-brick paved area surrounding the hole or two brick foot-stands (Figures 3.2 and 3.3). These are the most common arrangements in private houses of all periods. However, higher status buildings tended to have more elaborate and permanent toilet features. The six 3rd millennium BC toilets in Tell Asmar's Northern Palace had baked-brick seats, comprising a low stack of bricks to either side of a channel that sloped into the drain.[46] In the mid-2nd millennium BC palace at Nuzi, there were similar baked-brick toilet seats, including one that had a marble slab 'splash-back'.[47]

Although I focus here on southern Mesopotamia, the region's neighbours to the north saw similar developments in toilet features, although often with greater use of stone. Room C6 in the service wing of the late-3rd millennium BC palace at Tell Mozan, northeast Syria, had a 2-metre deep baked-brick shaft,[48] as well as a drain that led to an adjacent room, implying this was a combination lavatory and bathroom. Toilets in the mid-2nd millennium BC palace and residences at Alalakh in southeast Turkey are claimed as early flush toilets.[49] Sixteen toilets were recovered during the initial excavation at this site, most debouching into drains that ran below an outer wall and into the street but a few into cesspits. They had brick foot-stands and plastered floors with channels connected to stone and plastered drains or occasional terra-cotta pipe drains with interlocking segments. The walls of these toilet rooms were often plastered or stone-orthostat-lined.

Toilets and Health

The overall picture of sanitation in urban southern Mesopotamia is of a geographically widespread engagement with the problem of human waste and very similar solutions to the problem in the use of two types of drains below squat toilet installations. However, although toilets are found across the region

---

[45] Heller 1999.

[46] Delougaz et al 1967, pp. 144, 175, 176.

[47] Starr 1939: 144, Pl. 15A. These seats are similar to the foot-stands but are higher and clearly for sitting, not squatting.

[48] Buccellati, G., Kelly-Buccellati, M., 'The royal palace at Urkesh and the daughter of Naram-Sin', *Annales Archeologiques Arabes Syriennes* 44 (2001): 63–69.

[49] Fink 2008.

and throughout many periods of occupation, they are few in number. Even given the biases of preservation and excavation, there are simply not enough toilets per neighbourhood to make them anything but a minority solution. The individuals provided with toilets within any house may have enjoyed improved health over their non-provisioned neighbours, but there would still have been an overall health impact derived from the limited density of toilets in a neighbourhood or community.

If toilets were few in number, what were the alternatives? Given the size of many cities and the distance of many houses from the urban edge or other open-air potential toilet areas, it is probable that many houses had a toilet room but that this had a temporary container rather than a deep permanent drain (comparable to the modern bucket latrine). These waste containers would have been periodically emptied, possibly merely at the nearest edge of the city, and perhaps in a designated area that could be mined for fertilizer, either by its owners or by any member of the community. Such a strategy is similar to that described in many areas for the accumulation and removal of 'night soil' (e.g., Washington, DC, in the nineteenth century).[50] In Mesopotamia, there do not seem to have been professional waste removers nor state-managed collection and removal of lavatory contents. As with sewerage, this mode of waste management would have been resolved at the household level.

Access to clean water, significantly lacking in Mesopotamian cities, adds a further impact on health; waste removal and clean water provision are ideally provided together. In Mesopotamian cities, the nearest water may have been a river channel or canal at a significant distance from many houses. Wells are rare in south Mesopotamia although they are present in the north, e.g., Nuzi[51] and Tell Hamoukar.[52] Collection of water from river or canal would have been a daily chore, probably performed by women or older children, and therefore rarely documented. Given the difficulty of transport, it is likely that water was used carefully. Collection of water would also have been dangerous to health; the low topographic gradient of southern Mesopotamia meant that rivers and canals were sluggish, offering friendly breeding grounds for infectious diseases that are associated with water-based life cycles, such as malaria and schistosomiasis.

---

[50]   Crane, B.D., 'Filth, garbage and rubbish: refuse disposal, sanitary reform, and nineteenth-century yard deposits in Washington, DC', *Historical Archaeology* 34 (2000): 20–38.

[51]   Starr 1939, pp. 56–57.

[52]   Gibson, M., al-Azm, A., Reichel, C., Quntar, S., Franke, J., Khalidi, L., Hritz, C., Altaweel, M., Coyle, C., Colantoni, C., Tenney, J., Abdul Aziz, G., Hartnell, T., 'Hamoukar: a summary of three seasons of excavation', *Akkadica* 123 (2002): 11–34, see p.15.

Manuring and 'Provisional Refuse'

The low number of toilets per house, and house distance from open areas, together hint that the majority of human waste was provisionally accumulated in bucket latrines and physically removed, to the edge of the city or elsewhere. Waste may even have been a valuable agricultural resource in a region in which soil fertility was variable and the intensity of agriculture was high.

Surveys in northern Mesopotamia (north Iraq and northeast Syria) have identified a secondary phase of urbanism during the 3rd millennium BC; this was accompanied by new settlement patterns and greater site and regional densities of population. Archaeologically visible results of this re-urbanisation include 'hollow ways', shallow depressions created by frequent traffic of humans and animals from settlements to fields and between settlements.[53] These hollow ways, and the urban settlements themselves, are also associated with rings of low-density sherd scatter that reflect the removal of occupational debris and waste from the sites and its spreading on fields, or 'manuring'.[54] Together, the hollow ways and sherd scatters reflect agricultural intensification and a perverse increase in the value of human waste and rubbish. Such revalued rubbish has been termed 'provisional refuse', or rubbish that is retained specifically for re-use.[55]

Manuring traces are not visible in southern Mesopotamia, where dissection of the landscape by irrigation canals and a dense history of pre-modern and modern agricultural use have created an obscuring palimpsest. But the possibility exists that this practice occurred in the south; yearly flooding replenished field fertility to an extent, but the demands of urbanism and a rapidly-expanding bureaucracy may have exceeded any fertility gains. Reducing fallowing and increased soil salinisation were known problems from at least the later 3rd millennium BC. No pre-manuring rubbish or manure collection piles have been identified in southern Mesopotamia, but they are also unknown from northern Mesopotamia, where landscape evidence supports this practice. Our lack of evidence may be a problem of scale. Collection and composting before manuring was preferred in imperial Rome,[56] and the process has been intensively examined for Roman/Early

---

[53]   Ur, J., 'CORONA satellite photography and ancient road networks: a northern Mesopotamian case study', *Antiquity* 77 (2003): 102–115; Wilkinson, T.J., 'Extensive sherd scatters and land-use intensity: some recent results', *Journal of Field Archaeology* 16 (1989): 31–46; Wilkinson, T.J., 'Linear hollows in the Jazira, Upper Mesopotamia', *Antiquity* 67 (1993): 548–562.

[54]   Wilkinson, T.J., 'The structure and dynamics of dry-farming states in upper Mesopotamia', *Current Anthropology* 35 (1994): 483–520; Wilkinson 1989.

[55]   Schiffer, M., *Behavioral Archaeology* (New York: Academic Press, 1976); Needham, S., Spence, T., 'Refuse and the formation of middens', *Antiquity* 71 (1997): 77–90.

[56]   Taylor, C., 'The disposal of human waste: a comparison between ancient Rome and medieval London', *Past Imperfect* 11 (2005): 53–72, see p. 57.

Byzantine Sagalassos in southwest Turkey,[57] where such activities took place in an abandoned and repurposed latrine, a relatively small space. Mesopotamian manure collection areas also may have been small and less likely to have a noticeable impact on the archaeological record. As active and rapidly-changing functional locations, they would be relatively ephemeral. And if manuring storage is located in urban edge zones, these are areas that are traditionally unexcavated.

Manuring adds to urban and rural health risks. Although faecal contamination of plants grown in manured soil may vary, the presence of untreated sewage on fields would be a risk to farmers through direct contact. As manuring material dried, it could be inhaled by anyone living near to such fields, in both rural and urban communities. And with the strong winds and sporadic sandstorms in the region, air-borne contamination could have been very widespread.

Rubbish Mounds in Mesopotamia

Many archaeological deposits are inherently rubbish: discarded food, ashes, production debris, or broken artefacts. Streets, alleys, courtyards, and even 'clean' rooms were gradually in-filled with layered rubbish deposits of varying intensities in most regions of the world. In Mesopotamia, such discard practices and in-filling, together with the practice of using previous mud-brick buildings as foundations for subsequent structures, created distinctive 'tell' mounds. But not all rubbish became stratigraphy. There is a widespread assumption, based in modern observation of Middle Eastern villages, that settlement edges were also utilised for rubbish dumping, particularly of larger broken items, sharp objects, or smellier waste, including human waste. The Neolithic town of Çatal Höyük in Anatolia had distinct midden areas within the settlement, separate from the houses but in close proximity to them.[58] These middens contained human and animal coprolites as well as household rubbish.[59] Thus a village could have a number of distinct middens, each belonging to one or more households, or communal. But adaptations must be made when villages grow to cities. With larger human groups and their associated intensity of production, the quantity of rubbish increases exponentially. And even as rubbish generation swells, the distance to the convenient settlement edge midden or middens grows. In addition, space in that settlement edge or peri-urban zone could be under high demand and could see rapidly changing use for

[57]   Baeten, J., Marinova, E., De Laet, V., Degryse, P., de Vos, D., Waelkens., M., 'Faecal biomarker and archaeobotanical analyses in sediments from a public latrine shed new light on ruralisation in Sagalassos, Turkey', *Journal of Archaeological Science* 39 (2012): 1143–1159.

[58]   Shillito, L.-M., Matthews, W., Almond, M., Bull, I., 'The microstratigraphy of middens: capturing daily routine in rubbish at Neolithic Çatalhöyük, Turkey', *Antiquity* 85 (2011): 1024–1038.

[59]   Shillito et al. 2011, 'Biomolecular and micromorphological analysis'.

industry or additional housing. Excavations within cities reveal that street, alley and house discard and accumulation persisted, but the middens at the settlement edge changed in scale and nature.

Three case studies of ancient cities allow exploration of large-scale rubbish dumping and management. In each city, there were large rubbish deposits distinguished by deep sloping layers of soil with extremely high densities of diverse material finds. The potential for disease in these piles of rubbish and human (and animal) waste should have been high, although the arid climate might have mitigated this effect to an extent. As well as the potential for pathogen transference by direct contact and inhalation, rubbish piles would have been homes for disease-bearing insects and rodents. They seem to reflect the textual mentions of rubbish piles as homes for social transgressors, yet in each case, subsequent use of the area for burials and incorporation of the dumps into the urban landscape reveal a revaluing of rubbish.

Ur, South Iraq

Ur lies at the southern edge of the Mesopotamian alluvial plain, with occupation from at least the 5th through the 1st millennia BC. It was the capital of a powerful dynasty during the late 3rd millennium BC (Ur III Period) and was for most of its history a flourishing city with an important temple to the Moon God. Ur is best known for its stepped ziggurat/ temple tower and rich 'Royal Cemetery', the burial place of an elite sector of society during the mid-3rd millennium BC.[60] It is the location of this Royal Cemetery that bears further examination, with regard to the issue of urban rubbish management.

The Royal Cemetery is currently near the centre of the ancient city, but it is probable that the settlement was significantly smaller in the 3rd millennium BC than in the 1st millennium, when it acquired its current plan. The density, nature and slope of deposits in the cemetery location imply that this was a peri-urban zone during the 5th through mid-3rd millennia BC.[61] The initial function appears to have been for pottery production: a deep layer of debris, comprising kilns and enormous numbers of broken sherds and wasters, testifies to long-term industrial use of the area from late 5th through early 3rd millennia BC. Such industries are rarely located within settlements due to their ash, smoke and danger, supporting the theory that this area was at the city edge. Industrial use was followed by mixed rubbish dumping across the early to mid-3rd millennium BC; various deposits were identified, including building rubble and quantities of broken pottery, with other layers of 'dark-coloured rubbish and ashes'[62] that suggest household and other organic waste. In various sub-layers within these deposits were clay model

---

[60] Woolley, C.L., *The Royal Cemetery, Ur Excavations 2* (London: British Museum, 1934).

[61] Woolley 1934; Woolley 1956.

[62] Woolley 1956, p. 5.

chariots, miniature pottery vessels, and a great many discarded cuneiform tablets and clay container sealings, perhaps from the nearby temple.

These rubbish and industrial deposits covered an area about 120 x 50 m and in places were up to approximately 10 m deep. There are at least some episodes of rubbish dumping within the accumulation that seem to have been of large quantities of material in a fairly short time; this is indicated by the depth of layers that can be dated to within a few years by the similarity of artistic style on the incorporated container sealings. Both contents and scale suggest an administrative role in the dumping, as the source of the debris and as managers of the work. The Royal Cemetery graves were then dug into the upper layers. Despite a radical change in function, no attempt was made to move the earlier rubbish; indeed the height and scale of the dumps may have been embraced as providing maximum visibility for an important ritual.

Time does not stop for rubbish after discard. Rubbish itself decays further, particular elements of rubbish may be extracted and re-used as part of a 'refuse-cycle',[63] and rubbish mounds may be repurposed and revalued. The biography of the Ur rubbish dumps, originally dedicated to discard of negative-value materials, was unusually broken *c.* 2450 BC by this change in use of the space for elite burials. The growth of the city and its greater density may have meant that open areas were scarcer, even while shifts in leadership and ideology demanded visible public performance space. The Ur rubbish dumps thus provide insight into the necessity of changes in discard patterns with urban growth. The shift to burial use implies that a new rubbish dump was created, presumably at the new edge of the growing city and at an even greater distance from houses.

Abu Salabikh, South Iraq

Abu Salabikh is a town in the central alluvial plain, with settlement dating mainly to the mid-3rd millennium BC, *c.* 2600–2400 BC. Excavations recovered houses and many sub-floor graves. Rubbish accumulation in the houses exhibits the expected gradual build-up of thin layers and lenses, with occasional larger accumulations in abandoned houses.[64]

Near the houses was a public administrative or religious building, proposed as the source of a large part of an adjacent 'Ash Tip', an area (approximately 32 x 16 m, and 5.5 m deep) of dense sloping layers of ashy soil and incinerated waste. Like the Ur rubbish, some layers within this Ash Tip included higher than normal numbers of miniature vessels, clay discs, human and animal figurines, and clay

---

63   Needham 1997.
64   Postgate, J.N., 'Excavations at Abu Salabikh, 1978–79', *Iraq* 42 (1980): 87–104; Green, A. (ed.), *Abu Salabikh Excavations Volume 4; The 6G Ash Tip and Its Contents: Cultic and Administrative Discard from the Temple?* (London: British School of Archaeology in Iraq, 1993).

container sealings.[65] And like the contents of the rubbish layers at Ur, many items here can be associated with administrative buildings, and their quantities imply a deliberate and managed discard system. Yet there were also tools such as grinding stones and flints, which reflect a source in more quotidian contexts. A complete equid skeleton provides a reminder that cities needed places for discard of dead animals. This equid was discarded a mere 12 m from a still-occupied building and would have been a significant health risk as it decayed, from insects, rodents, and possibly larger scavenging mammals.

Here also, the rubbish heap was later repurposed for graves of infants, children and adults. Although not as rich or as many as in the Ur Royal Cemetery, the grave goods included pottery, beads and tools that indicate the dead were interred with the usual respectful rituals and were not low status. The Abu Salabikh rubbish mound underlines the conclusion from Ur that Mesopotamian urban residents' discard practices needed to be flexible as urban growth changed the use of living spaces. Its close proximity to houses indicates that our assumptions that urban rubbish would have been discarded at a distance from living spaces is not always warranted.

Tell Brak, Northeast Syria

Tell Brak, in northeast Syria, was one of the region's earliest cities, with urban scale, religious and secular institutions, and complex economic behaviour by *c.* 3800 BC. It has a core settlement on a densely occupied high mound, surrounded by a less densely occupied Outer Town. The edge of this Outer Town was demarcated by seven small sub-mounds. One of these, Tell Majnuna at the city's northern edge, was created entirely from repeated episodes of rubbish dumping across approximately three centuries of the mid-4th millennium BC (*c.* 3900–3600 BC). The mound was at least 3 hectares in extent and up to 7 m deep, or roughly 180,000 cubic metres and about 270 million kg. Sixteen archaeological trenches, together with inspection of a cross-section through the mound created by modern construction, revealed no traces of architecture. The 100% rubbish composition of this mound is entirely unexpected. Well-defined mounds are the typical ancient settlement marker for Mesopotamia and when excavated usually prove to be composed of stratified architecture and occupational debris. The assumption that 'tells equal settlements' forms the basis for surface survey-derived reconstruction of regional settlement patterns. At least some of the Majnuna rubbish mound was created by the collection and special deposition of 'feasting garbage', comprising large quantities of distinctively butchered animal bones and open ceramic plates. The animal bones exhibit the typical high wastage marker of feasting events, some elements being discarded whole with little evidence of actual consumption; likewise, some of the ceramics in these layers were discarded nearly complete,

---

[65] Green 1993.

with only minor chips. These feasting deposits were stratigraphically closely associated with mass graves of humans killed in violent conflict.[66]

However, these burial-and-feasting deposits were covered by numerous other large-scale deposits of 'normal' rubbish, each comprising ashy soil, broken ceramics, worn-out or broken tools, lithic debitage, lost single beads, clay container sealings, figurines, and kitchen waste, including animal bones and archaeobotanical remains. A single source for rubbish should yield a limited range of artefact types and broken pieces that can be rejoined. This is not the case for any Majnuna layer other than the special feasting discard deposits. Each 'normal' deposit includes rubbish from households, such as pottery sherds, figurines, food refuse, and broken or lost tools. But each also includes materials from production centres or workshops, such as lithic debitage and ceramic wasters. And finally, rubbish from institutions is represented in particular by the container sealings. The stratigraphic layering, however, indicates that the deposition was not piecemeal and prolonged but was performed in a series of large-scale but relatively rapid sessions. The paradox of the varied contents and homogenous deposition method can be resolved if there was an administered and concerted effort to gather rubbish from across the site, from all types of contexts. The scale of the rubbish mound and of the distinct layers within it suggests that communal labour was regularly mobilised for its creation and that the mound was a solution to a growing urban problem.

What do these three rubbish dumps have in common? The contents are mixed materials that appear to represent the full range of urban rubbish. Each contains elite, institution-related material (tablets or sealings), together with domestic rubbish such as broken ceramics and food debris, as well as discard from craft production of basic items such as tools. From 3rd millennium BC Egypt to 19th century AD Washington, DC, 'elite' wealthy residences and similar contexts (e.g., temples) are generally associated with less rubbish than houses of working class or non-elites.[67] It is not the case that elites throw out less, but that they discard it beyond the house or temple. That 'elite' rubbish must go somewhere. The high percentage of elite items in these three cases is therefore understandable and need not imply ownership; however, it does suggest a degree of rubbish management.

The rubbish piles are evidence of a negative aspect, the accumulation of waste within the settlement that required maintenance and removal. But they also project a positive aspect, the conscious creation of an urban landscape feature. While Tell Majnuna's visibility may have been the highest, since it stood at the edge of the settlement, the rubbish piles at Ur and Abu Salabikh were adjacent to important buildings and were or became central to the settlement. Unlike modern landfill

---

[66]   McMahon, A., Weber, J., Soltysiak, A., 'Late Chalcolithic mass graves at Tell Brak, Syria, and violent conflict during the growth of early city-states', *Journal of Field Archaeology* 36 (2011): 201–220.

[67]   Hoffman, M.A., 'The social context of trash disposal in an early dynastic Egyptian town', *American Antiquity* 39 (1974): 35–50; Crane 2000.

sites that aim to make garbage invisible, the use of these Mesopotamian rubbish mounds celebrates their scale and volume. What may have begun as the outcome of rubbish management became symbolic of urban success.

Conclusion

Rubbish and human waste were an early and endemic problem associated with urban growth. The absence of civic infrastructure to provide clean water and to remove waste and rubbish would have rendered the Mesopotamian urban populations vulnerable to water- and air-borne diseases. It was left to the individual and household to develop solutions; toilets were never completely embraced and water acquisition was never efficiently resolved. Individuals may have developed tolerable solutions, but the uneven uptake of those solutions left the larger urban group at risk. However, rubbish and waste deposits could be 'valuable', in that waste was probably collected and used to increase soil fertility. Rubbish could also be strategically placed or used to alter the urban landscape.

Chapter 4

Latrines and Wastewater Sanitation Technologies in Ancient Greece

Georgios P. Antoniou and Andreas N. Angelakis

'… all the sewers were still working! It was very interesting for me to see the water in the drainages and sewers so big that a man could enter. I doubt if there are other examples of ancient sewerages working after 4 thousand years'.

Angelo Mosso, during his visit to the palace of Phaistos in the early 1900s.[1]

Introduction

The aim of this paper is to demonstrate the archaeological evidence for latrines, sewers and drains in ancient Greece. This will enable us to understand better what facilities were available in different time periods, how design changed over time, how common such sanitation facilities were, and social attitudes to private and communal latrine use. The resulting body of evidence helps us to place into context the efforts made by those in the past to deal with human waste.

In order to understand how sanitation in classical Greece evolved, it is useful to appreciate what existed in other cultures of the ancient world, especially those around the Mediterranean. The earliest well-known multiple flushing lavatories attached to a sophisticated sewage system that have so far been identified in the world were located in the ancient cities of Harappa and Mohenjo-daro in Indus Valley, dating from the mid-3rd millennium BC.[2] Closer to the Mediterranean, in ancient Egypt there were cesspool lavatories located indoors for wealthy houses and temples, and outdoors for other dwellings. Excavations have revealed that underneath a wooden or stone slab seat was a hole leading to a cesspool, which was either filled with sand or emptied every few days onto nearby fields using the human waste as fertiliser.[3] At Abusir, a brass drainpipe running from the upper temple was found along the connecting masonry causeway to the outer temple on the river. At the temple of King Suhura at Abusir stone basins in niches on the

---

[1]   Mosso, A., *Escursioni nel Mediterraneo e gli Scavi di Creta* (Milan: Fratelli Treves, 1907).

[2]   Pruthi, R.K., *Prehistory and Harappan Civilization* (Delhi: APH, 2004), p. 106.

[3]   James P., Thorpe N., *Ancient Inventions* (New York: Ballantine Books, 1995), p. 442–56.

walls were used as lavatories, and pipes of beaten copper were used to empty the waste. In addition to these lavatories, a portable lavatory consisting of a wooden stool with a large slot in the middle for use with a pottery vessel beneath was discovered in the tomb of Kha.[4] Recent study has demonstrated human intestinal parasites among the Essene sect at Qumran, near the Dead Sea.[5] Living about 2,000 years ago, the Essenes seem to have used a hatchet to bury their faeces just below surface soil. However, a stone lavatory seat with keyhole-shaped defecation opening was recovered from a house in Jerusalem dating to *c.* 500–700 BC, confirming the presence of such technology by that date.[6]

The presence or absence of lavatory sewerage with flushing technology is that which distinguishes the majority of the earlier simple lavatory structures from the more innovative constructions of later antiquity.[7] Despite advances in engineering, the application of simpler lavatory constructions continued throughout most of antiquity. From the early Minoan era (*c.* 3200–2300 BC) issues related to water supply were considered of great importance and were accordingly developed.[8] Distinct from the flushing lavatory constructions of the Indus Valley civilisation, the history of water supply and wastewater engineering on Crete dates back more than *c.*4,500 years.[9]

Here we explore the evidence for sewers, lavatories, and other sanitation technologies in ancient Greece, compare how these technologies varied over time in different regions of Greece, and how their design and use evolved in the context of ancient Greek civilisations, focusing mostly on the engineering evolution through the centuries. The major archaeological sites considered in this study are shown in Figure 4.1.

---

[4]   James and Thorpe 1995, p. 442–56.

[5]   Harter, S., Bouchet, F., Mumcuoglu, K.Y., Zias, J., 'Toilet practices among members of the Dead Sea Scroll sect at Qumran (100BC-68AD)', *Revue de Qumran* 21 (2004): 579–84; Zias, J.E., Tabor, J.D., Harter-Lailheugue, S., 'Toilets at Qumran, the Essenes, and the scrolls, new anthropological data and old theories', *Revue de Qumran* 22 (2006): 631–640.

[6]   Cahill, J., Reinhard, K., Tarler, D., Warnock, P., 'It had to happen: scientists examine remains of ancient bathroom', *Biblical Archaeological Review* 17 (1991): 64–9.

[7]   Antoniou, G.P., 'Lavatories in ancient Greece', *Water Science and Technology: Water Supply* 7 (2007): 155–164; Antoniou, G.P., 'Ancient Greek lavatories: operation with reused water', in L.W. Mays (ed.), *Ancient Water Technologies* (Dordrecht: Springer, 2010), pp. 67–86.

[8]   Angelakis, A.N., Spyridakis, S.V., 'Wastewater management in Minoan times', in E. Diamadopoulos and G.P. Korfiatis (eds), *Proceedings of the Meeting on Protection and Restoration of Environment* (Chania: Technical University of Crete, 1996) pp. 549–558.

[9]   Angelakis, A.N., Koutsoyiannis, D.,, Tchobanoglous, G., 'Urban wastewater and stormwater technologies in the ancient Greece', *Water Research* 39 (2005): 210–220.

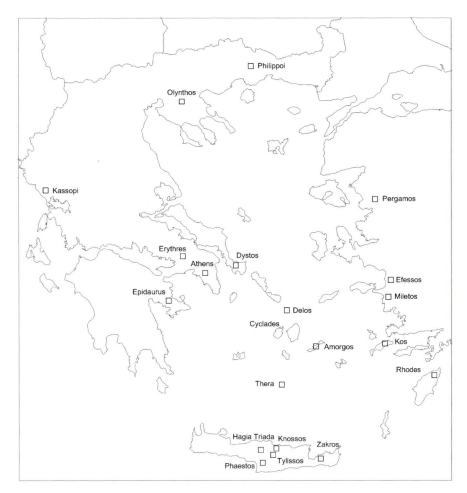

Figure 4.1.   The major archaeological sites discussed in this paper.

Sanitation in the Minoan Period

Archaeological evidence indicates that during the Bronze Age complex water management and sanitary techniques were practised in several settlements on the island of Crete, the home of the Minoans.[10] Increasing cultural complexity can be observed throughout the third and second millennia BC, but great progress was made in Crete, especially in the Middle Bronze Age (*c.* 2100–1600 BC), when the

    [10]   Angelakis, A.N., Koutsoyiannis, D., 'Urban water resources management in ancient Greek times', in B.A. Stewart and T. Howell (eds), *The Encyclopedia of Water Sciences* (New York: Markel Dekker, 2003), pp. 999–1008.

population in its central and southern regions increased, towns were developed, the first palaces were built, and Crete achieved a prosperous and uniform culture. In the early phases of the Late Bronze Age (*c.* 1600–1400 BC), Crete appears to have reached its peak, as evidenced by the larger houses and more luxurious palaces.[11] At this time, the flourishing arts, improvements in metalwork, along with the construction of better-equipped palaces, and a comprehensive road system, reveal a wealthy, highly cultured, well-organised society and government in Crete. However, one of the notable characteristics of the Minoan and Mycenaean civilisations were the architectural and hydraulic functions of sanitary structures such as sewers, drains, bathrooms, and lavatories.[12]

The construction of palaces reveals a notable development in water management in the urban context. Moreover, during the Middle Minoan and the beginning of the Late Minoan periods (*c.* 2000–1500 BC) a cultural explosion occurred on the island. A striking indication of this is manifested in the complex water management techniques practised in Crete at that time. These included various types of water resources, such as wells and ground-water hydrology, aqueducts, and domestic water supply applicable to local conditions in terms of climate and geomorphology. Additionally, the construction and use of sanitary facilities, even the recreational uses of water, signify attitudes to life and taste.[13] Numerous advanced clean water and waste water systems including aqueducts, cisterns, filtering systems, rainfall-harvesting systems, terracotta pipes for water supply, fountains, baths, sewers, and lavatories were in use in Minoan palaces and other settlements.[14]

The Minoans introduced many innovations, particularly in the management of water and wastewater. The palaces of the Minoans were very open in their design, served as community centres, and people could walk into any room they wanted. In the palaces, they had running water and flushing lavatories. This innovation was helpful because all of the waste would go outside of the building, and be away from the living places. In their houses, their bathtubs were mobile. This allowed them to move their bathtubs into different rooms and bring the tub to the person,

---

[11]　Koutsoyiannis, D., Zarkadoulas, N., Angelakis, A.N., Tchobanoglous, G., 'Urban water management in ancient Greece: legacies and lessons', *ASCE, Journal of Water Resources Planning & Management* 134 (2008): 45–54.

[12]　Angelakis, A. N., Spyridakis, S. V., 'The status of water resources in Minoan times: a preliminary study', in A.N. Angelakis and A.S. Issar (eds), *Diachronic Climatic Impacts on Water Resources with Emphasis on Mediterranean Region* (Heidelberg: Springer-Verlag, 1996), pp. 161–191.

[13]　Lyrintzis, A.,Angelakis, A.N., 'Is the "Labyrinth" a water catchment technology? A preliminary approach', in A.N. Angelakis and D. Koutsoyannis (eds), *IWA Specialty Conference: 1st International Symposium on Water and Wastewater Technologies in Ancient Civilizations* (Iraklion: National Foundation for Agricultural Research, 2006), pp. 163–174.

[14]　Angelakis et al. 2005.

not the person to the tub. To serve their gods, the Minoans had ritual baths in their palaces.[15]

One of the salient characteristics of Minoan civilisation was the hydraulic function of the storm water and wastewater in the palaces and cities. In the entire structure of the Minoan palace nothing is more impressive than the elaborate sewerage system that runs throughout its domestic quarter and adjoining halls. Evans[16] and MacDonald and Driessen,[17] described the course of these sewers and drew plans of what they considered to have been their original form. Such a plan of the entire sewerage system of Knossos has been published by Angelakis and Spyridakis.[18] This plan provides visitors with a basic orientation of the site and helps them to view the entire network in an integrated manner. A stone-by-stone description of the sewerage system with reference to the architecture above has also been attempted by MacDonald and Driessen.[19] The total extent of the sewerage system, including outlets and tributaries, exceeds one hundred and fifty metres. The modest size of the channels and other obstacles prevented a more thorough examination.

Besides the innovative structures from Minoan Crete, many remains of similar constructions that incorporate flushing technology have been found in the ancient Greek world. Fresh or reused water was employed for this type of flushing. The hygiene installations can be viewed as a characteristic factor indicating higher living standards and economic prosperity, both in domestic and public settings; lavatories often demonstrate luxury elements.[20] The sanitary facilities had been widely applied in domestic-residential buildings. It is evident that during the Hellenistic period great technical and functional progress had occurred in these kinds of structures. It is interesting to note that many of the terms used for defecation in ancient Greek are still in use in the modern Greek language.[21]

---

[15]   Angelakis, A.N., Lyrintzis, A.G., Spyridakis, S.V., 'A brief history of water and wastewater technologies in Minoan Crete, Greece', in I. Koyuncu, Z. Sen, S. Ozturk, M. Altinbas, and I. Ozturk (eds), *Proceedings of the 3rd IWA International Symposium on Water and Wastewater Technologies in Ancient Civilizations* (Istanbul: Istanbul Technical University, 2012), pp. 208–216; Angelakis et al. 2005.

[16]   Evans, S.A., *The Palace of Minos at Knossos: a Comparative Account of the Successive Stages of the Early Cretan Civilization as Illustrated by the Discoveries* (New York: Hafner, 1964), pp. 225–41.

[17]   MacDonald, C.F., Driessen, J.M., 'The drainage system of the domestic quarter in the palace at Knossos', *Annual of the British School at Athens* 83 (1988): 235–358.

[18]   Angelakis and Spyridakis 1996, 'The status of water resources'.

[19]   MacDonald and Driessen 1988.

[20]   Antoniou 2007.

[21]   Angelakis et al. 2005.

Sewerage and Drainage Systems

It is clear that during the Minoan era extensive systems and elaborate structures for water supply, irrigation and drainage were planned, designed and built to supply the growing population centres and agriculture with water.[22] In several Minoan palaces discovered by archaeologists in the 20th century, one of the most important elements was the provision and distribution of water and the transfer of sewerage in drains by means of hydraulic systems. Rainwater from the flat roofs of the palace at Knossos was carried off by vertical pipes; one of these, located in the eastern wing, emptied into a stone sewer head from which a stone channel carried the flow of storm water.[23]

The plumbing arrangements and especially the sewers in the Minoan cities were carefully planned. In the palace of Minos, surface water from a part of the Central Court was handled by a very capacious underground channel built of stone and lined with cement. It ran beneath the passage leading from the north entrance and received inflowing water from various channels. The most fully explored plan of the palace sewerage system was the portion that ran beneath the floors of the Residential Quarter. This formed a great loop with its high point located under the light-well, next to the Grand Staircase, and emptied via a combined channel down the slope to the east of the palace.[24] In the area of the Hall of the Double-Axes and the Queen's Hall with its associated chambers, it received the wastewater of no less than five light-wells. It also served a lavatory on the lowest floor, and was connected with three vertical shafts. The latter received storm water from the roof and were probably connected with lavatories on the upper floors. The sewers were built of stone blocks lined with cement and measured about 78 by 38 cm per section.[25] They were large enough to permit men to enter them for cleaning or maintenance; in fact, manholes were provided for that purpose, and airshafts at intervals also helped with ventilation.[26] Covered stone, slab-built sewerage systems are evident in many cities to carry away sewage and rain water. The remains at Knossos palace show clearly how rainwater collected from the roof by way of light-wells was used to flush out sewage from bathrooms and lavatories. Evans and MacDonald and Driessen[27] described the course of these facilities and drew plans of what they considered to have been their original form. Such a plan of the entire sewerage and drainage system of Knossos is illustrated in Figure 4.2.

---

[22]   Angelakis and Koutsoyiannis 2003.

[23]   Angelakis et al. 2005.

[24]   Angelakis and Spyridakis 1996, 'The status of water resources'.

[25]   Evans 1964, 226–241.

[26]   Graham, J.W., *The Palaces of Crete* (Princeton: Princeton University Press, 1987), p. 219–221.

[27]   Evans 1964; MacDonald and Driessen 1988.

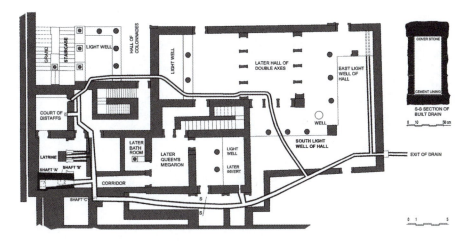

Figure 4.2.   The sewerage and drainage system of Knossos beneath the
Domestic Quarter. Adapted from Evans 1964.

Other Minoan palaces and cities were also equipped with elaborate storm
drainage and sewer systems (Figure 4.3).[28] Open terracotta and stone conduits
were used to convey and remove rainwater and limited quantities of wastewater.
However, terracotta pipes were scarcely used for this purpose. Larger sewers
were used in Minoan palaces at Knossos and Phaistos. It has been argued that
these large sewers may have led to the concept of the labyrinth, the subterranean
structure in the form of a maze that hosted the mythical hybrid monster known as
the Minotaur.[29] More on Minoan conduits has been reported by Angelakis et al.[30]

The sewerage system of Zakros was quite dense and of high water-engineering
standards for its time.[31] As at Knossos and other Minoan cities, Zakros provides
us with well-preserved remains of sophisticated networks in which there were
descending shafts and well-constructed stone sewers, large enough to permit the
passage of a man. Yet, there is evidence to suggest that the entire system was not
completely effective in times of heavy or extended storms. Due to the location of
the site on a natural slope, the eventual disposal of wastewater and storm water

---

[28]   MacDonald C. F.,Driessen, J.M., 'The storm drains of the east wing at Knossos',
Bulletin de Correspondance Hellénique Suppl. 19 (1990): 141–146.

[29]   Angelakis et al. 2005.

[30]   Angelakis, A.N., Koutsoyiannis, D., Papanikolaou, P., 'On the geometry of the
Minoan water conduits', in I. Koyuncu (ed.), *Proceedings of the 3rd IWA International
Symposium on Water and Wastewater Technologies in Ancient Civilizations* (Istanbul:
Istanbul Technical University, 2012), pp. 172–177.

[31]   Platon, M., 'New indications for the problems of purgatory cisterns and bathrooms
in Minoan World', in *Proceedings of the 6th International Cretologic Congress* (Chania:
Literary Association Chrysostomos, 1990), A2:141–155 (in Greek).

Figure 4.3.   Parts of Minoan sewerage and drainage systems: (a) central
system at Phaistos palace and (b) at the 'Little palace' at Knossos.
Copyright permission A.N. Angelakis.

into the sea was most likely. Platon noted three basic types of conduits in the
sewerage system of Zakros: a clay-conduit in reversed π-shape, another built up
with stones and a third, narrow type, constructed with stones but open at the top.[32]
A small section of the Zakros sewerage system, as it appears today, is shown in
Figure 4.4a.

One of the most advanced Minoan sanitary and storm sewer systems was
discovered in Hagia Triadha, close to the south coast of Crete west of Phaistos.[33]
The Italian writer Angelo Mosso who visited the villa of Hagia Triadha at the
beginning of the 20th century and inspected the storm sewer system (Figure 4.4b)
noticed that all the sewers of the villa functioned perfectly and was amazed to see
storm water coming out of sewers, 4,000 years after their construction.[34]

---

[32]   Platon 1974.
[33]   Angelakis et al. 2005.
[34]   Mosso 1907; Gray, H.F., 'Sewerage in ancient and medieval times', *Sewage Works
Journal* 12 (1940): 939–946.

Figure 4.4.   Parts of Minoan sewerage and drainage systems: (a) in Zakros and
(b) Hagia Triada. Copyright permission A. N. Angelakis.

Minoan Toilets or Lavatories

The first sophisticated drainage systems that were constructed in Minoan Crete date from *c*. 2500 to 1600 BC. Thus lavatories were flushed and connected to the drainage and sewerage systems. Comparable to the contemporary Indus Valley's civilisation in South Asia (*c*. 2600–1900 BC), streets were built on a grid pattern and networks of sewers were constructed under them. Lavatories were flushed with water. There is the possibility that the sanitation ideas of these two civilisations may have spread through the Egyptians, where the homes of the wealthy included bathrooms and lavatories. Lavatories seats were made of limestone.

No public lavatories were present in Minoan Crete, while in a number of houses the lavatory was quite clearly located in the private living rooms (e.g., Knossos, Phaistos, Tylissos, Malia, and Gournia). In most cases the evidence for the identification of a lavatory was from the existence of a sewer at the floor level passing through the exterior wall and connecting with the outside central sewerage and drainage system. However, in some homes there are also traces of some sort of provision for a stone or wooden seat.

One of the most interesting rooms on the ground floor in the residential quarter of the Knossos palace was identified as a lavatory. Remains of a clay tube were found just outside the door of the room. It is thought that water was poured through a hole in the floor immediately outside the lavatory door, while an under-floor channel linked the hole with the vertical clay pipe under the lavatory seat.[35] The lavatory could thus be flushed even during a rainless summer, either by an attendant outside the lavatory or by the user. The lavatory in the residential quarter of the Palace of Minos in Knossos is probably the earliest flush lavatory in history.[36]

---

[35]   Castleden, R., *Minoans: Life in Bronze Age Crete* (London: Routledge, 1993).
[36]   Angelakis et al. 2005 p. 212 fl.

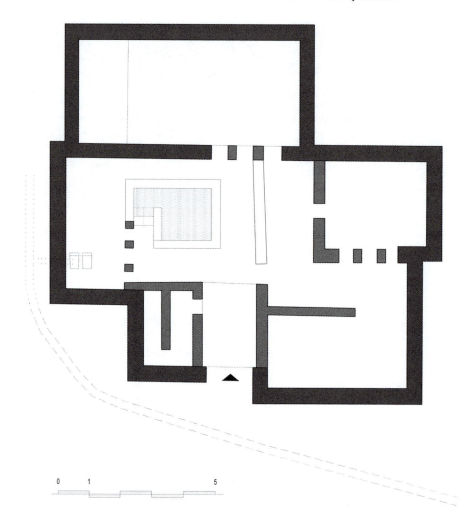

Figure 4.5 (a) Toilet in House Da, Malia: (a) Layout of the house (After Graham
1987) and (b) a recent photo. Copyright permission
A. N. Angelakis.

At certain times of the year the drains in the palace of Minos may have been
adequately flushed through by the rainfall that fell into the light-wells, but in
general it was supposed that water was poured into the lavatories to flush them. It
was also observed that there was sufficient space at the end of the seat at Queen's
Hall lavatory in Knossos for a large pitcher.[37] The lavatory is similar in function to

---

[37]   Graham 1987, pp. 108–110.

Figure 4.5 (b)

that of the so-called Queen's Hall, those found in the Phaistos and Malia palaces, as well as those in some Minoan cities and houses.

Fortunately, one of the houses near the palace at Malia, known as Da, contains a lavatory seat in nearly perfect condition, since it was made out of stone, not of wood like the seat at the palace of Minos in Knossos. This stone seat was 68.50 cm long by 45.50 cm wide front to back, and its surface was 34–38 cm above the floor (Figure 4.5). It was built directly against an outside wall through which a large sewer passed.[38] Like that in Knossos, the structure was evidently intended for use as a seat rather than to squat on. Thus, it resembles the 'Egyptian' toilet more than the so-called 'Turkish' type found in the palaces at Mari in Syria and Alalakh in Turkey.[39] However, there is a substantial difference between those lavatories and the Minoan lavatories, due to their flushing processes and their connections to the sewers. A similar lavatory to that discovered in the Palace of Minos in Knossos has been discovered in the west side of the so-called Queen's Apartment at Phaistos. It was connected to a closed sewer, part of which still exists. Another lavatory

[38]   Graham 1987, p. 110.
[39]   Angelakis et al. 2005.

and sewer was discovered in House C at Tylissos.[40] In addition, most Minoan lavatories were located near or next to the bathrooms, such as those in Queen's Hall at Knossos, Queen's Apartment at Phaeitos, and in House Da at Malia.

Some palaces had lavatories with flushing systems operated by pouring water into a conduit.[41] The best example of such an installation was found in the island of Thera (Santorini) in the Cyclades.[42] This is the best-preserved example belonging to *c.* 1550 BC, in the Bronze Age settlement of Akrotiri, which shares the same cultural context as that of Crete.

The Minoan and Mycenaean civilisations shared some common practices when it came to sanitation. Both had baths that fitted the human body, and drainpipes for vertical water transfer. However, in Mycenaean culture there was no running water in lavatories, and their bathtubs were not portable like the those of the Minoans. The palaces of the Minoan and Mycenaean civilisations both had large columns and throne rooms and they also both painted their walls with scenes from nature. However, the Mycenaeans burnt oils to please their gods, instead of taking ritual baths. Also, they had protective fortresses instead of community centres. Both Minoan and Mycenaean civilisations were writing in straight lines on clay tablets, on which they also wrote about religion. However, the Mycenaeans used Linear B (letters and characters) that has been translated, allowing us to understand their rituals better, whereas Minoans used pictures, which make it difficult for us to understand their views on sanitation.[43]

The Evolution of the Typical Ancient Greek Lavatories

The design of a typical lavatory in ancient Greece seems to have been completed by the 4th century BC, and incorporated all the pre-existing design features of that type. Some documentation for similar installations in the Minoan and the Mycenaean period has already being discussed.[44] Even though lavatories were mentioned in the texts, we have not found any public or private lavatories dated in the Classical period (5th–4th centuries BC).[45] Despite the absence of flushing lavatories in excavations from this time period, cesspits (κοπρών – kopron) have been found in the course of excavations by the American School of Classical Studies in houses of this period in Athens (specifically north of Areios Pagos).

---

[40]   Angelakis and Spyridakis 1996 'The status of water resources'.

[41]   Angelakis et al. 2005.

[42]   Palyvou, C., *Akrotiri Thera: an Architecture of Affluence 3500 years old* (Philadelphia: INSTAP, 2005), pp. 41–42, 51–53.

[43]   Bengtson, H., *Griechische Geschichte*, 9th edition (Munich: Beck, 2002), pp. 8–15.

[44]   Angelakis et al. 2005: 212.

[45]   Neudecker, R., *Die Pracht der Latrine: zum Wandel Öffentlicher Bedürfnisanstalten in der Kaiserzeitlichen Stadt München* (Munich: Pfeil, 1994), pp. 14, 16, 88, 157; Vatin, C., 'Jardins et services voirie', *Bulletin de Correspondance Hellénique* 100 (1976): 555–64.

Similarly, on Rhodes small rectangular constructions under the streets just outside the houses are believed to be *koprons* (cesspools).[46]

Containers of clay for defecation are known – κοπροδόχοι – *koprodochoi* – (amides or skoramides from Athens) as well as anatomically shaped earthen seats (from Olynthus, Figure 4.6, right images), which look like modern lavatory seats.[47] In these seats the absence of a base combined with the form of the lower edge (Figure 4.6, left images) suggests they were either used over cesspits or along with some other mechanism for the collection and drainage of excrement. The presence of such utensils in Olynthus, which was destroyed by Philipp II in 348 BC, could easily date them to the 5th century BC. In addition, at Olynthus an earthen clay utensil with a sewerage pipe also made of clay was found on floor. Its shape, according to the excavator, suggests that it was used along with another component that was not preserved, such as a wooden seat or small relevant board.[48] Finally, recent discoveries in Epidaurus, specifically at the foundations of Avaton, seem to include one of the first equivalent stone examples of a lavatory seat.

It seems that chamber pots or portable vessels were the most commonly used kind of lavatory during the Classical period, despite the development of earlier flushing Minoan constructions. Study of the time, when lavatories with this mature design appeared, suggests that this is most likely to have happened in the early 4th century BC. The key evidence for this hypothesis is the absence of excavated lavatories dating to the 5th century BC (although they were reported in the ancient texts) together with their appearance at the end of that century in Thera, Amorgos and Delos. Small public lavatories rather than private ones can be identified in ancient Thera.[49]

Several similar installations in Minoan Crete[50] are very early examples to be considered as one of the first links in their evolutionary chain. Despite this, it must be borne in mind that some knowledge of complex lavatory design must have been passed down through the centuries as they later reappeared. Numerous lavatories have been found in mansion houses, dwellings and public buildings in Delos demonstrating the importance of the island for the study of ancient lavatories.[51] Moreover, the economic and social evolution of Delos during the post-Peloponnesian war period as a commercial and naval centre of the Helladic

---

[46] Filimonos (Φιλήμονος), M., 'Τα αστικά απορρίμματα στην αγροτική παραγωγή. Η μαρτυρία της αρχαίας Ρόδου', in I. Λυριτζής και Α. Σάμψων (eds), *Αρχαιολογία και Περιβάλλον στα Δωδεκάνησα. Έρευνα και Πολιτισμικός Τουρισμός*. Διεθνές Συνέδριο, Τμήμα Μεσογειακών Σπουδών, Εργαστήριο Αρχαιομετρίας. Έκδοση Πρακτικών (Ροδος, 2000) (in Greek).

[47] Robinson, D., *Olynthos VIII* (Baltimore: Johns Hopkins, 1938), pp. 205–6, and Pl. 54 and 55.

[48] Robinson 1938, p. 205–6.

[49] Gaertringen, J.F.W.R.A.H., *Thera 3* (Berlin, 1899), Plan II, F 136, 141.

[50] Angelakis et al. 2005: 212.

[51] Antoniou 2007.

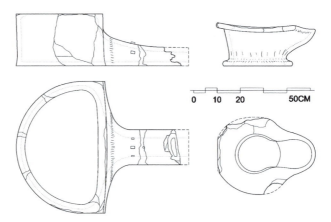

Figure 4.6.   Earthen lavatory seat and defecation vessel, Olynthus. After
Robinson 1938

space justifies that importance. This society of prosperous tradesmen and sailors
was a logical place to confront a problem that challenged all ancient cities and
highlighted the critical issue of hygiene. The significance of Delos for the evolution
of the typical layout of the ancient Greek lavatory is important, and is worthy of
detailed historical investigation.

The usual layout of the lavatory was formed during the following centuries in
the greater Hellenic region with numerous examples, not only on the islands but
also on the mainland. The technologies and techniques used for the design and
construction of the lavatories during that period are distinct from those used at
earlier cultural periods. In addition to that, it is evident that such advanced sanitary
systems are being found even in ordinary houses and not only in palaces as in
Minoan and Mycenaean civilisations. Many lavatories dated to the 2nd century
BC have been preserved in residences (Delos, Thira, Amorgos, Dystos, Kassopi,
and Erythrai) and in public buildings (especially Gymnasia and Palaestrae). The
public examples present more complicated layout and technical details. It seems
that an evolution of these technologies follows the improvement of the cultural
and social achievements of the late Classical and early Hellenistic periods, along
with the increased prosperity of the Hellenic world combined with the campaigns
of Alexander. These technologies are characteristic of the contemporary attitudes
to sanitation, representing the efforts of their designers and constructors to
achieve high sanitary standards. Considering the constructions in Delos, with
the numerous domestic lavatories as well as those in Dystos and Kassiope, it is
obvious that sanitation had become essential for the people of that period and not
a luxury. Moreover the widespread significance of sanitation should be related to
the increased social status of the upper middle class of that period.

Description of the Typical Lavatory

Existing evidence suggests that the main differences between private and public lavatories in the early periods were their size, represented by the number of defecation holes, and the existence or absence of continuous water flow. Private lavatories were generally single, whereas public facilities were communal, sometimes for tens of users at a time. It is also noteworthy that in Thira there are a large number of public lavatories,[52] while in Delos private lavatories dominate.

The Sewage Pipe Network

The layout of multiple lavatories was largely determined by the perimetric channel present under the defecation benches. At public lavatories, the channel was usually supplied with naturally flowing water. In contrast, such water flow was present in few private residential lavatories, and in some cases it was linked with the kitchen or the bath tub. In many examples of naturally flowing water supply for flushing, the water was reused following another household activity. In most residences, it was connected to pipes from the bathroom or the kitchen, in Delos and Ostia, respectively.[53] In cases of a continuous flow irrigation system from a stream, there is an inflow and outflow channel. However, in cases where the flushing was performed with the reused domestic water out of the kitchen or the bath, there was only the outflow duct and a 'flushing hole' at one edge of the lavatory.

The requirements for outflow of sewage meant that the lavatory was typically located at the periphery of the building, adjacent to a street. Even though the location of the lavatory in the house's layout should be examined in comparison with the distinction between 'public' and 'private' sectors within the residence, as in the Maison du Diadumene in Delos,[54] it appears that the most important aspects for latrine positioning were engineering issues such as convenient sewage outflow (e.g. Maison du Diadumene in Delos),[55] and the flowing water intake (as in Ithidiki's house in Amorgos, Figure 4.8, and at Philippoi, Figure 4.9).[56] The sewage drained through ditches along the streets or even in open spaces in cases of small houses (e.g. in Dystos).[57] Sometimes the household lavatory was placed at a corner of the building, while an alternative for residences, particularly at Delos was its location in a small room near the entrance. This may be a practical consequence

---

[52] Gaertingen 1899, Plan II.

[53] Chamonard, J., *Le Quartier du Theatre*, Collection Exploration Archéologique de Délos no.8, 3 vols (Paris: Boccard, 1922–1924); Hoepfner, W. (ed.), *Geschichte des Wohnens*, vol. 1 (Stuttgart: Deutsche Verlags-Anstalt, 1999), p. 895f.

[54] Chamonard 1924.

[55] Chamonard 1924, Figure 7.

[56] Antoniou, G.P., 'Ancient Greek lavatories: operation with reused water', in L.W. Mays (ed.), *Ancient Water Technologies* (Dordrecht: Springer, 2010), pp. 67–86.

[57] Hoepfner 1999, pp. 359, 362, 366.

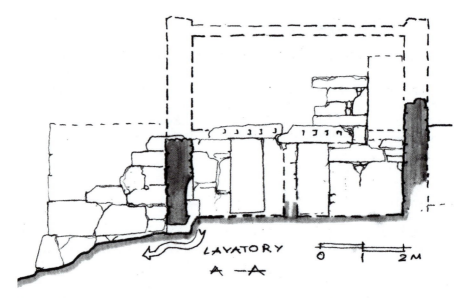

Figure 4.7.   Section of the ruined house at Dystos. (after Hoepfner 1999)

Figure 4.8.   Lavatory of Ithidiki's residence in Minoa, Amorgos. Copyright
                permission by G. Antoniou.

Figure 4.9.   Lavatories at the Gymnasium of Philippoi. The Gymnasium's
entrance is at the top right of the picture. Copyright permission by
G. Antoniou.

of the typical placement of the cesspit (κόπρωνας – kopronas) by the entrance of Athenian houses.[58] The pipe network and the sewers reduced the likelihood that house modifications such as additions of lavatories could be undertaken in existing buildings. Therefore only a few buildings seem to have been equipped with a lavatory added after their construction. One such example was at the Stoa of Kotys in Epidaurus.[59]

In most cases sewerage connected the lavatory outflow channel to the town's drains in a nearby street, while there were cases where no sewerage was provided outside the house. The case of the lavatory in a house of Dystos highlights the effect of the terrain on such constructions.[60] The inclination of the ground led to a layout with similarities to the lavatory in Minoa's Gymnasium. However, the main difference is that in Dystos there was no natural water flow and also the sewerage

---

[58]   Thompson, H., Wycherlay, R., *The Agora of Athens XIV* (Princeton: ASCSA, 1972), pp. 177–9, f. 42.

[59]   Antoniou 2007.

[60]   Hoepfner 1999, pp. 359–366f.

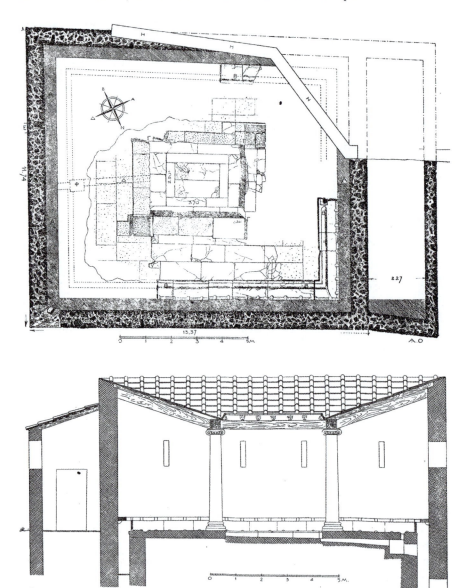

Figure 4.10.   The lavatory outside Roman Agora, Athens: (a, top) plan and (b, bottom) restored longitudinal section. (Orlandos 1940.)

emptied freely into the space just outside the house, without any conduit.[61] In Erythres, the lavatory was placed in the corner of the atrium on the narrow side of room, just opposite the door. The sewage was just directed outside of the building without connecting to further drainage channels.[62]

Perimetric Channel

The perimetric channel or ditch often lay along three sides of the latrine chamber, in a U shape, and was typically uncovered. In smaller private lavatories it was usually located along two sides, in an L shape.[63] Extremely small examples have a simple linear ditch. In contrast, in the later large public lavatories it lay along all four sides (Athens, Philippoi, and the Asklipieia in Kos, Pergamon, and Epidaurus).[64] In those cases, the part in front of the door was completely covered so no one trod in the water.

The input of water, either through a flowing channel or carried within a container, was generally located opposite the sewage outflow. In some cases, such as Philippoi and at the Stoa of Kotys in Epidaurus,[65] they were constructed in such positions where the turbulence increased the velocity of the water and therefore improved the flushing of the lavatory. The channel was designed to optimise the natural flow of water, either by initially having significant height on entry to the room (Roman Agora, Athens, Figure 4.10) or by adjusting the lavatory's floor to a lower level (Philippoi, Figure 4.9).

Lavatory Seats

The bench-shaped seat was typically made out of stone slabs ranging from 10 to 20 cm thick and from 45 to 50 cm wide, and positioned roughly 45 to 50 cm above the floor. The length varied depending upon the size of lavatory and the number of defecation apertures in each slab and on the distance between them. This distance varied between 1.20 m in Minoa, Amorgos, to 2.30 m in the Philippoi's lavatory.[66]

Under every lavatory seat, even in the simplest ones, was a vertical slab that covered the space between the floor and the seat. The typical height of 45 cm mentioned above is as high as a chair. This not only hid the faeces from view, but

---

[61]　Hoepfner 1999, p. 359, haus J, Figure 7.
[62]　Hoepfner 1999, p. 450f.
[63]　Hoepfner 1999, p. 523f, Figure 8.
[64]　Orlandos, A., 'The role of the Roman building located northern of horologe of Andronikos Kiristos', *Proceedings of the Athens Academy* (1940): 251–260 (in Greek); Lemerle, P., 'Palestre romaine à Philippes', *Bulletin de Correspondance Hellénique* 61 (1937): 86–102, Pl. IX; Schatzman, P., *Kos* (Berlin: Deutsches Archäologisches Institut, 1932), Tf. 34, pp. 68–69; Antoniou 2007.
[65]　Antoniou 2007.
[66]　Lemerle 1937, Pl. IX, XI.

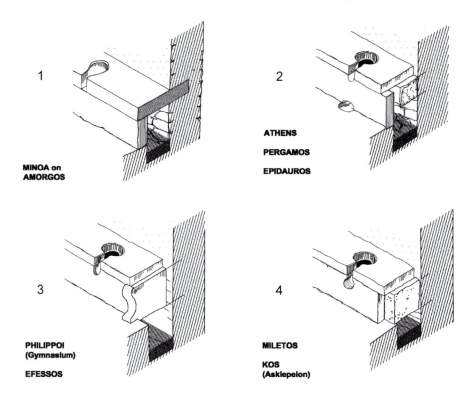

Figure 4.11.   Design and type of support for lavatory seats. Copyright
                permission G. Antoniou.

supported the weight of the person sitting on the lavatory. The support for lavatory seats was not uniform, and four types can be distinguished (Figure 4.11). The basic types are:

- Type 1: Cantilevered stone slab protruding out of the wall. This type occupied two of the three sides of the lavatory of the Gymnasium in Minoa, Amorgos. The other side was supported by an unarticulated stone bracket.
- Type 2: In this type, the seat slab was also supported by stone cantilever beams that were shorter and narrower than the seat. Characteristic examples were at the Asclepieia of Pergamon and Epidaurus. All of them were cantilevered, and most were covered except for the type in Philippoi and Efessos.
- Type 3: Similar to the previous type, but where the stone joists protrude out of the vertical plates and have been formed as neck mouldings of benches and exedras. Characteristic examples are those in Philippoi and Efessos.
- Type 4: Finally the freely supported slab over stone beams, which may or may not be cantilevered was characterised by the invisible beams, covered

by the vertical slab that filled the void in front of the seat. It was the most typical form and the joists were roughly as high as is the seat from the floor. The stone of the beams was mostly made of cheaper stone than the visible structure. Later in original Roman lavatories it was made from a small brick wall, penetrated in its lower part by the perimetric channel so as not to impede flow of the sewage, incorporating in the typical construction the technical achievements in brick and cement mortar techniques of that period.

Defecation Openings

In public lavatories the number of lavatory seats and the distance between them varied. In the Gymnasium of Minoa on the island of Amorgos the defecation openings were 85 cm apart, while in the Roman Agora of Athens they were just 51 cm. It seems that in large public lavatories that catered for more people the seats were placed more densely. In most Roman lavatories there was also a dense arrangement of openings.[67]

The shape, contour and design of the lavatory seats were all quite impressive. They maintained the keyhole-shaped outline of the opening used previously but also added slanting contours to their sides. The width between the slant and the stone openings varied from 4 cm in Minoa to only 1 cm in the Roman Agora of Athens. There is a hypothesis that this contour was for an earthenware cover[68] but that seems unlikely, since one of the two known clay covers, that of Philippoi, does not have an equivalent edge. Another interpretation is that this slanting was curved in order to make the seat more comfortable than would be the case with a sharp edge. There was quite a variety in the shape of the openings. The rough but more ergonomic elliptical shape found on the island of Amorgos becomes an object of formalisation in the Roman period. The prolongation of the opening up to the front edge of the seat contributes to these variations. It can be noted that the form of openings remained substantially the same during the lifetime of that particular type of building.

Auxiliary Elements

Many adjoining constructions were created for hygienic purposes, as the lavatory evolved in design. Despite their small size these auxiliary elements reveal the efforts made towards improved sanitary standards, as was mentioned before. Some lavatories incorporated holes for dripping urine.[69] The small holes for drainage of urine on the floor of the Roman Agora lavatory in Athens are remarkable. The small perimetric channel of continuous water flow, with half pipe cross-section,

---

[67]   Hoepfner 1999, pp. 726f, 730f.
[68]   Lemerle 1937, pp. 86–102.
[69]   Orlandos 1940, Figure 52.

was widely built (e.g. in Athens, Figure 4.9, and Kos[70]). Some researchers have suggested that this channel may have been used for the cleaning of σπογγιά – sponge on a stick, the lavatory paper of the time.[71]

In the central area of many communal lavatories there was a small shallow reservoir. In Athens (Figure 4.10) and Ephesus it was surrounded by a colonnade like a Greek κατάκλειστον – katakleiston or a Roman impluvium (covered area around an uncovered space, as in Figure 4.10b). It is quite possible that this was not its only use. It is worth noting that a slant of roughly 1.5% was present in the central reservoir in the lavatories at Epidaurus. It may be that it was used for the washing of sponges. A similar small central reservoir existed in a public lavatory in Thera and perhaps had an equivalent function.[72] Besides these elements there were also constructions like the small sedimentation tank of the lavatory in Asclepeion on Kos. The shape and position of the lavatory's layout suggests that the tank also regulated the flow of the water in the small perimetric channel.[73] There are also some traces indicating ventilation such as on the island of Amorgos, but this feature requires more extensive research.

Most ground plans have a simple rectangular shape in both public and private lavatories. At the known lavatories of Athens, Philippoi, Efessos and Epidaurus there was also a rectangular lobby with the entrance at the narrow side, and the door to the main chamber at the long side.[74] The evolution of the ground plan of the lavatory in the Imperial era, led to more complex shapes and imposing layouts, along with the increased scale.

Public Lavatories

One of the earliest contoured public lavatories was that of Minoa's 'Gymnasium' (probably a mansion house) on the island of Amorgos (Figure 4.12). It was small in size and built contemporary with the 'Gymnasium' at its southwest corner, and dated to the mid 4th century BC. Apart from the surviving roof and the benches on three sides it was also characterised by the large conduit that supplied it with naturally flowing water. The sewerage used a well-shaped conduit, which was parallel to the south wall of Gymnasium. This is thought to have dated from the end of 4th century BC.[75] It has survived in very good condition, although only half of the monolithic floor still exists. In contrast, the door has remained almost intact and only two pieces of the doorjamb have fallen down.

---

[70] Schatzman 1932, Tf 34a.
[71] Antoniou 2007, p. 155.
[72] Gaertingen 1899, Figure 141.
[73] Schatzman 1932, Tf 34 b, and #3 in 34a.
[74] Orlandos 1940; Lemerle 1937; Antoniou 2007.
[75] Neudecker 1994, pp. 14, 16, 88, 157.

Figure 4.12.   Restored view of the 'Gymnasium's' lavatory on Amorgos.
Copyright permission by G. Antoniou.

The public lavatories of Thera were small in size but abound all over the
excavated part of the ancient city.[76] Despite their public use, they were small
in size. Even though they were built abutting residences, their access was only
from communal areas such as the street. Only the ditches and sewers have been
preserved, as the seats and defecation openings have not survived. In the light of
this it is possible that these public lavatories had seats that were not made of stone.
After use, the waste was then channelled through ditches into the streets.

In Delos, public lavatories have been found in the Palaestrae and the
Gymnasium. In the Palaestra of the Lake (Figure 4.9), there were three spaces,
formed after the rearrangement of the original classical building, that are believed
to have been public lavatories.[77] The neighbouring smaller and newer Palaestra has
a lavatory as well. In both buildings lavatories have been placed in the perimeter,
and particularly near the path of some drainage. The north eastern lavatory of

[76]   Gaertingen 1899, Plan II.
[77]   Chamonard 1924.

the Lake's Palaestra was probably supplied by the water from the bath or even the colonnaded atrium. In the south western lavatory there was probably a small rectangular reservoir in the middle.

The double public lavatory of Asclepeion of Pergamon was characterised by its layout, which is more complicated than the usual rectangular form as is evident from its ground plan. In the Asclepeion of Kos, the public lavatory was part of a later extension of the lower perimetric portico towards the west. Here it is significant that the monolithic reservoir that drained the water from the small perimetric half pipe for the washing of σπογγιά (sponghia) to the main conduit, also provided water that was reused inside the lavatory itself.[78] At the Ventio's Thermae in Ephesus the traditional Greek typology was maintained inside a typical Roman building. They were characterised by the rectangular impluvium that was quite monumental for the size of the chamber situated by the entrance of the Thermae.[79] In the Gymnasium of Philippoi the typical Greek layout was predominant, despite the later Roman modification of the building (Figure 4.9). Also the placement resembled that of the lavatory of Kotys portico in Epidaurus.

In Athens, two public lavatories dating from the Roman period have also been preserved, in the south eastern corner of the Attalos' Stoa and east of the Roman Agora (Figure 4.10). Both ground plans have an almost square shape. The Roman market's lavatory was a mature construction of that period, since it was built after the Agora. Apart from the rectangular entrance lobby it was also characterised by the deep conduit underneath the benches and the impluvium at the centre of the room. From the surviving remains it appears to have had 62 defecation openings, which correspond to matching urinal holes on the floor.[80]

The public lavatory at Epidaurus, at the east end of Kotys portico, appears to have been one of the later buildings of this type in Greece.[81] It had a rectangular ground plan and was supplied with naturally flowing water, thought to have been channelled from the north eastern baths. It is believed to have been built when the portico was partly standing, and the poor construction includes stones of other collapsed buildings of the sanctuary. The elongated shallow tank in the middle, made of tiles, had a small sewerage pipe ending at the main perimetric conduit.

The Communal Use of Lavatories

Most of the ancient names for lavatory mentioned at the beginning of this article refer to a private space (the part –από -apo). The earlier examples of single defecation vessels (e.g., in Olynthus) or single cesspits (e.g, in Athens) indicate how privacy was an intrinsic element of the word for lavatory in the Classical Period. Despite this, the excavation at many private lavatories clearly

---

[78]   Schatzmann 1932, Tf 34 a,b; Antoniou 2007, p. 161, Figure 12.
[79]   Scherrer, P., (ed.), *Ephesus: the New Guide* (Vienna: Ege Yayinlari, 2000), p. 168.
[80]   Orlandos 1940, p. 251–260.
[81]   Antoniou 2007.

demonstrates evidence for their simultaneous use by more than one person. Even in residences where the inhabitants numbered 5–10 people, there were lavatories with two to four defecation openings, such that we can conclude the lavatories were used simultaneously by more than one person. Research has approached the use of private and public spaces by gender[82] but it is unclear whether there was a simultaneous usage of the domestic lavatory by residents of different sexes. At public lavatories there is also no doubt that they were used by dozens of people, often more than fifty. This was a practice that expanded during the Roman era and survived in many Byzantine and medieval lavatories of the Eastern Mediterranean area, including monasteries[83] and castles such as Mytilene (at the 16th century semi-subterranean refuge).

Lavatory capacity can be classified according to the number of lavatory seats, which corresponds to the maximum number of users at any one time:

a. The very small domestic lavatories used by two or three people of the house (e g. Figure 4.7 and[84])
b. Moderate-sized domestic lavatories with more than four defecation seats.
c. Small public lavatories with evidence for at least four users at a time (e.g. in the 'Gymnasium' of Minoa in Figure 4.7, and in Palaestrae in Delos).
d. Large public lavatories used by more than ten or twenty people. These were generally constructed during the Roman period (Figures 4.10 and[85]).

Lavatories of the Roman Period

With the spread of Roman culture throughout the empire, awareness of the design of effective private and public lavatories spread too. Public lavatories flourished during the Roman era, and these can be classified into three typical forms with the following examples: (a) the lavatory of Pompei's Palaestra, (b) the complex of Triklinon in Ostia,[86] and (c) the Largo Argentina lavatory in Rome. Therefore, in the 1st and 2nd century BC, lavatories were built in monumental forms and sizes, equivalent to other constructions of the Romans. It is clear that the Roman influence on such technologies was significant. Roman engineers, with their devotion to useful public works, were critical agents for the construction of numerous public lavatories all across their Empire. Moreover the size of these

---

[82]   Trümper, M., 'Gender and space, "public" and "private"', in S.L. James and S. Dillon (eds), *A Companion to Women in the Ancient World* (Oxford: Wiley-Blackwell, 2012), pp. 288–303.

[83]   Myriantheos, M., 'The bastion at the SE side of the Sinai monastery wall', in *Proceeding of 7th Symposium of Byzantine Archaeology and Art* (Athens, ΧΑΕ, 1987), p. 55 (in Greek).

[84]   Hoepfner 1999, p. 359, Haus J.

[85]   Orlandos 1940.

[86]   Hoepfner 1999, pp. 726f, 730f.

lavatories was adjusted to accommodate the growing cities of that era and their increasing population. The typical lavatory form was incorporated not only in most Roman Thermae but also other public buildings such as Gymnasia and Palaestrae. This was similar to the later Hellenistic period, but on a larger scale. Finally, all Roman mansion houses and villas had a proper lavatory, usually operated with running water.

The element of running water, provided to Roman cities by their aqueducts, is critical for the expansion of the size of the lavatories. In many cases it replaced the reused water supply that was a quite familiar water source for the earlier centuries. Technological improvements by the Romans to typical ancient Greek lavatories included their more widespread existence, their larger size to cater for a greater proportion of the population, and the use of running water from aqueducts to flush the facilities all year round. This was typical of the Roman approach to improving the conditions of everyday life. During the years of Emperor Vespasian's rule, lavatories became an important source of income for the imperial funds, since they began to charge an entrance fee.[87]

Conclusion

It is clear that the shape, the layout and the structural design of lavatories in antiquity depended on human anatomy, hygienic requirements, constructional restrictions from available materials, and the presence of water. The design of the seat and defecation openings, separate holes for male urination, methods for flushing away faeces, and the interconnection of both private and public facilities to the main sewers of the town all gradually evolved over time. Construction materials used at different times include wood, clay, stone, cement and brick. The evolution from the typical form of the ancient lavatory over the centuries is highlighted by the application of Roman engineering, in relation not only to their construction materials but also to the size of public multi-user lavatories.

It has been shown that in ancient Greece, extensive drainage and sewerage systems and elaborate sanitary and flushing structures were in use.[88] Such technologies were developed in prehistory, as early as 2100–1600 BC in the Minoan civilisation on Crete. In their palaces flushing waste from toilets into sewers was performed at a basic level with a jug of water in the summer, and storm water in the winter rains. The Hellenistic period (4th–1st centuries BC) should be considered as the most progressive time in the design of sanitary and sewerage engineering during antiquity. By the 4th century BC anatomically

---

[87]   Kline, A.S. (ed.), *Suetonius: the Lives of the Twelve Caesars*. VIII, Vespasian XXIII, (2010) http://www.poetryintranslation.com/PITBR/Latin/Suethome.htm.

[88]   De Feo, G., Mays, L.W., Angelakis, A.N., 'Water and wastewater management technologies in ancient Greek and Roman civilizations', in P. Wilderer (ed.), *Treatise on Water Science*, vol. 1 (Oxford: Academic Press, 2011), pp. 3–22.

shaped toilets seats are being found across Greece, and by the 2nd century BC many private houses and public buildings had lavatories. This change seems to reflect the increasing social status and income of the middle classes at that time. Private houses sometimes flushed their toilets by connecting them to waste water sources such as bathtubs and sinks. Improved understanding of hydraulic and sanitary principles occurred during the Hellenistic and Roman periods and this facilitated the development of communal latrines in towns.[89] As cities grew in size the pressure of larger populations resulted in the construction of communal latrines with seats that were more densely packed together.

The Romans subsequently applied these earlier techniques to larger constructions for a greater number of users at one time, using the advantages of their building methods with concrete based walls and vaulted roofing. In addition, due to their improved aqueduct technology they could provide continuously flowing water to most public lavatories. Some public lavatories survived past the fall of the ancient world and were in use during the first part of the Byzantine period. The customs of the new religion of the Byzantine Empire, Christianity, led to modifications in some of the structures, to give more privacy and sex segregation. In light of this historical and archaeological evidence, it seems that modern progress in urban water and wastewater technology, as well as in hygienic living, is not as evolutionarily significant as many tend to believe.[90]

---

[89]   Angelakis et al. 2005; Koutsoyiannis et al. 2008.

[90]   Koutsoyiannis, D., Angelakis, A.N., 'Hydrologic and hydraulic sciences and technologies in ancient Greek times', in B.A. Stewart and T. Howell (eds), *The Encyclopedia of Water Sciences* (New York: Markel Dekker, 2003), pp. 415–417.

Chapter 5

A Tale of Two Cities: The Efficacy of Ancient and Medieval Sanitation Methods

Craig Taylor

Introduction

A society's methods of dealing with sanitation is inextricably linked with public health. Most modern societies effectively deal with the proper disposal of garbage, animal and human waste, and other types of refuse by transporting sewage through underground drains, providing services to remove domestic garbage, and implementing laws designed to reduce the amount of garbage and animal waste thrown or deposited in public spaces. If there is an absence of unpleasant odours and sights, as well as minimal danger for an outbreak of disease, then most communities are generally satisfied with the methods of waste disposal. The primary concern of city officials, then, is to ensure that public health is not at risk.

To ensure that all different types of waste are properly disposed of in both developed and developing modern countries, particular criteria are frequently imposed.[1] The most stringent criteria are applied in the case of sewage (human excreta) and rubbish (all other types of waste). For instance, the practice in developing countries whereby excreta is re-used as fertiliser is now deemed hazardous because human waste contains pathogens that will seep into the soil and therefore crops. Since this is clearly harmful to humans, such practices would not meet the criteria for an effective sanitation system.[2] To avoid endangering public health, extra steps must be taken to kill these pathogens, such as implementing oxidation ponds, heat, and the frequent turning of sewage so oxygen can properly infiltrate the waste.[3] If these steps are followed, there is a more effective sanitation system in place and therefore sanitation criteria are more easily met.

---

[1] Nimpuno, K., 'Criteria for evaluating excreta disposal techniques', in A. Pacey (ed.), *Sanitation in Developing Countries* (Chichester: Wiley, 1978), pp. 43–48; Salvato, J.A., *Environmental Sanitation* (New York: Wiley, 1958), p. 186.

[2] Shuval, H.I., 'Parasitic disease and waste-water irrigation', in A. Pacey (ed.), *Sanitation in Developing Countries* (Chichester: Wiley, 1978), pp. 210–15, see p. 201.

[3] Conference Working Group, 'Composting as a treatment process', in A. Pacey (ed.), *Sanitation in Developing Countries* (Chichester: Wiley 1978b), pp. 205–7; Shuval 1978, p. 213.

The rigorous standards of safe waste disposal in modern societies cannot, however, be applied to those of the ancient and medieval world because what is presently considered unsanitary or dirty may not have been considered as such in the past. The characterisation of a nuisance differed from century to century, city to city, and individual to individual. For example, *garum*, a putrid fish sauce used in many ancient Roman dishes, was not considered a foul odour by the Romans.[4] Each nuisance can also produce a different reaction in individuals. For instance, pigs can be offensive to smell (they may stink), to sight (they are destructive and thus can be detrimental to the appearance of buildings) or to hearing (they are noisy). The urban attitudes towards waste were also quite different from rural attitudes, as dunghills were a nuisance in the city but not in the countryside.[5] Smell also produced different responses in past societies. Every city had a variety of different smells, both good and bad, with each part of the city having its own distinctive smell. In both Imperial Rome and medieval London odour could be tied to a social class, profession, or even conjure up feelings of emotion. In Rome good, sweet smells could be associated with love. In both Rome and London the smell of perfume was associated with the wealthy while the smell of offal was tied to the profession of butchers.[6] In the medieval period nice smells were also associated with holiness and priests, while bad smells were associated with the devil, projecting the idea that cleanliness was close to godliness.[7] Therefore, some of the nuisances and smells that annoy many modern urban populations were an accepted part of everyday life in ancient cities. People simply had a higher tolerance to the unsanitary conditions of their city and therefore the rigorous standards of proper waste disposal used for modern societies would seem irrelevant and impossible to reach for those in the past.[8]

Although common sense dictates that all societies desire the removal of objectionable odours and sights, ancient and medieval societies appear, on the surface, to have been less concerned with public health issues. In fact, evidence suggests that many communities were aware that an unsanitary environment posed a potential health concern, but they probably did not understand the science behind how dangerous it was to public health.[9] For example, prior to the 19th century

---

[4]   Classen, C., Howes, D., Synnott, A., *Aroma: the Cultural History of Smell* (London: Routledge, 1994), p. 22.

[5]   Cockayne, E., *Hubbub: Filth, Noise and Stench in England* (New Haven: Yale University Press, 2007), pp. 18–21.

[6]   Classen et al. 1994, pp. 17, 18, 28, 33–35.

[7]   Douglas, M., *Purity and Danger: an Analysis of Concepts of Pollution and Taboo* (London: Routledge, 2005), p. 9; Rawcliffe, C., *Urban Bodies: Communal Health in Late Medieval English Towns and Cities* (Woodbridge: The Boydell Press, 2013), pp. 222–223; Classen et al. 1994, pp. 51–54.

[8]   Cockayne 2007, pp. 242–243; Classen et al. 1994, p. 55

[9]   Magnusson, R., *Water Technology in the Middle Ages: Cities, Monasteries, and Waterworks After the Roman Empire* (Baltimore: Johns Hopkins University Press, 2001), p. 28; Rawcliffe 2013.

there was the commonly held belief that miasma, or bad air, drifting from corpses, gutters, ditches, privies, and so on, caused disease and sickness.[10] Since it would be unreasonable to apply modern criteria to ancient and medieval communities, a more appropriate set of criteria is required to determine whether ancient and medieval communities had satisfactory sanitation systems for their time period. In creating such criteria, two points must be considered. The first is that, despite their higher tolerance towards waste, we would expect that most citizens would have preferred not to see and smell it. The second is that, although ancient and medieval people may not have understood the scientific reasoning between waste and its bacterial effect on public health, they generally realised the hazards such unhealthy environments created, and would have desired to alleviate these conditions.

For ancient and medieval societies, I would argue that proper sanitation methods would have been successful when 1) there were adequate public and private facilities available for the removal and disposal of waste with no danger to the individual; 2) the removal of waste was supplied by city services, there were regulations to ensure the efficient collection and removal of said waste with little inconvenience for the individual, and these regulations were enforced; 3) waste did not give rise to a nuisance due to odour, unsightly appearance or negative impact on the health of the individual; 4) waste did not contaminate any drinking water supply or food supply; and 5) waste did not contaminate the waters of any bathing facility, waterfront, or stream used for public, financial, or recreational purposes. These five points are derived from the notion that the average person living in the ancient or medieval world would have wanted to inhabit an urban environment governed by these requirements regarding sanitation and public health.

In this paper I hope to determine whether or not ancient and medieval urban societies were able to meet these criteria. I will use the cities of Imperial Rome and late medieval London as test cases because they both had major disposal problems and we have relatively good evidence available. At its height, the city of Imperial Rome had a population nearing one million while medieval London had a population of around one hundred thousand. As it is estimated that the average person generates 50 grams of solid waste per day, the city of Rome would have produced 50,000 kilograms of solid waste a day and London 5,000 kilograms a day.[11] This, together with the production of other types of waste, such as environmental matter (leaves, dirt, excess rainwater, etc.), animal waste, and industrial and domestic rubbish, required that both cities have adequate sanitation systems. Using the criteria set out above, this study will uncover the efficacy of each city's sanitation system. One might hypothesise that medieval London would have had superior sanitation methods, as the city adjusted and improved upon the problems and issues experienced by Imperial Rome. Besides determining this notion, the differences and similarities in their approach to handling sanitation will also be examined.

---

10   Rawcliffe 2013, pp. 124–125; Cockayne 2007, pp. 206 and 212.
11   Scobie, A., 'Slums, Sanitation and Mortality', *Klio* 68 (1986): 399–433, see p. 413.

Comparative Assessment of the Five Criteria

1) There will be adequate public and private facilities available for the removal and disposal of waste with no danger to the individual

Rome

Did ancient and medieval societies have adequate facilities, meaning more than one option located throughout the city, for removing and disposing of waste? Roman cities had two primary drainage systems: 1) underground drains and 2) open sewers and gutters. Rome had a well-constructed system of underground channels, which began with the major drain of the city, the *Cloaca Maxima*, constructed in the 6th century BC.[12] Originally an open sewer used to drain the marshy land in the *Forum Romanum* and the *Suburba*, it became a system of underground paved sewers connected to many other drains, such as the *Lacus Servilius*, by the late Republic (*c*.1st century BC). Gutters running alongside city streets collected excess rainwater, spillage from water fountains, as well as any garbage lying in the street. All of this found its way into these underground drains through openings in the street and would then be carried into the Tiber River.[13]

Most cities, such as Pompeii, Herculaneum and even Roman London, possessed underground drains, and so closely followed the example of Rome in how to deal with the problems of sanitation.[14] However, Roman cities more typically had open sewer channels,[15] and it is probable that Rome itself would have had some open sewer channels in various parts of the city. Open sewers provided the same function as underground drains: the collection of waste and various types of rubbish. Typically open sewers contained excrement, hay, straw, stones and clay.[16] Being open they were much more accessible to citizens who could easily dispose of their waste and rubbish. Whether a city had an open sewer or an underground

---

[12]   Pliny the Elder, *Histoire Naturelle*, Livre XXXV, trans. R. Bloch, (Paris: Les Belles Lettres, 1981), 36.24.106–107.

[13]   Gowers, E., 'The Anatomy of Rome from Capitol to Cloaca', *Journal of Roman Studies* 85 (1995): 23–52, see p. 25; Robinson, O., *Ancient Rome: City Planning and Administration* (London: Routledge, 1992), p. 117.

[14]   Hodge, A.T., *Roman Aqueducts and Water Supply* (London: Duckworth, 1995), pp. 337–40.

[15]   Jackson, R., *Doctors and Diseases in the Roman Empire* (London: British Museum Publications, 1988), p. 52; Breeze, D.J., 'The Roman Fort on the Antonine Wall at Bearsden', in D.J. Breeze (ed.), *Studies in Scottish Antiquity* (Edinburgh: Donald, 1984), pp. 32–68; Pliny the Younger, *The Letters of the Younger Pliny*, trans. B. Radice, (London: Heinemann, 1969),10.98.

[16]   Leyerle, B., 'Refuse, filth, and excrement in the homilies of John Chrysostom', *Journal of Late Antiquity* 2 (2009): 337–356, see p. 339.

Figure 5.1   Latrine in the Hadrianic Baths at Lepcis Magna in Libya (Author's own photograph).

drain, they were typically connected to local streams and ditches, which carried away sewage and rubbish from the city.[17]

Rome also possessed numerous public facilities designed to collect an assortment of waste before it was carried out by the city's drainage systems. One such facility was the public latrine (Figure 5.1). There were approximately 144 public latrines in Rome by the 4th century AD.[18] Despite the high number, only two latrines have been discovered in Rome, but the ancient writer Cassius Dio[19] identifies another one in the *Curia Pompeia*. Whether or not the two latrines uncovered in Rome connected to an underground drain was never reported, but, surprisingly, the evidence regarding public latrines from other Roman cities indicate that many did not connect to the main sewer. Instead the sewage from public latrines was typically collected in cesspits.[20] These cesspits had a broad

---

[17]   Cilliers, L.,Retief, F.P., 'City planning in Graeco-Roman times with emphasis on health facilities' *Akroterian* 51 (2006): 43–56, see p. 49; Jackson 1988, p. 52.

[18]   Scobie 1986, p. 413; Robinson 1992, p. 120.

[19]   Cassius Dio, *The Roman History: the Reign of Augustus*, trans. I. Scott-Kilvert, (Harmondsworth: Penguin, 1987), 47.19.

[20]   Dodge, H., "Greater than the pyramids': the water supply of ancient Rome', in J. Coulston and H. Dodge (eds), *Ancient Rome: the Archaeology of the Eternal City*

function for inhabitants since individuals would dump more than just human faecal waste into them, such as unwanted babies and the corpses of gladiators, which were also sometimes discarded on dung and garbage heaps.[21]

Other locations for latrines were within the baths at Rome. The latrines in baths were designed both for the patrons and for those living in the surrounding areas.[22] Many baths had drains that connected to the main sewers and so their latrines would also have been connected.[23] Besides being ideal facilities for disposing of sewage, public latrines were also social places. They were places where gossip and dinner invitations could be exchanged.[24] Although some public latrines had a vestibule placed before the entrance in order to prevent onlookers from the streets, inside there were no permanent barriers between the seats. Patrons therefore depended on their voluminous clothing to provide some semblance of privacy.[25] Often a latrine could accommodate 10 to 20 persons at one time and therefore striking up a conversation with your neighbour was probably a common practice.[26] A benefit of conversation, whether fortuitous or not, was it helped mask the embarrassing sounds often created by those using the latrine.

Other public facilities available to Roman citizens were the *amphorae* (terracotta jars). These were sometimes placed in front of fuller's shops so that they could collect urine from passing citizens to be used for mordanting certain dyestuffs.[27] This was not only an adequate facility for the disposal of human waste, but also a prosperous business, so much so that in the 1st century AD the

---

(Oxford: Oxford University School of Archaeology, 2000), pp. 166–209, see p. 192; Van Vaerenbergh, J., 'The latrines in and near the Roman baths of Italy: a nice compromise with a bad smell', in G. Wiplinger (ed.), *Cura Aquarum in Ephesos* (Leuven: Peeters, 2006), pp. 453–59, see p. 457; Leyerle 2009, p. 341.

[21]   Juvenal, *Juvenal and Persius*, trans. S.M. Braund, (Cambridge: Loeb, 2004), 6.602; Scobie 1986, p. 419.

[22]   Van Vaerenbergh 2006, p. 453.

[23]   Koloski-Ostrow, A.O., 'Cacator cave malum: the subject and object of Roman public latrines in Italy during the first centuries BC and AD', in G.C.M. Jansen (ed.), *Cura Aquarum in Sicilia* (Leiden: Peeters, 2000), pp. 289–95, see p. 291; Koloski-Ostrow, A.O., 'Location and Context of Toilets', in G.C.M. Jansen, A.O. Koloski-Ostrow and E.M. Moormann (eds), *Roman Toilets, Their Archaeology and Cultural History* (Leuven: Peeters, 2011), pp. 113–14, see p. 113.

[24]   Martial, *Epigrams*, 3 vols. trans. D.R. Shackleton Bailey, (Cambridge: Loeb, 2002–6), 11.77.1–3.

[25]   Kamash, Z., 'Interpreting the archaeological evidence: latrines and the senses' in G.C.M. Jansen, A.O. Koloski-Ostrow and E.M. Moormann (eds), *Roman Toilets, Their Archaeology and Cultural History* (Leuven: Peeters Press, 2011), pp. 181–83.

[26]   Koloski-Ostrow, A.O., 'Finding social meaning in the public latrines of Pompeii', in N. de Haan and G.C.M. Jansen (eds), *Cura Aquarum in Campania* (Leiden: PVBA, 1996), pp. 79–86; Jackson 1988, p. 51.

[27]   Jansen, G.C.M., 'Systems for the disposal of waste and excreta in Roman cities: the situation in Pompeii, Herculaneum and Ostia', in X.D. Raventós and J-A. Remolà (eds), *Sordes Urbis: La Elimanación de Residuos en la Ciudad Romana. Actes de La Reunión de*

emperor Vespasian put a tax on it.[28] Men were probably the primary contributors to *amphorae*. As with the use of public latrines, these types of public facilities may not have embarrassed the citizens of Rome, since they just accepted it as a part of everyday life. Lastly, men must simply have relieved themselves outdoors. Those living in rural areas could easily relieve themselves in fields.[29] In the city, however, it was more difficult. Literary writers list different locations, such as alleys, behind statues, behind bushes, on tombs, and in public fountains, as frequent spots for men to relieve themselves.[30] Although not an ideal situation, the outdoors was a sufficient facility, primarily for men, to dispose of waste.

Private facilities were also available to the citizens of Rome. Within Roman tenement buildings individuals could use chamber pots, which could be emptied in a variety of different ways. Some tenement buildings supplied a vat placed under the well of the staircase.[31] If the tenement building had no vat, an individual could empty their chamber pot into the nearest dung heap, into the public latrines, into open sewers, or into the street gutters. Another alternative was to throw the excrement into designated wagons, which passed through the streets during the day.[32] A last option, for the especially lazy individual, was to empty the chamber pot out of the window onto the street where it was hoped it would find its way into the gutter.[33]

Private Roman residences could have chamber pots, but they could also have latrines that connected either to the main city drains or emptied into cesspits. Due to the inaccessibility of Roman houses in the archaeological record at Rome, we have very few examples of houses connected to drains.[34] More evidence for this design feature, however, is found at other Roman sites, such as Pompeii.[35] A pipe that connected to the main city drain, if it was not a part of the original construction, may not have been a common feature because of the cost of installing it. Although there are no monetary figures recorded in the ancient sources for such an undertaking, tearing up the road, connecting a pipe from the house to the sewer

---

Roma (15–16 de noviembre de 1996), (Roma: L'Erma di Bretschneider, 2000), pp. 37–49, see pp. 40 and 46; Scobie 1986, p. 408.

[28] Suetonius, *The Twelve Caesars*, trans. R. Graves, (London: Penguin, 1989), *Divus Vespasianus*, 23.

[29] Jansen 2000, p. 37.

[30] Petronius, *Petronius: Satyricon and Seneca: Apocolocyntosis*, trans. M. Heseltine and W.H.D. Rouse, (Cambridge: Loeb, 2005), *Satyricon*.71.8; Juvenal 2004, 1.131; Scobie 1986, p. 416.

[31] *Corpus Inscriptionum* Latinarum.VI.2979.

[32] *Lex Julia municipalis* 66–67 = *Corpus Inscriptionum Latinarum*.I.2.593.

[33] Juvenal 2004, 3.269–305.

[34] Gowers 1995, p. 27.

[35] Jashemski, W.F., 'The Excavation of a shop-house garden at Pompeii (I.xx.5)', *American Journal of Archaeology* 81 (1977): 217–227, see p. 217; Jansen, G.C.M., 'Private toilets at Pompeii: appearance and operation', in S.E. Bon and R. Jones (eds), *Sequence and Space in Pompeii* (Oxford: Oxbow, 1997), pp. 121–34, see p. 131–3.

and then reconstructing the road would probably have been costly. Therefore, instead of a pipe connecting to the city drains, Roman houses more often had their latrines connected to cesspits.[36] Cesspits were holes dug into porous rock, reaching a possible depth of 11 feet. Quite often they were located next to the kitchen, enabling residents to throw in domestic waste, such as bones and pottery fragments.[37] Thus private cesspits were convenient and adequate facilities for disposing of many different types of waste.

Besides human and animal excrement, Roman streets could accrue much rubble from building construction. Although much of the rubble could be re-used in making roads and other structures, a large amount required adequate facilities for its disposal,[38] without which the rubble, along with various other types of waste, would continue to amass and street levels would rise. It was also important that the streets did not become blocked to both foot and cart traffic.[39] The solution was to place excess rubble in wagons. Piling rubble into wagons allowed it to be easily and quickly removed from the city, ensuring that it would not cause traffic problems.

One issue concerning the use of sanitation facilities was the danger of personal injury. Night was very dark because there was not much lighting available in the streets.[40] Some of the sewers running along the streets were very large and open, so there was the danger of falling in and hurting oneself.[41] Another very real danger was the presence of thieves and gangs of juveniles roaming the streets of Rome at night beating and robbing people, possibly heading to the latrines. The Roman biographer Suetonius writes: 'one of [the emperor Nero's] games was to attack men on their way home from dinner, stab them if they offered resistance, and then drop their bodies down the sewers.'[42] Of course Suetonius is known for his exaggerations, but whether Nero engaged in these activities or not, incidents like these could occur, prompting one to dump waste out of the window rather than chance a journey to the latrine. Therefore, despite the steps taken to provide satisfactory sanitation facilities, not all dangers were prevented.

---

[36]   Sperber, D., *The City in Roman Palestine* (New York: Oxford University Press, 1988), p. 137.

[37]   Jansen 2000, p. 38; Scobie 1986, p. 410.

[38]   Rodríguez-Almedia, E., 'Roma, una città self-cleaning?' in X.D. Raventós and J-A. Remolà (eds), *Sordes Urbis: La Elimanación de Residuos en la Ciudad Romana* (Roma: L'Erma di Bretschneider, 2000), pp. 123–27.

[39]   Liebeschuetz, W., 'Rubbish disposal in Greek and Roman cities' in X.D. Raventós and J-A. Remolà (eds), *Sordes Urbis: La Elimanación de Residuos en la Ciudad Romana* (Roma: L'Erma di Bretschneider, 2000), pp. 51–61, see pp. 54 and 59.

[40]   Cilliers and Retief 2006, p. 46.

[41]   Sperber 1998, p. 140.

[42]   Suetonius, *Nero*.26.

London

Roman London had its own underground drains, and, much like the *Cloaca Maxima* at Rome, these drains emptied into the main river, the Thames, and its tributaries. Unfortunately for London citizens, by the medieval period these underground passageways became unused and fell into disrepair.[43] As they were no longer functioning, medieval London citizens had only one other drainage system available to them: the open sewer. This system was equally effective as the open sewers used in Roman cities. Businesses, such as butcher shops, and ordinary citizens could deposit their sewage and rubbish into these channels, and since in London open sewers connected directly with rivers and streams, the sewage and rubbish was carried away from the city. Many of London's public latrines were constructed over open sewers. Written sources have provided evidence for three public latrines in medieval London: one on Temple Bridge (or pier) south of Fleet street, one at Queenhithe, and one on London Bridge. On London Bridge there were tenement buildings and approximately 138 shops by 1358. With many London citizens frequenting the shops on the bridge, the public latrines here were especially busy. However, archaeological evidence has discovered at least 13 other latrines situated within the city, such as the one at London wall and that at Philipslane in Cripplegate Ward. Similar to the latrine on London Bridge, these were also over a source of water, meaning they had a ready clearance of sewage.[44]

Although placing latrines directly over running water was the most efficient sanitation method for London, the city preferred public latrines to be over cesspits, as this polluted waterways less. Ernest Sabine figures that a cesspit would cost around four pounds to make, factoring in the need to dig up the dirt, take away the earth, and find lime, sand and other materials for its construction.[45] Though expensive, cesspits were especially easy to construct on private property or in tenement buildings and thus very convenient. They could also be used for more than just the deposit of human faecal waste. A latrine cesspit at Southampton revealed kitchen garbage, dead carcasses of family pets (which included dogs, cats, ferrets and even a monkey), pottery, shoes, metal objects and wood.[46]

One last option as a public facility was the outdoors. Alleys and fields were the most probable locations for public urination and it was likely more convenient for men. This was a practice that was not sanctioned by the public, however. In

---

[43]   Harrison, M., *London Beneath the Pavement* (London: Peter Davies, 1961), p. 35; Home, G., *Roman London AD 43–457* (London: Eyre and Spottiswoode, 1948); Merrifield, R., *London: City of Romans* (London: Batsford, 1983).

[44]   Sabine, E., 'Butchering in mediaeval London', *Speculum* 8 (1933): 335–353, see p. 343; Sabine, E., 'Latrines and cesspools of mediaeval London' *Speculum* 9 (1934): 303–321, see p. 307–8; Barron, C.M., *London in the Later Middle Ages: Government and People, 1200–1500* (Oxford: Oxford University Press, 2004), p. 256.

[45]   Sabine 1934, p. 315.

[46]   Magnusson 2001, p. 157.

1307 Thomas Scott, as documented in the *Calendar of Early Mayors' Court Rolls*, quarrelled with two citizens because they

> protested against his stopping, not evidently in a frequented thoroughfare, but in a certain lane, when it would have been 'more decent' for him to have gone to the common privies of the city.[47]

London citizens obviously believed that urinating in public was distasteful, not because it was unsanitary, but because it was a private activity to be done in public latrines, or at home.[48] Unlike at Rome then, privacy was more of a concern in medieval London, as divisions between the seats in small privies found in the towers or turrets of a castle and in monasteries reveal.[49] Walls placed between seats were common in the city as well. The *London Assize of Nuisance*, a text outlining the regulations concerning walls, gutters, privies, windows and pavements, as well as the procedures to be followed in assizes, records that a London tenement building in 1333 experienced a privacy issue regarding their common cesspit. One tenant complained that a party wall and roof that once enclosed the cesspit were removed by Joan de Arementers and William de Thorneye so that the extremities of those sitting upon the seats could now be seen, 'a thing which is abominable and altogether intolerable'.[50] Using the latrine was a private matter and no one else should have to observe the activities within. This inclination towards privacy might also explain why there was only mention of three public latrines in London historical sources, whereas archaeological records demonstrate there were at least 16 latrines.

London citizens also had private facilities available for disposing sewage. These were usually latrines that connected to open sewers, ditches, cesspits, or street gutters by way of pipes or drains. Of course these worked more effectively if there was a constant flow of water to remove the sewage, such as the Thames, the Fleet, or the Walbrook, but ditches were just as convenient. Private latrines would have been more common in the larger homes of the wealthy, but the poorer citizens of London could also construct private latrines in their tenement buildings. In 1314 Alice Wade attached a wooden pipe from her private privy to the gutter running under the street. This was done in the hope that the excess rainwater from the roofs and streets would help cleanse her privy.[51] Applying some ingenuity gave those living in tenement buildings an option that did not require leaving their homes. Those without these inventive disposal systems relied on the chamber pot. Using chamber pots, of course, meant they had to be emptied,

---

[47] Sabine 1934, p. 307.
[48] Barron 2004, p. 261.
[49] Magnusson 2001, p. 156.
[50] Chew, H.M., Kellaway, W. (eds), *London Assize of Nuisance* 1301–1431 (London: London Record Society, 1973), pp. x and 79.
[51] Chew and Kellaway 1973, p. 45.

and this could be accomplished in cesspits, open sewers, ditches, or the rivers and streams. Businesses and citizens of London could also put their waste into wagons, dung-boats, or just outside of their doors to be picked up by carts.[52] This would all then be carried outside of the city or sold to farmers as fertiliser.[53] If these options were not convenient, a tenant could also just dump waste out the window and onto the street.

As in Rome, the streets at night in medieval London posed many dangers. Travelling to a latrine in the dark could end in death, as happened to John de Abyndon when he was killed heading to the one situated in London wall within Cripplegate Ward at the head of Philipslane in 1290–91.[54] The chance of personal injury or death was not worth risking an expedition to the public latrine at night and therefore many chose the much safer option of emptying their chamber pots out of windows. Another danger associated with cesspits was that floorboards, if not properly maintained, could rot causing people to fall through. This exact scenario, recorded in the *Calendar of the Coroners Rolls of the City of London*, befell Richard the Rayker, who died after he fell into a cesspit when rotten planks gave way under his seat.[55] Therefore, despite the existence of many public facilities, there were some dangers associated with using them.

Both Imperial Rome and medieval London provided adequate sanitation facilities designed to collect sewage and different types of rubbish. Since Rome had a much larger population it is not surprising that it offered more public facilities, especially latrines, than medieval London. Although both offered many facilities throughout the city they could still be dangerous. Falling into open sewers or cesspits was a real risk, and heading to the latrine at night was always a challenge. What is startling is that London did not take advantage of the underground drains that ran under the city. Assuredly they would have required fixing and cleaning, but they would have provided an added sanitation system to help alleviate the accumulation of sewage and rubbish deposited in the ditches and open sewers. Although never taking advantage of an underground sanitation system, London still managed to provide reasonable alternatives to its citizens. Therefore, both Rome and London offered adequate facilities for the removal and disposal of waste and rubbish.

---

[52]   Sabine 1933, p. 357; Sabine, E., 'City cleaning in mediaeval London' *Speculum* 12 (1937): 19–43.

[53]   Halliday, S., *The Great Stink of London* (Stroud: Sutton, 2001), p. 31.

[54]   Sabine 1934, p. 306.

[55]   Sabine 1934, p. 317; Magnusson 2001, p. 155.

2) The removal of waste will be supplied by city services; there will be regulations to ensure the efficient collection and removal of said waste with little inconvenience for the individual; and these regulations will be enforced

Rome

Rome has shown that it satisfied the first criteria in providing adequate public and private facilities for the removal or disposal of waste, but these needed constant cleaning. In part, Rome would have depended on Mother Nature to help clean gutters, streets, drains and open sewers. Besides rain and wind, animals and insects such as worms, beetles, mosquitoes, flies, dogs and even pigs all played a role in removing waste.[56] For instance dogs ate food scraps, human excrement, and even corpses that were dumped in the streets.[57]

The city of Rome, however, did not depend solely on Mother Nature. The Romans used other sources of water to help flush the streets, gutters and drains.[58] Runoff from fountains and basins helped flush the accumulation of dirt, rubbish and sewage in the streets into the sewers and drains. Consequently, careful attention was paid to the construction of open sewers in order that waste could more easily be flushed out of the city, such as using the natural slope of the site.[59] Water from baths also contributed to cleaning drains and sewers. As many latrines connected to baths, bath water helped flush the sewage out into the Tiber River.

As much of the city's waste found its way into the Tiber, the emperor Tiberius in the early 1st century AD created a commission called the *cura riparum et alvei Tiberis* that was in charge of the river's maintenance.[60] Although its duties were originally more concerned with preventing the river from flooding than removing human waste, in the 2nd century AD, the Emperor Trajan added the responsibility of the sewers.[61] On a few occasions the accumulation of waste in the river resulted in the dredging of the Tiber.[62] Controlling the flooding of the Tiber was a necessity, because floods caused by storms could scour the insides of drains, creating the danger of collapse and rendering the drains inoperable. An added danger, besides the destruction of sewer walls, was the collapse of buildings above the street.[63]

---

[56]   Leyerle 2009, p. 340.

[57]   Martial, *Epigrams*.1.83, 3.82, 7.20, 12.48.8; Petronius, *Satyricon*.134.1; Suetonius, *Divus Vespasianus*.5.

[58]   Frontinus, *Strategems and Aqueducts of Rome*, trans. C.E. Bennett, (Cambridge: Loeb, 2003), *De aquae ductu urbis Romae*.2.111.

[59]   Jansen 2000, p. 40.

[60]   Tacitus, *The Annals of Imperial Rome*, trans. M. Grant, (London: Penguin, 1989), 1.76; Cassius Dio.57.14.7–8.

[61]   *Inscriptiones Latinae Selectae*, 3 vols, (1892–1916): Herman Dessau (ed.), Berlin. *ILS*.5930 & 5932 = *Corpus Inscriptionum Latinarum*.VI.31549 & 31553.

[62]   Suetonius, *Divus Augustus*.30; **SHA,** *Aurelian*.47.2–3, 1932.

[63]   Ulpian, *Digest*.43.23.1–2 in Scott, S.P., (ed.), *The Civil Law* (New York: AMS Press, 1973).

Besides the board of commissioners, the *aediles* (supervisors of public works) were responsible for the upkeep of the city, which presumably included keeping streets clean.[64] Together, the *aediles* and the board of commissioners probably designated, ordered or hired individuals or groups to deal with sanitation removal. This may have included limiting the offensive sights and smells produced by butcher shops and tanneries,[65] removing corpses found in the streets, or on dung and garbage heaps, and removing construction rubble. In the case of the latter, Caesar had decreed that heavy wagon transport should not be allowed in the city at certain times of the day except for those carrying building resources in, or rubble out of the city of Rome.[66] Elsewhere, such as at Antioch, peasants were forced to take out rubble with their donkeys and carts.[67]

Rome also provided services for the removal of human waste. One such service was the *stercorarii*.[68] They collected human waste in their wagons during the day, while other wheeled traffic, except if carrying rubble, was not allowed in the city.[69] Although human excrement was thrown into these wagons, it is unclear whether or not excrement left on the street by animals, such as dogs, horses, cats, and so on, was picked up by the *stercorarii*, left there to degrade, washed away, or picked up by the owners of these animals. Whatever excrement found its way onto the wagons of the *stercorarii* was taken and sold to farmers as fertiliser, thus providing two services.

As for who cleaned the sewers, the earliest source mentioning this is the early 2nd century AD writer Pliny the Younger, who described how convicts were forced to clean the sewers below the surface.[70] Convicts were not the only ones cleaning sewers. The Edict of Prices, issued by Diocletian in 301 AD, established that the pay of a *cloacarius* (person cleaning sewer) was 24 *denarii* a day,[71] indicating that some made a living cleaning sewers. These sewer workers may also have emptied and cleaned out the cesspits, whose contents could then be sold to farmers. Cleaning sewers and cesspits was a dangerous occupation. If not regularly maintained the build-up of rubbish and waste in these facilities would create a foul atmosphere, creating a very dangerous environment for these sewer cleaners, some of whom died from choking fumes.[72] An accumulation of sewage

---

[64]   Cicero, *De Re Publica, De Legibus*, trans. C.W. Keyes, (Cambridge: Loeb, 1928). *De Legibus*.3.3.6–9; Varro, *On the Latin Language*, trans. R.G. Kent, (Cambridge: Loeb, 1999), *De lingua Latina*.5.14.81; Suetonius, *Divus Vespasianus*.5.

[65]   *Corpus Inscriptionum Latinarum*.VI.975; Martial, *Epigrams*.6.93.

[66]   Liebeschuetz 2000, p. 53.

[67]   Libanius, *Opera*, vol.III, Orationes XXVI-L, (Hildesheim: G. Olm, 1963), 50.17; Liebeschuetz 2000, p. 52.

[68]   Cicero, *On Old Age, On Friendship, On Divination*, trans. W.A. Falconer, (Cambridge: Loeb, 2001). *De divinatione*.1.27.57.

[69]   *Lex Julia Municipalis* 66–67 = *Corpus Inscriptionum Latinarum*.I.2.593

[70]   Pliny the Younger, *The Letters of the Younger Pliny*.10.32.2.

[71]   Sperber 1998, p. 139.

[72]   Leyerle 2009, p. 339; Scobie 1986, p. 412.

and rubbish would also clog underground drains, making them useless. Regular cleaning would allow a close inspection of the drains, enabling workers to catch any possible structural weaknesses that would cause the drains and the buildings above to collapse. Although sewer workers were a necessity in Rome and other Roman Imperial cities, they were despised. The late 4th century AD Christian writer John Chrysostom considered cleaning sewers to be a lowly profession, likely in part due to the stench associated with it.[73]

The services provided for cleaning private latrines, cesspits and in front of private property are uncertain. Rubbish thrown or dropped onto the streets may have been the responsibility of the building owner if it was in front of their property. As for the latrines and cesspits located on private property, the owners may have cleaned them and afterwards sold the sewage as fertiliser, or used it for their own gardens.[74] It is more likely, however, that most Romans paid someone to remove human waste from their cesspits, as a graffito from Herculaneum recording a payment of 11 *asses* for its removal proves.[75] It is possible that the *stercorarii* were the ones providing this service, but there may have been other unrecorded groups offering this service to private individuals. Regardless of who cleaned these facilities, there were services available for those in the private sector.

The city of Rome provided many different services to deal with sanitation removal. Undoubtedly not all Romans used these services, as many urinated wherever they pleased. To discourage this activity warnings and threats were erected. At Pompeii, an inscription placed above a public fountain prohibited people from polluting the water, while in some alleys, graffiti on the walls warned off those wishing to urinate with threats from the god Jove.[76] Others simply dumped sewage and rubbish wherever they pleased. In these situations the city depended on Mother Nature to aid in clean-up. However the city still attempted to dissuade individuals from haphazardly tossing out waste, particularly through windows. In the 3rd century AD, the jurist Ulpian writes on how to catch and prosecute those individuals responsible for tossing sewage out of windows.

> If the apartment [*cenaculum*] is divided among several tenants, redress can be sought only against that one of them who lives in that part of the apartment from the level of which the liquid has been poured. If the tenant, however, while professing to have sub-let [*cenacularium exercens*], has in fact retained for himself the enjoyment of the greater part of the apartment, he shall be held solely responsible. If, on the other hand, the tenant who professes to have sub-let has in fact retained for his own use only a modest fraction of the space, he and

---

[73]   Leyerle 2009, pp. 339 and 341.
[74]   Dodge 2000, p. 192–193; Jansen 2000, p. 38; Van Vaerenbergh 2006, p. 457.
[75]   Scobie 1986, p. 414.
[76]   Scobie 1986, p. 416; Jansen 2000, p. 40.

his sub-tenants shall be jointly held responsible. The same will hold good if the
vessel or the liquid has been thrown from a balcony.[77]

Despite such harsh preventative measures, it was probably very difficult to
determine exactly where the sewage originated. Therefore the onus was placed
on the pedestrians to pay attention while walking. John Chrysostom felt that
the passer-by had to be very careful when walking and in fact put blame on the
individual if they got dumped on.[78]

London

London also provided adequate sanitation services. Certainly, as at Rome, Mother
Nature played an integral role in the clean-up of gutters, streets, and open sewers.
Rain, wind, animals and insects all would have helped London become cleaner, but
the city did not depend solely on them. Services specialising in sanitation removal,
city regulations and fines were all employed in the attempt to adequately remove
sewage and rubbish with little inconvenience to the individual, and to ensure that
there was a satisfactory standard of public health. When a London citizen had
a complaint regarding sanitation the law stipulated that the nuisance had to be
against the law and to have caused some type of damage. The complaint was then
brought before an assembly and if the plaintiff won his case the defendant had 40
days to correct the nuisance.[79]

As London had public and private latrines constructed over waterways, the
constant flow of running water removed a good portion of the sewage and rubbish.
However, if the streams and rivers became clogged someone needed to clean
them. Early on city officials may have appointed a variety of different individuals
or groups to undertake this, but in 1385 the appointment of a Sergeant of the
Channels was created, who was probably solely responsible for the upkeep of
these streams and rivers.[80] The latrines positioned over cesspits would have to be
emptied periodically when full, for which professional cleaners were hired.[81] This
was not a desirable job, since there was a stigma attached to it, and, if not careful,
death could result from the choking fumes.[82] However, those who did accept this
responsibility demanded a higher wage than other unskilled workmen.[83] Accounts
of privy cleaning recorded in London between 1382 and 1419 report that there
were different prices charged for this service. The prices ranged from 3s 4d a tun
to 4s and 4s 8d, depending on the amount of sewage that needed removing. This

---

[77]   Ulpian, *Digest*.9 3, 5, 1–2 in Scott 1973.
[78]   Leyerle 2009, p. 340.
[79]   Chew and Kellaway 1973, p. xii-xx.
[80]   Amulree, Lord, 'Hygienic Conditions in Ancient Rome and Modern England',
Medical History 17 (1973): 244–255, see p. 252; Rawcliffe 2013, p. 135.
[81]   Barron 2004, p. 259.
[82]   Magnusson 2001, p. 155; Barron 2004, p. 256.
[83]   Magnusson 2001, p. 158.

changed in 1466 when the city authorities granted John Lovegold a monopoly on cleaning privies because Lovegold explained 'that the business hitherto been done imperfectly and at an exhorbitant charge'.[84] This monopoly was granted to him for ten years.

Other professional cleaners included the officially employed 'rayker' in each of London's wards, who was responsible for picking up the sewage and rubbish left in the streets. After collecting the waste, the intention was to deposit it in dumps by the river.[85] The carts provided could not handle all of the city's refuse and by 1357 the streets were so filled with waste that citizens began to complain about the odour.[86] Therefore, the city designated extra wagons and dung-boats to help carry the waste outside of the city. Wagons could even be commandeered to help take away rubbish.[87] Anything not picked up was presumably crushed into the ground, or hopefully removed by Mother Nature.

Regulations, outlined in the *London Assize of Nuisance*, concerning the construction of cesspits on private property were also put in place to make latrines more effective and less dangerous. The regulations were different depending on the type of construction material used, but if the cesspit was lined with stone

> its mouth should be two and a half ft. from a neighbor's land even though there were a stone wall between them; if not so lined it should be three and a half ft. from a neighbor's land.[88]

These rules were put in place because if too close, sewage could rot the timbers of a neighbour's cellar and creep into the room, as it did in 1301, when William de Bethune complained that the sewage from the cesspit of his neighbour, William de Gartone, was penetrating into his cellar. Even if the cesspit had been built 40 years prior to the current occupancy, it still had to follow the distance regulations. If it did not then the cesspit had to be removed at a cost to the current resident, as John de Langeley learned in 1306 when it was discovered his was built too close to the wall of his neighbour, Richer de Refham, and he was given 40 days to remove it. In some circumstances, even if the cesspit was constructed according to the specific regulations, it could still be removed if it had not been periodically cleaned and therefore created an obnoxious smell, which disturbed neighbours. Henry de Ware had to remove his because the stench from it was penetrating into the tenement of Isabel, widow of John Luter. Therefore he was ordered to remove the nuisance in 40 days.[89] These harsh regulations were probably meant to persuade London

---

[84]   Sabine 1934, p. 316.
[85]   Harrison 1961, p. 35; Amulree 1973, p. 252.
[86]   Trench R., Hillman, E., *London Under London: a Subterranean Guide* (London: Murray, 1985), p. 59; Sabine 1937: 27;
[87]   Sabine 1937, p. 39; Barron 2004, p. 262.
[88]   Chew and Kellaway, 1973, p. xxv.
[89]   Chew and Kellaway 1973, pp. 1, 21 and 88.

citizens to regularly clean their cesspits using the services available to them. One might think that Henry de Ware, had he habitually cleaned his latrine more often, would not have had to remove his properly constructed cesspit.

Unfortunately, the city could not completely prevent its citizens from circumventing these services. Some London citizens used easier, less inconvenient methods to dispose of waste. This forced the city to establish rules and regulations to help curb these practices. Placing latrines over waterways was a logical system, as the water helped carry waste away from the city. However, after the Black Death, city officials believed that the filth deposited in these places was one of the causes for its uncontrolled spread. Thus laws were enforced in order to keep waterways and ditches clean and less clogged.[90] The ultimate goal was to encourage London citizens to use the sanitation services the city provided. Proclamations in 1357 forbade anyone to dump waste into any of the waterways under penalty of imprisonment and severe punishment. Then in 1383 London decided to further regulate the construction of latrines over waterways by allowing

> persons having houses abutting on the water-course to have latrines built over the stream, provided they did not 'throw rubbish or other refuse through the same, whereby the passage of the said water' might be stopped.[91]

Those that were built over water had to pay two shillings a year to help clean the waterway. This was not very effective because in 1477 the

> common council passed an ordinance forbidding the making of any 'priveye or sege' not only over Walbrook but also upon any of the town ditches, and ordering the abatement of those already in existence.[92]

Also in this year, some courses, such as the Walbrook, were bricked up.[93] All of this was done with the expectation that citizens would discard their waste in the designated dumps outside of the city, or in the carts and dung-boats the city provided as sanitation services. The city also began cleaning the filth that had accumulated in the waterways, with tolls issued to those vessels using them. What these regulations accomplished was to force citizens to find new dumping spots. Eventually the city issued laws forbidding dumping at some of these new places, but this only caused a renewed dumping into the Thames. Although the city offered some sanitation services to the public, London citizens did not believe they were convenient and so resorted to other means.

Those who chose to throw or sweep waste onto the streets rather than use any of the city services could also be fined. In London, the *Letter Books* indicate

---

[90]   Trench and Hillman 1985, p. 29.
[91]   Sabine 1934, p. 310.
[92]   Sabine 1934, p. 310.
[93]   Sabine 1937, p. 34.

that the fine by the end of the 14th century was two shillings.[94] Fines for offences such as this were issued in other medieval towns as well. In 1421 the citizens of Coventry were obliged to clean the street in front of their property or be fined.[95] Catching those who littered in London was not an easy task and so to encourage others to turn in such offenders the city passed an ordinance to reward informers 2s 4d.[96] The regulation was either extremely successful or people rarely turned others in, because a survey in 1421, in Wardmote, showed that very few charges were brought against London citizens for dumping waste in the streets.[97] Other rules governing street cleanliness included forbidding poulters to pluck birds in the streets.[98] London officials provided adequate sanitation services and so encouraged citizens to use them by levying fines upon those choosing to dump waste wherever they pleased.

After the Black Death, city officials also attempted to control how waste was disposed by certain businesses, such as butchers and tanners.[99] Butchers initially discarded their waste in places such as streams and designated pits. However, from the Black Death until 1391, they were forced to work and dump their wastes outside of the city. After prices of beef increased, the city allowed them back in, but they were relegated to the banks of the River Thames. As well as being welcomed back into the city, butchers were given specific instructions on how to dispose of their waste. The Statute of Winchester in 1391 stipulated that all of their offal had to be cut into small pieces, and then had to be placed in boats and tossed into the middle of the Thames when the water was at ebb-tide. The Statute also stated that only butchers were given this privilege.[100] The city was attempting to provide a sanitation service satisfactory to both the butchers and the people, without greatly compromising public health.

These were the best services London could provide for cleaning and removing waste from within the city. The time of day most of this removal occurred is unclear, but butchers were required to bring their waste through the city during the evening,[101] thus it was probable that other waste was also carted out of the city during the night. Removing waste at night would be less offensive to the public's senses and less obstructive to traffic.[102] If done during the day, traffic could be slowed when the carts, overloaded, spilled rubbish out of the sides into the streets.

---

94   Sabine 1937, p. 29; Amulree 1973, p. 252.
95   Jørgensen, D., 'Cooperative sanitation: managing streets and gutters in late medieval England and Scandinavia', *Technology and Culture* 49 (2008): 547–567, see p. 558.
96   Sabine 1937, p. 29; Amulree 1973, p. 252.
97   Amulree 1973, p. 252.
98   Barron 2004, p. 263.
99   Keene, D., 'Rubbish in medieval towns', in A.R. Hall (ed.), *Environmental Archaeology in the Urban Context* (London: Council for British Archaeology, 1982), pp. 26–30, see p. 27; Sabine 1933; Barron 2004, p. 264.
100   Sabine 1933, p. 349; Rawcliffe 2013, pp. 148–149.
101   Sabine 1933, p. 353.
102   Sabine 1934, p. 316; Barron 2004, p. 259.

Although this problem was corrected by passing a rule making the sideboards of these designated carts two and a half feet high, it was still more efficient to remove waste at night.[103] Another advantage to moving waste out of the city at night was that the latrines were substantially less busy in the evening compared to the daytime.

The sanitation services provided by both Imperial Rome and medieval London were broadly comparable in that they both offered many options to their citizens. Besides relying on Mother Nature, professionals cleaned waterways, emptied cesspits and carried waste away from the city in wagons at designated times of the day. It was an undesirable occupation that had a stigma attached to it and the risk of death was ever present, but one could make a living from it. Both cities also had problems with citizens using their own, apparently more convenient, methods to dispose of waste. Again both cities tried to deal with these problems by issuing laws and fines to offenders. One noticeable difference, however, was that London appeared to have a more difficult time providing accommodating city services, as well as appropriate locations for disposing of sewage and rubbish. London would close one location off, instructing its citizens to go elsewhere, only to eventually close this new location as well. Many frustrated individuals then dumped their waste in prohibited areas, due to a lack of convenient services and available options. Struggling to provide convenient sanitation services for the public did not seem to be a significant problem in Rome, but it is hard to believe that the Romans never experienced similar troubles.

3) Waste will not give rise to a nuisance due to odour, unsightly appearance or negative impact on the health of the individual

Rome

Rome provided many different services and facilities for sanitation removal. However, did these adequately prevent sanitation from becoming a nuisance due to odour, sight or public health? The advantages of carrying sewage away in underground drains resulted in a lower probability of obnoxious odours and sights, as well as a much lower risk to public health. One problem, however, regarding pipes and drains connecting to the main sewer was that the Romans did not have traps, resulting in the smell of human waste re-entering the facilities – though perfumes and incense may have helped to combat these smells.[104] Another problem was that when the Tiber River flooded every year,[105] the *Cloaca Maxima* became backfilled with water, clogging it with the waste previously dumped into the river and, subsequently, any pipes connected to it would also become

---

[103]   Barron 2004, p. 262.

[104]   Scobie 1986, p. 413; Classen et al. 1994, p. 18–19.

[105]   Livy, *History of Rome*, Books 35–37, trans. E.T. Sage, (Cambridge: Loeb, 1997), 35.9.2, 35.21.5; Pliny the Elder, *Histoire Naturelle*.36.24.105; Claudius Dio.53.33, 54.25, 55.22, 56.27.

clogged. This would have created a terrible mess as waste re-entered the facilities where they originated. A third problem with pipes connecting to the main sewer was that anything living in the drains, such as vermin, was able to crawl into the houses. The early 3rd century AD writer Aelian even relates an urban myth whereby an octopus swims up a house drain every night to feed on the pickled fish belonging to the merchants that lived there. Only after the third visit was the octopus successfully killed.[106] All of these potential scenarios probably led many private homeowners to avoid connecting their latrines to the main sewer.[107]

While Roman latrines were functional, the archaeological evidence suggests that most were poorly ventilated with only small windows placed very high, offering little light or air.[108] That being the case, the smell within latrines was quite obnoxious, explaining why they are often located near the *palaestra* (open-air exercise ground) of the bath.[109] Another concern regarding public, and private, latrines was the kind of materials available for self-cleansing. The literary evidence suggests that a sponge on the end of a stick performed the function of modern toilet paper for the Romans.[110] Whether these sponges were communal or if each user had his own is unclear. However, Seneca tells a story about a *bestiarius* (wild-beast hunter) who commits suicide rather than fight to the death in the arena, by gaining permission to relieve himself and then stuffing the latrine sponge down his throat.[111] This tale would suggest that the sponge was communal as the man needed to go to the latrine in order to obtain his instrument of death. In some parts of the Roman Empire there is also evidence for the use of moss as toilet paper, but this could only be an option in certain regions where moss grew in sufficient quantities, such as in York in Britain.[112] Many latrines also had a small channel running around the room at floor level which presumably was used either for rinsing one's sponge, catching spillage, and/or washing one's hands.[113] Since the re-use of a sponge is clearly unhygienic, latrines, although suitable for disposal of waste, could nevertheless still be potentially hazardous to one's health.

---

[106]   Aelian, *De Natura Animalium*, trans. A.F. Scholfield, volume III, (Cambridge: Loeb, 1959), 13.6.

[107]   Ingemark, C.A., 'The octopus in the sewers: an ancient legend analogue', *Journal of Folklore Research* 45 (2008): 145–170, see p. 156; Gowers 1995, p. 27.

[108]   Van Vaerenbergh 2009, p. 456.

[109]   Taylor, C., *The Design and Uses of Bath-House Palaestrae Roman North Africa* (University of Alberta: Unpublished PhD Thesis, 2009); Van Vaerenbergh 2009, p. 453; Kamash 2011, p. 182.

[110]   Martial, *Epigrams*.12.48.7.

[111]   Seneca, *Epistles*.70.20.

[112]   Breeze 1984, p. 56.

[113]   Shanks, H., 'The puzzling channels in ancient latrines', *Biblical Archeology Review* 28 (2002): 49–51; Wilson, A., 'Toilets' in G.C.M. Jansen, A.O. Koloski-Ostrow and E.M. Moormann (eds), *Roman Toilets, Their Archaeology and Cultural History* (Leuven: Peeters, 2011), pp. 99–105, see pp. 102–3; Jackson 1988, p. 51.

Underground drains were not as dangerous to public health as were open sewers and gutters running along the streets. The latter needed a constant flow of running water, supplied by rain, spill-off from basins and fountains, or bath water, in order to clear the accumulated waste. These methods would not have been completely effective and so would have required sewer workers to clear them with poles and mattocks.[114] If not regularly cleaned the sewage and rubbish would have created an unpleasant sight and odour, and would attract animals, rodents, bacteria and insects, which all increased the chance of disease. If open sewers were believed hazardous enough to health, a cover could be constructed over them. This action was contemplated at Amastris, when the emperor Trajan wrote to Pliny the Younger to cover the open sewer there, if he deemed it necessary for the benefit of public health.[115]

Cesspits had problems comparable to those of open sewers and gutters. As cesspits were holes dug into porous rock, liquids could escape but solids had to be periodically removed. The danger of death for those cleaning them has already been discussed, but even if cesspits were frequently cleaned, remnants of solids could become stuck in gaps along the walls, attracting insects, breeding bacteria and causing an objectionable odour. Meanwhile the liquids seeping into the soil were also unhygienic. Chamber pots and the vats in tenement buildings also needed a thorough washing, otherwise there was the potential of lingering odours and bacteria.

Any rubbish and human waste left in the streets, alleys, or in *amphorae*, created offensive and unsanitary conditions. Furthermore, the smell of urine was very putrid, and urine left sitting throughout the day in the *amphorae* of fullers on public streets would have given off a continuous smell unless emptied periodically. Another hazard was that the terracotta jars were quite porous and thus would leak or sweat, and if cracked could break, releasing their contents into the street.[116] The waste deposited elsewhere outdoors would not have been easily cleaned. Liquids would seep into the soil, while solids were left for decomposition, hopefully picked up by those responsible for cleaning the streets or eaten by insects and other creatures. Even when sewage and rubbish was properly placed on the wagons of the *stercorarii*, the smell emanating from the wagons as it travelled through the streets wafted throughout the neighbourhoods and would have created an unpleasant sight. Roman streets could, therefore, have been potentially hazardous to public health.

London

Although London also offered various sanitation facilities and many services, the city struggled to provide the most convenient services and locations for disposal. This resulted in the constant sight and smell of waste, and ultimately

---

[114] Leyerle 2009, p. 339.
[115] Pliny the Younger, *The Letters of the Younger Pliny*.10.98–99.
[116] Martial. *Epigrams*. 6.93.

created a greater risk to public health, especially when latrines were situated over waterways and ditches. Although the water flushed away some of the waste in the open sewers, not all of it was removed and the heavier items could easily clog up the channels, which, in turn, could catch other sewage, creating an unpleasant sight and odour.[117] This possibility in fact occurred in the Fleet River by the end of the 13th century, becoming so bad that the White Friars complained to the King and parliament that the river was giving off putrid exhalations.[118] The situation in ditches was much worse as there was no water to flush away the waste deposited here. One such example occurred in the Fleet prison ditch.

> The Fleet ditch, which encloses the Fleet prison and was built for its safety and is now so obstructed by dung from privies built thereon and other filth thrown into it as to cause a reasonable fear of the escape of prisoners and a grave danger to their health by reason of the infection of the air and the abominable stenches, and further to enquire by a jury of London and the suburbs as to the names of those who have built privies thereon or have thrown filth therein, the sheriffs having been ordered to assist and to summon the said jury.[119]

It seem that the waterways and ditches in London were consequently foul smelling, unpleasant to look at, and breeding grounds for disease.

After London officials ruled that waterways were not to be used as sanitation facilities, citizens turned to using dung and rubbish heaps, demonstrating that they would rather deal with the smell and waste rather than cart it off themselves.[120] Over time these areas became very hazardous to public health in addition to being a nuisance. One of these locations was at Tower Hill, and by 1371–72 it was so tainted that the citizens living in close proximity complained about the disgusting odour.[121] Instead of removing areas that bred disease and created unpleasant odours and sights, the city simply forced citizens to create new areas throughout the city. These areas were very unsanitary, as were the wagons and boats used to carry the waste and rubbish out of the city to these heaps. London did, however, attempt to lessen the smell of waste being carried through the streets by collecting it at night.

Cesspits were another health hazard. As in Rome they needed regular cleaning, otherwise, like the one owned by Henry de Ware, the smell emanating from them would become obnoxious and a nuisance to neighbours. In addition, if they were not constructed according to proper city regulations they could rot the timbers and allow sewage to creep into adjacent properties, or, worse, the floorboards could

---

[117]   Magnusson 2001, p. 258.

[118]   Wright, L., *Clean and Decent: the Fascinating History of the Bathroom and the Water Closet* (London: Routledge and Kegan Paul, 1960), p. 34.

[119]   Flower, C.T. (ed.), *Public Works in Mediaeval Law*, vol. II, (London: Quaritch, 1923), pp. 32, CXXXIII.

[120]   Classen et al. 1994, p. 55.

[121]   Sabine 1937, p. 38.

decay causing patrons to fall into the filth. Not everyone had cesspits, so some, such as Alice Wade mentioned earlier, opted to connect pipes from their premises to gutters or open sewers. Although ingenious, this expedient could clog up the gutters and sewers thereby creating a mess.

Those without privies or makeshift latrines resorted to tossing or placing waste outdoors. Throwing it out of the window, or piling it outside your door to be picked up by wagons during the evening, created a great nuisance to passers-by, as they had to see and smell all the waste before the doors of tenement buildings.[122] Adding to the unsanitary conditions in medieval London streets were those who urinated in public, animal faeces, dead animals, and the sawdust, straw, dust and ash from households.[123] The biggest polluters of streets were the butchers.[124] Even after butchers were moved out of the city they still produced an abundance of obnoxious waste that the city could not properly dispose of. After every epidemic disease outbreak, butchers were among the first to be blamed because of the unsanitary conditions they created.[125]

Dirt and disease was prevalent throughout the streets of medieval London, yet using baths was not a common activity for most citizens. Bathing was considered a sensual pastime, and it was believed that water corrupted the body making it vulnerable to unhealthy air and disease.[126] Baths also had a stigma attached to them, since they were mostly used for prostitution. Caroline Barron believes that the baths would not have improved public health anyway.[127] She is probably correct in her estimation because many diseases easily passed through water.[128] In order to become clean the poor washed in waterways or in ditches, while the rich washed in basins at home or used perfumes to mask and dispel odours.[129] Although there was soap, it was expensive so not often used.[130] Thus when London citizens washed one wonders exactly how clean they became. Medieval London may have been more sanitary than Imperial Rome in its use of cleansing materials. Evidence from cesspits in Dublin and Oslo shows that moss was used for cleansing during the medieval period, while small pieces of cloth, discovered in the privies of monasteries, suggests their use as toilet paper.[131] Although these were perhaps better options than Rome's use of the sponge, London citizens do not seem to

---

[122] Sabine 1934, p. 306.
[123] Rawcliffe 2013, pp. 127–128.
[124] Keene 1982, pp. 26–28.
[125] Sabine 1933, p. 348.
[126] Classen et al. 1994, p. 70.
[127] Barron 2004, p. 259.
[128] Salvato, J.A., *Environmental Engineering and Sanitation* (New York: Wiley, 1982), pp. 28–35.
[129] Classen et al. 1994, p. 71.
[130] Barron 2004, p. 258.
[131] Greig, J., 'Plant Resources', in G.G. Astill and A. Grant (eds), *The Countryside of Medieval England* (Oxford: Blackwell, 1992), pp. 108–27, see p. 125; Magnusson 2001, p. 159.

have been greatly concerned with personal hygiene despite the presence of dirt and disease.

Although both Rome and London provided adequate facilities and services, the problems of obnoxious odours and inappropriate sights were always an issue. Whether sewage and rubbish were in open sewers, cesspits, or in the streets, they continually offended the citizen's sensibilities. Each city had problems uniquely their own, such as Rome's problems associated with the annual flooding of the Tiber River, and London's problems of filth-filled ditches, but the results were similarly disappointing, as neither city could effectively solve them. Despite their common problems, there were areas where sanitary conditions were superior in one city than the other. At Rome, the underground drains helped remove much of the odour and sight of sewage, while in London, moss, if available, and cloth were much more sanitary than a communal sponge. In the end, however, the pervasive sight and odour of sewage and rubbish increased the risk of disease and infection in both cities.

4) Waste will not contaminate any drinking water supply or food supply

Rome

The drinking water at Rome was first drawn from wells, springs and the Tiber River.[132] As the city grew so did the demand for water. This was met with the construction of large aqueducts, which brought water from far distances and then distributed it at baths, basins or into pipes ensuring that the Romans had a relatively clean source of water for drinking. Once drawn, however, water was open to many carriers of bacteria found in the streets and even within the household. As the warning on the fountain in Pompeii suggests, citizens would urinate in or near some of these water sources, therefore contaminating them. Furthermore, the porous nature of cesspits meant liquids escaped into the soil and potentially into the groundwater. More contamination occurred when the Tiber flooded and filled the cesspits with water. This meant these liquids could easily find their way into the wells and springs used for drinking. In addition, cesspits situated in the kitchen of private homes would have attracted insects and other carriers that could come into contact with drinking water and food.

Human waste that was removed and subsequently used as fertiliser was a practical solution to dealing with sanitation. However, the use of human waste as fertiliser is now regarded as a public health hazard.[133] Unless processed correctly, many pathogens can infiltrate the soil and enter crops thus endangering public health. The ancient sources suggest that when farmers obtained human waste they

---

[132]   Frontinus, *De Aquae Ductu Urbis Romae*.4.1.

[133]   Conference Working Group, 'Re-use policies and research needs', in A. Pacey (ed.), *Sanitation in Developing Countries* (Chichester: Wiley 1978a), pp. 201–5.

should place it into a pit for an unspecified amount of time for decomposition.[134] Varro, a 1st century BC writer, stated that in order to get good manure, the pit should also be protected from the sun, presumably believing that it was better to use rotten than fresh manure.[135] We now know that heat is actually required in order to kill most of the pathogens, and that the waste should also be turned over repeatedly to be even more effective.[136] Since the Romans were unaware that these steps were necessary they unintentionally reintroduced harmful pathogens into the crops. These same precautions were required for those who used human waste as fertiliser for city or private gardens.

London

Early in the 13th century London had pipes carrying water into the city from the Tyburn River and these were closely guarded. Although one could get a licence to tap into the pipes, many illegally siphoned the water off.[137] Regardless of who used the water or how they got it, once drawn the water was easily contaminated by bacteria in the air from the sewage and rubbish lying in the streets. The water from the Tyburn was not the only source of water for London citizens. A much more polluted source came from the water drawn from many of the local wells and rivers, including the Thames.[138] These sources of water were constantly spoiled from dyers and their chemicals, the blood and hair from the carcasses of butchers' animals, and the sewage and rubbish tossed in by citizens.[139] In addition, liquids from cesspits drained into the local drinking water quite easily because 'sloping for miles from the north of the city down to the Thames River lay a thin layer of clay over deep gravel'.[140] City officials recognised that continually dumping sewage and rubbish into waterways was creating unsanitary conditions and polluting their drinking water. Enacting laws to prohibit citizens from doing this should have helped, but some, such as butchers, were still allowed to dump their wastes into the Thames, demonstrating that officials did not fully realise the potential hazards to public health caused by waste thrown into the river. The dangers of using sewage as fertiliser for growing crops at Rome, not properly processed, have already been mentioned, and so the same standards equally apply to the city of London.

The sanitation methods used in Imperial Rome and medieval London could not prevent their food and water from being contaminated. When food was processed, bacteria on the feet of flies could easily contaminate it. The contamination of food could, however, begin at the growing stage if improperly processed sewage was

---

134   *Cato and Varro: On Agriculture*, trans. W.D. Hooper and H.B. Ash (Cambridge: Loeb, 1999), Varro, *De Re Rustica*.1.13.4; Cato, *De Re Rustica*.2.3.

135   Varro, *De Re Rustica*.1.13.4.

136   Conference Working Group 1978a, p. 206; Shuval 1978, pp. 210–15.

137   Barron 2004, p. 256.

138   Barron 2004, p. 225; Sabine 1937, p. 37.

139   Keene 1982, p. 27; Sabine 1933, p. 346; Trench and Hillman 1985, pp. 32 and 59.

140   Sabine 1934, p. 318.

used as fertiliser. Cesspits were designed to allow liquids to escape, and these found their way into the rivers and wells, which supplied drinking water to many citizens. Ralph Jackson believes that in Rome most people would have built up a resistance to certain gastrointestinal diseases such as dysentery if they did not die from it as an infant.[141] Although probably true, for those in Imperial Rome and medieval London, the contamination of food and drinking water was still a risk to public health, and probably contributed to outbreaks of epidemic disease in both cities. Ultimately, whether or not Rome and London understood the risks to public health, both could not prevent the contamination of their food and water, even when water was piped in from cleaner sources.

5) Waste will not contaminate the waters of any bathing facility, waterfront, or stream used for public, financial, or recreational purposes

Rome
The Romans had sufficient facilities and services, but could not satisfactorily prevent the presence of obnoxious smells and sights. They also did not fully recognise the potential health hazards created by some of their methods. Food and drinking water could easily be affected, and ignorance concerning how bacteria spread meant recreational water sources also became contaminated. In the Roman world the baths were very popular and frequented by men and women, healthy and sick. Recognising that the sick and healthy should not bathe at the same time, the emperor Hadrian ordered that the sick use the baths first in the morning before the eighth hour.[142] This effectively removed the sick from the sight of the healthy. However, the sick could still easily pass some of their ailments to other bathers who used the same facilities later. Although the Romans recognised the existence of ailments such as diarrhoea and dysentery, they were not aware of just how easily they passed through water.[143] Thus whether bathing at the same time or later, the healthy could still catch these ailments persisting in the communal bath water.

Further public health problems ensued when this bath water was diverted into drains for the purpose of cleaning them. Though an extremely effective sanitation method, this potentially contaminated water flushed out drains and streets, picking up other pathogens from sewage and rubbish. All of this water eventually found its way into the Tiber and although the drinking water at Rome primarily came from outside of the city, the Tiber was still used for bathing, swimming, and fishing. The 3rd century AD doctor Galen recognised the effects that this dirty water had on the fish in the Tiber. He noted that the quality of fish caught upstream from the *Cloaca*

---

[141]   Jackson 1988, p. 53.
[142]   SHA, *Hadrian*.22.7, (1976).
[143]   Celsus, *De Medicina*, trans. W.G. Spencer, (Cambridge: Loeb, 1935) 2.8.30–33; Pliny the Elder, *Naturalis Historia*.27.6.21, 27.105.129; Salvato 1982, pp. 28–35.

Maxima was better than those caught downstream.[144] Furthermore, the constant dumping of sewage and rubbish into the Tiber caused problems for navigation and so the river needed to be dredged from time to time.[145]

London

The waterways in London acted as more than just simple depots for sewage and rubbish. They were used for recreational and business purposes as well. Since baths had the stigma of prostitution associated with them, many turned to the waterways to bathe.[146] Although bathing still allowed London citizens to get marginally cleaner, the water from these streams and rivers was contaminated with many different types of microorganisms. These polluted waterways also continued to supply fish for many citizens. Lastly, clogged river channels slowed and prevented proper navigation. In 1372 the king noted that the channel of the Thames had been narrowed so much by the continual dumping of waste that it was causing a great hindrance to shipping.[147] By repeatedly dumping waste into waterways, it not only affected one of London's drinking sources, but also its primary source for bathing, fishing, and shipping.

It is not surprising that the waters of bathing facilities, beaches, and streams used for public, business, and recreational purposes were contaminated due to the sanitation methods employed by Imperial Rome and medieval London. Societies from the past often used streams, rivers, lakes, and other water sources for many purposes. The most common function was for drinking, but bathing, fishing, recreation, and shipping would also occur. Although both cities transported water from significant distances, many of the poor still relied on the local waterways for everyday needs. These unavoidable needs meant that many Roman and London citizens were exposed to infectious diseases contaminating the water.

Conclusion

After this examination of the sanitation systems employed by Imperial Rome and medieval London we are in a position to suggest whether or not they satisfied the five criteria established at the outset. Both Rome and London provided different types of facilities spread throughout the city. Some, such as latrines and cesspits, were specifically designed to collect waste, while others, such as the outdoors, were just convenient facilities. Certain dangers associated with using some sanitation facilities, such as falling into open sewers, were always possible, but if one paid attention and avoided using them at night, the danger was significantly

---

[144]   Galen, *On the Properties of Foodstuffs*, trans. O. Powell, (Cambridge: Cambridge University Press, 2003), 6.722–3k.

[145]   Suetonius, *Divus Augustus*.30; SHA, *Aurelian*.47.2–3, (1932).

[146]   Barron 2004, p. 258.

[147]   Sabine 1937, p. 39.

reduced. One major difference between the two cities was that Rome used both underground drains and open sewers, while London used only open sewers. Although Rome provided an additional sanitation system for its citizens, the open sewer London employed was suitably adequate. Overall, therefore, both Imperial Rome and medieval London sufficiently satisfied the first criterion.

Although both cities satisfied the second criterion, Rome did so somewhat more successfully than London. Both supplied a variety of sanitation services, since commissions and city officials, such as the *aediles* or the Sergeant of the Channels, had responsibilities specifically dealing with sanitation. There were also individuals responsible for cleaning cesspits, drains and streets. Moreover, Imperial Rome and medieval London both instituted regulations to encourage citizens to use proper sanitation facilities so that all types of waste could be more easily removed from the city. Fines were also levied at both cities to enforce these regulations. The evidence, however, suggests that London struggled more than Rome to keep its citizens from tossing and dumping waste in non-designated sanitation facilities. This was, in part, due to the city constantly closing areas designated for sanitation, thus causing a great inconvenience for citizens, as they continually sought new dumping locations. Regardless of this one complication, London, as well as Rome, passed the second criterion.

Although both cities met the first two criteria, it was virtually impossible for them to completely remove the sight and smell of waste from public awareness since most complaints about sanitation deal with the issues of offending smells and undesirable sights, even though there was a much higher tolerance. Thus both failed to meet the third criterion. Rome and London provided facilities and services, but if these facilities were not frequently cleaned or effectively washed, obnoxious odours could persist. The accumulation of sewage and rubbish in the streets not picked up, eaten by scavengers, or washed away, further added to an unpleasant appearance and odour. Without frequent and meticulous cleaning, neither city was able to completely remove waste from the public's view.

If an ancient or medieval society's primary concern with sanitation systems was the public's senses, then it is not surprising that both cities failed to meet the final two criteria. Although both Rome and London recognised that an unsanitary environment endangered public health, neither properly understood the causes underlying these unsanitary conditions, as the belief was that bad air caused disease and sickness. Sewage and rubbish was consistently deposited into waterways and although city officials recognised that an accumulation of waste impacted navigation, and that fish found downstream were of lower quality than those found upstream, they failed to recognise the effects that contaminated drinking water had upon health. This also explains why nothing was done to prevent the liquids in cesspits from penetrating groundwater, nor to properly treat human waste before using it as fertiliser. Even when clean water was channelled from outside of the city, to be drawn at fountains or piped into private homes, it was then open to the bacteria spread on the feet of flies. Although both Rome and London desired an environment favourable to public health, neither understood that by failing to prevent their water from being contaminated they simply could not attain this goal, and so both failed to achieve the fourth and fifth criteria.

I would argue that the five criteria established in this paper would have been desired by anyone living in either Imperial Rome or medieval London. Proper sanitation facilities and services were crucial for the health of citizens. What these criteria reveal, however, is that both cities' idea of public health was primarily concerned with the public's senses. Had all five criteria been successfully attained then both may have achieved a relatively high standard of public health for their time. Interestingly, both cities passed and failed the same criteria, with Rome being slightly more successful in keeping human waste from the public's senses. These achievements notwithstanding, not until a society realises that contaminated water and improperly treated sewage actually increase the risk of disease for the public, can any society successful pass all five criteria. Although these criteria set much lower standards than those of the present day, these minimal standards are still required to properly determine how ancient and medieval cities handled the problems of sanitation and to adequately assess the effectiveness of their methods.

Chapter 6

Sewers, Cesspits and Middens: A Survey of the Evidence for 2000 Years of Waste Disposal in York, UK

Allan R. Hall and Harry K. Kenward

Introduction

In a paper now over 20 years old, Peter Addyman[1] addressed the question of public health through the two millennia of York's history, drawing on an accumulating body of evidence from archaeological excavations in the city from the 1970s onwards. Our aim in this paper is to update Addyman's account, at least with respect to sanitation and waste disposal more generally, using information gained during the investigation of hundreds of samples of archaeological deposits from dozens of sites during the life of the Environmental Archaeology Unit (1975–2003) at the University of York. Working within an integrated team, it was possible to study macroscopic plant remains (fruits and seeds, fragments of leaf and moss and so on), insects and other macroscopic invertebrates, the microscopic eggs of intestinal parasites, and the remains of vertebrates of all kind, including humans. We recognise a characteristic set of plant and invertebrate remains as constituting an 'indicator group'[2] for faecal material, although most of the individual components could have other origins; only the eggs of intestinal parasites (Table 6.1) necessarily originated in faeces of some kind, although identification of the host is not always certain and these tiny eggs were liable to be redeposited easily. The results are exemplified by publications

---

[1]   Addyman, P.V., 'The archaeology of public health at York, England', *World Archaeology* 21(1989): 244–64.

[2]   Kenward, H., Hall, A., 'Enhancing bioarchaeological interpretation using indicator groups: stable manure as a paradigm', *Journal of Archaeological Science* 24 (1997): 663–73; Kenward, H., Hall, A., 'Dung and stable manure on waterlogged archaeological occupation sites: some ruminations on the evidence from plant and invertebrate remains', in R.L.C. Jones (ed.), *Manure Matters* (Farnham: Ashgate, 2012), pp. 79–95.

dealing with material from Roman levels at 24–36 Tanner Row (Hall et al. 1990)[3] and from Anglo-Scandinavian deposits at 16–22 Coppergate and other sites.[4]

Roman York

Like Addyman, we shall follow a chronological path, beginning with the foundation of the Roman city of *Eboracum* in AD 71. Most striking for much of the Roman town is the lack of survival of evidence for organic occupation waste: in the greater part of the city for which we have explored Roman levels, waste has either simply not survived (through decay since deposition or levelling during development during the Roman period), or it was never there in the first place. Dobney et al.[5] have reviewed the nature of the evidence from bioarchaeology for Roman York, emphasising this problem. Our view of the Romans as having well-organised waste disposal is borne out by the excavation of an impressive stone-lined sewer under Church Street, within the Roman fortress (see plates in[6]). However, in other parts of the settlement where such large-scale sewerage did not extend, waste must have been removed by other means as there is no evidence that it was left near to habitation in significant amounts or for long periods. We do not, for example, have a single convincing example of a well-preserved organic deposit in a cesspit from the first four centuries of York's past. A single pit fill from a site on the fringes of the Roman town, in Peasholme Green, stands as evidence for faecal material in the form of mineral-replaced and concreted plant remains including fruit stones such as *Prunus* (for example plums and sloes; Figure 6.1) and corncockle (*Agrostemma githago* L.) seed fragments.[7] It

[3]   Hall, A.R., Kenward, H.K., *Environmental Evidence from the Colonia: General Accident and Rougier Street*. The Archaeology of York series 14(6) (London: Council for British Archaeology, 1990).

[4]   Hall, A.R., Kenward, H.K. 'Setting people in their environment: plant and animal remains from Anglo-Scandinavian York', in R.A. Hall, D.W. Rollason, M. Blackburn, D.N. Parsons, G. Fellows-Jensen, A.R. Hall, H.K. Kenward, T.P. O'Connor, D. Tweddle, A.J. Mainman and N.S.H. Rogers, *Aspects of Anglo-Scandinavian York*. The Archaeology of York series 8(4) (York: Council for British Archaeology, 2004), pp. 372–426 and references pp. 507–21; Kenward, H.K., Hall, A.R., *Biological Evidence from Anglo-Scandinavian Deposits at 16–22 Coppergate*. The Archaeology of York series 14(7) (York: Council for British Archaeology, 1995).

[5]   Dobney, K., Hall, A., Kenward, H., 'It's all garbage ... A review of bioarchaeology in the four English Colonia towns', in H. Hurst (ed.), *The Coloniae of Roman Britain: New studies and a review*. Journal of Roman Archaeology Supplementary Series 36 (Gloucester: Journal of Roman Archaeology, 1999), pp. 15–35.

[6]   Whitwell, J.B., *The Church Street Sewer and an adjacent Building*. The Archaeology of York series 3(1) (London: Council for British Archaeology, 1976).

[7]   Hall, A., Kenward, H., Jaques, D., Carrott, J. (2000), 'Technical Report: Environment and industry at Layerthorpe Bridge, York (site code YORYM 1996.345)', *Reports from the Environmental Archaeology Unit, York* 2000/64.

Figure 6.1.   A sloe (*Prunus spinosa* L.) fruitstone embedded in a faecal
concretion from Anglo-Scandinavian 16–22 Coppergate. The
'flesh' (mesocarp) of the stone is also preserved in this case. The
stone is about 10 mm in length. (Photograph: Philippa Tomlinson)

must, however, be said that few excavations have revealed substantial remains of
domestic dwellings of the period.

Where there *are* surface accumulations of organic material from the Roman town,
these have been shown largely to comprise of stable manure, as at 24–30 Tanner Row,
within the civilian settlement (Colonia) SW of the Ouse,[8] and more recently at a site
in Spurriergate, at the edge of the fortress on the NE bank (unpublished). Obviously
the waste from the stabling of equines – which are the animals presumed to have
produced the material in question – was much more tolerable than the equivalent
waste from human occupants, and certainly it had somewhat different (but at the
time apparently unappreciated) health implications in terms of transfer of harmful
bacteria and of endoparasites. No Roman dumps are known outside the urban area
of York or on the riverfronts, the latter in contrast with London and Lincoln. The

---

[8]   Hall and Kenward 1990. See Figure 6.2 (beetle head) as an example of the remains
of a beetle typical of herbivore dung.

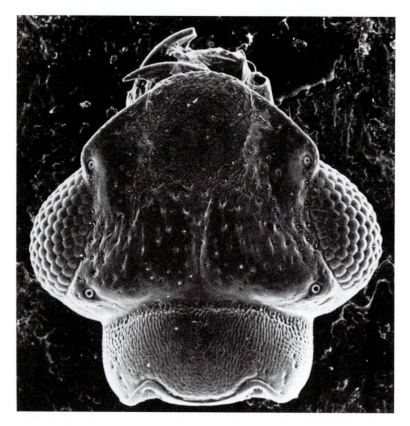

Figure 6.2.   Head of the rove beetle *Oxytelus sculptus* Gravenhorst from
Roman 24–30 Tanner Row: a common denizen of stable
manure and cesspits in York. Width across eyes about 0.6 mm.
(Photograph: Enid Allison and Harry Kenward)

substantial organic deposits at Tanner Row may have been dumps on the edge of the
occupied area, perhaps serving as landfill to raise the ground.

In reviewing records of eggs of human intestinal parasites (the whipworm,
Trichuris trichiura and the roundworm, *Ascaris lumbricoides*), we were surprised
by the paucity of records for Roman York. As for the post-medieval period (below)
it seems more likely that this is a result of a combination of often poor preservation
and rarity of analyses, and not just simply a low level of infestation.

Returning to the sewer, it must be remarked that its potential as a source of
evidence for waste from the inhabitants using it has not been sufficiently realised.
Buckland[9] reported a wide variety of remains preserved in samples of its fills, but

---

[9]   Buckland, P.C., *The Environmental Evidence from the Church Street Roman Sewer
System*. The Archaeology of York series 14(1) (London: Council for British Archaeology, 1976).

the presence of some Australasian insects, which certainly arrived in Britain in the early modern period, casts frustrating doubt on the dating of the remains as a whole. It may be that the extensive unexplored parts of the Roman sewer system will prove to contain uncontaminated deposits that can be investigated in future.

After the Romans

For the Anglian period, between the end of Roman York towards the end of the 5th century AD and the coming of the Vikings in the mid-9th century, the archaeological record is tantalisingly sparse, and with it the record for many kinds of biological remains. Fortunately at an excavation at 46–54 Fishergate, away from the Roman and medieval centre of the city, a number of pit fills (and fills of some other features) can be shown to have contained remnants of plant foods preserved by mineral replacement, in which some of the soft tissues had become impregnated by calcium phosphate. This kind of preservation is very typical of cesspits, where high concentrations of calcium and phosphate occur: see[10] for studies of the processes involved. Every gradation can occur from the presence of small amounts of mineral replacement within material that is essentially preserved by anoxic waterlogging, through the formation of 'concretions' of waterlogged material bound together by calcium phosphate into more or less amorphous lumps ('faecal concretions', commonly encountered towards the edges of cesspits), to assemblages of plant material preserved by mineral replacement alone. At Fishergate only the most extreme case was observed. This may relate to ground conditions in which continuous waterlogging did not occur,[11] although another variable to consider is the rate at which waste was deposited. If this site was occupied only seasonally, for example, as a trading settlement, or was simply not very densely settled, it is possible that conditions were hardly ever suitable for mineral replacement to take place. At any rate, the amounts of mineral-replaced plant material were small. The study of insects, too, offered little evidence for foul matter. However, some of the assemblages of bones, especially those of fish, gave rather clearer evidence of faeces, in the form of remains likely to have been ingested and subsequently voided.[12]

---

[10]   McCobb, L.M.E., Briggs, D.E.G., Evershed, R.P., Hall, A.R., Hall, R.A., 'Preservation of fossil seeds from a 10th century AD cess pit at Coppergate, York', *Journal of Archaeological Science* 28 (2001): 929–40.; McCobb, L.M.E., Briggs, D.E.G., Hall, A.R., Kenward, H.K., 'Preservation of invertebrates in 16th century cesspits at St Saviourgate, York', *Archaeometry* 46 (2004): 157–69.

[11]   Allison, E.P., Hall, A.R., Jones, A.K.G., Kenward, H.K., Robertson, A., 'Report on plant and invertebrate remains', in R.L. Kemp (ed.), *Anglian Settlement at 46–54 Fishergate*. The Archaeology of York series 7(1) (York: Council for British Archaeology, 1996), p. 85–105.

[12]   O'Connor, T.P., *Bones from 46–54 Fishergate*. The Archaeology of York series 15(4) (London: Council for British Archaeology, 1991).

Viking Age York

The contrast between the evidence from Fishergate and that from the mid-9th to late 11th century (Anglo-Scandinavian or 'Viking') occupation at 16–22 Coppergate[13] could hardly be greater. Here, very many of the pits contained fills rich in organic material preserved by anoxic waterlogging, much of which was human faecal waste – to judge from the characteristic assemblages of wheat/rye 'bran' (and other plant foods), weed seed fragments (from the milling of grain contaminants), intestinal parasite eggs (Table 6.1), and a wide variety of insects characteristic of foul matter, especially the puparia (resting stage) of flies and a suite of foul-matter beetles. Cesspits were common towards what is supposed to be the street frontage along the north edge of the site during the earliest phase of occupation,[14] though exactly where the inhabitants using those cesspits lived is unknown. Later, when a series of four contiguous tenements was laid out and the street front was formed by two ranks of wooden buildings, cesspits were located towards the rear of the buildings in an area of yards.[15] No obvious evidence survives for superstructures around these cesspits so it is possible they were open to the skies with perhaps just wicker screens; the suite of beetles found in them rather suggests this.[16]

To give an idea of the prevalence of cesspits – or at least of pits that served as cesspits at some stage in their life – we can note that a total of 50 layers from Anglo-Scandinavian Coppergate were recorded as containing large concentrations of wheat/rye bran. Of these, all but three were pit fills, and represented a total of 30 pits. Of the 50 layers rich in bran, 22 also yielded abundant seed fragments of corncockle (see below). Analysis of eggs of intestinal parasitic worms from the same samples showed that in almost all cases the whipworm (*Trichuris*, Figure 6.3) was present, often in large numbers and, in more than two-thirds, eggs of the roundworm *Ascaris* were also present (though, as is usually the case in material thought to represent human faecal waste, in very much smaller concentrations).

Most of these pits contained puparia of flies, including the house fly (*Musca domestica* Linnaeus), which are known to carry disease organisms, and it is quite probable that the beetles, too, would have been minor agents of disease dispersal.[17] A common fly in cesspits of this period and later was *Thoracochaeta zosterae*

---

[13]   Hall, A.R., Kenward, H.K., Williams, D., Greig, J.R.A., *Environment and Living Conditions at Two Anglo-Scandinavian Sites*. The Archaeology of York series 14(4) (London: Council for British Archaeology, 1983); Kenward, H.K., Hall, A.R., *Biological Evidence from Anglo-Scandinavian Deposits at 16–22 Coppergate*. The Archaeology of York series 14(7) (York: Council for British Archaeology, 1995).

[14]   Kenward and Hall 1995, Figure 130.

[15]   Kenward and Hall 1995, Figure 141.

[16]   Carrott, J., Kenward, H., 'Species associations among insect remains from urban archaeological deposits and their significance in reconstructing the past human environment', *Journal of Archaeological Science* 28 (2001): 887–905.

[17]   Kenward, H., Large, F., 'Insects in urban waste pits in Viking York: another kind of seasonality', *Environmental Archaeology* 3 (1998): 35–53.

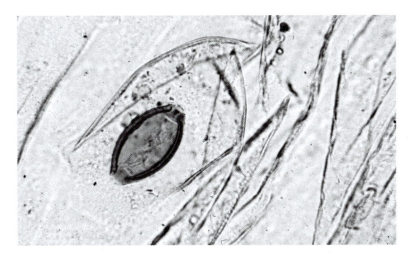

Figure 6.3.   Whipworm (*Trichuris*) egg within a leaf-margin tooth of
leek (*Allium porrum* L.) from an Anglo-Scandinavian cesspit
deposit at 16–22 Coppergate. The egg is about 50 μm in length.
(Photograph: Philippa Tomlinson)

(Haliday), now usually found in stranded seaweed and originally misidentified
as a species more likely to be found in faeces, the latrine fly *Teichomyza fusca*
Macquart.[18] As an aside, isotopic analysis of material from medieval Oxford has
shown that *T. zosterae* was exploiting organic material locally, and had not been
imported with seaweed;[19] the same is undoubtedly true for the vast majority of
inland archaeological sites.

A topic of endless fascination in relation to the use of all these cesspits is the
nature of materials used as 'sanitary wipes'. The most likely candidates are textiles,
on the one hand, and moss, on the other. We are not convinced – given the lack
of any high concentrations of textile fragments in pit fills – that they served this
purpose on a regular basis and, indeed, Walton[20] seems to regard textile scraps at
the Coppergate site as casual discards. Moss, by contrast, is regularly recorded in
these pit fills, sometimes in very high concentrations, and is surely there because it
was brought into Jorvik (Viking York) for wiping bottoms. The species concerned

[18]   Belshaw, R., 'A note on the recovery of *Thoracochaeta zosterae* (Haliday) (Diptera:
Sphaeroceridae) from archaeological deposits', *Circaea* 6 (1989): 39–41.

[19]   Webb, S.C., Hedges, R.E.M., Robinson, M., 'The seaweed fly *Thoracochaeta
zosterae* (Hal.) in inland archaeological contexts: $\partial^{13}C$ and $\partial^{15}N$ solves the problem',
Journal of Archaeological Science 25 (1998): 1253–57.

[20]   Walton, P., *Textiles, Cordage and Raw Fibre from 16–22 Coppergate*. The
Archaeology of York series 17(5) (London: Council for British Archaeology, 1989).

are typical of woodland floors and tree trunks,[21] and a similar suite is recorded from pit fills from this and later medieval periods across Northern Europe.

There were various gullies or drains at Anglo-Scandinavian Coppergate, some of them originating within buildings,[22] but there is no good evidence from the plant and animal remains in their fills that they carried human waste; most seem to have been backfilled with an assortment of waste material such as the dyebath residues mentioned below. These drains, some tentatively identified as 'open sewers' by Addyman,[23] almost certainly carried rainwater or groundwater away; those within buildings were situated in basements that were surely liable to seepage.

There were also small patches of filth on floors and external surfaces, on the evidence of localised concentrations of fly puparia or occasionally intestinal worm eggs. These puparia usually seem to have been *in situ* but the worm eggs are perhaps as likely to have resulted from redeposition of material from earlier cesspits through the digging of new ones. Floors and external surfaces at sites such as Coppergate were constantly built up by the informal deposition of waste, much of it a potential source of infective agents. Among this material were some substantial accumulations of waste from dyebaths at Coppergate and other Viking Age sites in York, likely to have been most unsavoury – though, like some cesspit fills, some may have been sufficiently toxic that even flies would have been unable to breed in them! We might suspect that a large proportion of waste in most areas in the Anglo-Scandinavian period – and in at least some areas in all periods – ended up on surfaces and decayed into the general build-up that became York's exceptional archaeological archive.

From the Neolithic period onwards, organic waste produced in small settlements was almost certainly transported to agricultural land as fertiliser, but this may have been impracticable for a town of thousands of inhabitants such as Jorvik (Viking York), explaining the abundance of cesspits and their fills. Indeed, there seems to be no evidence of any formal waste disposal system in Anglo-Scandinavian York, although if 'town dumps' existed they may have been overlooked or, if close to one of the rivers, flushed away. An example that may represent disposal of waste into the river at this period comes from excavations by Layerthorpe Bridge, where several organic deposits proved to be rich in very decayed tree bark. This, and the remains of a beetle with a predilection for stored skins, have been interpreted as indicative of tan-bath waste, a very noxious kind of effluent.[24] It is worth noting that, while this disposal site was downwind of the town (leather tanning being an

---

[21]   Kenward and Hall 1995, p. 745.

[22]   Kenward and Hall 1997: 663–73, see Figure 159.

[23]   Addyman 1989, pl.3.

[24]   Hall et al. 2000; Hall, A., Kenward, H. 'Can we identify biological indicator groups for craft, industry and other activities?', in P. Murphy and P.E.J. Wiltshire (eds), *The Environmental Archaeology of Industry*. Symposia of the Association for Environmental Archaeology 20 (Oxford: Oxbow, 2003), pp. 114–30; Hall, A., Kenward, H., 'Plant and invertebrate indicators of leather production: from fresh skin to leather offcuts', in

especially noisome business), the waste was being dumped upstream of the town centre, contributing to the likely pollution mentioned below.

Many other (much smaller) excavations of Viking Age deposits in the centre of York have revealed further examples of cesspits with the same suites of organisms occurring repeatedly (discussed as a group by[25]; records of parasite eggs from these sites are listed in Table 6.1). Good examples have been examined at 2 Clifford St,[26] and 28–9 High Ousegate.[27] At a further site in this group, at 4–7 Parliament St, two of the four samples examined were rich in the classic 'faecal' suite of remains but also contained quantities of uncharred cereal chaff, perhaps pointing to the presence of faeces from livestock, most likely pigs.[28] There are substantial difficulties in distinguishing the eggs of the *Trichuris* and *Ascaris* species that infect pigs and humans, as they are of very similar size and shape to one another.[29]

Unlike nearby Coppergate, an early excavation of Anglo-Scandinavian deposits at 6–8 Pavement[30] yielded no evidence for pits containing waste – the deposits excavated here seemed primarily to have formed as floors. Even at Pavement, though, there were occasional concentrations of insects indicating rather foul conditions. Intriguingly, an object formed of concreted faecal material was recovered from one of these layers and appears to represent a single (large) human stool.[31] Unlike the usual faecal concretions recovered from cesspits, this object offered the opportunity to explore the diet and worm burden of a single individual rather than a potentially 'averaged' sample of faeces from a random concretion or unconcreted fills from a pit.

One of the constants – or nearly so – of faecal concretions and 'unmineralised' parts of faecal deposits from Anglo-Scandinavian York (and indeed many other sites of this period and the Middle Ages in York and elsewhere) is the presence of

---

R. Thomson and Q. Mould (eds), *Leather Tanneries: The Archaeological Evidence* (London: Archetype, 2011), pp. 9–32.

[25]   Hall and Kenward 2004, pp. 372–426 and references pp. 507–21.

[26]   Hall, A.R., Kenward, H.K. (2000), 'Technical Report: Plant and invertebrate remains from Anglo-Scandinavian deposits at 4–7 Parliament Street (Littlewoods Store), York (site code 99.946)', *Reports from the EAU, York* 2000/22.

[27]   Kenward, H., Hall, A., Jaques, D., Carrott, J., Cousins, S. (2003), 'Assessment of biological remains from excavations at Waterstones bookshop, 28–29 High Ousegate, York (site code: 2002.475)', *Palaeoecology Research Services Report* 2003/50.

[28]   Hall and Kenward 2000; Hall and Kenward 2004, pp. 407–8; Kenward and Hall 2012, pp. 79–95.

[29]   Kenward, H. (2009), 'Invertebrates in archaeology in the north of England', *(English Heritage) Research Department Report Series* 12/2009 (available online at http://services.english-heritage.org.uk/ResearchReportsPdfs/012_2009WEB.pdf), p.24–5.

[30]   Hall et al. 1983.

[31]   Jones, A.K.G., 'Report on a coprolite from 6–8 Pavement', in A.R. Hall, H.K. Kenward, D. Williams and J.R.A. Greig, *Environment and Living Conditions at Two Anglo-Scandinavian Sites*. The Archaeology of York series 14(4) (London: Council for British Archaeology, 1983), pp. 225–9.

milled weed seeds, as mentioned above. These are from seeds unavoidably mixed with the cereal crop and evidently ending up in the flour-based products whose bran forms a large part of the surviving material (virtually all of it has been identified as 'wheat/rye', these two not being distinguishable microscopically). There are at least two implications concerning past health from these observations. The first is that the diet – insofar as it is represented by the large bulk of bran – contained plenty of insoluble fibre. At the time these deposits were first being studied in the late 1970s, the vogue for a high-fibre diet to combat what were perceived as a variety of diseases consequent on the large-scale consumption of refined foods lacking dietary fibre was being taken seriously by the medical profession and filtering into the popular consciousness. It is perhaps difficult now to remember, for example, how rare it was at that time to find bread on the supermarket shelves that was both brown and contained a good quantity of fibre. Brown rice was still very much the preserve of a relatively few people, regarded as eccentrics. People in Viking Age York certainly seem to have had a high-fibre diet, perhaps essential in easing the passage of the fish bones and fruit stones which are common in faecal deposits from the period and clearly were regularly swallowed.

By contrast with the evidence from the ground, the presence of milled weed seeds is something that is extremely rare in even the most rustic of modern 'granary' loaves. Many of the seeds were probably of little consequence to the consumers, or may even have been nutritious, but one particular species, corncockle (*Agrostemma githago* L.), was probably injurious.[32] The large black seeds of this plant must at least have made brown flour grey and imparted a disagreeable odour;[33] but more significantly corncockle seeds contain considerable quantities of saponins, a group of substances that are injurious to cell walls and therefore toxic when eaten by mammals. What is not entirely clear – the now very old (mainly mid-19th century) literature is ambivalent on the subject – is how far the poisonous effects were mitigated by baking, or boiling in the case of foods like porridges and frumenty. Certainly at times corncockle has been used as a famine food,[34] though seemingly after treatment with steam, which presumably made it less harmful. It has also been suggested that consuming corncockle in bread and other flour-based products may actually have counteracted some of the effects of an intestinal worm burden; certainly Foster and Duke[35] refer to the use of powdered corncockle seed (albeit uncooked) as a vermifuge in North America – where the plant, and presumably its use for this purpose, was brought from Europe.

---

[32]   Hall, A.R., '…The cockle of rebellion, insolence, sedition…', *Interim: Bulletin of the York Archaeological Trust* 8 (1981): 5–8.

[33]   Long, H.C., *Plants Poisonous to Livestock* (Cambridge: Cambridge University Press, 1917).

[34]   Maurizio, A., *Die Geschichte unserer Pflanzennahrung von den Urzeiten bis zur Gegenwart* (Berlin: P. Parey, 1927).

[35]   Foster, S., Duke, J.A., *A Field Guide to Medicinal Plants and Herbs of Eastern and Central North America*. 2nd edition (Boston: Houghton Mifflin, 1999).

On the topic of vermifuges, we might in theory hope to be able to detect their use in the past through examination of the contents of cesspits. In practice, however, the actual use of any of the wide range of plants mentioned in the literature of herbal medicine as having been employed thus would be very hard to detect. The parts used or the way in which they were used (typically leaves, prepared as powders, or as decoctions) simply would not leave a trace in the ground recognisable by the methods of low-power microscopy currently routinely used to study macroscopic plant remains in cesspit fills. The growing application of biomolecular analyses of archaeological organic residues may eventually cast some light on this and various other questions regarding diet and disease.

After the Norman Conquest

Our knowledge of the cesspits of post-Conquest York comes from a variety of sites, although most studies have been on a small scale (for example, the medieval levels at Tanner Row and Rougier Street).[36] To judge from the lack of structures other than wicker or barrel linings, these earlier post-Conquest cesspits continue the tradition of the Anglo-Scandinavian period. There are several examples of the seats from latrines of the early part of this period (Figure 6.4), although they are sometimes incorrectly referred to as if they were Anglo-Scandinavian.[37] Through time, stone- and brick-lined (external) cesspits and (internal) garderobes became more common and eventually the norm. In one case where a large quantity of material was examined, from excavations of the College of the Vicars Choral in The Bedern, dating to the 14th–17th centuries, brick-lined latrines[38] were rich in food plants, especially seeds and fruit stones of fig, grape, wild strawberry, coriander, and fennel, as well as 'bran', and generally yielded at least a few intestinal worm eggs. In contrast to this evidence for faeces, many of the pits had an insect fauna predominantly of beetles likely to have lived within buildings – these pits were, after all, associated with buildings of good quality – and only occasionally yielded more than a few fly puparia or significant populations of foul-matter beetles.[39] Pits

---

[36] Hall and Kenward 1990.

[37] Murray, H., *Where to go in York: The History of the Public Conveniences in the City of York* (York: Voyager, 2000), p. 1.

[38] Addyman 1989, pl. 11.

[39] Hall, A.R., Kenward, H.K., Robertson, A. (1993a), 'Investigation of medieval and post-medieval plant and invertebrate remains from Area X of the excavations in The Bedern (south-west), York (YAT/Yorkshire Museum sitecode 1973–81.13 X): Technical report', *Ancient Monuments Laboratory Report* 56/93; Hall, A.R., Kenward, H.K., Robertson, A. (1993b), 'Investigation of medieval and post-medieval plant and invertebrate remains from Area IV of the excavations in The Bedern (north-east), York (YAT/Yorkshire Museum sitecode 1976–81.14 IV): Technical report', *Ancient Monuments Laboratory Report* 57/93; Hall, A.R., Kenward, H.K., Robertson, A. (1993c), 'Investigation of medieval and post-medieval plant and invertebrate remains from Area II of the excavations in The Bedern

of this period sometimes yield larger numbers of puparia, including *Thoracochaeta zosterae*, mentioned above. Another example, from the late 14th century, was a stone-lined cesspit from a site in Low Petergate. Its fills contained the usual mélange of plant foods, including bran, with milled weed seeds, but there was also evidence from the insect fauna for the disposal of floor sweepings from the adjacent building.[40] As for Anglo-Scandinavian York, infestation by *Trichuris* and *Ascaris* seems to have been very common, eggs having been found in a substantial proportion of the deposits investigated.

There seems to have been some dumping in the open air as well as in pits. William the Conqueror caused the damming of the River Foss by the building of one of his two castles in York, leading to the formation of the 'King's Pool', a large shallow lake on the SE side of the city. This seems to have become a focus for waste disposal throughout the medieval period and later, and it seems that the shore adjacent to the core of the city gradually extended into the lake through the dumping of urban ejectamenta. We cannot determine how much of a health hazard this dumping represents, although it must have led to significant water pollution (a point to which we return later). Similarly, we are not sure if it was officially sanctioned to make new ground, the defensive pool now being redundant, or represents 'fly tipping'. There is no bioarchaeological evidence for dung in the streets heaped against houses as described by King from documentary sources for early post-medieval Prescot in Merseyside,[41] and implicit in the presence of garderobes within the city walls of medieval York, including the bars,[42] but how might we ever detect it? It is most unlikely that waste of this kind would ever be sealed into an archaeological sequence in a form where studies of plant and animal remains would give an unequivocal identification, though biomolecular analyses might reveal concentrations of coprosterols or bile acids.[43]

(north-east), York (YAT/Yorkshire Museum sitecode 1976–81.14 II): Technical report', *Ancient Monuments Laboratory Report* 58/93.

[40]   Hall, A., Kenward, H., Girvan, L., McKenna, R. (2007), 'Investigations of plant and invertebrate macrofossil remains from excavations in 2004 at 62–8 Low Petergate, York (site code 2002.421)', *Reports from the Centre for Human Palaeoecology, University of York* **2007/06**.

[41]   King, W., 'How high is too high? Disposing of dung in seventeenth-century Prescot', *The Sixteenth Century Journal* 23 (1992): 443–57.

[42]   Murray 2000, p. 2.

[43]   Bethell, P.H., Goad, L.J., Evershed, R.P., 'The study of biomarkers of human activity: the use of coprostanol in the soil as an indicator of human faecal material', *Journal of Archaeological Science* 21 (1994): 619–32; Dickson, J. H., Brough, D.W., 'Biological studies of a Pictish midden', in U. Körber-Grohne and H. Küster (eds), *Archäobotanik*. Dissertationes Botanicae series no. 133 (Berlin: J. Cramer, 1989), pp. 155–66.; Knights, B.A., Dickson, C.A., Dickson, J.H., 'Evidence concerning the Roman military diet at Bearsden, Scotland, in the 2nd century AD', *Journal of Archaeological Science* 10 (1983): 139–52.

Figure 6.4.   12th century wooden toilet seat from 16–22 Coppergate. The scale is 20 cm long. (Photograph: York Archaeological Trust)

There were at least some communal 'facilities' in York from the later Middle Ages onwards,[44] which demonstrates that the community was attempting to put a stop to *al fresco* defecation and urination. Sabine[45] refers to a medieval 'great well' or cesspool in London but there does not seem to have been an equivalent on such s scale in York, perhaps because most of the town was close to one or other of the rivers running through it.

While there is effectively no documentary evidence that reflects on mundane details of life – and health – in pre-Conquest York, the rise of bureaucracy following the Norman settlement led to the creation of an ever-growing documentary trail. York does not have the richest archive, but there is plenty that has a bearing on the topic at hand. We will not review this – or the documentary evidence for plagues – as we are concerned with biological evidence that has been recovered from archaeological deposits, but useful sources include compilations by Palliser[46]

---

[44]   Murray 2000.

[45]   Sabine, E.L., 'Latrines and cesspools of mediaeval London', *Speculum* 9 (1934): 303–21, see p. 305.

[46]   Palliser, D.M., 'Epidemics in Tudor York', *Northern History* 8 (1973): 45–63; Palliser, D.M., 'Civic mentality and the environment in Tudor York', *Northern History* 18 (1982): 78–115.

Figure 6.5.   Remains of a Victorian system of tipping-flush communal toilets at
Hungate. (Photograph: York Archaeological Trust)

and Cooper.[47] Although only peripherally concerned with archaeological evidence,
Murray's very readable account of the history of public conveniences in York also
deserves further mention here.[48]

The Recent Past

Recent excavations in York at Hungate have given us the opportunity to explore
sanitation in the city in the much more recent past. Within a block of badly made
mid-19th terraced brick houses lay a yard with a communal latrine, serving five
households, immediately behind the back wall of the houses. Later, by the time the
houses were 'accommodating' 11 households with perhaps as many as 50 people,
the cesspit was replaced by a system in which a row of large metal buckets on
pivots became filled with rainwater and, when full, tipped and flushed the effluent.[49]
In the absence of piped water, this cannot have been very efficient much of the
time in an area of predominantly low rainfall – the smell must have been revolting

---

[47]   Cooper, T.P., 'The medieval highways, streets, open ditches and sanitary conditions
of the City of York', *Yorkshire Archaeological Journal* 22 (1913): 270–86.

[48]   Murray 2000.

[49]   Hunter-Mann, K., 'Scratching the surface of Early Modern York: the Block E
excavation, Hungate', *Yorkshire Archaeology Today* 12 (2007): 12–14, see Figure 6.5.

and disease transmission by flies rife. There are almost no records of intestinal parasite eggs from the post-medieval period (Table 6.1), but we suspect that this is not because infestation levels dropped significantly, but because preservation is generally poorer and rather few deposits have been examined for worm eggs.

Some General Issues

One of the most important sources of human disease is contaminated water. Unfortunately we know very little about water supplies in York's more remote past. We do know that there were excellent deep wells in Roman York,[50] and there has been speculation concerning the existence of an aqueduct to the city.[51] Addyman illustrates one of the Roman water pipes recovered from the city.[52] For later periods, up till the installation of piped water in the 19th century, wells and the rivers appear to have been the only water sources, although rainwater may have been collected in cisterns. The last of these may have provided water of moderate potability, but at least some supposed wells of the Anglo-Scandinavian and medieval periods seem to have been located worryingly close to cesspits, and the quality of river water may usually have been questionable, bearing in mind the discharge from sewers in the Roman period and the likely dumping of foul waste at this and later periods. There are hints of a decline in water quality in the Ouse from studies of fish bones and bivalve molluscs,[53] but this is an area in need of a good deal of further study. That the Ouse was badly polluted by human waste from 'privies and jakes' along its margins within the city seems certain; Murray[54] refers to ordinances in 1579 to have them removed. York's other river, the Foss, has a more limited flow and there is archaeological evidence for waste dumping into it at some period (see above), so it was surely severely polluted. There is certainly evidence from the Foss for Anglo-Scandinavian or early post-Conquest flax retting,[55] which generates extremely foul water. Again, there is room

---

[50]   Carver, M.O.H., Donaghey, S., Sumpter, A.B., *Riverside Structures and a Well in Skeldergate and Buildings in Bishophill*. The Archaeology of York series 4(1) (London: Council for British Archaeology, 1978); Hall, A.R., Kenward, H.K., Williams, D., *Environmental Evidence from Roman Deposits at Skeldergate*. The Archaeology of York series 14(3) (London: Council for British Archaeology, 1980); Kenward, H.K., Hall, A.R., Jones, A.K.G., *Environmental evidence from a Roman well and Anglian pits in the Legionary Fortress*. The Archaeology of York series 14(5) (London: Council for British Archaeology, 1986).

[51]   Buckland 1976.

[52]   Addyman 1989, pl.4.

[53]   Hall and Kenward 1990, p. 386; Kenward and Hall 1995, p. 780; O'Connor, T.P., *Bones from Anglo-Scandinavian levels at 16–22 Coppergate*. The Archaeology of York series 15(3) (London: Council for British Archaeology, 1989), p. 198.

[54]   Murray 2000, p. 3.

[55]   Hall et al. 2000.

for further study of the margins of the Foss around the King's Pool through the post-Conquest period.

We mentioned above the contamination of bread by weed seeds, but it is quite likely that, in the Roman and post-Norman Conquest periods, contamination by grain pests was prevalent (the typical grain pests seem to have been very rare or more probably absent in Anglo-Scandinavian times[56]). There are records of abundant grain weevils (*Sitophilus granarius* (L.)) and other grain pests in deposits interpreted as the remains of stored grain as well as more generally through occupation layers. In the latter case, the most likely explanation for their presence is that they arrived in stable manure, infested grain having been fed to horses (the importance of the grain pests in the Roman period in Britain is discussed by Smith & Kenward[57]). Grain pests are sometimes found in cesspit fills, but it is not clear whether they had been through the human digestive tract first – it has been shown by Osborne[58] that insects are not significantly damaged by such a journey. On the other hand it seems fairly certain that most of the bean weevils (*Bruchus rufimanus* Boheman) *had* been swallowed inside pulses; indeed, some of the fossils are of individuals whose cuticles had not hardened so that they were certainly still inside their host seeds when they died. Species association analysis suggested that *Bruchus* tended to occur with a group of insects found especially in cesspit fills at Anglo-Scandinavian Coppergate.[59]

Although somewhat peripheral to the topic of waste disposal, it is worth mentioning that there are numerous records of human ectoparasites from Roman, Anglo-Scandinavian and later York.[60] These include large numbers of human fleas (*Pulex irritans* Linnaeus), the larvae of which develop in accumulations of filth. As an example, *P. irritans* was consistently present in and around the Anglo-Scandinavian buildings at 16–22 Coppergate, while *Pediculus humanus*, the human louse, was found in over 50 layers.[61] The comparative rarity of *P. humanus* in the ground probably reflects differential preservation rather than a difference in levels of infestation of people. Both of these ectoparasites are implicated in disease transmission, of course, and both must have been almost inevitable companions of people in the past.

---

[56]   Kenward 2009.

[57]   Smith, D., Kenward, H., 'Roman grain pests in Britain: implications for grain supply and agricultural production', *Britannia* 42 (2011): 243–62.

[58]   Osborne, P.J., 'An insect fauna from a modern cesspit and its comparison with probable cesspit assemblages from archaeological sites', *Journal of Archaeological Science* 10 (1983): 453–63.

[59]   Carrott and Kenward 2001: 887–905.

[60]   Kenward 2009, p. 339ff.

[61]   Kenward and Hall 1995, pp. 488–91 and 700–3.

Bones of food animals are a major component of the archaeological build-up in York as in other towns.[62] Most of these probably represent cooked 'post-consumer' waste that would not generally have been a significant health hazard – and was clearly tolerated, given the frequency with which bones occur in floors and other surface-laid deposits. More serious may have been various components of butchery and skin processing. These will have attracted a range of specialist scavengers that could subsequently disseminate disease organisms, although only gut contents and skin scrapings may have generally been discarded, everything else ending up as glue or stew. We have yet to recover convincing evidence of such vile material.

The remains of animals were not the only organic 'waste' likely to have been recycled. Many other materials will have had a secondary use, for example as food for livestock, absorptive litter in stables, make up for roads and other surfaces, manure, or fuel. In some of these cases the material will have been effectively lost to the bioarchaeological record of the occupation site – manure taken out to fields, for example, is evidenced only by potsherds and other durable material, or possibly through biochemical markers, in cultivated soils. Stable manure is a special case deserving a little further consideration. As noted above, while foul and produced in enormous quantities at some periods, it is much more tolerable close to human occupation. It must be for this reason – and the fact that it may often be 'self-preserving' – that its remains are so often found in urban deposits. This is fortuitous, since the numerous materials it may contain and their diverse origins can provide many insights into wider aspects of the past than just the stabling of equines.[63]

We have mentioned above that much of the organic waste deposited on surfaces, but also in cuts into well-drained substrates, will have decayed so as to leave only residues that are not easily identified. In consequence, we can rarely be sure that absence of evidence of filth in the archaeological record is truly evidence of absence in the past. However, it seems very probable that some parts of York at most periods did not have more than traces of decaying organic matter exposed to the air. Much of the core of Roman York, with its technologically advanced sewer system, surely falls in this category. But would any filth have survived if it were deposited on metalled surfaces? Unless very large quantities were deposited quickly, most would surely have dispersed naturally, even if not swept up. There is a hint from within the Roman fort at Carlisle that there may have been horse

---

[62] O'Connor, T.P., *Bones from the General Accident Site, Tanner Row.* The Archaeology of York series 15(2) (London: Council for British Archaeology, 1988); O'Connor 1989; Bond, J.M., O'Connor, T.P., *Bones from Medieval Deposits at 16–22 Coppergate and other Sites in York.* The Archaeology of York series 15(5) (York: Council for British Archaeology, 1999).

[63] Kenward and Hall 1997: 663–73; Hall, A., Kenward, H., 'Disentangling dung: pathways to stable manure', *Environmental Archaeology* 1 (1998): 123–6; Kenward and Hall 2012, pp. 79–95.

manure on surfaces, from the strong statistical association between grain beetles (which probably arrived within faeces) and dung beetles,[64] though it is uncertain for how long such dung lingered. We have yet to discover parallel evidence from York.

People living in clean zones of towns and, in the Roman period, in military establishments, may not have been immune to the effects of the filth exposed in less salubrious areas nearby, however. Apart from the smell, their homes and barracks would certainly have been invaded by the abundant flies emerging from cesspits and middens. Thus even the occupants of the religious houses with drains and an inherent regime of cleanliness were probably subject to fly-borne disease.

We have very briefly surveyed 2000 years of the disposal of organic waste in York, but what of future studies in this area? We are not optimistic that the archive of organic material under the city will survive or be studied. Many of the deposits rich in delicate biological remains such as plant tissues and insect fragments are not within stable water-tables, which would favour their continued survival, but in deposits that appear to have perched water-tables or that hold water like sponges.[65] Changing groundwater regimes are suspected to be leading to the decay of these richly organic deposits.[66] At the same time, the nature of British archaeology has changed radically, from a regime under which there were often intensive studies of large corpora of material to one in which there are numerous but usually very superficial and unpublished studies of small excavations.[67] There are rays of hope, however. The many small excavations do, at least, offer a more or less random sample of 'keyholes' into the past and, with pressure from local planning offices, some property developers are still prepared to fund large-scale excavations with a research component. Recent excavations at Hungate, York, represent just such a case.

---

[64] Kenward, H., Carrott, J., 'Insect species associations characterise past occupation sites', *Journal of Archaeological Science* 33 (2006): 1452–73.

[65] Kenward, H.K., Hall, A.R., 'Easily decayed organic remains in urban archaeological deposits: value, threats, research directions and conservation', in O. Brinkkemper, J. Deeben, J. van Doesburg, D. Hallewas, E.M. Theunissen and A.D. Verlinde (eds), *Vakken in Vlakken. Archeologische Kennis in Lagen.* Nederlandse Archeologische Rapporten 32 (Amersfoort: Rijksdienst voor het Oudheikundig, 2006), pp. 183–98.

[66] Kenward, H., Hall, A., 'Decay of delicate organic remains in shallow urban deposits: are we at a watershed?', *Antiquity* 74 (2000): 519–25; Kenward, H., Hall, A., 'Urban organic archaeology: an irreplaceable palaeoecological archive at risk', *World Archaeology* 40 (2008): 584–96.

[67] Hall, A.R., Kenward, H.K., 'Development-driven archaeology: bane or boon for bioarchaeology?', *Oxford Journal of Archaeology* 25 (2006): 213–24.

Acknowledgements

The authors would like to thank all the people with whom they have worked with over nearly four decades in the University of York and York Archaeological Trust; they are too numerous to mention individually. York Archaeological Trust (through the good offices of Christine Kyriacou) kindly made some figures available to us.

Table 6.1   Representative records of presumed human intestinal parasites from archaeological deposits in York.[68] Many records for the medieval/post-medieval transition could not be included because dating was too broad.

Date	Site	Parasites	Deposit type
Roman	24–30 Tanner Row (pre-buildings)	traces T, A	ditch fills
	24–30 Tanner Row (Colonia)	abundant T, A	drain fills
	The Bedern (Fortress)	traces T, A	well backfill
Anglian	Blue Bridge Ln	traces T	pit fill
	36–54 Fishergate	traces T, A	various deposits, including dog coprolites
Anglo-Scandinavian	6–8 Pavement	abundant T, A	human coprolite
	16–22 Coppergate	abundant T, A	pit fills and various other deposits, including traces in floors
	4–7 Parliament St	abundant T, A	?pit fills
	2 Clifford St	traces T, A	pit fills
	28–9 High Ousegate	sometimes abundant T, A	pit fills
	118–126 Walmgate	sometimes abundant T, A	various
	7–9 Aldwark	sometimes abundant T, A	pit fills
	NCP Car Park, Skeldergate	sometimes small numbers T, A	pit fills
	1–9 Micklegate	sometimes abundant T, A	pit fills
Norman and later medieval	7–9 Aldwark	some T, A	pit fills
	The Bedern	some T	pit fills
	Davygate	some T, A	concretions
	former Presto supermarket (George Hudson St)	some T, A	pit fill

---

[68]   Kenward, H. (2009), 'Invertebrates in archaeology in the north of England', *(English Heritage) Research Department Report Series* 12/2009. (available online at http://services.english-heritage.org.uk/ResearchReportsPdfs/012_2009WEB.pdf)

Date	Site	Parasites	Deposit type
	62–8 Low Petergate	abundant T, some A	pit fills and other layers
	Merchant Adventurers' Hall	some T	levelling/dumps
	50–2 Monkgate	some T	pit fill
	44–5 Parliament Street	sometimes abundant T, traces A	pit fills
	17–21 Piccadilly (Reynard's Garage)	traces T, A	pit fill
	5 Rougier St	traces T	pit fill
	St Andrewgate	some T, ?A	dump
	9 St Saviourgate	abundant T, some A	pit fills
	Swinegate area	traces T, A	various deposits
	NCP Car Park, Skeldergate	some T, A	layers, pit fills
	7–15 Spurriergate	sometimes abundant T, A	pit fills and other deposits
	24–30 Tanner Row	traces T, A	pit fills
	47–55 Tanner Row	traces T	pit fill
	1–2 Tower Street (Castle Garage)	traces T, A	fills of large ditch/ moat
	41–9 Walmgate	traces T, A	pit fill
Post-medieval to modern	9 St Saviourgate	abundant T, some A	pit fills

(Copies of the unpublished *Reports from the Environmental Archaeology Unit, York* and *Palaeoecology Research Services Report* series are available as pdfs from http://www.york.ac.uk/inst/chumpal/EAU-reps/eaureps-web.htm and *Reports from the Centre for Human Palaeoecology* are available at http://www.york.ac.uk/inst/chumpal/CHPReps/CHP-reps-web.htm)

Chapter 7

Human Intestinal Parasites and Dysentery in Africa and the Middle East Prior to 1500

Evilena Anastasiou and Piers D. Mitchell

Introduction

Africa and the Middle East are arguably the most important regions of the world for the study of human disease. Humans evolved in east Africa, and then migrated around the planet in sequential waves over the last 100,000 years, so it is understandable that this region is inexorably linked with the biological and cultural evolution of our species.[1] Africa and the Middle East have been the locations for some of the most important cultural developments in human history, as the civilisations that flourished in this area were the first to develop agriculture, social and political complexity, and technological innovation.[2]

This paper will discuss the evidence for the presence of endoparasites and ectoparasites in Africa and the Middle East from the earliest prehistory up to the 15th century AD. This date has been chosen as the 15th century saw the voyages of exploration across the Atlantic to the Americas, as well as an expansion of voyages around the coasts of Africa to Asia, so potentially leading to the spread of parasites and a change in the previous distribution of species. Reconstructing the parasitic past of the region is of great importance for demonstrating the associations that existed between parasitism, ecology, large-scale cultural change, technology and migration throughout human history. At the same time, many of the parasitic diseases that are still important health stressors today originated in Africa. The reconstruction of the continent's parasitic past has the potential to illuminate the antiquity of human–parasite co-evolution and to demonstrate the factors that originally facilitated the transmission of important parasitic organisms from animals to humans.

Although paleoparasitology is now more than a century old and despite the important conclusions that can be drawn from the reconstruction of the parasitic

---

[1] Lewin, R., Foley, R., *Principles of Human Evolution* (Oxford: Blackwell, 2003); Pasternak, C., *What Makes Us Human?* (Oxford: Oneworld, 2007).

[2] Harris, H.D., *The Origins and Spread of Agriculture and Pastoralism in Eurasia: Crops, Felds, Flocks and Herds* (London: UCL Press, 1996); Rodda J.C., Ubertini, L. (eds), *The Basis of Civilization: Water Science?* (Wallingford: International Association for Hydrological Science, 2004).

past of Africa and the Middle East, most paleoparasitological studies have been focused on the Americas and Europe. As a result, our knowledge of ancient parasites in Africa and the Middle East is limited to only a few areas of the region. This paper will try to underline the necessity for further targeted research in the area by highlighting the current state of paleoparasitological research, and give an initial interpretation of the paleoparasitological evidence from the Middle East and Africa.

Paleoparasitology

This field investigates human and animal parasites from archaeological contexts and aims to identify the parasite species that infected past communities during their history. By determining which parasite species were present in different regions in the past, paleoparasitology provides us with information on the health status, the dietary habits, the food preparation methods and the hygiene conditions that prevailed in the cultures of antiquity.[3] Using information regarding the geographical distribution of the parasites and the peculiarities of their life cycles, we can also infer the migration routes chosen by past populations, and the impact that migration events and long-distance trading may have had in the cultures of antiquity.[4] Finally, by studying the parasitic evidence from archaeological and paleontological contexts, paleoparasitology reconstructs the prehistoric and historic distribution of parasites, and provides evidence for the antiquity and pathogenicity of different parasite species.[5]

In order to identify these parasites, we must extract their remains from mummies, coprolites and soil samples from latrines, cesspools and burials.

---

[3]   Reinhard, K., 'Archaeoparasitology in North America', *American Journal of Physical Anthropology* 82 (1990): 145–63; Reinhard, K., Araújo, A., 'Archaeoparasitology', in D.M. Pearshall (ed.), *Encyclopaedia of Archaeology* (New York: Elsevier, Academic Press, 2008), pp. 494–501; Calagero, S., Reinhard, K., Vinton, S.D., 'Inca expansion and parasitism in the Lluta Valley: preliminary data', *Memórias do Instituto Oswaldo Cruz* 98 (Suppl. 1) (2003): 161–63.

[4]   Mitchell, P.D., Anastasiou, E., Syon, D., 'Human intestinal parasites in crusader Acre: evidence for migration with disease in the medieval period', *International Journal of Paleopathology* 1 (2011): 132–37; Montenegro, A., Araújo, A., Eby, M., Ferreira, L.F., Hetherington, R., Weaver, J.A., 'Parasites, paleoclimate, and the peopling of the Americas', *Current Anthropology* 47 (2006): 193–200; Araújo, A., Reinhard, K., Ferreira, L.F., Gardner, S.L., 'Parasites as probes for prehistoric human migrations?', *Trends in Parasitology* 24 (2008): 112–15.

[5]   Araújo, A., Ferreira, L.F., 'Paleoparasitology and the antiquity of human host-parasite relationships', *Memórias do Instituto Oswaldo Cruz* 98 (Suppl. 1) (2000): 89–93; Araújo, A., Reinhard, K., Bastos, O.M., Costa, L.C., Pirmez, C., Iniquez, A., Vicente, A.C., Morel, C.M., Ferreira, L.F., 'Paleoparasitology: perspectives with new techniques', *Revista do Instituto de Medicina Tropical de São Paulo* 40 (1998): 371–76.

However, due to the physical nature of most parasites only a number of parasite species can be extracted and identified from the archaeological record. For example, ectoparasites (lice, ticks, mites) can be identified when the skin, hair or clothes of mummified bodies is examined. In burials that have decomposed to just leave the bones and teeth, the ectoparasites have generally decomposed as well. In contrast, because the larvae and adult worms of the endoparasites rarely survive decomposition outside of a mummified body, only those endoparasites that release eggs from their human host into the environment can be identified paleoparasitologically. Consequently, the intestinal parasites that release eggs through the faeces into the environment are the most commonly identified ancient parasite species. Nonetheless, in the category of species that can be identified, one must also include the blood trematodes and the lung and liver trematodes that release eggs through faeces or urine and the vector-borne parasitic diseases, such as filariasis, malaria, trypanosomiasis and leishmaniasis, that can be identified from mummified bodies if immunological and molecular methods such as ELISA (Enzyme-linked immunosorbent assay) and PCR (polymerase chain reaction) are employed.

Paleoparasitology appeared as a new branch of parasitology at the beginning of the 20th century when Ruffer, using a new technique to rehydrate desiccated tissues, claimed to have found the eggs of *Schistosoma haematobium* in the kidneys of two Egyptian mummies of the twentieth dynasty (1250–1000 BC)[6]. No images of these eggs were included in his article, but since subsequent researchers have also found this species in ancient Egypt, it seems quite likely that he was correct. Despite the fact that the first paleoparasitological study analysed Egyptian material, the development into an independent field with its own rigorous methodology largely took place in the Americas. Here researchers from North and South America worked extensively from 1960 onwards to establish the methodology of the field[7] and to reconstruct the parasitic environment of the Amerindian populations prior to the arrival of the Europeans.[8]

---

[6] Ruffer, M.A., 'Note on the presence of Bilharzia haematobia in Egyptian mummies of the Twentieth Dynasty', *The British Medical Journal* 1 (1910): 16.

[7] Callen. E.O., Cameron, T.W.M., 'A prehistoric diet revealed in coprolites', *New Scientist* 8 (1960): 35–40; Reinhard, K., Confalonieri, U., Herrmann, B., Ferreira, L.F., Araujo, A., 'Recovery of parasite remains from coprolites and latrines: aspects of paleoparasitological technique', *Homo* 37 (1986): 217–39.

[8] Araújo, A., Confalonieri, U., and Ferreira, L.F., 'Oxyurid (Nematoda) eggs from coprolites from Brazil', *Journal of Parasitology* 68 (1982): 511–12; Araújo, A., Ferreira, L.F., Confalonieri, U., Nunez, L., Filho, B. R., 'The finding of Enterobius vermicularis eggs in pre-Columbian human coprolites', *Memórias do Instituto Oswaldo Cruz* 80 (1985): 141–43; Reinhard, K., Hevly, R.H., Anderson, G.A., 'Helminth remains from prehistoric Indian coprolites on the Colorado Plateau', *Journal of Parasitology* 73 (1987): 630–39; Reinhard, K., Clary, K.H., 'Parasite analysis of prehistoric coprolites from Chaco Canyon, New Mexico', in N.J. Atkins (ed.), *A Biocultural Approach to Human Burials from Chaco Center 9* (Santa Fe: National Park Service, 1986), pp. 177–86.

In Europe, paleoparasitology has focused on the interpretation of the parasitic remains in terms of the depositional processes that created different archaeological sites,[9] on the epidemiology of helminth infections during the medieval period in northern Europe, and on the antiquity of various parasites, such as taeniid tapeworms, whipworms and roundworms in Europe.[10]

Finally, another important focus of research into ancient parasites has been in East Asia, where since the 1970s studies have been carried out in China, Korea and Japan, focusing on the distribution and origins of indigenous parasitic species, as well as their impact on the daily life of the past.[11]

Reflecting the history of the field's development and in part the particular interests of parasitologists, only a few studies have been carried out in regions other than the Americas, Europe and East Asia. As a result our knowledge about the parasitic past of other geographical areas (Asia, Oceania, Africa, the Middle East) has been very limited.

In the next sections the evidence that is available for ancient parasites in the Middle East and Africa will be discussed, in order to highlight that although research in the area has been geographically limited, important conclusions can be drawn regarding how humans first contracted their parasites, the impact of these parasites upon health, and the daily life of the communities that flourished in the region. The importance of the evidence from the Middle East and Africa is

---

[9]   Jones, A.K.G., 'Human parasite remains: prospects for a quantitative approach', in R.A. Hall and K.H. Kenward (eds), *Environmental Archaeology in the Urban Context* (London: Council for British Archaeology, 1982), pp. 66–70; Bouchet, F., Guidon, N., Dittmar, K., Harter, S., Ferreira, L.F., Chaves, M.S., Reinhard, K., Araújo, A., 'Parasite remains in archaeological sites', *Memórias do Instituto Oswaldo Cruz* 98 (Suppl. 1) (2003): 47–52.

[10]   Herrmann, B., 'Parasite remains from medieval latrine deposits: an epidemiologic and ecologic approach', *Actes des Troisiemes Journees Anthropologiques, Notes et Monographies Techniques* 24 (1988): 135–42; Aspöck, H., Auer, H., Picher, O., '*Trichuris trichiura* eggs in the neolithic glacier mummy from the Alps', *Parasitology Today* 12 (1996): 255–56; Aspöck, H., Auer, H., Picher, O., 'Parasites and parasitic diseases in prehistoric human populations in central Europe', *Helminthologia* 36 (1999): 139–45.

[11]   Matsui, A., Kanehara, M., Kanehara, M., 'Paleoparasitology in Japan: discovery of toilet features', *Memórias do Instituto Oswaldo Cruz* 98 (Suppl. 1) (2003): 127–36; Wei, D.X., Yang, W.Y., Huang, S.Q., Lu, Y.F., Su, T.C., Ma, J.H., Hu, W.X., Xie, N.F., 'Parasitological investigation on the ancient corpse of the Western Han Dynasty unearthed from tomb No. 168 on Phoenix Hill in Jiangling County', *Acta Academiae Medicinae Wuhan* 1 (1981): 16–23; Wei, O., 'Internal organs of a 2100-year-old female corpse', *The Lancet* 302 (1973): 1198; Shin, D.H., Oh, S.C., Chung, T., Yi, S.Y., Chai, Y.J., Seo, M., 'Detection of parasite eggs from a moat encircling the royal palace of Silla, the ancient Korean kingdom', *Journal of Archaeological Science* 36 (2009): 2534–39; Seo, M., Shin, D.H., Guk, S.M., Oh, C.S., Lee, E.J., Shin, M.H., Kim, M.J., Lee, S. D., Kim, Y.S., Yi, Y.S., Spigelman, M., Chai, J.Y. 'Gymnophalloides seoi eggs from the stool of a 17th century female mummy found in Hadong, Republic of Korea', *Journal of Parasitology* 94 (2008): 467–72.

the best advocate for further research in the area, as only when a comprehensive spatiotemporal map of the parasitic environment is available will the evidence be interpreted to its full potential.

Ancient Parasites in Africa

Africa is the place where our biological evolution took place, and as such paleoparasitology has a central role in the reconstruction of the evolutionary history of parasites and humans. The relationship between parasites and hosts can be as long as the life of a host species and so it has been argued that human evolution and parasitic infections have run hand in hand over the past 5 million years.[12] According to the co-evolutionary theory, human parasites can be categorised with respect to their co-evolution with their human hosts, as either heirloom or souvenir parasites.[13]

The heirloom parasites are those inherited from our primate ancestors; they have been shared by pre-hominins and modern ape ancestors and remained with hominins even after speciation.[14] As a result, some of the heirloom species of human parasites, such as the pinworms, hookworms and whipworms, are shared by humans and their closely related primates (for example, chimpanzees). The souvenir parasites are those acquired from animals with which humans have come into contact at some point in our evolutionary travels, in the way we might pick up a souvenir on holiday.[15] All souvenir parasites appear to be zoonoses, whose primary hosts were animals who interacted with humans and this allowed the parasite to switch species.

Therefore, the categorisation of the human parasites as either heirlooms or souvenirs reflects the long co-evolution between humans and their parasites, as each parasite species found today in humans is a species either inherited from our ancestors or acquired during our biological and social evolution.[16] For example,

---

[12]   Cox, F.E.G., 'History of human parasitology', *Clinical Microbiology Reviews* 15 (2002): 595–612.

[13]   Sprent, J.F.A., 'Evolutionary aspects of immunity of zooparasitic infections', in G.J. Jackson (ed.), *Immunity to Parasitic Animals* (New York: Appleton, 1969), pp. 3–64; Kliks, M.M., 'Paleoparasitology: on the origins and impact of human-helminth relationships', in N.A. Croll and J.H. Cross (eds), *Human Ecology and Infectious Disease* (New York: Academic Press, 1983) , pp. 291–313.

[14]   Araújo et al. 1998; Armelagos, G.J., Brown, P.J., Turner, B., 'Evolutionary, historical and political economic perspectives on health and disease', *Social Science and Medicine* 61 (2005): 755–65.

[15]   Armelagos et al. 2005; Kliks, M.M., 'Helminths as heirlooms and souvenirs: a review of New World paleoparasitology', *Parasitology Today* 6 (1990): 93–100.

[16]   Mitchell, P.D., 'The origins of human parasites: exploring the evidence for endoparasitism throughout human evolution', *International Journal of Paleopathology* 3 (2013): 191–98; Araújo et al. 2008.

it is easy to imagine that when the *Homo* species migrated out of Africa they carried with them their heirloom parasites. As our ancestors explored new habitats their parasites were spread to these new areas, if the environmental conditions allowed their survival. However, some parasites that were no longer viable in the local environment may have died out in these new regions. While our ancestors explored new food sources and environments they were also exposed to new parasite species, by coming into contact with animals that acted as reservoirs for these novel parasitic diseases.

Consequently, the analysis of paleontological and paleolithic contexts from Africa has the potential to illuminate the early associations between humans and their parasites, as humans evolved in Africa and subsequently migrated out of the continent. Despite the wealth of information that can be concluded from the parasitological record of the region, in Africa ancient parasite research has been focused mainly on the region of Egypt (Table 7.1) with only a handful of studies analysing samples from Sudan (Table 7.2) and South Africa (Table 7.3).

In Egypt the evidence consists of intestinal, blood-borne and tissue endoparasites, as well as ectoparasites (head lice *Pediculus humanus capitis*).[17] The finds date from the 4th millennium BC up to the 6th century AD. The intestinal parasites identified from Egypt are common and widely distributed species such as *Ascaris lumbricoides* (roundworm),[18] *Enterobius vermicularis* (pinworm)[19], *Diphyllobothrium* sp. (fish tapeworm),[20] *Strongyloides stercoralis* (threadworm)[21] and *Taenia* sp. (beef/pork tapeworms).[22] In contrast, the tissue-dwelling parasites identified in the region include those with worldwide distribution and those

---

[17]   Palma, R.L., 'Ancient head lice on a wooden comb from Antinoe, Egypt', *Journal of Egyptian Archaeology* 77 (1991): 194.

[18]   Harter, S., Le Bailly, M., Janot, F., Bouchet, F., 'First paleoparasitological study of embalming rejects jar found in Saqqara, Egypt', *Memórias do Instituto Oswaldo Cruz* 98 (Suppl. 1) (2003): 119–21.

[19]   Horne, P.D., 'First evidence of Enterobiasis in ancient Egypt', *Journal of Parasitology* 88 (2002): 1019–21.

[20]   Harter, S., *Implication de la Paléoparasitologie dans l'Etude des Populations Anciennes de la Vallée du Nil et du Proche-Orient: Etudes de Cas* (PhD Thesis: Université de Reims Champagne-Ardenne, 2003).

[21]   Tapp, E., 'Disease and the Manchester mummies – the pathologist's role', in A.R. David and E. Tapp (eds), *Evidence Embalmed: Modern Medicine and the Mummies of Ancient Egypt* (Manchester: Manchester University Press, 1984), pp. 99–101.

[22]   Bruschi, F., Maseti, M., Locci, M.T., Ciranni, R., Fornaciari, G., 'Cystercercosis in an Egyptian mummy of the late Ptolemaic Period', *American Journal of Tropical Medicine and Hygiene* 74 (2006): 598–599; Harter 2003; Le Bailly, M., Mouze, S., Rocha, G.C.D., Heim, J.-L., Lichtenberg, R., Dunand, F., Bouchet, F., 'Identification of *Taenia* sp. in a mummy from a Christian necropolis in El-Deir, oasis of Kharga, ancient Egypt', *Journal of Parasitology* 96 (2010): 213–215.

restricted to Africa. Species found in ancient Egypt include *Trichinella spiralis*[23] (trichinosis), the tropical and subtropical filarial worms (such as *Wuchereria bancrofti*)[24] and the Guinea worm *Dracunculus medinensis*.[25] The trematodes *Fasciola* sp. that parasitise the liver and intestines of their host[26] and the blood trematodes *Schistosoma* sp. that cause bilharzia have also been identified in Egypt.[27] The mosquito-borne protozoon *Plasmodium falciparum* has been found, which is the form of malaria most likely to cause death.[28] The sandfly-borne protozoon *Leishmania donovani* has also been identified, which causes visceral leishmaniasis.[29] Toxoplasmosis (*Toxoplasma gondii*) has also been identified in a mummy using a DNA analysis.[30]

[23] Hart, G.D., Millet, N.B., Rideout, D.F., Scott, J.W., Lynn, G.E., Reyman, T.A., Boni, U.D., Barraco, R.A., Zimmerman, M.R., Lewin, P.K., Horne, P.D., 'Autopsy of an Egyptian mummy (Nakht-R.O.M.-1)', *Canadian Medical Association Journal* 117 (1977): 461–76.

[24] Tapp, E., Wildsmith, K., 'The autopsy and endoscopy of the Leeds mummy', in A.R. David and E. Tapp (eds), *The Mummy's Tale: The Scientific and Medical Investigation of Natsef-Amun, Priest in the Temple at Karnack* (London: Michael O'Mara, 1992), pp. 132–153.

[25] Isherwood, I., Jarvis, H., Fawcitt, R.A., 'Radiology of the Manchester mummies', in A.R. David and E. Tapp (eds), *Evidence Embalmed: Modern Medicine and the Mummies of Ancient Egypt* (Manchester: Manchester University Press, 1984) pp. 25–64; Horne, P., Redford, S., 'Aspergillosis and dracunculiasis in mummies from the tomb of Parannefer', *Paleopathology Newsletter* 92 (1995): 10–12.

[26] Harter 2003.

[27] Deelder, A.M., Miller, R.L., de Jonge, N., Krijger, F.W., 'Detection of schistosome antigen in mummies', *The Lancet* 335 (1990): 724–5; Reyman, T.A., 'Schistosomal cirrhosis in an Egyptian mummy', *Yearbook of Physical Anthropology* 20 (1976): 356–358; Hart et al. 1977.

[28] Bianucci, R., Mattutino, G., Lallo, R., Charlier, P., Jouin-Spriet, H., Peluso, A., Higham, T., Torre, C., Rabino Massa, E., 'Immunological evidence of Plasmodium falciparum infection in a child mummy from the Early Dynastic Period', *Journal of Archaeological Science* 35 (2008): 1880–1885; Hawass, Z., Gad, Y., Ismail, S., Khairat, R., Fathalla, D., Hasan, N., Ahmed, A., Elleithy, H., Ball, M., Gaballah, F., Wasef, S., Fateen, M., Amer, H., Gostner, P., Selim, A., Zink, A., Pusch, C.M., 'Ancestry and pathology in King Tutankhamun's family', *Journal of the American Medical Association (JAMA)* 303 (2010): 638–647; Khairat, R., Ball, M., Chang, C.-C.H., Bianucci, R., Nerlich, A.G., Trautmann, M., Ismail, S., Shanab, B.M.L., Karim, A.M., Gad, Y.Z., Pusch, C.M., 'First insights into the metagenome of Egyptian mummies using next-generation sequencing', *Journal of Applied Genetics* (2013): doi.org/10.1007/s13353–013–0145–1.

[29] Zink, A., Spigelman, M., Schraut, B., Greenblatt, C.L., Nerlich, A.G., Donoghue, H.D., 'Leishmaniasis in ancient Egypt and upper Nubia', *Emerging Infectious Diseases* 12 (2006): 1616–17.

[30] Khairat et al. 2013.

Table 7.1　　Ancient Parasites in Egypt

Species	Location	Date	Source
Ascaris lumbricoides (roundworm)	Saqqara	715–656BC	Harter et al. ref. 18
Diphyllobothrium latum (fish tapeworm)	Unknown	400–300BC	Harter ref. 20
Dracunculus medinensis (Guinea worm)	Valley of the Nobles Hawara	1450BC 1000–770BC	Horne and Redford ref.25 Isherwood et al. ref.25
Echinococcus granulosus (hydatid worm)	Unknown	Mummy of unknown date	Tapp ref.21
Enterobius vermicularis (pinworm)	Dakhleh Oasis	395BC-30AD	Horne ref.19
Fasciola sp. (liver fluke)	Unknown	2400–1750BC 400–300BC 275BC–350AD	Harter ref.20 Harter ref.20 Harter ref.20
Filarial worm	Karnack	1200BC	Tapp and Wildsmith ref.24
Leishmania donovani (visceral leishmaniasis)	Thebes West	2050–1650BC	Zink et al. ref.29
Pediculus humanus capitis (head louse)	Antinoe	400–600AD	Palma ref.17
Plasmodium falciparum (malaria)	Gebelein Valley of the Kings Unknown	2820–2630BC 1550–1324BC 3rd intermediate- Roman period	Bianucci et al. ref 28 Hawass et al. ref.28 Khairat et al. ref.28
Schistosoma haematobium (bladder fluke)	Unknown Thebes Amarna	3200BC 1198–1150BC 1200BC	Deelder et al. ref.27 Deelder et al. ref.27 Reyman ref.27
Schistosoma sp. (bilharzia)	Thebes	1200BC	Hart et al. ref.23
Strongyloides stercoralis (threadworm)	Karnack	600BC	Tapp ref.21
Taenia sp. (beef/pork tapeworm)	Thebes Unknown El-Deir	1200BC 200–100BC 300–500AD	Hart et al. ref.23 Bruschi et al. ref.22 Le Bailly et al ref.22
Toxoplasma gondii (toxoplasmosis)	Unknown	3rd intermediate – Roman period	Khairat et al ref.30
Trichinella spiralis	Thebes	1200BC	Hart et al. ref.23

As far as Sudan and South Africa are concerned, their paleoparasitological record is more limited than that of Egypt. In Sudan the evidence dates from the 4th millennium BC up to the 10th century AD and includes worms such as *Diphyllobothrium latum, Dicrocoelium* sp., *Fasciola* sp., *Taenia* sp. and

Schistosoma mansoni.[31] In South Africa paleoparasitological studies have identified eggs of *Ascaris lumbricoides, Trichuris trichiura* and *Dicrocoelium* sp. from contexts dated from the 8th millennium BC up to the 13th century AD.[32]

Table 7.2   Ancient Parasites in Nubia/Sudan

Species	Date	Source
Dicrocoelium sp. (lancet liver fluke)	3365–1750BC	Harter ref.20
Diphyllobothrium sp. (fish tapeworm)	700–300BC	Harter ref.20
Fasciola sp. (liver fluke)	2400–1750BC 700–300BC 300–600AD	Harter ref.20 Harter ref.20 Harter ref.20
Leishmania donovani (visceral leishmaniasis)	550–750AD	Zink et al. ref.29
Taenia sp. (beef/pork tapeworm)	2400–1750BC 700–300BC 300–600AD	Harter ref.20 Harter ref.20 Harter ref.20
Schistosoma mansoni (bilharzia)	350–550AD 550–950AD	Hibbs et al. ref.31 Miller et al. ref.31 Hibbs et al. ref.31

Table 7.3   Ancient Parasites in South Africa

Species	Location	Date	Source
Ascaris lumbricoides (roundworm	Kruger Cave, Rustenburg	8000–5000BC	Evans et al. ref.32
Dicrocoelium sp. (lancet liver fluke)	K2, Greefswald	1000–1300AD	Dittmar and Steyn ref.32
Trichuris trichiura (whipworm)	Kruger Cave, Rustenburg K2, Greefswald	8000–5000BC 1000–1300AD	Evans et al. ref.32 Dittmar and Steyn ref.32

---

[31]   Harter 2003; Hibbs, A.C., Secor, W.E., Gerven, D.V., Armelagos, G.J., 'Irrigation and infection: the immunoepidemiology of schistosomiasis in Ancient Nubia', *American Journal of Physical Anthropology* 145 (2011): 290–98.; Miller, R.L., Armelagos, G.J., Ikram, S., Jonge, D.N., Krijger, F.W., Deelder, A.M., 'Paleoepidemiology of Schistosoma infection in mummies', *British Medical Journal* 304 (1992): 555–556.

[32]   Evans, A.C., Markus, M.B., Mason, R.J., Steel, R., 'Late stone-age coprolite reveals evidence of prehistoric parasitism', *South African Medical Journal* 86 (1996): 274–75; Dittmar, K., Steyn, M., 'Paleoparasitological analysis of coprolites from K2, an iron age archaeological site in South Africa: the first finding of Dicrocoelium sp. eggs', *Journal of Parasitology* 90 (2004): 171–73.

As is evident from Tables 7.1–7.3, a plethora of species has been identified despite the limited number of paleoparasitological studies that have been carried out in Africa. This reflects the high level of species richness encountered in the parasitic past of the continent. Today, many parasitic diseases remain endemic in Africa and they are noted to have a major impact upon health as measured with DALYs (Disability Adjusted Life Years).[33] Since these same diseases have been shown to exist in Africa for thousands of years, it is quite likely that they had similar effects upon the health of our ancestors.

The multitude of different insect vectors that are endemic in Africa, the tropical and subtropical climate of the region, along with the fact that our biological evolution took place in east Africa, explain the long-term association between humans and parasites in the area, as well as the diversity of parasitic species in the past and present of the continent.

Genetic Evidence for the Origin of Important Parasite Species in Africa

In the last few decades, genetic studies of parasite genome and phylogenetic analysis of different parasite species have demonstrated that many of the parasitic diseases that are important health stressors today had their origins in Africa, further explaining the extremely rich parasitic environment of the continent. The origins of some of the most common and important parasite species will now be discussed in order to highlight the long-term associations that exist between parasitic infection and Africa. This section will explore the origins of *Plasmodium falciparum,* of the Schistosoma group, and of the *Taenia* tapeworms as demonstrated by the genetic evidence. This will provide a detailed view of the origins, the evolution, phylogeny and divergence of these important parasitic diseases.

Plasmodium Falciparum (Malaria)

The evolution of *Plasmodium falciparum* has been a great source of debate for geneticists. Although the origins of the parasite are traced back to Africa, the timing of the pathogen's origin is not as easily defined, because different views about the origins of the pathogen have been supported by its genetic nucleotide sequence diversity.[34] *Plasmodium falciparum* exhibits great variation in antigenic, drug resistance and pathogenesis determinants, consistent with an ancient origin of the pathogen, but DNA variation at synonymous nucleotide sites is virtually

---

[33]   World Health Organization, WHO, 'The World Health Report', http://www.who.int/whr/2004/en/report04_en.pdf.

[34]   Conway, D.J., 'Tracing the dawn of Plasmodium falciparum with mitochondrial genome sequences', *Trends in Genetics* 19 (2003): 671–74; Hume, J.C.C., Lyons, E.J., Day, K.P., 'Human migration, mosquitoes and the evolution of Plasmodium falciparum', *Trends in Parasitology* 19 (2003): 144–49.

absent, more compatible with a recent origin of the parasite.[35] Despite the controversy, molecular studies on the genome of *Plasmodium falciparum* by Volkman et al. support the hypothesis of a recent common progenitor of all of the extant *Plasmodium falciparum* and of a high mutation rate for the creation of microsatellite repeats, hence reconciling the differences encountered in the variation of different sites in the parasite genome.

Further information on the origins and divergence of *Plasmodium falciparum* derived from the analysis of orthologous gene sequences of *Plasmodium* lineages by Silva et al.[36] Their study supported the hypothesis that humans are the reservoir for infection of the African apes by *Plasmodium falciparum* and not the opposite. Moreover, the study suggested that the last common ancestor of *Plasmodium falciparum* and *Plasmodium reichenowi*, the equivalent chimpanzee parasite, lived around the same time as the human–chimpanzee divergence, therefore, suggesting that *Plasmodium falciparum* is as old as the hominid lineage. In the same study, Silva et al. also concluded that *Plasmodium vivax* was split from *Plasmodium knowlesi*, the monkey parasite, much earlier than the split between *Plasmodium falciparum* and *Plasmodium reichenowi*, at the time of the separation of the Great Apes and the Old World monkeys.

Schistosoma Species (Blood Flukes)

Today, almost ninety different species of schistosoma are generally recognised. These parasitise birds, mammals and reptiles, and are classified into four groups: the *Schistosoma mansoni*, *Schistosoma japonicum*, *Schistosoma haematobium* and *Schistosoma indicum* groups. The classification of schistosoma into these four groups is based on their geographic location, the spination of their eggs and the species of their intermediate snail host.[37] The human schistosomes belong to the *Schistosoma mansoni*, *Schistosoma japonicum* and *Schistosoma haematobium* groups and are the *Schistosoma haematobium*, *Schistosoma mansoni*, *Schistosoma*

---

[35] Conway 2003; Volkman, S.K., Barry, A.E., Lyons, J.E., Nielsen, K.M., Thomas, M.S., Choi, M., Thakore, S.S., Day, K.P., Wirth, D.F., Hartl, D.L., 'Recent origin of Plasmodium falciparum from a single progenitor', *Science* 293 (2001): 482–84.

[36] Silva, J.C., Egan, A., Friedman, R., Munro, J.B., Carlton, J.M., Hughes, A.L., 'Genome sequences reveal divergence times of malaria parasite lineages', *Parasitology* 138 (2011): 1737–49.

[37] Agatsuma, T., Iwagami, M., Liu, C.X., Rajapakse, R.P.V., Mondal, M.M.H., Kitikoons, V., Ambus, S., Agatsuma, Y., Blair, D., Higuchi, T., 'Affinities between Asian non-human Schistosoma species, the S. indicum group, and the African human Schistosomes', *Journal of Helminthology* 76 (2002): 7–19; Morgan, J.A.T., Dejong, R.J., Kazibwe, F., Mkoji, G.M., Loker, E.S., 'A newly-identified lineage of Schistosoma', *International Journal of Parasitology* 33 (2003): 977–85; Snyder, S., Loker, E.S., 'Evolutionary relationships among the Schistosomatidae (Platyhelminthes: Digenea) and an Asian origin for Schistosoma', *Journal of Parasitology* 86 (2000): 283–88.

japonicum, *Schistosoma mekongi*, *Schistosoma intercalatum*, *Schistosoma malayensis*, *Schistosoma guineensis* and *Schistosoma mattheei*. [38]

Due to the variety of different schistosoma species their relationship has been a long studying issue, with molecular phylogenetic studies[39] and studies of mitochondrial gene order raising several interesting points.[40] According to genetic evidence the seven species of the *Schistosoma haematobium* group cluster close together, as well as the examined species of the *Schistosoma mansoni* group. On the other hand the *Schistosoma japonicum* group separates consistently from the rest of the schistosoma species, has a basal position, and represents a monophyletic group within the schistosoma. The *Schistosoma indicum* group is most probably paraphyletic and separates between the three indoplanorbis transmitted species – *Schistosoma indicum*, *Schistosoma spindale* and *Schistosoma nasale* – that have close affinities with the *Schistosoma haematobium* group, and the *Schistosoma incognitum*, the only member of the group that is transmitted by lymnaeid snails.[41]

In terms of the origins and the biogeography of the different schistosoma, a minimum of three colonisation events are necessary to explain the current distribution of species. Although the molecular evidence suggests that an Asian origin of the schistosomes is much more likely than an African one, the direction of the colonisation events remains difficult to ascertain.[42]

In answering the question about the directionality of the colonisation events of the schistosoma, Morgan et al. in a molecular analysis of combined nuclear and mitochondrial DNA proposed three possible scenarios to explain the biogeography of the species.[43] The first suggests that schistosoma colonised Africa from Asia in three separate occasions giving rise to the African lineages. The second scenario proposes that they colonised Africa twice, once to give rise to the long tail-stem lineage, and then to give rise to the ancestor of *Schistosoma mansoni*, *Schistosoma indicum* and *Schistosoma haematobium* groups, and finally that the *Schistosoma indicium* lineage re-colonised Asia. Finally, the third scenario proposes that schistosoma colonised Africa only once and then re-colonised Asia at least twice giving rise to *Orientobilharzia* sp., *Schistosoma incognitum* and *Schistosoma indicum* groups.

---

[38]   Gunn, A., Pitt, S.J., *Parasitology: An Integrated Approach* (Chichester: Wiley-Blackwell, 2012), p. 100.

[39]   Snyder and Loker 2000; Agatsuma et al. 2002.

[40]   Le, T.H., Blair, D., McManus, D.P., 'Mitochondrial genomes of human helminths and their use as markers in population genetics and phylogeny', *Acta Tropica* 77 (2000): 243–56.

[41]   Agatsuma et al. 2002; Morgan et al. 2003; Snyder and Loker 2000.

[42]   Morgan, J.A.T., Dejong, R.J., Snyder, S.D., Mkoji, G.M., Loker, E.S, 'Schistosoma mansoni and Biomphalaria: past history and future trends', *Parasitology* 123 (2001): 211–28.

[43]   Combes, C., 'Where do human Schistosomes come from? An evolutionary approach', *Trends in Ecology and Evolution* 5 (1990): 334–37.

The timing of these colonisation events is also difficult to postulate, but according to Despres et al. the timing of the divergence of the different intermediate hosts of the schistosoma can be used to trace back the separation and divergence of the different schistosoma groups.[44] Therefore, the divergence between the Africa and Asian species could have happened 24–70 million years ago. Separation of the two African groups (*Schistosoma mansoni* and *Schistosoma haematobium*) can be dated 10–30 million years ago, and divergence within the African clades to 1–10 million years ago for the *Schistosoma mansoni* and 1–6 million years ago for the *Schistosoma haematobium* group.[45] Finally, human acquisition of the African schistosomes is believed to have happened through lateral transfer from other animals and, in the case of *Schistosoma haematobium*, possibly from ungulates.[46]

Taenia Tapeworms

It was previously thought that human infection with the *Taenia* tapeworms came about after the Neolithic Revolution, as a result of the domestication of the cow and pig, which are intermediate host for these parasites.[47] However, the phylogenetic analysis of *Taenia* sp. by Hoberg et al. demonstrated that *Taenia solium*, *Taenia saginata* and *Taenia asiatica* did not parasitise humans after the domestication of their intermediate swine and cattle host respectively, but they rather started to parasitise hominins 1–2.5 million years ago.[48] Based on the genetic evidence, Hoberg et al. proposed that a host-switching event occurred among hyena and lion tapeworms to ancestors of modern humans. This event was quite likely triggered by human ancestors scavenging the buffalo, wart hog, and other prey that also served as intermediate hosts of *Taenia*. Hoberg proposes that the main reasons for the host-switching of the *Taenia* sp. were climate changes and the shifting ecological conditions near the Pliocene-Pleistocene transition.[49] At the same time, the shift in the diet of the hominins from a herbivorous to an omnivorous one allowed *Taenia* sp. to parasitise a new host. Hoberg at al. also argue that it is possible to suggest that two independent events of host-switching from felids (*Taenia saginata*) and hyaenids (*Taenia solium*) to human ancestors happened prior to the advent of animal domestication.

---

[44]   Despres, L., Imbert-Establet, D., Combes, C., Bonhomme, F., 'Molecular evidence linking hominid evolution to recent radiation of Schistosomes (Platyhelminthes: Trematoda)', *Molecular Phylogenetics and Evolution* 1 (1992): 295–304.

[45]   Despres et al. 2002; Morgan et al. 2001.

[46]   Combes 1990.

[47]   Cameron, T.W.M., *Parasites and Parasitism* (New York: John Wiley and Sons, 1956).

[48]   Hoberg, E.P., Alkire, N.L., Queiroz, A., Jones, A., 'Out of Africa: origins of the Taenia tapeworms in humans', *Proceedings of the Royal Society B: Biological Sciences* 268 (2001): 781–87.

[49]   Hoberg, E.P., 'Phylogeny of Taenia: species definitions and origins of human parasites', *Parasitology International* 55 (2006): S23-S30.

Ancient Parasites in the Middle East

Until the last decade there have been extremely few studies of ancient parasites in the Middle East, and these were limited to Israel. Nevertheless, the last decade has seen a number of new studies focusing on the parasitic past of the region and today our understanding of the parasitic environment of ancient Middle East is considerably better and encompasses different areas in Cyprus (Table 7.4), Iran (Table 7.5), and Israel (Table 7.6).

Table 7.4   Ancient Parasites in Cyprus

Species	Location	Date	Source
Ascaris lumbricoides (roundworm)	Shillourokambos	8300–7000BC	Guilaine et al. ref.51
	Khirokitia	7000–6000BC	Guilaine et al. ref.51
	Saranda Kolones	1200AD	Anastasiou and Mitchell, ref.52
Diphyllobothrium sp. (fish tapeworm)	Unknown	7600–7500BC	Harter, ref.20
Fasciola sp. (liver fluke)	Shillourokambos	8300–7000BC	Guilaine et al. ref.51
	Khirokitia	7000–6000BC	Guilaine et al. ref.51
Taenia sp. (beef/pork tapeworm)	Shillourokambos	8300–7000BC	Guilaine et al. ref.51
	Khirokitia	7000–6000BC	Guilaine et al. ref.51
Trichuris trichiura (whipworm)	Shillourokambos	8300–7000BC	Guilaine et al. ref.51
	Khirokitia	7000–6000BC	Guilaine et al. ref.51
	Saranda Kolones	1200AD	Anastasiou and Mitchell, ref.52

In Iran, in a recent paleoparasitological study,[50] whipworms (*Trichuris* sp.), roundworms (*Ascaris* sp.), tapeworms (*Taenia* sp. or *Echinococcus* sp.), the lancet liver fluke (*Dicrocoelium* sp.) and the horse (*Oxyuris equi*) and human pinworm (*Enterobius vermicularis*) were all identified from soil samples recovered from an ancient salt mine. The mine is situated in Chehrabad in Northwestern Iran and it is dated to between 2500 and 1500BP. The identified species provide the first evidence for human and animal parasitism in Iran, and provide important insights into the hygiene conditions and dietary habits of the miners.

---

[50]   Nezamabadi, M., Aali, A., Stöllner, Th., Mashkour, M., Le Bailly, M., 'Paleoparasitological analysis of samples from Chehrabad salt mine (Northwestern Iran)', *International Journal of Paleopathology* 3 (2013): 229–233.

Our knowledge of the parasitic past of Cyprus comes from two aceramic Neolithic sites, Khirokitia[51] and Parekklisha–Shillourokambos,[52] as well as from the crusader period castle of Saranda Kolones.[53] The paleoparasitological analysis of samples from the Neolithic sites identified eggs of roundworm (*Ascaris lumbricoides*), beef/pork tapeworm (*Taenia* sp.) and whipworm (*Trichuris* sp.) in both sites, whereas eggs of *Diphyllobothrium* sp., *Toxocara* sp. and *Fasciola* sp. were found in the samples from Shillourokambos (Table 7.4).[54] The analysis of the samples from Saranda Kolones revealed the presence of whipworms and roundworms, and provided the first evidence for the parasitic environment of Cyprus, in periods later than the Neolithic.

Table 7.5   Ancient Parasites in Iran

Species	Location	Date	Source
Ascaris sp. (roundworm)	Chehrabad	1500–500BC	Nezamabadi et al. ref.54
Dicrocoelium sp. (lancet liver fluke)	Chehrabad	1500–500BC	Nezamabadi et al. ref.54
Echinococcus sp. (hydatid worm)	Chehrabad	1500–500BC	Nezamabadi et al. ref.54
Enterobius vermicularis (pinworm)	Chehrabad	1500–500BC	Nezamabadi et al. ref.54
Taenia sp. or *Echinococcus* (tapeworm/hydatid worm)	Chehrabad	1500–500BC	Nezamabadi et al. ref.54
Trichuris trichiura (whipworm)	Chehrabad	1500–500BC	Nezamabadi et al. ref.54

---

[51]   Le Brun, A., 'At the other end of the sequence; the Cypriot Aceramic Neolithic as seen from Khirokitia', in S. Swiny (ed.), *The Earliest Prehistory of Cyprus: From Colonization to Exploitation* (Boston: American School of Oriental Research, 2001), pp. 109–18.

[52]   Guilaine, J., Le Brun, A., Mort, F.L., Vigne, J.D., Bouchet, F., Harter, S., 'Premières données parasitologiques sur les populations humaines précéramiques Chypriotes (VIIIe et VIIe millénaires av. J.-C.)', *Paléorient* 31 (2005): 43–54.

[53]   Anastasiou, E., Mitchell, P.D., 'Human intestinal parasites from a latrine in the 12th century Frankish castle of Saranda Kolones in Cyprus', *International Journal of Paleopathology* 3 (2013): 218–23.

[54]   Guilaine et al. 2005; Harter 2003.

In Israel (Table 7.6), parasitological studies have been carried out in Nahal Hemar cave,[55] Nahal Mishmar valley,[56] Jerusalem,[57] Acre,[58] Masada[59] and Qumran.[60] Whipworms (*Trichuris trichiura*) have been identified in all sites but Masada, while in Jerusalem the dog tapeworm (*Echinococcus granulosus*) and the beef/pork tapeworm (*Taenia* sp.) were also present.[61] In Qumran, the parasitological studies revealed the presence of roundworms (*Ascaris lumbricoides*), whipworms (*Trichuris trichiura*), beef/pork tapeworms (*Taenia* sp.), pinworms (*Enterobius vermicularis*) and head lice.[62] In Nahal Mishmar Valley *Entamoeba histolytica, Giardia duodenalis,* and *Trichuris trichiura* were allegedly identified but the absence of any images in the paper of the structures seen on microscopy means these diagnoses must be viewed with caution.[63] In any case, the pathogenic *Entamoeba histolytica* and non-pathogenic commensal organism *Entamoeba dispar* appear identical on microscopy, so can never be distinguished with simple microscopic observation. In Masada head and body lice were recovered from combs and textiles.[64] In terms of chronology, the samples from Nahal Hemar cave

---

[55]   Mumcuoglu, K.Y., Zias, J., 'Pre-Pottery Neolithic B head lice found in Nahal Hemar Cave and dated 6900–6300 BCE (uncalibrated)', *Atikot* 20 (1991): 167–168.

[56]   Witenberg, G., 'Human parasites in archaeological findings', *Bulletin of the Israel Exploration Society* 25 (1961): 86.

[57]   Cahill, J., Reinhard, K., Tarler, D., Warnock, P., 'It had to happen: scientists examine remains of ancient bathroom', *Biblical Archaeological Review* 17 (1991): 64–69; Zias, J.E., Mumcuoglu, K.Y., 'Case reports on paleopathology: calcified hydatid cysts', *Paleopathology Newsletter* 73 (1991): 7–8.

[58]   Mitchell, P.D., Stern, E., 'Parasitic intestinal helminth ova from the latrines of the 13th century crusader hospital of St. John in Acre, Israel', in M. La Verghetta and L. Capasso (eds), *Proceedings of the XIIIth European Meeting of the Paleopathology Association, Chieti, Italy* (Teramo: Edigrafital, 2001), pp. 207–13; Mitchell, P.D., Tepper, Y., 'Intestinal parasitic worm eggs from a crusader period cesspool in the city of Acre (Israel)', *Levant* 39 (2007): 91–95; Mitchell, P.D., Stern, E., Tepper, Y., 'Dysentery in the crusader kingdom of Jerusalem: an ELISA analysis of two medieval latrines in the city of Acre (Israel)', *Journal of Archaeological Science* 35 (2008): 1849–53.

[59]   Mumcuoglu, K.Y., Zias, J., 'Head lice, Pediculus humanus capitis (Anoplura:Pediculidae) from hair combs excavated in Israel and dated from the first century BC to the eighth century AD', *Journal of Medical Entomology* 25 (1988): 545–47; Mumcuoglu, K.Y., Zias, J., Tarshis, M., Lavi, M., Stiebe, G.D., 'Body louse remains in textiles excavated at Masada, Israel', *Journal of Medical Entomology* 40 (2003): 585–87.

[60]   Harter, S., Bouchet, F., Mumcuoglu, K.Y., Zias, J. E., 'Toilet practices among members of the Dead Sea scrolls sect at Qumran (100 BCE-68 CE)', *Revue de Qumran* 21 (2004): 579–84; Zias, J.E., Tabor, J.D., Harter-Lailheugue, S., 'Toilets at Qumran, the Essenes, and the scrolls: new anthropological data and old theories', *Revue de Qumran* 22 (2006): 631–39.

[61]   Cahill et al. 1991.

[62]   Harter et al. 2004; Zias, et al. 2006; Mumcuoglu and Zias 1988.

[63]   Witenberg 1961.

[64]   Mumcuoglu and Zias 1988; Mumcuoglu et al. 2003.

are dated to 6900–6300BC, those from Jerusalem are dated to the 7th–6th century BC and 1st century AD, those from Nahal Mishmar Valley are dated to the 2nd century AD, and the samples from Qumran are dated to the 1st century BC–1st century AD.

Table 7.6   Ancient Parasites in Israel

Species	Location	Date	Source
Ascaris lumbricoides (roundworm)	Qumran Acre	100BC-100AD 1200–1291AD	Harter et al. ref.60 Mitchell et al. ref.4
Dicrocoelium sp. (lancet liver fluke)	Qumran	100BC-100AD	Zias et al., ref.60
Diphyllobothrium latum (fish tapeworm)	Acre	1200–1291AD	Mitchell and Stern, ref.58 Mitchell et al., ref.4
Echinococcus granulosus (hydatid worm)	Jerusalem	1–100AD	Zias and Mumcuoglu, ref.57
Entamoeba histolytica (dysentery)	Nahal Mishmar Acre	160AD (possible case) 1200–1291AD	Witenberg, ref.56 Mitchell et al. 2008 ref.58
Enterobius vermicularis (pinworm)	Qumran	100BC-100AD	Zias et al., ref.60
Giardia duodenalis (dysentery)	Nahal Mishmar Acre	160AD (possible case) 1200–1291AD	Witenberg, ref.56 Mitchell et al. 2008, ref.58
Pediculus humanus capitis (head louse)	Nahal Hemar Masada Qumran	6900–6300BC 100BC-800AD 100BC-100AD	Mumcuoglu and Zias, ref.55 Mumcuoglu and Zias, ref.59 Mumcuoglu and Zias, ref.59
Pediculus humanus humanus (body louse)	Masada	100BC-800AD	Mumcuoglu et al., ref.59
Taenia sp. (beef/pork tapeworm)	Jerusalem Qumran Acre	700–500BC 100BC-100AD 1200–1291AD	Cahill et al., ref.57 Harter et al., ref.60 Mitchell and Tepper, ref.58
Trichuris trichiura (whipworm)	Jerusalem Nahal Mishmar Acre	700–500BC 160AD 1200–1291AD	Cahill et al., ref.57 Witenberg, 1961, ref.56 Mitchell and Tepper, ref.58

In Acre, samples were analysed from two cesspools and one latrine, dated to the 13th century AD, when the city was under the control of the crusaders. During the paleoparasitological analysis, eggs of roundworm (*Ascaris lumbricoides*), whipworm (*Trichuris trichiura*) (Figure 7.1), beef/pork tapeworm (*Taenia* sp.)

and fish tapeworm (*Diphyllobothrium latum*) (Figure 7.2) were identified.[65] The presence of the protozoa *Giardia duodenalis* and *Entamoeba histolytica* in medieval Acre was also demonstrated using the biomolecular technique of ELISA

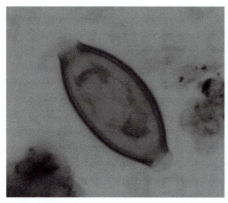

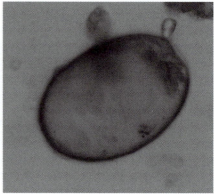

Figure 7.1.
Egg of *Trichuris trichiura* (whipworm) from a 13th century latrine in crusader period Acre, Israel. Size 53 x 23 μm. The faecal–oral transmission indicates limited effective sanitation in this population.

Figure 7.2.
Egg of *Diphyllobothrium latum* (fish tapeworm) from a 13th century latrine in crusader period Acre, Israel. Size 61 x 44 μm. This is compatible with human migration from northern Europe, where it was common.

In Syria the only ancient parasite study has been undertaken at the chalcolithic site of Tell Zeidan, located on the confluence of the Euphrates and Balikh rivers between 5800 and 4000BC. Twenty-six burials dating from 4500-4000BC underwent analysis of their pelvic soil and one was positive for schistosomiasis.[66] The egg identified was a terminal spined schistosome, likely to be either *S. intercalatum* or *S. haematobium*. This is the earliest case of schistosomiasis so far identified in the world.

The Importance of the Paleoparasitological Record from Africa and the Middle East

Although the range of time periods and geographical regions represented by the samples could be more comprehensive, a variety of different species have been

---

[65]   Mitchell and Stern 2001; Mitchell and Tepper 2007; Mitchell et al. 2011.

[66]   Anastasiou, E., Lorentz, K.O., Stein, G.J., Mitchell, P.D. 'Prehistoric schistosomiasis parasite found in the Middle East'. *Lancet Infectious Diseases* 14 (2014): 553-4.

extracted from the archaeological record that furthers our understanding of the communities that flourished in the region. In this section the evidence from Africa and the Middle East will be interpreted in terms of health, diet, hygiene, migration and environment in order to reconstruct aspects of life among our ancestors.

Health Consequences

The most obvious inference that can be drawn from the reconstruction of the parasitic environment of a past society relates to the health status of the community, as the presence of any parasite species provides direct evidence for a specific parasitic infection. Our knowledge of the effects that different parasite species may have had upon human health in the past is based on the symptoms and the pathology they cause today in modern populations. Although the possibility that ancient parasite species may have affected humans differently in the past cannot be excluded, there is clearly very little we can do currently to determine whether that may have been the case.

In the Middle East and Africa a variety of different parasite species have been identified, each of which provokes a different physiological response to the host. From the identified species, some cause health problems directly, such as the dog tapeworm (*Echinococcus granulosus*) that causes hydatid disease, and the filarial worms (e.g., *Wuchereria bancrofti, Loa loa*) that cause elephantiasis or blindness. Other species, like whipworm and roundworm, contribute to malnutrition and childhood stunting in heavy infections.

In this section the pathognomonic characteristics of each of the species that have been extracted from the archaeological record of the Middle East and Africa will briefly presented.

From the identified species, a mild infection with *Ascaris lumbricoides, Trichuris trichiura* and *Enterobius vermicularis* is mostly asymptomatic. Nevertheless, in a malnourished individual, infection with roundworms or whipworms may aggravate his/her nutritional deficiencies, as the parasite absorbs the nutrients before the host is able to process them. A heavy infection with pinworms may lead to intestinal damage and bacterial infection, due to the ulcerations of the intestinal mucosa caused by the attachment of the adult worms on the intestines.

The protozoa *Giardia duodenalis* and *Entamoeba histolytica* cause dysentery with symptoms of diarrhoea, vomiting, dehydration, intestinal pain, dehydration, and weight loss. The tapeworms *Diphyllobothrium* sp. and *Taenia* sp. cause minor problems in moderate infections, such as abdominal pain, nausea and diarrhoea. Nonetheless, heavy infection with *Diphyllobothrium* sp. causes pernicious anaemia due to vitamin B12 deficiency, while infection with the eggs of *Taenia solium* causes cysticercosis. The pathogenesis of cysticercosis depends on the site of infection. Although cysticercosis of the muscles, skin, or liver causes moderate symptoms, cysticercosis of the eye can cause severe damage to the retina and cysticercosis of the brain can cause seizures, central nervous system malfunction, blindness, and limb paralysis. Similarly, infection with the eggs of the dog tapeworm *Echinococcus granulosus* causes hydatid disease, whose pathogenesis depends on the location of the cysts in the human body and on their size, which can become quite large.

As far as *Fasciola hepatica* and *Dicrocoelium* sp. are concerned, moderate infections are generally asymptomatic. Heavy infections may cause biliary colic, abdominal pain, enlarged liver and spleen, severe anaemia and jaundice. *Trichinella spiralis* may cause intestinal inflammation and diarrhoea immediately after infection, while in more severe cases, the migration of the larvae through the liver, heart and lungs to the muscles may cause pneumonia, encephalitis and meningitis. In the case of *Strongyloides stercoralis* severe infection may cause chest pain during the migration of the larvae through the lungs and abdominal pain when the larvae become established in the intestines.

Among the species of worms identified in archaeological contexts in Africa, *Schistosoma* sp., the filarial worms, the Guinea worm and the *Plasmodium falciparum* have the most direct and severe consequences upon the health status of the infected individuals. Therefore, it can be hypothesised that these parasite species probably had the most severe and debilitating effects upon the past cultures that flourished in the Middle East and Africa too.

Schistosomiasis, caused by one of the human schistosoma, is today one of the most important water-borne chronic parasitic diseases, with more than 240 million people infected in the endemic regions.[67] The pathogenesis of schistosomiasis, although having small differences depending on the causative agent, can be divided into three phases: initial, intermediate and final. The initial phase is characterised by skin rash, abdominal pain and enlargement of the liver and spleen for all the species involved. During the intermediate phase pathological changes are caused in the intestines or the urinary tract due to the production of eggs by the adult worms. Anaemia is common from the chronic loss of blood at the locations where the worms are located (bladder or intestines). The final phase of schistosomiasis damages the renal and gastrointestinal systems, with periportal cirrhosis of the liver in the case of *Schistosoma mansoni,* neurological damage in the case of *Schistosoma japonicum* and kidney damage in the case of *Schistosoma haematobium.*

The filarial worms *Wuchereria bancrofti, Brugia malayi* and *Brugia timori* cause lymphatic filariasis (elephantiasis), a disease that blocks the flow of lymph through the body and results in chronic severe oedematous swelling that can become severely debilitating for the infected individual. Moreover, the filarial worms *Loa loa, Onchocerca volvulus* and *Mansonella streptocerca* cause subcutaneous filariasis, which in *Loa loa* results in lymphedema (swollen limbs), and in *Onchocerca volvulus* results in blindness. Furthermore, infection with the Guinea worm *Dracunculus medinensis* causes severe allergic reactions, with

---

[67]   Schmidt, G.D., Roberts, L.S., *Foundations of Parasitology*, 7th edn. (New York: McGraw-Hill, 2006), p. 256.

rashes, diarrhoea, dizziness and edema. More severely, the parasite can also cause arthritis or paralysis of the spinal cord if the adult worms die inside the joints.

Finally, *Plasmodium falciparum,* identified in Egypt, causes malignant malaria, which is the most dangerous and life-threatening form of the disease. Despite effective modern treatments it remains the most serious and debilitating parasitic disease, with 216 million infections recorded in 2010 and 655,000 resulting deaths.[68] These numbers paint a very grave picture upon the health consequences that the disease had in antiquity, when it was not only incurable but may also have been more widespread. Indeed, as evident from ancient medical texts from the Middle East and Africa, malaria was recognised as a severe health problem due to its high toll on human lives.[69]

Hygiene Conditions

Besides the associations between parasitism and health, the parasite remains can also be used as a proxy for the reconstruction of the hygiene conditions that prevailed in a community. Every parasite species has a specific life cycle and is thus restricted by the limitations that its life cycle imposes. Certain species, such as the roundworms and whipworms, have a faecal–oral transmission and are prevalent in conditions of limited sanitation. As a result, their presence in an archaeological context reflects the hygiene conditions of that community and allows for certain conclusions to be drawn regarding the sanitation habits of the community in question (Figure 7.1).

From the species that have been identified in Africa and the Middle East, *Ascaris lumbricoides*, *Trichuris trichiura*, *Enterobius vermicularis*, *Giardia duodenalis* and *Entamoeba histolytica* all have a faecal–oral transmission and thus are prevalent in conditions of poor sanitation and hygiene, where inadequate disposal of the faecal material, contamination of food and water supplies with faecal waste, use of human faeces as fertiliser and geophagy by children (eating soil) are prevalent. *Strongyloides stercoralis* is also associated with poor standards of hygiene, since it infects people that contract the juveniles of the parasite in contaminated water and soil. *Fasciola* sp. is transmitted when certain vegetation (like watercress, water chestnut, or bamboo) is eaten without being properly washed, and thus the presence of these parasites in a community is closely associated with inadequate sanitation.

The identification of faecal–orally transmitted parasites from Africa and the Middle East is dated from the Neolithic to the medieval period. This continuous

[68]   World Health Organization, WHO, 'Malaria, Fact Sheet', http://www.who.int/mediacentre/factsheets/fs094/en/index.html.

[69]   Bruce-Chwatt, L.J., 'Paleogenesis and paleo-epidemiology of primate malaria', *Bulletin of World Health Organization* 32 (1965): 363–87; Hoeppli, R., 'The knowledge of parasites and parasitic infections from ancient times to the 17th century', *Experimental Parasitology* 5 (1956): 398–419.

presence of faecal–orally transmitted helminths in the area is extremely interesting, as it demonstrates that the level of sanitation of the communities in question did not change significantly throughout antiquity, even following the invention of latrines. Contamination of the food and water resources with faecal material, ineffective disposal of faecal waste, consumption of unwashed vegetables, use of human faeces as fertiliser and eating with unwashed hands are all factors facilitating the transmission of the aforementioned species, and as such they can be used to describe the living conditions of the societies of the Middle East and Africa, where these species have been identified.

Dietary Habits

One of the most important insights that paleoparasitology provides into the lifestyle of past communities relates to the dietary habits and food preparation methods of the societies under study. Parasite species with complex life cycles require one or more intermediate hosts in order to reach adulthood and are often transmitted to the definitive host (e.g., humans) through predation of the intermediate host (e.g., a tasty animal). Consequently, the identification of parasites that are transmitted to humans through the consumption of their intermediate host reflects the dietary habits and the food preparation methods of the community in which they are present. For example, the beef tapeworm (*Taenia saginata*) and the pork tapeworm (*Taenia solium*) require cattle and swine respectively as intermediate hosts to complete their life cycles and are transmitted to the definitive human host through the consumption of raw, salted, dried, smoked or poorly cooked beef and pork.

Consequently, the identification in the Middle East and Africa of the *Taenia* tapeworms, *Trichinella spiralis* and *Diphyllobothrium* sp. – parasites that are transmitted to humans through the consumption of poorly cooked meat and, in the case of *Diphyllobothrium,* poorly cooked fish – can be used to indicate the dietary habits and food preparation methods of the societies that flourished in the area. Based upon the available paleoparasitological evidence, it can be argued that the consumption of poorly cooked, salted, dried or raw meat (pork and beef) was not uncommon throughout antiquity in the area. The consumption of poorly cooked fish by people who then migrated to medieval Acre as indicated by the presence of *Diphyllobothrium latum* will be discussed in more detail in the next section, as it provides evidence for migration.

Migration

Ancient parasites can also provide information about the migration routes chosen by historic and prehistoric populations. The constraints imposed upon the parasite species by their biology and life cycle, alongside their specificity to particular hosts, are factors that explain why the parasite evidence can be used to trace human migration events. If they are found in a region where the environment is incompatible with their life cycle, then they must have been brought there in the body of a migrating human.

Paleoparasitological studies have already been used to trace new migration routes to the New World during prehistory,[70] and to identify the presence of foreigners in France in 1450–1555AD[71] and in California in the 19th–20th century AD.[72] In the paleoparasitological corpus of the Middle East the identification of the fish tapeworm in crusader period Acre [73] provides evidence for the migration of Europeans into the Middle East as part of the crusades (Figure 7.2).

Previous studies have focused on different time periods from prehistory up to the modern era (up to the 19th century AD) and have identified eggs of the fish tapeworm in contexts from northern Europe and Scandinavia.[74] This geographic distribution of the fish tapeworm mainly in the northern parts of the northern hemisphere reflects its life cycle characteristics, as well as the dietary habits of the cultures in which the parasite has been identified. On one hand, the preparation of fish prior to its consumption is important for whether the fish tapeworm eggs can survive, since although cooking the fish kills the eggs, eating it raw, smoked or pickled does not. Eating raw or preserved fish was widespread in northern Europe and Scandinavia in the past and in part explains the wide distribution of the parasite in these regions.[75] The life cycle of the fish tapeworm requires the presence of two intermediate hosts, the first of which must be a copepod (tiny shrimp) and the second a freshwater fish. Therefore, in areas without freshwater lakes or rivers, or in areas where the bodies of fresh water do not support the presence of either the copepods or the freshwater fishes that are necessary for the completion of the parasite's life cycle, the parasite cannot become endemic.

---

[70]   Montenegro et al. 2006.

[71]   Bouchet, F., Harter, S., Paicheler, J. C., Araújo, A., Ferreira, L. F., 'First recovery of Schistosoma mansoni eggs from a latrine in Europe (15–16th centuries)', *Journal of Parasitology* 88 (2002): 404–05.

[72]   Reinhard, K., Araújo, A., Sianto, L., Costello, J.G., Swope, K., 'Chinese liver flukes in latrine sediments from Wong Nom's property, San Bernandino, California: archaeoparasitology of the Caltrans District Headquarters', *Journal of Parasitology* 94 (2008): 300–03.

[73]   Mitchell, et al. 2011; Mitchell and Stern 2001.

[74]   Sianto, L., Chame, M., Silva, C.S.P., Goncalves, C.L.M., Reinhard, K., Fugassa, M., Araújo, A., 'Animal helminths in human archaeological remains: a review of zoonoses in the past', *Revista do Instituto de Medicina Tropical de São Paulo* 51 (2009): 119–30; Goncalves, C.L.M., Araujo, A., Ferreira, L.F., 'Human intestinal parasites in the past: new findings and a review', *Memórias do Instituto Oswaldo Cruz* 98 (Suppl. 1) (2003): 103–118; Yeh, et al. 2014.

[75]   Buxton, M., Walker, H., 'Fish-eating in medieval England', in H. Walker (ed.), *Food and Cookery: Fish Food from the Waters* (Totnes: Prospect Books, 1998) pp. 51–59; Gifford, C., *Food and Cooking in Viking Times* (London: Wayland, 2009); Hagen, A., *Anglo-Saxon Food and Drink: Production, Processing, Distribution and Consumption* (Hockwold cum Wilton: Anglo Saxon Books, 2006).

In Israel the fish tapeworm is not endemic today and was very rare in archaeological latrines and coprolites before the medieval period. However, eggs of the *Diphyllobothrium* genus have been recovered from prehistoric Cyprus and occasionally from ancient Egypt. The identification of *D. latum* eggs in two crusader period latrines provides evidence for one of the most important migration events in history. During the crusader period a great number of Europeans travelled to the Latin states of the East, either as part of military campaigns, as pilgrims, or for trade, and although many of them returned to Europe soon after their journey a significant number settled in the East.

Despite the fact that the crusades have often been blamed for the spread of disease during the medieval period[76] there has been only limited research into the issue.[77] As a result little is known about the diseases that may have been spread due to the crusades, their directionality (towards Europe or towards the Latin East) and their impact.[78] Therefore, the identification of the fish tapeworm in a crusader period cesspool from Acre provides an important insight towards understanding the relationship between the crusades and disease transmission.

The presence of fish tapeworm in Acre illustrates that at least one parasitic disease was introduced to the crusader states from northern Europe (even if it did not then become endemic in the locals there) and that its impact may have been disadvantageous for the infected crusader soldiers. The evidence from Acre demonstrates the importance of paleoparasitology for inferring the impact that migration events had in the introduction of new pathogens into a geographical region. In extending this point, the parasitic evidence from Acre also demonstrates the importance of the paleoparasitological record for tracing human migration events and long-distance trading. In the case of Acre the paleoparasitological record complements the historical and archaeological evidence in reconstructing one of the most important migration events in history.

Environment and Activities

In modern times a common method by which people contract schistosomiasis in Africa and the Middle East is when farmers wade in water irrigation channels

---

[76]   Hudson, E.H., 'Treponematosis and pilgrimage', *American Journal of Medical Science* 246 (1963): 645–56; Nozais, J.P., 'The origin and dispersion of human parasitic disease in the Old World (Africa, Europe and Madagascar)', *Memórias do Instituto Oswaldo Cruz* 98 (Suppl. 1) (2003): 13–19; Zinsser, H., *Rats, Lice and History* (London: Macmillan Press, 1985), p. 125.

[77]   Mitchell, P.D., 'The spread of disease with the crusades', in B. Nance and E.F. Glaze (eds), *Between Text and Patient: The Medical Enterprise in Medieval and Early Modern Europe* (Florence: Simsel, 2011), pp. 309–330.

[78]   Mitchell, et al. 2011; Mitchell, P.D., 'The myth of the spread of leprosy with the crusades', in C. Roberts, K. Manchester, M. Lewis (eds), *The Past and Present of Leprosy* (Oxford: Archaeopress, 2002) pp. 175–81.

supplying their crops. Snails of the bulinus group living in the warm fresh water act as an intermediate host for the parasite. In the ancient Middle East crop irrigation was first developed around 5500BC, and it spread across the region.[79] The chalcolithic case of schistosomiasis from Syria dates from 4500-4000BC, once crop irrigation had become well established.[80] It is possible, therefore, that the individual who suffered with schistosomiasis at Tell Zeidan may have contracted it from either wading in a natural water source, or in a man made irrigation channel. If the latter, this could be one of the earliest examples of a man-made technology (crop irrigation) leading to increased risk of developing a disease.

Future Directions in the Paleoparasitology of the Middle East and Africa

One of the most important inferences that can be drawn from ancient parasites relates to the impact that social organisation, urbanisation and large-scale cultural changes had on the transmission and distribution of the parasitic diseases. The most commonly cited example of how the parasite remains can be used to trace the interaction between health, social complexity and large-scale social and habitual changes is the Neolithic Revolution. Studies since the 1980s[81] of the parasitic environment between Amerindian hunter-gatherers and agriculturalists demonstrated that the significant changes in diet, settlement patterns and social organisation caused by the advent of agriculture triggered one of the most important transitions in the parasitoses of man. After the advent of agriculture, the domestication of plants and animals, the increase in population size and density and the inception of sedentism and of social stratification increased the number of certain parasitic and infectious diseases.[82] The proximity of habitation to the domesticated animals seems to have created a cluster of disease vectors, while the proximity of the living areas to the water sources facilitated their contamination with human waste. Moreover, the utilisation of human faeces as fertiliser, the lack of anti-helminthic compounds in cultivated food, as well as the disturbance of the environment through agriculture, were all factors that aided the diffusion of parasites in sedentary communities.[83]

---

[79] Helbaek, H. 'Samarran irrigation agriculture at Choga Mami in Iraq', *Iraq* (1972): 25-48.

[80] Anastasiou et al., 2014.

[81] Reinhard, K.J., 'Cultural ecology of prehistoric parasitism on the Colorado Plateau as evidenced by coprology', *American Journal of Physical Anthropology* 77 (1988): 355–66.

[82] Armelagos et al. 2005.

[83] Reinhard 1988; Pearce-Duvet, J.M.C., 'The origin of human pathogens: evaluating the role of agriculture and domestic animals in the evolution of human disease', *Biological Reviews* 81 (2006): 369–82.

Although the Fertile Crescent in the Middle East is the birthplace of agriculture,[84] no paleoparasitological studies have been carried out to the present day comparing the parasitic environment of the hunter-gatherers in the paleolithic Middle East with that of the first agricultural settlements in the fertile crescent. It is therefore necessary to address the impact that agriculture had on the parasitic environment of human societies with data from the area where agriculture first emerged, in order to highlight the immediate changes that agriculture introduced on parasitism. By demonstrating the differences between the parasitic environment of pre-Neolithic and Neolithic settlements when agriculture first emerged, it will become possible to determine the first and most important change that one of the largest cultural and social advancements in human history had upon the parasitic environment.

The first complex societies in the world, the first true cities and the first technological innovations in the form of man-made water irrigation systems were developed in Ubaid period Mesopotamia and in pre-dynastic Egypt. Consequently, the reconstruction of the parasitic environment of the Middle East and Africa during the early periods of the development of social and political complexity and during the dawn of technological advancement will shed light upon the associations that existed between the transmission of parasitic diseases and large-scale changes in social complexity and technological advances.

Only a few studies have investigated the interaction between parasitism and technological innovation. Hibbs et al.,[85] in their comparative study of the prevalence of *Schistosoma mansoni* in the Wadi Halfa and Kulubnarti populations of ancient Nubia (350–950AD), demonstrated that schistosomiasis was more prevalent in the Wadi Halfa population that utilised extensively saqia irrigation technology. Their study demonstrated that the technological advancements brought with saqia irrigation facilitated the transmission of schistosomiasis, since it created additional habitats for the intermediate snail host of schistosomiasis.

Despite the importance of the conclusions that these studies have in illuminating the associations between social complexity, political leadership, technological innovation and transmission of parasitic disease, in the Middle East and Africa these studies are still scarce. Therefore, we should now focus upon research that investigates the changes that our cultural and technological evolution brought to the parasitic environment of our ancestors.

Conclusion

It can be seen that Africa and the Middle East were key regions of the world for human evolution. The concurrent evolution of human parasites which have changed with us in order to remain a viable species is a fascinating topic. The available genetic evidence has highlighted how many of these parasites evolved

---

[84] Harris 1996.
[85] Hibbs et al. 2011.

from those which infected the troupes of early apes that foraged in the tropical jungles, or the carnivore species that hunted on the east African plains. This paper has presented the known evidence for ancient human parasites from the Middle East and Africa to highlight the important steps that have been made towards reconstructing the parasitic environment of the region. This demonstrates the broad range of serious parasitic diseases that were present there in the past, which would have had serious effects upon the health of our ancestors. We have also shown how finding ancient parasites in regions incompatible with the constraints of their life cycle can give us evidence for the migration of peoples in the past.

However, vast regions of Africa remain unstudied, most notably in the west and central regions of the continent. Many fascinating research questions can only be understood once studies have been undertaken there, and this will undoubtedly take many years. The challenging terrain and dense forests, heavy rainfall, and volatile political environment of many countries make such research highly challenging for archaeological parasite studies.

Chapter 8

Parasitism, Cesspits and Sanitation in East Asian Countries Prior to Modernisation

Min Seo and Dong Hoon Shin

Introduction

Different types of microbes and parasites are excreted in human faeces and transmitted to other people through the ingestion of contaminated water and food, inducing various intestinal diseases. However, the study of the history of waterborne diseases and of the close correlation between them and states of sanitation has suffered from a relative lack of documentation, especially as researchers delved more deeply into the past. In this context, archaeoparasitology, the study of coprolites and sediments from archaeological sites, can provide rare opportunities for studying ancient parasites. The resulting discoveries provide invaluable clues about human sanitary practices and health in the past.[1]

Archaeoparasitological studies conducted in Europe and the Americas were focused on the recovery and diagnosis of parasite eggs from ancient or medieval samples. The researchers showed that the examination of coprolites and sediments from archaeological sites could provide information on the relationships between parasitic diseases in the past and the cultural development of human society.[2] Indeed, in recent years a series of archaeoparasitological reports have proved to be useful for understanding the history of parasitic infection among different human populations.[3] Such reports found that certain types of parasitic infections, in their emergence, transmission and overall pathology, seemingly have been significantly influenced by social changes of human history. Unsurprisingly then, the historical-contextual development of sanitation as a means of controlling parasitism has

---

[1] Reinhard, K.J., 'Archaeoparasitology in North America', *American Journal of Physical Anthropology* 82 (1990): 145–163.

[2] Bouchet, F., Guidon, N., Dittmar, K., Harter, S., Ferreira, L.F., Chaves, S.M., Reinhard, K., Araújo, A., 'Parasite remains in archaeological sites', *Memórias do Instituto Oswaldo Cruz* 98 (Suppl. 1) (2003): 47–52; Reinhard, K.J., Araújo, A., 'Archaeoparasitology' in D.M. Pearsall (ed.), *Encyclopedia of Archaeology* (New York: Elsevier, 2008), pp. 494–501.

[3] Ferreira, L.F., Britto, C., Cardoso, M.A., Fernandez, O., Reinhard, K., Araújo, A., 'Paleoparasitology of Chagas disease revealed by infected tissues from Chilean mummies', *Acta Tropica* 75 (2000): 79–84.

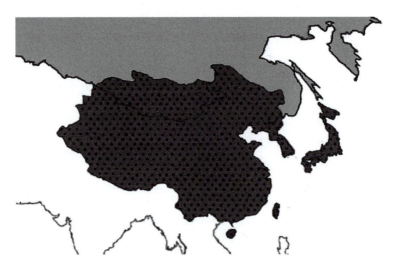

Figure 8.1.   Geography of East Asia. Korea, China, Japan, Mongolia and
                Taiwan (marked by dots) make up the region. A part of the Russian
                Federation (i.e., Siberia, shaded in grey), known as North Asia,
                was also dealt with in this study.

been one of the commonest themes that the archaeoparasitologists of Europe and
the Americas have studied.[4]

East Asia covers about 28 per cent of the Asian continent, and is home to 22
per cent of the entire world's population (Figure 8.1). The rich natural and cultural
heritage of East Asian countries suggests that research in this region should make
a very important contribution to the global body of knowledge on sanitation and
parasitism in human history. Without the East Asian contribution, any understanding
of the links between parasitism, sanitation and social development in the broad
context of human history would remain incomplete. Since the pattern of parasite
infection in pre-modern Asian societies could serve as an invaluable point of
reference for related studies, this paper aims to bring together and interpret the
previous studies on sanitation and parasitism in pre-modern East Asian societies.

Chronological and Geographical Scope

The peoples of East Asia have experienced different socio-cultural evolutions
over recent millennia, in contrasting natural environments such as temperate,
subtropical, desert, steppe, taiga and tundra zones. There were agrarian societies

---

[4]   Reinhard and Araújo 2008.

that emerged in China at least nine thousand years ago,[5] while nomadic peoples have dominated the steppe grasslands in the northern territories (e.g. Mongolia), and hunter-gatherers have wandered in parts of Manchuria and Siberia until quite recently. Studies on sanitation and parasitism in the context of various societies might well show differences in each population native to temperate or subtropical forest zones. However, our current knowledge focuses mainly on reports from Korea, China and Japan, simply because most of the relevant research in East Asia has originated there until now.

Archaeoparasitology in East Asia

In Europe, many aspects of people's lives underwent rapid changes wrought by historical events such as the Reformation, the Age of Reason, the Age of Enlightenment and, eventually, the Industrial Revolution.[6] The industrial revolution, with its advanced technology, brought profound and sweeping improvements in public sanitation and health. Modern biological samples unearthed from archaeological sites accordingly show relatively lower prevalence of parasitic infection compared with ancient and medieval specimens from European countries. We suspect that the same changes in the prevalence of parasite infection were also occurring in East Asian societies after the rapid modernisation of the area.

As for the awareness of parasitism in primitive East Asian societies, study of mid-twentieth century tribesmen in Southeast Asia is very illuminating.[7] The tribesmen clearly knew of the existence of some roundworm parasites (such as *Ascaris lumbricoides* and *Enterobius vermicularis*), indicating that the concept of parasitism was not nonsensical to them, even without scientific knowledge. Extant East Asian historical texts also provide invaluable information on prevailing knowledge of parasitism in pre-modern societies. Considering that these texts were in a position of unchallenged academic authority among the pre-modern Korean people, the ideas on parasitism found therein should have been the dominant thinking in Korea until Western medicine finally supplanted it. For instance, in a 17th century medical textbook (*Donguibogam* in Korean) that was written by a famous court physician of the Joseon Dynasty, the contemporary science on parasitism of pre-modern Korea is in evidence:

---

[5]   Barnes, E., *Diseases and Human Evolution* (Albuquerque: University of New Mexico Press, 2005), p. 49.

[6]   Palmer, R.R., Colton, J., *A History of the Modern World* (New York: Alfred A. Knopf, 1971).

[7]   Hoeppli, R., 'Some early views on parasites and parasitic infections shared by the people of Borneo, Malaya and China', *Proceedings of the Alumni Association of Malaya* 7 (1954): 3–17.

Every kind of parasite is formed by inappropriately cooked meals (i.e., raw or undercooked, cold meat or fishes). At first, they aggregate; and then make heat. It makes changes, forming nine different types of parasites … . First of all, the length of a bokchung is 12 cm … Next, hoechung (Ascaris?) is measured at 30 cm, penetrating the heart, making the patient die. Third, baekchung, measured at 12 cm, can produce larvae. The patients die as the baekchung becomes mature. Next, yukchung, looking like an apricot, makes discomfort in the chest. The fifth one is pyechung (worm in the lung). Its looks like a silkworm, inducing patients' coughs. The sixth is wichung (worm in the stomach); it looks like a toad, causing hiccups, chest pain, and geophagia. Next, yakchung (weak worm) looks like a cucumber, causing sputum. The eighth is jukchung (red worm). It looks like meat, causing abdominal discomfort. Ninth, yochung (Enterobius vermicularis?) is like a worm in vegetables; very slender and small; living in the colon. It induces hemorrhoids when the symptoms are advanced.[8]

Such knowledge of parasitism should have been shared by peoples from other East Asian countries, in that traditional herbal medicines in those countries have a common academic root. Certainly, the herbal medicine of the Joseon society could not have been very effective, as the egg-positive rate for soil-transmitted helminthes among Koreans was very high (over 80 per cent) as late as 1948.[9] The pathology of parasitic infection seems not to have been fully understood by pre-modern East Asian peoples. The delayed introduction of modern parasitology and related medicine to the East Asian countries should have resulted in a higher prevalence of parasitic infection in the region until quite recently. Naturally enough, numerous parasite eggs should therefore have been observed in archaeological samples from the countries. Notwithstanding this, until recently there has been little archaeoparasitological research on East Asian samples, and most of them have been relatively simple surveys on the presence or absence of ancient parasite eggs in samples from archaeological sites. Archaeoparasitology in East Asia followed divergent development pathways, leading to different research achievements in particular countries. For instance, in Korea and China coprolites from mummies have been examined, whereas in Japan sediments from cesspits or toilets have been the main research focus.

In China since the 1950s a number of human mummies have been discovered in ancient and medieval tombs.[10] Most of the reports on the ancient parasite eggs

---

[8]   Heo, J., *Donguibogam* (Seóul, 1613), Book 6, Page 55–1.

[9]   Lee, S.-H., 'Transition of parasitic diseases in Korea', *Journal of Korean Medical Association* 50 (2007): 937–945.

[10]   Wei, D.X., Yang, W.Y., Huang, S.Q., Lu, Y.F., Su, T.C., Ma, J.H., Hu, W.X., Xie, N.F., 'Párasitological investigation on the ancient corpse of the Western Han Dynasty unearthed from tomb No. 168 on Phoenix Hill in Jiangling County', *Acta Academiae Medicinae Wuhan* 1 (1981): 16–23; Hu, S.Y., 'Study on the parasite eggs in an ancient corpse from Zhangguo Chu Tomb No. 1 in Mashan brick-field of Jiangling County, Hubei',

have concentrated on these mummies. A range of ancient parasite eggs were found when intestinal material was extracted from the mummies. The eggs of *Ascaris lumbricoides* (roundworm), *Clonorchis sinensis* (Chinese liver fluke), *Fasciolopsis buski* (giant intestinal fluke), and *Trichuris trichiura* (whipworm) were observed in coprolite samples from Song Dynasty (960–1279) and Ming Dynasty (1368–1644) mummies.[11] In the case of a female mummy from the Mawangtui tomb in Changsha (Han Dynasty, 202BC–220AD), the eggs of *Schistosoma japonicum* (oriental bilharzia), *T. trichiura,* and *E. vermicularis* (pinworm) were identified in the coprolite sample.[12] A mummified corpse dating to the Han Dynasty, recovered from a tomb on Phoenix Hill in Hubei Province, also yielded eggs of four different species: *S. japonicum, C. sinensis, Taeniarhynchus saginata* (or *Taenia solium*), and *T. trichiura.*[13] Parasitological studies have also been conducted on corpses discovered in Warring States tombs as well.[14] The archaeoparasitologists in China did not perform the studies using morphological techniques alone. Actually, the *C. sinensis* eggs found in the gall bladder of the Phoenix Hill mummy were further subjected to ancient DNA (aDNA) analysis.[15] In the study, the genomic DNA of *C. sinensis* was extracted and successfully sequenced for the internal transcribed spacers 1 and 2 (ITS1 and ITS2) in ribosomal RNA genes. Past studies on mummy coprolites in China certainly have provided invaluable information on the historical parasite infections of the ancient or medieval Chinese people.

Meanwhile, in contrast to those in China, researchers in Japan examined sediments collected from cesspits and other types of toilets discovered at archaeological sites, from the beginning of their archaeoparasitological studies.[16] At first, archaeologists in Japan were not sure if the ancient toilets could be located by microscopic examination of archaeologically obtained sediments. However,

---

Chinese Journal of Parasitology and Parasitic Disease 2 (1984): 8; Yang, W.Y., Wei, D.X., Song, G.F., Wu, Z.B., Teng, R.S., 'Parasitologic investigations on the ancient corpse of Chu dynasty the warring states unearthed from the Ma-zhuan tomb No. 1, Jiangling County', *Acta Academiae Medicinae Wuhan* 14 (1984): 43–45; Su, T.C., 'A scanning electron microscopic study on the parasite eggs in an ancient corpse from a tomb of Chu Dynasty, the Warring State, in Jiangling County, Hubei Province', *Journal of Tongji Medical University* 7 (1987): 63–64; Wu, Z., Guan, Y., Zhou, Z., 'Study of an ancient corpse of the Warring States period unearthed from Tomb No. 1 at Guo-Jia Gang in Jingmen City (a comprehensive study)', *Journal of Tongji Medical University* 16 (1996): 1–5, 10.

[11] Wei et al. 1981.

[12] Wei, O., 'Internal organs of a 2100-year-old female corpse', *The Lancet* 24 (1973): 1198.

[13] Wei et al. 1981.

[14] Hu 1984; Yang et al. 1984; Su 1987; Wu et al. 1996.

[15] Liu, W.-Q., Liu, J., Zhang, J.-H., Long, X.-C., Lei, J.-H., Li, Y.-L., 'Comparison of ancient and modern *Clonorchis sinensis* based on ITS1 and ITS2 sequences', *Acta Tropica* 101 (2007): 91–94.

[16] Matsui, A., Kanehara, M., Kanehara, M., 'Palaeoparasitology in Japan – discovery of toilet features', *Memórias do Instituto Oswaldo Cruz* 98 (Suppl. 1) (2003): 127–136.

after the archaeoparasitological technique pioneered in the UK was introduced to the Japan, this question was answered affirmatively. In 1992, when Fujiwara palace in the Nara Prefecture, one of the ancient capitals in history of Japan (AD 694 to 710), was excavated, the eggs of *A. lumbricoides*, *T. trichiura*, *Metagonimus yokogawai* (metagonimiasis), *C. sinensis* and *Taenia* spp. were identified in sediments from the site, confirming the existence there of the oldest cesspit toilet ever discovered in Japan.[17] From then on, the study on presumptive toilet sites by parasitological examination of sediments has been established in Japan as a distinctive research discipline: *toilet archaeology*.

The collaboration between archaeologists and parasitologists looks much smoother and more routine in Japan than in other East Asian countries. In other words, parasitological data acquired from ancient samples in Japan has been much more readily, effectively and fruitfully interpreted from the viewpoints of archaeology. For instance, ancient pork (*Taenia solium*) and beef (*Taenia saginatum*) tapeworm eggs were discovered in sediments from the cesspits of Koro-Kan, the 8th century guesthouse in Dazaihu City.[18] The eggs were not thought to have come from Japanese individuals, but rather from Chinese or Korean diplomatic delegates, because in ancient Japan, beef and pork were prohibited from human consumption by a Buddhism-inspired royal decree.[19] The study on a fish tapeworm (*Diphyllobothrium* sp.) infection, a risk associated with eating raw or undercooked cherry salmon, is another example of the collaboration between archaeologists and parasitologists in Japan. Whereas eggs of this parasite were discovered in sediments from a 12th century toilet of a local Samurai and merchant town site, they were not found in toilet sediments from a castle in the same area. Since the castle was a place for the officials who were dispatched there from the other regions of Japan in 8th to 9th century, the absence of eggs in the toilet sediments from the castle was due likely to the dietary habits of those officials, most of whom might not have been born or bred in the area and who therefore might very well have been unfamiliar with the dishes of raw cherry salmon popular there.[20] This so-called *toilet archaeology* in Japan seems to have become a particularly successful tool for the successful study on the sanitation and parasitism of the past.

The history of the archaeoparasitology in Korea, on the other hand, is relatively short, even compared with China and Japan. The earliest reports in Korea on the presence of parasite eggs in archaeological sediments were not made until quite recently. In 1997, *Ascaris* and *Trichuris* eggs were recovered at a wetland

---

[17]   Matsui et al. 2003.

[18]   Board of Education, Fukuoka City, *Kouro-kan III, Fukuoka City Archaeological Site Report No. 355 (Fukuokashi, Kouro-kan Ato III, Fukuoka-shi Maizo-Bunkazai Chosa houkokusho)* (Fukuoka City, Japan: Board of Education, 1993).

[19]   Matsui et al. 2003.

[20]   Matsui et al. 2003.

site, dating from about 100BC.[21] *Ascaris, Trichuris, Clonorchis* and two other unknown species of trematode eggs were also found in another archaeological site of Korea.[22] Subsequently, as it were in the wake of those initial pioneering forays, a series of studies on the ancient and medieval parasite samples have been initiated in Korea as well.[23]

As was the case in China, rapid archaeoparasitological progress in Korea was spurred by mummy discoveries at first. In general, mummies in the world are either the products of artificial embalming (such as Egyptian mummies) or of natural process under the driest or coldest environments (such as Taklamakan mummies or Otzi the Iceman). In contrast, as cultural tradition and climate conditions in Korea did not favour the mummification of dead persons, the discovery of Korean mummies seems to have been very exceptional. When the Korean mummies were discovered, textile historians carefully removed the clothing first because the mummies were heavily shrouded by them. After the investigation of textile historians was finished, parasitologists started to collect coprolite samples from the Korean mummies (Figure 8.2). To date, there have been twelve cases of such interdisciplinary examinations conducted in Korea (Table 8.1), which showed ancient parasite eggs of *T. trichiura, C. sinensis, Paragonimus westermani*

---

[21] Kwangju National Museum (KNM), 'Shinchang-dong wetland site I: report on the research of antiquities of the Kwangju National Museum', *Kwangju National Museum* 33 (1997): 159–166.

[22] Han, E.T., Guk, S.M., Kim, J.L., Jeong H.J., Kim, S.N., Chai, J.Y., 'Detection of parasite eggs from archaeological excavations in the Republic of Korea', *Memórias do Instituto Oswaldo Cruz* 98 (2003): 123–126.

[23] Seo, M., Oh, C.S., Chai, J.Y., Lee, S.J., Park, J.B., Lee, B.H., Park, J.H., Cho, G.H., Hong, D.W., Park, H.U., Shin, D.H., 'The influence of differential burial preservation on the recovery of parasite eggs in soil samples from Korean medieval tombs', *Journal for Parasitology* 96 (2010): 366–370; Seo, M., Shin, D.H., Guk, S.M., Oh, C.S., Lee, E.J., Shin, M.H., Kim, M.J., Lee, S.D., Kim, Y.S., Yi, Y.S., Spigelman, M., Chai, J.Y., '*Gymnophalloides seoi* eggs from the stool of a 17th century female mummy found in Hadong, Republic of Korea', *Journal for Parasitology* 94 (2008): 467–472; Lee, I.S., Lee, E.J., Park, J.B., Baek, S.H., Oh, C.S., Lee, S.D., Kim, Y.S., Bok, G.D., Hong, J.W., Lim, D.S., Shin, M.H., Seo, M., Shin, D.H., 'Acute traumatic death of a 17th century general based on examination of mummified remains found in Korea', *Annals of Anatomy* 191 (2009): 309–320; Shin, D.H., Chai, J.Y., Park, E.A., Lee, W., Lee, H., Lee, J.S., Choi, Y.M., Koh, B.J., Park, J.B., Oh, C.S., Bok, G.D., Kim, W.L., Lee, E., Lee, E.J., Seo, M., 'Finding ancient parasite larvae in the sample from a male living in the late 17th century Korea', *Journal for Parasitology* 95 (2009a): 768–771; Shin, D.H., Lim, D.S., Choi, K.J., Oh, C.S., Kim, M.J., Lee, I.S., Kim, S.B., Shin, J.E., Bok, G.D., Chai, J.Y., Seo, M., 'Scanning electron microscope study of ancient parasite eggs recovered from Korean mummies of the Joseon Dynasty', *Journal for Parasitology* 95 (2009b): 137–145; Shin, D.H., Oh, C.S., Chung, T.C., Yi, Y.S., Chai, J.Y., Seo, M., 'Detection of parasite eggs from a moat encircling the royal palace of Silla, the ancient Korean Kingdom', *Journal of Archaeological Science* 36 (2009c): 2534–2539.

(lung fluke), *Strongyloides* (threadworm), *Trichostrongylus*, *E. vermicularis*, *A. lumbricoides*, *M. yokogawai*, and *Gymnophalloides seoi.*[24]

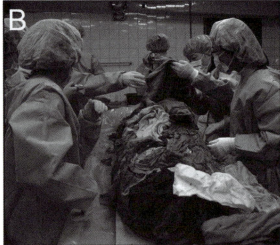

Figure 8.2. A. Finding the Korean mummy at archaeological excavation. B. Removal of shrouds from Korean mummy. After textile specialists carefully removed the clothes, biological sampling was undertaken in the controlled environment of a laboratory.

---

[24]   Seo, M., Guk, S.M., Kim, J.L., Chai, J.Y., Bok, G.D., Park, S.S., Oh, C.S., Kim, M.J., Yi, Y.S., Shin, M.H., Kang, I.U., Shin, D.H., 'Paleoparasitological report on the stool from a medieval child mummy in Yangju, Korea', *Journal of Parasitology* 93 (2007): 589–592; Seo et al. 2008; Seo et al. 2010; Lee et al. 2009; Shin et al. 2009a; Shin et al. 2009b; Oh, C.S., Seo, M., Chai, J.Y., Lee, S.J., Kim, M.J., Park, J.B., Shin, D.H., 'Amplification and sequencing of *Trichuris trichiura* ancient DNA extracted from archaeological sediments', *Journal of Archaeological Science* 37 (2010a): 1269–1273; Oh, C.S., Seo, M., Lim, N.J., Lee, S.J., Lee, E.J., Lee, S.D., Shin, D.H., 'Paleoparasitological report on *Ascaris* aDNA from an ancient East Asian sample', *Memórias do Instituto Oswaldo Cruz* 105 (2010b): 225–228.

Table 8.1　　Parasite eggs observed in coprolites or sediments from
　　　　　　　Joseon mummies

Sample	Parasite	Reference
Yangju child	*Trichuris trichiura*	Seo et al. 2007, ref.24
		Shin et al. 2009b, ref.23
Yangju child	*Ascaris lumbricoides*	Seo et al. 2007, ref.24
Hadong	*Clonorchis sinensis*	Shin et al. 2009b, ref.23
	Clonorchis sinensis	Seo et al. 2008, ref.23
		Shin et al. 2009b, ref.23
Hadong	*Metagonimus yokogawai*	Seo et al. 2008, ref.23
Gangneung Choi	*Gymnophalloides seoi*	Shin et al. 2009b, ref.23
	Trichuris trichiura	Lee et al. 2009, ref.23
Seocheon	*Ascaris lumbricoides*	Seo et al. 2010, ref.23
		Oh et al. 2010b, ref.24
Seocheon	*Trichuris trichiura*	Seo et al. 2010, ref.23
Waegwan	*Clonorchis sinensis*	Oh et al. 2010b, ref.24
		Seo et al. 2010, ref.23
Waegwan	*Trichuris trichiura*	Seo et al. 2010, ref.23
SN 1–2	*Trichuris trichiura*	Seo et al. 2010, ref.23
SN 3–7–1	*Trichuris trichiura*	Seo et al. 2010, ref.23
SN 2–19–1	*Ascaris lumbricoides*	Seo et al. 2010, ref.23
SN 2–19–1	*Trichuris trichiura*	Seo et al. 2010, ref.23
SN 2–19–2	*Trichuris trichiura*	Seo et al. 2010, ref.23
SN 2–19–2	*Ascaris lumbricoides*	Seo et al. 2010, ref.23
HY HM (Yongin)	*Ascaris lumbricoides*	Seo et al. 2010, ref.23
		Shin et al. 2009b, ref.23
HY HM (Yongin)	*Trichuris trichiura*	Seo et al. 2010, ref.23
SN 2–19–2	*Paragonimus westermani*	Shin et al. 2009b, ref.23
	Trichuris trichiura	Oh et al. 2010a, ref.24
SN 2–19–2	*Ascaris lumbricoides*	Oh et al. 2010a, ref.24
Gongju 1–2 (Male)	*Ascaris lumbricoides*	Shin et al. 2009a, ref.23
Gongju 1–2 (Male)	*Trichuris trichiura*	Shin et al. 2009a, ref.23
	Paragonimus westermani	
	Strongyloides stercoralis	
	Trichostrongylus spp.	

　　Recently, archaeoparasitological studies in Korea have begun to be extended to the other types of samples, such as the sediments obtained from archaeological sites. From those studies we know that ancient parasite eggs were found only under very specific archaeological conditions in Korea. Since close correlation could be made between the preservation of ancient parasite eggs and certain types of cultural remains such as textiles, hair, and brain tissue, certain cultural and organic remains discovered in archaeological sites can be used as strong predictors of the existence of well-preserved ancient parasite eggs in the sediments from the same sites.[25] Although the prospect for archaeoparasitology appears to be bright in Korea, the great mass of research remains to be done in order to acquire detailed information about parasite infection patterns in pre-modern Korean society.

Historical Changes in Parasitism

Human parasitism is thought to have dramatically altered at major historical turning points of world civilisation, such as the beginning of agriculture, the domestication of animals, industrialisation and urbanisation. Columbus' discovery of America is a relatively recent example of how human diseases could be affected by changes in the interaction between people living in different regions of the world.[26] There is no reason to believe that the prevalence of certain types of parasitic infection in human populations has remained constant, and it is likely that it has modulated over the long history of social evolution. For instance, parasitism seems to have been less significant in hunter-gatherer bands because infection was limited by the low density of the diffusely scattered, small population groups. In contrast, parasitic infection is believed to have become more common in agricultural and industrial societies where human groups were much more highly concentrated within constricted areas such as towns.[27]

Studies in East Asia also have shown changes in parasitic infection patterns that occurred around the beginning of agriculture. According to researchers in Japan, parasite infection was not prevalent prior to the establishment of agrarian society in the country. Examining sediments from a San-nai Maruyama site (6,000–3,500 BP), they noted the absence of roundworm (*Ascaris*) eggs in the geological strata of non-agrarian Jomon society.[28]The common finding of Ascaris after the introduction of agriculture at Yayoi sites shows how this parasite benefitted from changes in human lifestyle.[29]

Parasitological studies on the coprolites of a 17th century Korean female mummy likewise showed the historical changes in the geographic distribution of parasitic infection.[30] Although *G. seoi*, a trematode parasite, currently was known to be distributed only in two western coastal counties in Korea,[31] we found their

---

[25]   Seo et al. 2010.

[26]   Cohen, M.N., Crane-Kramer, G., 'The state and future of paleoepidemiology', in C. Greenblatt and M. Spigelman (eds), *Emerging Pathogens* (Oxford: Oxford University Press, 2003), pp. 79–91.

[27]   Reinhard and Araújo 2008.

[28]   Matsui et al. 2003.

[29]   Matsui et al. 2003.

[30]   Seo et al. 2008.

[31]   Chai, J.Y., Park, J.H., Han, E.T., Shin, E.H., Kim, J.L., Hong, K.S., Rim, H.J., Lee, S.H., 'A nationwide survey of the prevalence of human Gymnophalloides seoi infection on western and southern coastal islands in the Republic of Korea', *Korean Journal of Parasitology* 39 (2001): 23–30.

eggs in the coprolites of the 17th century female mummy whose home county does not belong to a contemporary *G. seoi*-endemic area.[32] This means either that this person had travelled elsewhere and contracted the parasite, or that only a few centuries ago the distribution of *G. seoi* infection in Korea was not limited to a small area of two small counties as it is today, but might have been widely distributed on the coast of the Korean peninsula. The authors argued that parasitological studies on ancient samples in Korea can be performed not only to confirm the presence of specific parasitic infections in the past, but also to reconstruct the history of the influences of socio-cultural changes upon these diseases.

Researchers in East Asia have also employed biomolecular techniques in order to understand the changes of ancient parasites better. Phylogenetic analysis has been an essential and indispensable tool to those who are interested in the evolution of parasite species.[33] Since parasite eggs from archaeological sites are in a fragile or degraded condition or in relatively small quantities, aDNA extracted from such samples could not be easily analysed until DNA amplification was achievable by means of polymerase chain reaction (PCR). Although aDNA acquired from various parasite species has been much analysed, most of the pertinent studies have been limited to Europe and the Americas.[34] In order to redress this imbalance, parasite aDNA representing a wider geographic range, especially from East Asian countries, has recently been be analszed.[35]

---

[32]   Seo et al. 2008.

[33]   Hofreiter, M., Serre, D., Poinar, H.N., Kuch, M., Pääbo, S., 'Ancient DNA', *Nature Reviews Genetics* 2 (2001): 353–359.

[34]   Guhl, F., Jaramillo, C., Vallejo, G.A., Yockteng, R., Cárdenas-Arroyo, F., Fornaciari, G., Arriaza, B., Aufderheide, A.C., 'Isolation of Trypanosoma cruzi DNA in 4000-year-old mummified human tissue from Northern Chile', *American Journal of Physical Anthropology* 108 (1999): 401–407; Sallares, R., Gomzi, S., 'Biomolecular archaeology of malaria', *Ancient Biomolecules* 3 (2001): 195–213; Loreille, O., Roumat, E., Verneau, O., Bouchet, F., Hänni, C., 'Ancient DNA from *Ascaris*: extraction amplification and sequences from eggs collected in coprolites', *International Journal for Parasitology* 31 (2001): 1101–1106; Iñiguez, A.M., Reinhard, K.J., Araújo, A., Ferreira, L.F., Vicente, A.C.P., 'Enterobius vermicularis: ancient DNA from North and South American human coprolites', *Memórias do Instituto Oswaldo Cruz* 98 (2003): 67–69; Iñiguez, A.M., Reinhard, K., Carvalho Gonçalves, M.L., Ferreira, L.F., Araújo, A., Paulo Vicente, A.C., 'SL1 RNA gene recovery from Enterobius vermicularis ancient DNA in pre-Columbian human coprolites', *International Journal for Parasitology* 36 (2006): 1419–1425; Aufderheide, A.C., Salo, W., Madden, M., Streitz, J., Buikstra, J., Guhl, F., Arriaza, B., Renier, C., Wittmers, L.E., Fornaciari, G., Allison, M., 'A 9000-year record of Chagas' disease', *Proceedings of the National Academy of Sciences of the United States of America* 101 (2004): 2034–2039; Leles, D., Araújo, A., Ferreira, L.F., Vicente, A.C.P., Iñiguez, A.M., 'Molecular paleoparasitological diagnosis of *Ascaris* sp. from coprolites: new scenery of ascariasis in pre-Columbian South America times', *Memórias do Instituto Oswaldo Cruz* 103 (2008): 106–108; Liu et al. 2007.

[35]   Oh et al. 2010a.

The pioneering aDNA study for ancient parasite eggs from East Asia was conducted on *C. sinensis* eggs. An aDNA analysis on the internal transcribed spacers 1 and 2 (ITS1 and ITS2) at rRNA genes was performed on *C. sinensis* eggs taken from the gall bladder of an ancient mummy (buried in 167BC). In the study, although the ITS2 sequences obtained were identical to those from modern eggs of the same species, the authors found differences in 15 nucleotides in ITS1 sequences, demonstrating that the parasite had evolved over the last 2,000 years.[36] *Ascaris* aDNA has also been extracted from a Korean archaeological sample and sequenced. The sample comprised eggs found in sediments within the pelvis of a burial from the tomb of Joseon Dynasty (1392–1910). Two independent labs performed PCR with 18S rRNA (176 bp) and cyt B (98 bp) gene primers, conducting cloning and sequencing for the amplified DNA fragments.[37] This was the first report on *Ascaris* aDNA from an East Asian country, expanding the scope of genetic research on the species.

Amplification and sequencing of aDNA was also performed on an archaeological sample containing ancient *T. trichiura* eggs as well. Since a consensus sequence expressed 100 per cent homology with the contemporary *T. trichiura* in GenBank, but was distinct from that of *T. suis* and *T. muris,* authors showed that the molecular diagnosis of *Trichuris* spp. could be successfully performed by PCR amplification.[38] Archaeoparasitologists also undertook aDNA analysis on *P. westermani* from a 17th century Korean mummy. By microscopic observation, they discovered many eggs of *P. wesermani* in the mummy coprolite samples. When the ITS 2 gene was extracted, amplified and sequenced, they observed 100 per cent homology to the DNA sequences of modern *Paragonimus* from Korea and Japan, forming a cluster distinct from those of South Asian *Paragonimus*. This was the first ever report on ancient *Paragonimus* DNA from any archaeological site in the world. While aDNA analyses in East Asia have confirmed the scientific value of combining PCR-based detection with microscopic diagnosis of ancient parasite eggs,[39] even more detailed approaches to molecular analysis in forthcoming studies on ancient parasite eggs from the East Asian countries are under way.

Cesspits, Sanitation and Parasitism

Effective disposal of human waste was integral to the maintenance of public health in ancient and medieval urban communities. In consequence, parasitological studies in East Asia have expanded beyond the usual issues of the presence or absence of parasite eggs in coprolites to incorporate historical sanitary conditions in densely populated areas.

---

36 Liu et al. 2007.
37 Oh et al. 2010b.
38 Oh et al. 2010a.
39 Oh et al. 2010a; Oh et al. 2010b.

Collaborative archaeological/parasitological studies have documented efforts of historical East Asian societies to remove human waste from densely populated areas of the past. Actually, the removal of 'night soils' (human faeces) should have been one of the top priorities for ancient and medieval peoples living in large towns or cities. For example, when the sanitary conditions in a pre-agrarian settlement were examined by Japanese researchers, they found many human coprolites in Jomon shell middens but none at any of the other Jomon sites surveyed. The Jomon people, then, were likely to have defecated habitually onto shell midden, leaving the night soil subject only to natural decomposition.[40] However, the transition from pre-agrarian Jomon to full-agrarian Yayoi society, with the attendant advances in rice farming techniques and accompanying explosive population growth did not result in significant changes in disposal habits of night soils. Judging from the available archaeological evidence, very few toilets seem to have been constructed in the Yayoi villages. Human waste continued to be discharged into settlement-encircling moats, the special utility of which some researchers believed to have been the washing away of excrement during the rainy season.

An archaeoparasitological study at a royal palace in Korea made us rethink the ancient moat's role in East Asia once again.[41] Based on the historical records, royal families of the ancient Silla Dynasty (57BC–935AD) lived in Weolseong palace until the complete abandonment of the city in the 10th century AD.[42] Our archaeological excavation raised the question as to how human waste from the royal residences was disposed. The most probable answer is by use of a sewage canal that drained waste from toilets to the outside. Our discovery of many *Trichuris* eggs in the 8th century moat-floor sediments at Weolseong palace supports the hypothesis that toilet contents were continuously flushed through the sewage canal into the moat surrounding the ancient palaces.[43] This was further supported by archaeological evidence of a similar sewage canal discovered in the royal palace of the ancient Baekje Kingdom.[44] Even if moats encircling settlements in East Asia were designed originally for defensive purposes,[45] human excrement came to be allowed to accumulate in the stagnant water there, resulting in serious sanitary problems. Certainly, if the situation had deteriorated to this point, those living

---

[40]   Matsui et al. 2003.

[41]   Shin et al. 2009c.

[42]   Chang, K.H., *Gyeongju Weolseong eui josayeonguwa yeoksajeok euieui. Symposium of Gyeongju National Research Institute of Cultural Heritage. Gyeongju Weolseong eui eojewa oneul, gurigo mirae* (Gyeongju: Gyeongju National Research Institute of Cultural Heritage, 2007), pp. 9–22.

[43]   Shin et al. 2009c.

[44]   Buyeo National Research Institute of Cultural Heritage, *The Achievement and Significance of Excavation on the Wanggungri Site in Iksan* (Buyeo: Buyeo National Research Institute of Cultural Heritage, 2009), p. 428.

[45]   Kanazawa, I., Miyatake, Y., 'Insect remains', in *The Preliminary Report of the Excavations of Ikegami-Sone Site* (Osaka: Board of Education, Osaka Prefectural Government, 1990), pp. 107–16; Matsui et al. 2003.

in a settlement encircled by such a moat had to endure the spread of pathogens, obnoxious smells, and proliferations of mosquitoes.[46]

As an effective means of alleviating pollution caused by human wastes, the ancient Korean people devised an improved moat-drainage system comprising water inlets and outlets, which allowed for continuous unidirectional water flow drawn mostly from a nearby mountain area.[47] Similar water-flow arrangements might have been also provided for ancient Nara, one of the ancient capitals in Japan. Drainage gutters were dug alongside the streets, efficiently carrying rainwater and sewage away from every corner of the capital. The system seems to have functioned very well, particularly in light of the evidence showing other cities following Nara's lead.[48] Effective sanitation by means of flowing-water removal of excrement evidently might have been a high-priority of urban-planning for some ancient East Asian cities.

East Asian researchers also have studied the structure of toilets that were discovered in archaeological sites. Generally, upon the discovery of possible toilet remains at archaeological sites, parasitologists tried to confirm if any parasite eggs were extant in the relevant sediments. Based on affirmative answers, the egg-positive sites were intensively investigated by archaeologists, and finally toilet structures begin to be evaluated. Previous reports confirmed the existence of flushing toilets at East Asian archaeological sites. They found an advanced flushing toilet at ancient Makimuku site (dating from the early 3rd century AD) where human excrement seemed to have been washed away by water flow. Similar flushing toilets utilising water flow through a wooden conduit were also identified at ancient site of Nara in Japan.[49] In comparison, the use of constant-flow water to flush toilets has been archaeologically proven in the famous Roman aqueducts and public flushing toilets. Water was supplied in two channels, one for flushing, and the other for rinsing one's bottom.[50] This means that flushing toilets might have been commonly constructed in ancient societies around the world.

Meanwhile, considering that agrarian societies in East Asia must have used human excrement as a fertiliser, the cesspit toilet might also have been used as a good fertiliser store. The farmers must have carried away night soil from cesspit toilets to their farmlands.[51] In fact, a number of cesspit toilets have been discovered in archaeological sites in East Asia. In 2004, Korean archaeologists also found ancient toilets at the Wanggungri site, the royal palace of the ancient

---

[46]   Shin et al. 2009c.

[47]   Shin et al. 2009c.

[48]   Matsui et al. 2003.

[49]   Matsui et al. 2003.

[50]   Vuorinen, H.S., Juuti, P.S., Katko, T.S., 'History of water and health from ancient civilization to modern times', *Water Science & Technology* 7 (2007): 49–57; Vuorinen 2009.

[51]   Kurosaki, S., *The Toilet Features of the Fujiwara Palace Site* (Nara: Nabunken, 1992); Matsui et al. 2003.

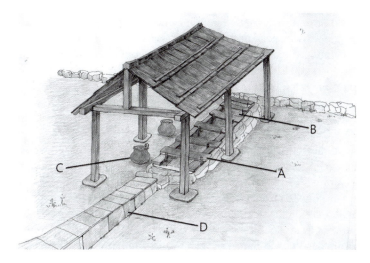

Figure 8.3.   Reconstructed toilet of Wanggungri, Korea. A, footholds; B,
cesspit; C, pot for cleaning device; D, drain connecting the toilet
to the outside of the royal residence. Courtesy of Buyeo National
Research Institute of Cultural Heritage.

Baekje Kingdom in the 7th century. Parasitological examination on the sediments
from the toilet-like structures showed many eggs of *Ascaris, Trichuris* and
Clonorchis spp. The archaeological sequence suggests that the ancient Korean
people dug the cesspit, erected pillars around it, and finally formed the toilet block
over it. One of the most interesting structures found at Wanggungri site was a
sewage canal connecting the toilets to the land outside the royal residence. Dirty
water from the toilets was likely to have been directed through it. Among the three
toilets discovered in the royal residence, the largest one was measured at 10.8
m in length, 1.8 m in width, and 3.4 m in depth. Judging from the presence of
small blocks within, it seems to have been used simultaneously by people of lower
social status. Another toilet was apparently reserved for use by dignitaries (Figure
8.3).[52] It appears that the efforts of archaeoparasitologists have been able to clarify
academic debates on the toilet structures in ancient East Asian towns and cities.

Prospects for Archaeoparasitology in East Asia

As a research tool for tracing sanitary practices and conditions in the past,
archaeoparasitological study has a long history. Even though the studies have
explored common questions on the biogeography and endemicity of parasite

---

[52]   Buyeo National Research Institute of Cultural Heritage 2009.

infections that have a relevance to public health,[53] each continent and country has developed independent academic traditions. Among these, we have summarised the history of archaeoparasitological studies on sanitation and parasitism in East Asian contexts. Even if archaeoparasitology in East Asian countries remains in its relative infancy, the findings so far represent a great start in efforts to answer questions as to how the pre-modern peoples in the region derived community-managed sanitation schemes to live better and healthier lives in such densely populated towns and cities.

Despite the encouraging achievements of East Asian archaeoparasitologists, we should note that most previous reports have concentrated on agrarian societies in Korea, Japan and China. Therefore, to acquire broader knowledge for archaeoparasitology regarding this area in the past, new studies should be extended to the nomadic and hunter-gatherer peoples in other sub-regions of the area. For example, studies of archaeological samples from North Asia (e.g., Siberia) might demonstrate differences in parasitological infection patterns compared with East Asian (agrarian) counterparts, thereby enriching our knowledge of sanitation and parasitism in human society as a whole. While there is clearly a long way to go, archaeoparasitology in East Asia is a quickly developing science nowadays, promising a bright future for research in each country.

Acknowledgements

This study was supported by the Conservation Technology Research and Development project funded by the National Research Institute of Cultural Heritage Administration (NRICH-1207-B03F).

---

[53]   Reinhard and Araújo 2008.

Chapter 9

New World Paleoparasitology

Adauto Araújo, Luiz Fernando Ferreira, Martin Fugassa, Daniela Leles,
Luciana Sianto, Sheila Maria Mendonça de Souza, Juliana Dutra,
Alena Iñiguez, Karl Reinhard

Introduction

The study of parasites found in archaeological material began with Sir Marc Ruffer in Egypt, when he described *Schistosoma haematobium* (bilharzia) eggs in mummies dated to 5,200 BP (before present).[1] Years later, in Europe, Lothar Szidat reported finding *Trichuris trichiura* (whipworm) and *Ascaris lumbricoides* (roundworm) eggs in the mummified bodies of a man and a girl found in a swamp in Prussia, dated to 600BC and 500AD.[2] However, it was up to researchers in the Americas to make important strides in the field of parasitic infections in archaeological remains. The initial work of Thomas Cameron and Eric Callen in coprolites from the Huaca Prieta archaeological site in Peru, introducing trisodium phosphate 0.5 per cent aqueous solution for rehydration of coprolites, based on the technique of van Cleave and Ross for recovering desiccated invertebrate specimens conserved in museums, allowed more advanced studies on parasites preserved in archaeological material.[3]

Initially, parasite findings in archaeological material reflected the sporadic collaboration between archaeologists and parasitologists, in which they described the parasites found and gave an interpretation of the findings. Pizzi and Schenone commented on finding *Trichuris trichiura* eggs and *Entamoeba coli* cysts in intestinal material from the mummified body of a child from the Inca period, preserved in ice in the Andes.[4] They raised the erroneous hypothesis that *Trichuris trichiura* infection had originated in the Americas. However, as highlighted by Szidat, trichuriasis

---

[1]   Ruffer, M.A., 'Note on the presence of *Bilharzia haematobia* in Egyptian mummies of the twentieth dynasty', *British Medical Journal* 1 (1910): 16.

[2]   Szidat, L., 'Uber die erhaltungsfahigkeit von helmintheneiern in vorand friihgeschichtlichen moorleichen', *Zeitschrift für Parasitenkunde* 13 (1944): 265–74.

[3]   Callen, E.O., Cameron, T.W.M., 'The diet and parasites of pre-historic Huaca Prieta Indians as determined by dried coprolites', *Proceedings of the Royal Society of Canada* 7 (1955): 51–2; Callen, E.O., Cameron, T.W.M., 'A prehistoric diet revealed in coprolites' *New Scientist* 8 (1960): 35–40; Van Cleave, H.J. Ross, J.A., 'A method for reclaiming dried zoological specimens', *Science* 105 (1947): 318.

[4]   Pizzi, T., Schenone, H., 'Hallazgo de huevos de *Trichuris trichiura* en contenido intestinal de un cuerpo arqueológico incaico' *Boletin Chileno de Parasitologia* 9 (1954): 73–5.

had already been recorded in the Old World at an earlier archaeological date than this mummy.[5]

The term paleoparasitology originated in Brazil with Luiz Fernando Ferreira, who was studying parasites in archaeological material at the Oswaldo Cruz Foundation.[6] This branch of parasitology and paleopathology, which also ended up as part of bioarchaeology, was created with the aim of establishing methods and techniques to study parasites found in archaeological material and paleontological material of both human and animal origin. The central objective is to study the origin and evolution of parasitic infections, with the definition of parasites including viruses, bacteria, protozoa, helminths, arthropods, fungi, and other forms of life that find their ecological niche in a given host.[7]

The study of infectious diseases has changed the previously accepted concepts on the origin of various organisms in the Americas. For example, it had been thought that tuberculosis was introduced by the arrival of the Europeans, and particularly in South America by the first Jesuit priests that came in the early colonial period in search of a healthy climate, not only to catechise, but to treat their own illness, whereby they ended up infecting the indigenous peoples. However, *Mycobacterium tuberculosis* infection, with its clinical manifestations, already existed in pre-Columbian America, as shown by findings in mummified bodies in Chile and Peru, as well as in other populations on the continent.[8]

Early 20th-century publications implicated the African slave trade in the introduction of a series of parasitic diseases, including intestinal parasites, but without any concrete evidence.[9] These concepts began to be challenged by methods from ethnographic and comparative parasitology, as reported by Olympio da Fonseca in studying fungal and hookworm infections and lice infestation among indigenous groups isolated from contact in South America, as previously shown by

------

[5]   Szidat 1944.

[6]   Ferreira, L.F., Araújo, A., Confalonieri, U., 'Subsídios para a paleoparasitologia do Brasil 1. Parasitos encontrados em coprólitos no município de Unaí, Minas Gerais', Abstracts, IV Congresso Brasileiro de Parasitologia, Campinas, (São Paulo, 1979), p. 56; Ferreira, L.F., Araújo, A., Confalonieri, U., 'Finding of helminth eggs in human coprolites from Unai, Minas Gerais, Brazil', *Transactions of the Royal Society of Tropical Medicine and Hygiene* 76 (1980): 798–800.

[7]   Ferreira, L.F., 'O fenômeno parasitismo', *Revista da Sociedade Brasileira de Medicina Tropical* 4 (1973): 261–77; Araújo, A., Jansen, A.M., Bouchet, F., Reinhard, K., Ferreira, L.F., 'Parasitism, the diversity of life, and paleoparasitology', *Memórias do Instituto Oswaldo Cruz* 98 (Suppl. 1) (2003): 5–11.

[8]   Prati, J.G., Souza, S.M.M., 'Prehistoric tuberculosis in America: adding comments in a literature review', *Memórias do Instituto Oswaldo Cruz* 98 (Suppl. 1) (2003): 151–9; Wilbur, A.K., Buikstra, J.E., 'Patterns of tuberculosis in the Americas: how can modern biomedicine inform the ancient past?', *Memórias do Instituto Oswaldo Cruz* 101 (Suppl. 2) (2006): 59–66.

[9]   Freitas, O., '*Doenças Africanas no Brasil*', Bibliotheca Pedagogica Brasileira, Brasiliana volume 51, série V, (São Paulo: Cia Editora Nacional, 1935), p. 21–30.

Samuel Darling and Fred Soper.[10] They were searching for data to use the presence of parasites in isolated groups as an indication of prehistoric migrations. Harold Manter reviewed the studies on hookworm infection, concluding that it would be very difficult to reach a definitive conclusion on pre-Columbian migrations, due to the lack of fossil parasites.[11] The only other research possibilities available at that time were based upon the written evidence of chroniclers from the colonial period, and artistic representations left by pre-Columbian peoples.[12]

However, the parasites found in present-day isolated human groups, the artistic representations, and other archaeological vestiges may not accurately reflect situations from the remote past. Contacts would have been possible between groups with different origins, and traces of such contacts could have survived until the present. For example, one should consider the territorial disputes between indigenous groups on the Brazilian coast at the time of the discovery and the retreat of the defeated groups into the interior, with the possible dispersal of parasites.[13]

Parasites preserved in archaeological material help answer questions as to the existence (or absence) of given parasitic infections in pre-Columbian populations.[14] However, other questions emerge, like those raised by Leles et al. on the under-diagnosis of *Ascaris lumbricoides* eggs in coprolites from South American archaeological sites.[15] As shown by paleoparasitological data (Tables 9.1 and 9.2, at the end of this chapter), most helminth infections were already widespread among pre-Columbian groups in both South America and North America.[16]

---

[10]   Fonseca Filho, O., 'Parasitological and clinical relationship between Asiatic and Oceanian tokelau and Brazilian chimbere of some Mato Grosso Indians' *Boletim do Museu Nacional* 6 (1930): 201–21; Fonseca Filho, O., *Parasitismo e Migrações Pré-Históricas* (Rio de Janeiro: Mauro Familiar Editora, 1972); Darling, S.T., 'Observations on the geographical and ethnological distribution of hookworms', *Parasitology* 12 (1921): 217–233; Soper, F., 'The report of a nearly pure *Ancylostoma duodenale* infestation in native South American Indians and a discussion of its ethnological significance', *American Journal of Hygiene* 7 (1927): 174–84.

[11]   Manter, H.W., 'Some aspects of the geographical distribution of parasites', *Journal of Parasitology* 53 (1967): 2–9.

[12]   Jarcho, S., 'Some observations on diseases in prehistoric North America', *Bulletin of the History of Medicine* 38 (1964): 1–19.

[13]   Medeiros, R.P., 'Povos indígenas do sertão nordestino no período colonial: descobrimento, alianças, resistência e encobrimento', *FUMDHAmentos* 2 (2002): 7–52.

[14]   Araújo, A., Ferreira, L.F., Confalonieri, U., 'A contribution to the study of helminth findings in archaeological material in Brazil', *Revista Brasileira de Biologia* 41 (1981): 873–81.

[15]   Leles, D., Araújo, A., Ferreira, L.F., Vicente, A.C.P., Iñiguez, A.M., 'Molecular paleoparasitological diagnosis of *Ascaris* sp. from coprolites: new scenery of ascariasis in pre-Colombian South America times', *Memórias do Instituto Oswaldo Cruz* 103 (2008): 106–8.

[16]   Ferreira et al. 1980; Ferreira, L.F., Araújo, A., Confalonieri, U., 'The finding of helminth eggs in a Brazilian mummy', *Transactions of the Royal Society of Tropical Medicine and Hygiene* 77 (1983): 65–7; Gonçalves, M.L.C., Araújo, A., Ferreira,

When the human species emerged in Africa and migrated outside the continent to colonise other parts of the world, it included individuals infected by parasite species inherited from their ancestors. However, new species of parasites were acquired over the course of their evolution, when human groups established themselves in new territories other than those from which they originated. Plants and animals were domesticated, and further parasite species started to infect humans when new habitats were settled and contacts with parasites from animal hosts were established. Parasite transfers occurred, and new species adapted to their human hosts as they occupied each new environment and territory.[17] *Homo sapiens* is indisputably one of the most successful species on Earth, having explored and dominated nearly everywhere on the planet. The history of the human species' long journey out of Africa to conquer new territories is extraordinary, but the history of the parasites that were transferred with us, and of others acquired over the course of our highly peculiar species' biological and social history, still remains to be studied in detail.

The parasite discoveries in archaeological material given here is intended to provide information on the conquest of the Americas in prehistoric times and on the way of life of the different human groups that lived there. Parasites can be used as tracers, or probes, of human migrations in the past and can indicate health and disease conditions in human groups during the human evolutionary process.[18] New approaches such as molecular biology techniques applied to diagnosis in paleoparasitology and imaging diagnosis in paleopathology, combined with traditional microscopic diagnostic techniques, have demonstrated parasite findings as biological markers of prehistoric migrations and health conditions in ancient

---

L.F., 'Human intestinal parasites in the past: new findings and a review', *Memórias do Instituto Oswaldo Cruz* 98 (Suppl. 1) (2003): 103–18; Fry, G.F., Moore, J.G., '*Enterobius vermicularis*: 10,000-year-old human infection', *Science* 166 (1969): 1620; Horne, P.D., 'A review of the evidence of human endoparasitism in the pre-Columbian New World through the study of coprolites', *Journal of Archaeological Science* 12 (1985): 299–10; Reinhard, K., 'Parasitology as an interpretative tool in archaeology', *American Antiquity* 57 (1992): 231–45; Reinhard, K.J., Anderson, G.A.A., Hevly, R.H., 'Helminth remains from prehistoric coprolites on the Colorado Plateau', *Journal of Parasitology* 73 (1987): 630–39.

   17   Kliks, M.M., 'Paleoparasitology: on the origins and impact of human-helminth relationships', in N.A. Croll and J.H. Cross (eds), *Human Ecology and Infectious Disease* (New York: Academic Press, 1983), pp. 291–313; Araújo, A., Reinhard, K., Ferreira, L.F., Gardner, S., 'Parasites as probes for prehistoric human migrations?', *Trends in Parasitology* 24 (2008a): 112–15; Araújo, A., Reinhard, K., Ferreira, L.F., 'Parasite findings in archaeological remains: diagnosis and interpretation', *Quaternary International* 180 (2008b): 1–4.

   18   Araújo et al. 1981; Araújo et al. 1988; Araújo et al. 2008a; Reinhard, K., Araújo, A., Ferreira, L.F., Coimbra, C.E., 'American hookworm antiquity', *Medical Anthropology* 20 (2001): 96–101.

populations.[19] They provide quite solid information and contribute to more precise knowledge of the past.

This article only considers infections and diseases caused by helminths and protozoa in the human host or with the potential to infect it, emphasising intestinal parasites that infected pre-Columbian populations and those introduced after the arrival of Europeans and Africans. Araújo et al. and Horne have previously reviewed intestinal helminthiases in pre-Columbian America, while Reinhard, Gonçalves et al., and Fugassa have also written subsequent evaluations.[20] However, new data continue to emerge, and in consequence our knowledge and understanding of the field is improving all the time.

Prehistoric Populations in the Americas, Paleoparasitology, and Paleoepidemiology

The New World is known as such because it was one of the last territories on Earth to be discovered and colonised by Europeans. However, America had been discovered long before the Europeans arrived. Peoples from Asia and possibly other parts of the world reached the continent many thousands of years ago.[21]

---

[19]   Iñiguez, A.M., Reinhard, K.J., Araújo, A., Ferreira, L.F., Vicente, A.C.P., '*Enterobius vermicularis*: ancient DNA from North and South American human coprolites', *Memórias do Instituto Oswaldo Cruz* 98 (Suppl. 1) (2003): 67–9; de Souza, S.M.M., 'Millenary Egyptian mummies – non invasive excursions', in H. Werner Jr. and J. Lopes (eds), *3D Technologies – Palaeontology, Archaeology, Fetology* (Rio de Janeiro: Livraria & Editora Revinter LTDA, 2009), pp. 77–104; Reinhard et al. 1987; Araújo, A., Reinhard, K., Bastos, O.M., Costa, L.C., Pirmez, C., Iñiguez, A.M., Vicente, A.C., Morel, C.M., Ferreira, L.F., 'Paleoparasitology: perspectives with new techniques', *Revista do Instituto de Medicina Tropical de São Paulo* 40 (1998): 371–76; Bouchet, F., Harter, S., Le Bailly, M., 'The state of the art of paleoparasitological research in the Old World', *Memórias do Instituto Oswaldo Cruz* 98 (Suppl. 1) (2003): 95–101.

[20]   Araújo et al. 1981; Horne 2005; Reinhard, K.J., 'Archaeoparasitology in North America', *American Journal of Physical Anthropology* 82 (1990): 145–63; Gonçalves et al. 2003; Fugassa, M.H., *Enteroparasitosis en Poblaciones Cazadoras-Recolectoras de Patagonia Austral* (PhD Thesis, Universidad Nacional de Mar del Plata, Argentina, 2006).

[21]   Meltzer, D.J., 'Peopling of North America', *Development in Quaternary Science* 1 (2003): 539–63; Neves, W.A., Hubbe, M., Pilo, L.B., 'Early Holocene human skeletal remains from Sumidouro Cave, Lagoa Santa, Brazil: history of discoveries, geological and chronological context, and comparative cranial morphology', *Journal of Human Evolution* 52 (2007): 16–30; Guidon, N., Pessis, A.M., 'Serra da Capivara National Park, Brazil: cultural heritage and society', *World Archaeology* 39 (2007): 406–16; Hubbe, M., Neves, W.A., Amaral, H.L., Guidon, N., '"Zuzu" strikes again: morphological affinities of the early Holocene human skeleton from Toca dos Coqueiros, Piaui, Brazil', *American Journal of Physical Anthropology* 134 (2007): 285–91; Pucciarelli, H.M., González-José, R., Neves, W.A., Sardi, M.L., Rozzi, F.R., 'East-West cranial differentiation in pre-Columbian populations from Central and North America', *Journal of Human Evolution* 54

The human groups that lived in South America before the European discovery were quite diversified, considering those living on the Pacific coast, like the Chichorro, and those on the Atlantic, builders of shell mounds (*sambaquis*). Between the two coasts there was a wide variety of cultures, as exemplified especially by various prehistoric populations in the Andean altiplanos with their constructions and social organisations, in contrast with the groups of hunter-gatherers and Neolithic agriculturalists living on the lowlands on the other side of the Andean cordillera, on the plains, in the scrub forest (*caatinga*), in the Chaco region on the coast, and in the cold southernmost regions or the hot rainforest.[22]

It is difficult to obtain consistent data for epidemiological studies of infectious diseases in ancient populations. It is more difficult, and in most cases impossible, to assess the impact of parasitic infections in hunter-gatherer populations, since representative samples of these populations in archaeological remains are extremely rare due to the absence of specific locations such as funeral sites, and latrines were not built in the region at that early date. In consequence, samples that are representative of prehistoric infectious disease events are rare. More common are series of human remains such as skeletons or scattered bones of different individuals, in which one can attempt to study diseases from pathological lesions on the skeletal remains.[23]

In order to advance this field, new approaches have been developed in paleoepidemiology, through the study of diseases in the past using a population focus.[24] Even so, paleoepidemiology provides a paleoreconstruction of what may have occurred in extinct populations. However, paleoparasitological methods have begun to contribute concrete evidence retrieved from archaeological or paleontological remains, adding data on the presence of parasitic infections in ancient populations to the biological knowledge of each parasite found. For example, recent contributions from the use of molecular biology techniques for

(2008): 296–30; Gaspar, M.D., Deblasis, P., Fish, S.K., Fish, P.R., 'Sambaqui (shell mound) societies of coastal Brazil', in H. Silverman and W.H. Isbell (eds), *Handbook of South American Archaeology* (New York: Springer, 2008), pp. 319–35; Dillehay, T., 'Probing deeper into first American studies', *Proceedings of the National Academy of Science of the United States of America* 106 (2009): 971–78.

22   Silverman, H., Isbell, W.H. (eds), *Handbook of South American Archaeology* (New York: Springer, 2008).

23   De Souza, S.M., de Carvalho, D.M., Lessa, A., 'Paleoepidemiology: is there a case to answer?', *Memórias do Instituto Oswaldo Cruz* 98 (Suppl. 1) (2003): 21–7.

24   El-Najjar, M.Y., Lozof, B., Ryan, D.J. 'The paleoepidemiology of porotic hyperostosis in the American Southwest: radiographical and ecological considerations', *American Journal of Roentgenology Radium Therapy Nuclear Medicine* 125 (1975): 918–25; Buikstra, J., Cook, D., 'Paleopathology: an American account', *Annual Review of Anthropology* 9 (1980): 433–70; de Souza et al. 2003; D'Anastasio, R., Staniscia, T., Milia, M.L., Manzoli, L., Capasso, L., 'Origin, evolution and paleoepidemiology of brucellosis', *Epidemiology and Infection* 7 (2010): 1–8.

parasite diagnosis in archaeological material, such as *Trypanosoma cruzi* infection, have shown that the latter may be as old as human presence in the Americas.[25]

The number of individuals in each prehistoric group varied in the different regions, and thus the conditions for the circulation of parasites and their population prevalence rates also varied. However, even with few individuals in each group, there was contact between them, and the conditions were created for given parasitic diseases to circulate, considering the population as a whole in a given region, as exemplified by the shell mounds (*sambaquis*) on the Brazilian coast. Gaspar et al. showed that on the southeast Brazilian coast, the shell mound inhabitants maintained contact between groups, which would have facilitated parasite circulation.[26]

Many of the human groups that inhabited the Andean region, both on the coast and the altiplano, culturally preserved their dead. Some artificially mummified them, such as the Chinchorro, while others offered their children and youth as sacrifices, preserving them magnificently by mummifying them in extremely cold and dry conditions.[27] Other groups living on the eastern side of the continent had a diversity of burial rituals. Some practised cremation, others transferred the bodies for secondary burial, and a few practised anthropophagic rituals.[28] Therefore, the remains vary greatly, but do not prevent tracing the impact of infectious diseases in these populations, as long as the cultural context is clearly known.[29]

In North America, an example is provided by the human groups that comprised the Ancestral Pueblo or Anasazi in the Southwest United States, including southern

---

[25]   Guhl, F., Jaramillo, C., Vallejo, G.A., Yockteng, R., Cardenas-Arroyo, F., Fornaciari, G., Arriaza, B., Aufderheide, A.C., 'Isolation of *Trypanosoma cruzi* DNA in 4,000-year-old mummified human tissue from northern Chile', *American Journal of Physical Anthropology* 108 (1999): 401–07; Ferreira, L.F., Britto, C., Cardoso, M.A., Fernandes, O., Reinhard, K., Araújo, A., 'Paleoparasitology of Chagas disease revealed by infected tissues from Chilean mummies', *Acta Tropica* 75 (2000): 79–84; Aufderheide, A.C., Salo, W., Madden, M., Streitz, J., Buikstra, J., Guhl, F., Arriaza, B., Renier, C., Wittmers Jr, L.E., Fornaciari, G., Allison, M., 'A 9,000-year record of Chagas' disease', *Proceedings of the National Academy of Sciences of the United States of America* 101 (2004): 2034–9; Lima, V.S., Iñiguez, A.M., Otsuki, K., Ferreira, L.F., Araújo, A., Vicente, A.C.P., Jansen, A.M., 'Chagas disease by *Trypanosoma cruzi* lineage I in a hunter-gatherer ancient population in Brazil', *Emerging Infectious Diseases* 14 (2008): 1001–2; Araújo, A., Jansen, A.M., Reinhard, K., Ferreira, L.F., 'Paleoparasitology of Chagas disease: a review', *Memórias do Instituto Oswaldo Cruz* 104 (2009): 9–16.

[26]   Gaspar et al. 2008.

[27]   Arriaza, B., *Beyond Death: the Chinchorro Mummies of Ancient Chile* (Washington, DC: 1995); Arriaza, B., Standen, V.G., Cassman, V., Santoro, C.M., 'Chinchorro culture: pioneers of the coast of the Atacama Desert' in H. Silverman and W.H. Isbell (eds), *Handbook of South American Archaeology* (New York: Springer, 2008), pp. 45–58.

[28]   Vilaça, A.M.N., 'Relations between funerary cannibalism and warfare cannibalism: the question of predation', *Ethnos* (Stockholm) 65 (2000): 83–106.

[29]   De Souza et al. 2003.

Utah and Colorado and northern Arizona and New Mexico. Exploring a semi-arid region, these groups adapted to the environment, leaving evidence of their use of natural resources and cultivated plants. In addition, by building elaborate housing on the rocky cliffs and plains, they also left latrine structures that they used to deposit faeces, leaving material that has only recently been appreciated as a source of priceless information on diet, environment, and parasitic infections, obtained by analysing the archaeological remains.[30]

The faeces found in archaeological or paleontological sites are called coprolites, and they can be preserved in mineralised or desiccated form, in this case whether in very dry, hot, or cold environments or in acid pH conditions, as in the European peat bogs. However, coprolites are not the only source for studying parasites. The soil sediments contained in the pelvic region of skeletons, on the surface of bones preserved in museums, as well as in sediments with organic content and discarded utensils, have shown the potential of studying parasites in various types of material found in archaeological sites.[31] Mummified bodies have been examined with imaging diagnostic techniques, facilitating the localisation of coprolite remains and avoiding unnecessary damage to the material.[32]

Paleoparasitological data show that many of the intestinal helminth infections found most commonly around the world at present already existed among prehistoric human groups in the Americas and were distributed relatively homogeneously among them.[33] However, whether transmitted through the consumption of wild game or domestic animals, other parasites were found to infect populations in the Americas and can be used as indicators of epidemiological transitions from the pre- to post-contact periods. Fugassa showed that among the groups that lived in the far South of Patagonia, the predominant parasite eggs were from animals eaten by these groups, while in coprolites and sediments from skeletons of Europeans, the predominant infection was with the roundworm *Ascaris lumbricoides*.[34]

Sianto et al. showed the potential for human infection with intestinal helminths from animals, such as *Echinostoma* sp., found in coprolites retained in

---

[30]   Reinhard 1990.

[31]   Reinhard, K.J., Geib, P.R., Callahan, M.M., Hevly, R.H., 'Discovery of colon contents in a skeletonized burial: soil sampling for dietary remains', *Journal of Archaeological Science* 19 (1992): 697–705; Shafer, H.J., Marek, M., Reinhard, K.J., 'Mimbres burial with associated colon remains from the NAN Ranch Ruin, New Mexico', *Journal of Field Archaeology* 16 (1989): 17–30; Fugassa, M.H., Sardella, N.H., Guichón, R.A., Denegri, G.M., Araújo, A., 'Paleoparasitological analysis applied to skeletal sediments of meridional Patagonian collections', *Journal of Archaeological Science* 35 (2008a): 1408–11; Harter, S., Le Bailly, M., Janot, F., Bouchet, F., 'First paleoparasitological study of an embalming rejects jar found in Saqqara, Egypt', *Memórias do Instituto Oswaldo Cruz* 98 (Suppl. 1) (2003): 119–21.

[32]   De Souza 2009.

[33]   Gonçalves et al. 2003.

[34]   Fugassa 2006.

megacolon lesions in a partially mummified body dated to 600 BP.[35] *Trypanosoma cruzi* infection was diagnosed in this same individual using molecular biology techniques, confirming a case of Chagas disease, an anthropozoonosis in groups of potter-farmers in central Brazil.[36]

Helminthiases and Intestinal Protozooses in Prehistoric America

Enterobius Vermicularis (Pinworm)

One of the most widely distributed parasites in all regions of the world occupied by humans is the pinworm nematode *Enterobius vermicularis*, with variable prevalence rates in different population groups.[37] *Enterobius vermicularis* infection can be transmitted directly from human host to host through the ingestion of eggs, without necessarily contaminating the soil. The female worms, when gravid and full of eggs, migrate to the perianal region where they release their eggs, which can contaminate the environment or the host's own hands, since the infection is characterised by perianal itching. The larvae also penetrate the anus, returning to the large intestine. External climate conditions have little or no influence on host-to-host transmission.

Enterobius vermicularis infection is believed to have originated in Africa and spread to other regions, accompanying the migratory process of human populations.[38] There are records of this parasitosis in North American

---

[35] Sianto, L., Reinhard, K.J., Chame, M., Mendonça, S., Gonçalves, M.L.C., Fernandes, A., Ferreira, L.F., Araújo, A., 'The finding of *Echinostoma* (Trematoda: Digenea) and hookworm eggs in coprolites collected from a Brazilian mummified body dated 600–1,200 years before present', *Journal of Parasitology* 91 (2005): 972–5; Sianto, L., Chame, M., Silva, C.S.P., Gonçalves, M.L.C., Reinhard, K., Fugassa, M.H., Araújo, A., 'Animal helminths in human archaeological remains: a review of zoonoses in the past', *Revista do Instituto de Medicina Tropical de São Paulo* 51 (2009): 119–30.

[36] Fernandes, A., Iñiguez, A.M., Lima, V.S., Souza, S.M., Ferreira, L.F., Vicente, A.C., Jansen, A.M., 'Pre-Columbian Chagas disease in Brazil: *Trypanosoma cruzi* I in the archaeological remains of a human in Peruaçu Valley, Minas Gerais, Brazil', *Memórias do Instituto Oswaldo Cruz* 103 (2008): 514–16.

[37] Gale, E.A.M., 'A missing link in the hygiene hypothesis?', *Diabetologia* 45 (2002): 588–94.

[38] Hoeppli, R., *Parasites and Parasitic Infection in Early Medicine and Science* (Singapore: University of Malaya Press, 1959), pp. 27–28, and 157; Hugot, J.P., Reinhard, K., Gardner, S.L., 'Human enterobiasis in evolution: origin, specificity and transmission', *Parasite* 6 (1999): 201–08; Reinhard, K.J., 'Cultural ecology of prehistoric parasitism on the Colorado Plateau as evidenced by coprology', *American Journal of Physical Anthropology* 77 (1988a): 355–66; Reinhard 1990; Araújo et al. 2008a; Glen, D.R., Brooks, D.R., 'Parasitological evidence pertaining to the phylogeny of the hominoid primates', *Biological Journal of the Linnean Society* 27 (2008): 331–54.

archaeological sites dated to as far back as 10,000 BP.[39] The record shows that pinworms intermittently infected ancient hunter-gatherers. After agriculture was established, pinworm became a constant and common parasite of Ancestral Pueblo people who inhabited the apartment-like villages. The crowding of people in these ancient villages promoted infection.[40] Indeed, pinworm prevalence in coprolites may serve as the best proxy indicator of levels of infectious disease.[41]

The same contrast was found in the number of *Enterobius vermicularis* eggs (Figure 9.1) per gram of faeces in coprolites of nomad and farmer-herder populations in sites in the Atacama Desert in northern Chile, dated to 6,000 BP.[42] Santoro et al. found an increase in pinworm prevalence after the Inca moved dispersed farmers into large villages in the Lluta River Valley near Arica, Chile.[43] However, it is surprising that the results are negative thus far for *Enterobius vermicularis* eggs in archaeological sites in Brazil.[44]

Refinement of the diagnosis has been possible with the use of molecular biology techniques. In some of the samples that tested negative on microscopic examination, it was possible to retrieve genetic material from this parasite, thus expanding its distribution in archaeological sites.[45] These analyses yielded haplotypes that showed different geographic origins for this parasite in the human groups that inhabited archaeological sites on the Pacific coast of Chile compared with desert sites in Arizona, United States.[46] However, even with molecular biology techniques, the evidence for *Enterobius vermicularis* infection in Brazilian sites is still negative thus far.

Due to its mechanism of transmission, *Enterobius vermicularis* or pinworm infection was able to accompany the prehistoric migrations from Africa during the peopling of the American continent, crossing the land and ice bridge at the

---

[39]   Fry and Moore 1969.

[40]   Reinhard, K.J., Bryant, V.M., 'Pathoecology and the future of coprolite studies', in A.W.M. Stodder (ed.), *Reanalysis and Reinterpretation in Southwestern Bioarchaeology* (Tempe: Arizona State University, 2008), pp. 199–216.

[41]   Reinhard 1992.

[42]   Ferreira, L.F., Araújo, A., Confallonieri, U., Nuñez, L., 'Infecção por *Enterobius vermicularis* em populações agro-pastoris pré-colombianas de San Pedro de Atacama, Chile', *Memórias do Instituto Oswaldo Cruz* 84 (suppl. 4) (1989a): 197–99.

[43]   Santoro, C., Vinton, S.D., Reinhard, K.J., 'Inca expansion and parasitism in the Lluta Valley: preliminary data', *Memórias do Instituto Oswaldo Cruz* 98 (suppl. 1) (2003): 161–3.

[44]   Araújo, A., Ferreira, L.F., Confalonieri, U., Nunez, L., Ribeiro Filho, B.M., 'The finding of *Enterobius vermicularis* eggs in pre-Columbian human coprolites', *Memórias do Instituto Oswaldo Cruz* 80 (1985): 141–43.

[45]   Iñiguez et al. 2003.

[46]   Iñiguez, A.M., Reinhard, K., Gonçalves, M.L.C., Ferreira, L.F., Araújo, A., Paulo Vicente, A.C., 'SL1 RNA gene recovery from *Enterobius vermicularis* ancient DNA in pre-Columbian human coprolites', *International Journal for Parasitology* 36 (2006): 1419–25.

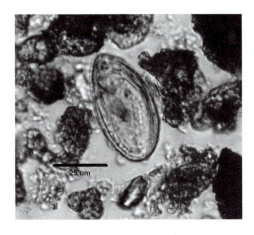

Figure 9.1.
Pinworm egg found in a human coprolite dated to the beginning of agriculture, Tulán 54, San Pedro de Atacama, Chile.

Bering Strait.[47] However, the evidence of two distinct prehistoric haplotypes in the ancient Americas could mean that pinworm arrived with two distinct prehistoric migrations.

The Introduction of Other Geohelminthiases

Other helminth species that also originated in our African ancestors could not have been introduced by this same route. This was due to the cold climatic conditions in the Bering Strait region that would have been hostile for the life cycle of the intermediate forms of the parasite while they matured in the soil.[48] Hookworms or Ancylostomidae (*Necator americanus, Ancylostoma duodenale*), threadworms (*Strongyloides stercoralis*), whipworms (*Trichuris trichiura*) and roundworms (*Ascaris lumbricoides)* are parasites known as geohelminths, whose life cycle necessarily includes a passage through soil and for which the temperature and humidity conditions are relatively restricted for their transmission.[49] Since they are helminth parasites that seem to have originated in the Old World, finding them in archaeological sites in America marks events involving a non-frozen environment and occupations that facilitate faecal contamination of hands or food.

Araújo et al. reviewed the geohelminth infections in prehistoric American populations and concluded that they can be used as markers of migrations by their human hosts.[50] They showed that hookworms (Figure 9.2), whose oldest

---

[47] Araújo et al. 2008b.

[48] Araújo et al. 1981; Araújo et al. 2008a; Araújo et al. 2008b.

[49] Camillo-Coura, L., 'Control of soil-transmitted helminthiasis: co-ordinated control projects' in D.W.T. Compton, M.C. Nesheim and Z.S. Pawlowski (eds), *Ascariasis and its Public Health Significance* (London: Taylor and Francis, 1985), pp. 253–63.

[50] Araújo et al. 2008a.

archaeological examples in the Americas go back 7,000 years,[51] must have been introduced by other migratory routes, not the Bering Strait Crossing.[52] Montenegro et al. simulated the paleoclimatic conditions for the Bering Strait Crossing where the migrants crossed during the peopling of the continent and concluded that the conditions were unfit for maintaining the hookworm life cycle.[53] The proposed alternatives are seafaring contacts or sailing across the Aleutian Islands, which would have allowed access to regions with appropriate conditions for the hookworm life cycle some 7,000 years ago.[54]

As for *Ascaris lumbricoides*, there is interesting speculation as to whether the infection originated from a swine parasite species or, on the contrary, whether the parasite began to infect swine after their domestication by humans.[55] Findings of *Ascaris* sp. eggs in France dated to 30,000 BP led to the hypothesis that *Ascaris* sp. of swine origin emerged later than that of human origin.[56] *Ascaris* sp. is a parasite commonly found in Old World archaeological sites, especially from Medieval Europe.[57] *Ascaris* sp. egg findings have also been reported in Asian countries, like China, Japan, and Korea, in samples mainly from mummified bodies and sediment from latrines and cesspits.[58] In Japan, this parasite's origin is associated with

---

[51]   Ferreira, L.F., Araújo, A., Confalonieri, U., Chame, M., Ribeiro, B.M., 'Encontro de ovos de ancilostomideos em coprólitos humanos datados de 7.230 +/- 80 anos, Piauí, Brasil' *Anais da Academia Brasileira de Ciencias* 59 (1987): 280–81.

[52]   Araújo et al. 1981; Araújo et al. 2008a; Reinhard et al. 2001.

[53]   Montenegro, A., Araújo, A., Eby, M., Ferreira, L.F., Heatherington, R., Weaver, A., 'Parasites, paleoclimate and the peopling of the Americas: Using the hookworm to time the Clovis migration', *Current Anthropology* 47 (2006): 193–200.

[54]   Araújo et al. 2008a.

[55]   Loreille, O., Bouchet, F., 'Evolution of ascariasis in humans and pigs: a multidisciplinary approach', *Memórias do Instituto Oswaldo Cruz* 98 (Suppl. 1) (2003): 39–46.

[56]   Bouchet, F., Baffier, D., Girard, M., Morel, P., Paicheler, J.C., David, F., 'Paléoparasitologie en contexte pléistocène: premières observations à la Grande Grotte d'Arcy-sur-Cure (Yonne), France', *Comptes Rendus de l'Académie des sciences* 319 (1996): 147–51.

[57]   Gonçalves et al. 2003; Bouchet et al. 2003.

[58]   Wei, O., 'Internal organs of a 2100-year-old female corpse', *The Lancet* 7839 (1973): 1198; Liangbiao, C., Tao, H., 'Scanning electron microscopic view of parasites worm ova in an ancient corpse', Acta Academica Sinicae 3 (1981): 64–5; Yang, W.Y., Wei, D.X., Song, G.F., Wu, Z.B., Teng, R.S., 'Parasitologic investigations on the ancient corpse of Chu dynasty the warring states unearthed from the Ma-zhuan tomb No. 1, Jiangling County', Acta Academiae Medicinae Wuhan 14 (1984): 43–45; Cheng, T.O., 'Glimpses of the past from the recently unearthed ancient corpses in China', Annals of Internal Medicine 101 (1984): 714–5; Su, T.C., 'A scanning electron microscopic study on the parasite eggs in an ancient corpse from a tomb of Chu Dynasty, the Warring State, in Jiangling County, Hubei Province', Journal of Tongji Medical University 7 (1987): 63–4; Han, E.T., Guk, S.M., Kim, J.L., Jeong, H.J., Kim, S.N., Chai, J.Y., 'Detection of parasite eggs from archaeological excavations in the Republic of Korea', Memórias do Instituto Oswaldo Cruz 98 (Suppl. 1) (2003): 123–26; Matsui, A., Kanehara, M., Kanehara, M., 'Paleoparasitology

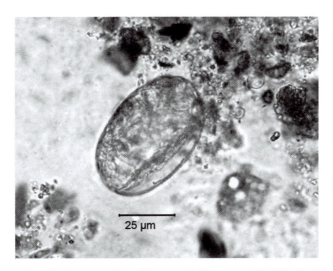

Figure 9.2.   Hookworm egg found in a partially mummified body dated 560 ± 40 BP from Peruaçu Valley, Minas Gerais, Brazil.

the introduction of rice farming by the Chinese.[59] In the last decade, molecular diagnosis has contributed to the study of this parasitosis in Europe, South America and Asia.[60] Recently, the use of molecular biology techniques and the possibility of comparing paleoepidemiology and modern epidemiology of the infection enabled us to improve our understanding of the origin of *Ascaris* sp. infection, and helped to conclude that *Ascaris lumbricoides* and *Ascaris suum* are a single species (named *Ascaris lumbricoides* as a priority name), infecting both humans and pigs.[61]

---

in Japan - discovery of toilet features', Memórias do Instituto Oswaldo Cruz 98 (Suppl. 1) (2003): 127–36.

[59]   Matsui et al. 2003.

[60]   Loreille, O., Roumat, E., Verneau, O., Bouchet, F., Hänni, C., 'Ancient DNA from *Ascaris*: extraction amplification and sequences from eggs collected in coprolites', *International Journal for Parasitology* 31 (2001): 1101–6; Leles et al. 2008; Seo, M., Guk, S.M., Kim, J., Chai, J.Y., Bok, G.D., Park, S.S., Oh, C.S., Kim, M.J., Yi, Y.S., Shin, M.H., Kang, I.U., Shin, D.H., 'Paleoparasitological report on the stool from a medieval child mummy in Yangju, Korea', *Journal of Parasitology* 93 (2007): 589–92; Shin, D.H., Chai, J.Y., Park, E.A., Lee, W., Lee, H., Lee, J.S., Choi, Y.M., Koh, B.J., Park, J.B., Oh, C.S., Bok, G.D., Kim, W.L., Lee, E., Lee, E.J., Seo, M., 'Finding ancient parasite larvae in a sample from a male living in late 17th century Korea', *Journal of Parasitology* 95 (2009): 768–71; Oh, C.S., Seo, M., Lim, N.J., Lee, S.J., Lee, E.J., Lee, S.D., Shin, D.H., 'Paleoparasitological report on *Ascaris* aDNA from an ancient East Asian sample', *Memórias do Instituto Oswaldo Cruz* 105 (2010b): 225–8.

[61]   Leles, D., Reinhard, K., Fugassa, M., Ferreira, L.F., Iñiguez, A.M., Araújo, A., 'A parasitological paradox: why is ascarid infection so rare in the prehistoric Americas?', *Journal of Archaeological Sciences* 37 (2010): 1510–20; Leles, D., Gardner, S.L.,

Intestinal Protozoa

Finding the cysts or other forms of intestinal parasitic protozoa in coprolites in the Americas is very rare.[62] Using serological techniques such as ELISA (enzyme-linked immunosorbent assays), some diagnoses have been made.[63] These show the presence of *Entamoeba histolytica* and *Giardia intestinalis* infection in human coprolites recovered from sites in Arizona.

Reviewing Diagnoses in the Paleoparasitological Record

The record of parasite species recovered from archaeological sites is large. Studies have been undertaken by a diverse range of specialists ranging from archaeologists to archaeobotanists to parasitologists. The research has appeared in a variety of formats ranging from unpublished theses, to site reports, to book chapters and peer-reviewed journal articles. Over the years, hypothesis and biases have changed. For example, early researchers were reluctant to report hookworm evidence in the Americas as such because there was a prevailing belief in the parasitological community that hookworm could not be present. This was eliminated in the classic debate between Ferreira et al. and Kliks.[64] However, earlier discoveries were either modified by the discoverer or greeted with trepidation by peer reviewers. For this reason, some parasitologists preferred to publish the detailed descriptions of their finds at a higher taxonomic level of 'strongylate nematode' rather than risk misidentification. Other finds are mentioned in archaeological texts with reference to an opinion of a parasitologist, but where no other detailed publication of that parasitologist exists. Therefore, some published records are simply anecdotal.

Reinhard, K., Iñiguez, A.M., Araújo, A., 'Are Ascaris lumbricoides and Ascaris suum a single species?' *Parasites & Vectors* 5 (2012): 42.

[62] Gonçalves et al. 2003; Fugassa, M.H., Sardella, N.H., Taglioretti, V., Reinhard, K., Araújo, A., 'Morphometric variability in oocysts of *Eimeria macusaniensis* (Guerrero et al. 1967) in archaeological samples from the Holocene of Patagonia, Argentina', *Journal of Parasitology* 94 (2008b): 1418–20.

[63] Gonçalves, M.L.C., Araújo, A., Duarte, R., Pereira da Silva, J., Reinhard, K., Bouchet, F., Ferreira, L.F., 'Detection of *Giardia duodenalis* antigen in coprolites using a commercially available enzyme-linked immonosorbent assay', *Transactions of the Royal Society of Tropical Medicine and Hygiene* 96 (2002): 640–43; Gonçalves, M.L.C., da Silva, V.L., de Andrade, C.M., Reinhard, K., da Rocha, G.C., Le Bailly, M., Bouchet, F., Ferreira, L.F., Araujo, A., 'Amoebiasis distribution in the past: first steps using an immunoassay technique', *Transactions of the Royal Society of Tropical Medicine and Hygiene* 98 (2004): 88–91; Allison, M.J., Bergman, T., Gerszten, E., 'Further studies on fecal parasites in antiquity', *American Journal of Clinical Pathology* 112 (1999): 605–09; Ortega, Y.R., Bonavia, D., '*Cryptosporidium, Giardia*, and *Cyclospora* in ancient Peruvians', *Journal of Parasitology* 89 (2003): 635–36.

[64] Ferreira et al. 1980; Ferreira et al. 2003; Klicks 1983.

Discoveries of parasites in unusual circumstances, for example tropical parasites in arctic sites or northern hemisphere species in South American sites, should be presented as provisional.

We are taking the opportunity here to present potential biases in the parasitological record from the Americas. Because of these considerations noted above, it is important to approach the record with a degree of healthy scepticism. We feel that the most secure identifications are those that have been accomplished by a trained parasitologist who has sought independent evaluation of his/her diagnoses. The secure identifications should be presented in a peer-reviewed outlet to ensure that errors are caught. Identifications should be accompanied by full analyses with illustrations.

A case in point is Reinhard and Clary's report of *Strongyloides* in the Chaco Canyon burials.[65] This report has several areas that could have been improved, and we can be honest about these as Reinhard (a co-author of this article) was a co-author of this Chaco Canyon paper. Firstly, it was completed at a time when the conventional wisdom stated that hookworm could not have been a prehistoric parasite in the Americas. As a master's student in 1984, Reinhard considered the importance of conventional wisdom compelling. Therefore, Reinhard did not include hookworm species in the differential diagnosis of the third stage larvae that he identified. Secondly, the identification was not independently evaluated by another parasitologist. Thirdly, the results were published in an unreviewed book. Recognising these deficiencies, Reinhard is currently having the same samples from the 1986 study re-examined independently by trained parasitologists as part of a re-evaluation of his past work aimed at eliminating the bias of changing conventional wisdom in his record of discoveries. The list of finds in Table 9.2 is annotated for some identifications that may be mistaken due to analyst bias.

There are anecdotal accounts in the older literature that have never been properly published in detail. A first example is the note of an acanthocephalan egg found in a coprolite excavated from Black Mesa, Arizona.[66] The note is not accompanied by any details of the analysis of the coprolite. Indeed, there is no substantiation that the coprolite is human. No independent paper was published on the egg. Therefore, this case is anecdotal and should be viewed as highly provisional. Another example is the Daws Island hookworm recovered from a coprolite.[67] There is some description of the find, but the specimen was sent

---

[65]   Reinhard, K.J., Clary, K.H., 'Parasite analysis of prehistoric coprolites from Chaco Canyon', in N.J. Akins (ed.), *A Biocultural Approach to Human Burials from Chaco Canyon, New Mexico* (Santa Fe: National Park Service, 1986), pp. 177–86.

[66]   Gummerman, G.J., Westfall, D.A., Weed, C.S., *'Archaeological Investigations on Black Mesa: The 1969–1970 Seasons* (Arizona: Prescott College Pr., 1972).

[67]   Rathbun, T.A., Sexton, J., Michie, J., 'Disease patterns in a formative period South Carolina coastal population', in P. Willey and F.H. Smith (eds), *The Skeletal Biology of Aboriginal Populations in the Southeastern United States* (Knoxville: Tennessee Anthropological Association, 1980), pp. 53–74.

to a parasitology lab and no publication appeared. Therefore, this too should be regarded as a provisional diagnosis.

We also present as provisional those case studies that report a parasite species at locations extensively studied by other parasitologists who did not report the same species, especially of common parasites. For example, Goncalves et al. reported an *Ascaris lumbricoides* egg from the Ancestral Puebloan site of Antelope House, Canyon de Chelly, Arizona.[68] Previously, four studies by various authors had all failed to note *Ascaris* at this site.[69] The discovery by Goncalves in the same coprolites analysed by other parasitologists suggest that either *Ascaris* sp. was extremely rare, or that one or more of them were in error. For this reason, the *Ascaris lumbricoides* egg found by Goncalves must be considered as provisional until verified by independent examination.

Discoveries of parasites in unexpected locations are always sensational. The cases of Allison et al.'s long-ignored discovery of hookworm in a pre-Inca Peruvian mummy and Ferreira et al.'s hotly debated hookworm discovery are cases in point.[70] Indeed, 20 years after their publication, these discoveries were still the focus of debate.[71] The lesson learned from this is that discoveries in unusual locales must be thoroughly described and verified by independent analyses. An example of a fully documented discovery in an unusual location is the Buldir Island hookworm.[72] Although peer-reviewed, the surprising nature of the discovery of parasites in an Arctic midden needs to be verified, especially as no images of this parasite were included in the paper.

It is important for readers to be aware that some work is being undertaken by untrained parasitologists on a contractual level. The work can be erroneous. For example, one such contractor reported the find of *Diphyllobothrium latum* eggs in prehistoric Chile.[73] The researchers seem to be unaware of the probability

---

[68]   Gonçalves et al. 2003.

[69]   Reinhard 1992; Fry, G., Hall, H.J., 'Human coprolites from Antelope House: preliminary analysis', *Kiva* 41 (1975): 87–96; Fry, G.F., Hall, H.J., 'Human coprolites', in D.P. Morris (ed.), *Archaeological Investigations at Antelope House* (Washington, DC: National Park Service, 1986), pp. 165–88; Reinhard et al. 1987.

[70]   Allison, M.J., Pezzia, A., Hasegawa, I., Gerszten, E., 'A case of hookworm infestation in a pre-Columbian American', *American Journal of Physical Anthropology* 41 (1974): 103–6; Ferreira et al. 1980; Ferreira et al. 1983.

[71]   Fuller, K., 'Hookworm: not a pre-Columbian pathogen', *Medical Anthropology* 17 (1997): 297–308.

[72]   Bouchet, F., Lefèvre, C., West, D., Corbett, D., 'First paleoparasitological analysis of a midden in the Aleutian Island (Alaska): results and limits', *Journal of Parasitology* 85 (1999): 369–72.

[73]   Cummings, L.S., Nepstad-Thornberry, C., Puseman, K., *Paleofeces from the Ramaditas Site in Northern Chile: Addressing Middle to Late Formative Period Diet and Health* (1999). Unpublished manuscript on file with Paleo Research Institute and Beloit College, Beloit, Wisconsin Stable. URL: http://core.tdar.org/document/378500, DOI: doi:10.6067/XCV8TQ60WS

that this species, which infects freshwater fish, did not exist in prehistoric Chile. Alternatively, *D. pacificum* is very common in the area from eating saltwater fish. Simple morphological examination of the eggs is used to separate the two species. The report mistakenly proposed that the prehistoric inhabitants were infected by eating lake fish. It specifies that the prehistoric people habitually fish in high Andean lakes. Of course, trained parasitologists realise that in South America diphyllobothriids did not infect lake fish in prehistoric times. Unfortunately, the archaeologist who paid for the work does not have this training and their interpretation of prehistory is being distorted by error. Contract workers do not publish their work, and therefore such errors cannot be caught in the peer-review system. Therefore, researchers must be aware that erroneous finds can be generated from the contract archaeology world.

Health Consequences of Parasitic Disease

A major potential contribution by paleoparasitology to studies of the occupation of archaeological sites relate to the standards of health of the human groups that lived there. In the past there have been few papers attempting to determine the effect of intestinal parasites upon the health of prehistoric populations.[74] This is a challenging area, as it can be difficult to determine whether one population was healthier than another from the study of just their skeletal remains.[75] When it comes to specific lesions on the skeleton, there is debate as to whether the bony lesions of porotic hyperostosis on the skull vault and cribra orbitalia in the skull orbits may be caused by different types of anaemia, and whether they may be a result of anaemia secondary to intestinal helminths.[76]

While it can be very difficult to establish paleoepidemiological parameters that can answer these questions, it is not always impossible. When favourable conditions for preservation are found, as in the archaeological sites in the southwestern United States, it is possible to gather data capable of shedding some light on the health and disease of individuals in a population.[77] In this case, the archaeoparasitological reconstruction produced data on the way of life of these

---

[74]   Reinhard 1992.

[75]   Wood, J.W., Milner, G.R., Harpending, H.C., Weiss, K.M., 'The osteological paradox: problems of inferring prehistoric health from skeletal samples', *Current Anthropology* 33 (1992): 343–58.

[76]   Martinson, E., *Assessing the Etiology of Cribra Orbitalia and Porotic Hyperostosis: A Case Study of the Chiribaya of the Osmore Drainage, Peru* (University of New Mexico: PhD Thesis, 2002); Walker, P.L., Bathurst, R.R., Richman, R., Gjerdrum, T., Andrushko, V.A., 'The causes of porotic hyperostosis and cribra orbitalia: a reappraisal of the iron-deficiency-anemia hypothesis', *American Journal of Physical Anthropology* 139 (2009): 109–125.

[77]   Reinhard and Bryant 2008; Reinhard, K.J., Araújo, A., Sianto, L., Costello, J.G., Swope, K., 'Chinese liver flukes in latrine sediments from Wong Nim's property, San

populations by exploiting evidence for parasitic infections. There seem to have been differences in the exposure to hookworm and pinworm infections in order to explain variation in the number of eggs found in coprolites studied by Reinhard.[78] One possible hypothesis is that children and women stayed longer inside the dwelling places, but the men wandered in search of game, leaving them less exposed to geohelminth infections.[79]

In South American archaeological sites, several hypotheses have been tested on the health and disease conditions of pre-Columbian populations. In the prehistoric groups that lived in the Atacama Desert, their exceptionally good preservation means that some inferences are possible on the relationship between the environment and the parasitic infections that affected them. Based on the El Niño climate phenomenon and its intermittent occurrence, as well as the parasite cycle in fish and mammals, it was possible to speculate on the prevalence of *Diphyllobothrium pacificum* infection at different moments in the past.[80] This tapeworm (cestode) has its life cycle in crustaceans, fish, and marine mammals in the Pacific Ocean, and it has the potential to infect humans when they eat contaminated fish. The larvae contained in the fish flesh develop into adult worms in the human intestine, reaching some 1 to 10 meters in length. They attach themselves to the intestinal mucosa and can cause discomfort, leading to complaints of abdominal pain. *Diphyllobothrium pacificum* infection was first noted in prehistoric populations that lived in Peru and Chile, and it proved to have been common in other prehistoric groups on the Pacific coast.[81] A combined study of climate factors generated by the El Niño phenomenon in the past and the presence of marine fish species led to the hypothesis of fluctuation in this infection's prevalence among prehistoric groups at different points in time, based upon the presence of different intermediate host fish species and the human host.[82]

Research began in Patagonia, attempting to determine moments of change, or epidemiological transitions, in the disease process before and after contact with

---

Bernardino, California: archaeoparasitology of the Caltrans District Headquarters', *Journal of Parasitology* 94 (2008): 300–3.

[78]   Reinhard, K.J., 'Effects of parasitism on Ancestral Pueblo maternal and infant health', *American Journal of Physical Anthropology* Suppl. 40 (2004): 179.

[79]   Reinhard 1988a.

[80]   Arriaza, B., Reinhard, K., Araújo, A., Orellana, N.C., Standen, V.G., 'Possible influence of the ENSO phenomenon on the pathoecology of diphyllobothriasis and anisakiasis in ancient Chinchorro populations', *Memórias do Instituto Oswaldo Cruz* 105 (2010): 66–72.

[81]   Patrucco, R., Tello, R., Bonavia, D., 'Parasitological studies of coprolites of pre-Hispanic Peruvian populations', *Current Anthropology* 24 (1983): 393–94; Ferreira, L.F., Araújo, A., Confalonieri, U., Nuñez, L., 'The finding of *Diphyllobothrium pacificum* in human coprolites (4100–1950 BC) from Northern Chile', *Memórias do Instituto Oswaldo Cruz* 79 (1984): 175–80; Santoro et al. 2003.

[82]   Arriaza et al. 2010.

the European colonists.[83] The prehistoric groups from the southernmost region of the American continent were exceptionally well adapted to the environment, but differed from each other in relation to the interactions that allowed them to subsist by exploring diverse ecosystems, such as the seacoast and the fields of Patagonia.[84] The paleoparasitological evidence shows changes beginning at the time of contact with the Europeans.[85] Human coprolites from sites in Patagonia yielded parasites resulting from the ingestion of animals infected with parasites, both capable of causing infection or disease in humans, called zoonoses, or simply parasites indicating the ingestion of animals, but incapable of establishing themselves in the human host.[86] The model used for prehistoric groups in Patagonia is very interesting and provides consistent information on the way of life of these populations and the changes brought by contact with the Europeans.

Considering the available information for Patagonia, it is possible to formulate paleoepidemiological scenarios, and, based on them, to consider the risks associated with various biocultural situations in diverse ecosystems and periods in the Holocene. It should be possible to interpret the evidence as it gradually accumulates, and to then improve our models. Based on ecological strategies of parasite dispersal,[87] criteria were defined to assess which aspects of biocultural information on human groups that existed in Patagonia during the Holocene could be relevant for the occurrence of various parasites. This required a broad approach to anthropological, archaeological, historical and ethnographic knowledge of the region.

According to conditions of agglomeration and mobility, tropism, the ecosystem occupied, and cultural behaviour (for example, hygiene, habitat and preparation of foods), a general table can be constructed that indicates probability of infection

---

[83]   Fugassa, M., Guichón, R.A., 'Modelos paleoepidemiológicos para el Holoceno patagónico', *7th Jornadas de Arqueología de la Patagonia*. 21–25 April 2008, Conference Proceedings Abstracts (Ushuaia, 2008), p. 30.

[84]   Borrero, L.A., 'Human dispersal and climatic conditions during Late Pleistocene times in Fuego-Patagonia', *Quaternary International* 53–53 (1999): 93–99; Guichón, R.A., Suby, J.A., Casali, R., Fugassa, M.H., 'Health at the time of Native-European contact in Southern Patagonia: first steps, results, and prospects', *Memórias do Instituto Oswaldo Cruz* 101 (Suppl. 2) (2006): 97–05.

[85]   Fugassa, M.H., Araújo, A., Guichón, R.A., 'Quantitative paleoparasitology applied to archaeological sediments', *Memórias do Instituto Oswaldo Cruz* 101 (suppl. 2) (2006): 29–33.

[86]   Fugassa et al. 2008b; Fugassa, M.H., Beltrame, M.O., Sardella, N.H., Civalero, M.T., Aschero, C., 'Paleoparasitological results from coprolites dated at the Pleistocene-Holocene transition as source of paleoecological evidences in Patagonia', *Journal of Archaeological Science* 37 (2010a): 880–4; Fugassa, M.H., Reinhard, K.J., Johnson, K.L., Gardner, S.L., Vieira, M., Araújo, A., 'Parasitism of prehistoric humans and companion animals from Antelope Cave, Mojave County, Northwest Arizona', *Journal of Parasitology* 97 (2011): 862–867.

[87]   Fugassa et al. 2006; Fugassa and Guichón 2008.

by groups of parasites. The dichotomous ordering of the factors identified and described thus far has provided various combinations that are interpreted as possible scenarios for parasite paleoepidemiology in Patagonia.[88] In general, the epidemiology of human groups in Patagonia is quite different from that of groups in other regions, as a result of the climate and biocultural conditions. Widely diverse and unusual parasite forms were able to infect human groups in Patagonia, including species that were able to proliferate due to favourable biocultural habits. The diversity of parasite forms found in hunter-gatherers in Patagonia offers a complex panorama that can be underestimated by conventional paleopathological studies, which emphasise just a few parasitoses that cause bone lesions from anaemia. Morbidity models, based upon more exhaustive models of occurrence, are needed to improve these theoretical proposals. Thus far, the empirical evidence brought by paleoparasitology is consistent with these models.

Parasites of Animals in Humans

Despite the difficulties involved in a paleoepidemiological approach to prehistoric groups in Brazil, a study was attempted in archaeological sites in the Serra da Capivara National Park in the semi-arid region of Northeast Brazil. With the retrieval of a considerable number of human and animal coprolites, it was possible to evaluate different parasitic infections in periods ranging from 30,000 BP to historical times and to estimate potential zoonotic infections in the region. The results showed that in addition to infections with intestinal helminths more common to humans, there was the potential for infections with specific animal helminths with the capacity to infect the human host.[89]

These studies on animal parasites found in humans demonstrate the use of food resources, often with the ingestion of the animal host whole and raw (without any cooking). Cases of ingestion of potential parasite vectors have also been recorded, like fragments of arthropods found in coprolites, showing their ingestion, intentional or not, by the human host.[90] Both Fugassa and Sianto et al. reviewed cases of animal parasites found in archaeological sites in the Americas.[91] In the case of animal parasites in human coprolites, it is necessary to distinguish between true infections, in which the parasite installs itself and lays eggs and

---

[88]   Fugassa and Guichón 2008.

[89]   Sianto, L., '*Parasitismo em Populações Pré-Colombianas: Helmintos de Animais em Coprólitos de Origem Humana do Parque Nacional Serra da Capivara, PI, Brasil*', (Escola Nacional de Saúde Pública, Fundação Oswaldo Cruz, Rio de Janeiro: PhD Thesis, 2008).

[90]   Johnson, K.L., Reinhard, K., Sianto, L., Araújo, A., Gardner, S.L., Janovy Jr, J., 'A tick from a prehistoric Arizona coprolite', *Journal of Parasitology* 94 (2008): 296–98.

[91]   Fugassa 2006; Sianto et al. 2009.

leaves larvae, from cases of pseudo-parasitism, in which eggs are found in the faeces, but infection does not occur and the eggs disappear within a few days.

As an example of pseudo-parasitism, *Calodium* sp. (*Capillaria* sp.) eggs have been found in coprolites in Argentina and in modern-day indigenous communities in Brazil.[92] Humans can be infected by two routes: by ingesting the poorly cooked flesh of wild animals, in which pseudo-parasitism occurs, or by ingesting embryonated eggs present in the soil, leading to capillariasis, which is usually fatal. Carvalho-Costa et al. recently identified a case of pseudo-parasitism in an 85-year-old woman in a community of indigenous descent in the Upper Rio Negro in the Brazilian Amazon.[93] Since the woman had eaten tapir (*Tapirus terrestris*) meat just a few days before the stool test and this animal had been identified as a host for the parasite, the authors concluded that tapir was the source of the infection.

Conclusion

In prehistoric America, evidence has been shown for the presence of helminths that originated in the Old World and that accompanied their human hosts along migrations across the continents, as well as for the presence of other types of parasite that they encountered while exploring their new environment. Paleoparasitology has the ability to retrace the various events in which these disease transfers occurred, in addition to identifying moments of change in parasitic infections due to contacts between different human ethnic groups, especially when Europeans conquered the American continent. Together with paleogeography, paleoparasitology is capable of situating parasitic infections in human groups in time and space and tracing their paths in prehistory. In combination with paleoepidemiology, paleoparasitology helps us to reconstruct possible scenarios that explain the impact of parasitic diseases on the ancient inhabitants of the Americas.

---

[92] Fugassa, M.H., Araújo, A., Sardella, N., Denegri, G.M., 'New paleoparasitological finding in caves from Patagonia, Argentina', *Paleopathology Newsletter* 137 (2007): 17–21; Fugassa, M., Taglioretti, V., Gonçalves, M.L.C., Araújo, A., Sardella, N.H., Denegri, G.M., '*Capillaria* spp. findings in Patagonian archaeological sites: statistical analysis of morphometric data', *Memórias do Instituto Oswaldo Cruz* 103 (2008c): 104–5; Lawrence, D.N., Neel, J.V., Abadie, S.H., Moore, L.L., Adams, L.J., Healy, G.R., Kagan, I.G., 'Epidemiologic studies among Amerindian populations of Amazonia III. Intestinal parasitoses in newly contacted and acculturating villages', *American Journal of Tropical Medicine and Hygiene* 29 (1908): 530–7; Coimbra Jr, C.E.A., Mello, D.A., 'Enteroparasites and *Capillaria* sp. found in Indians of the Suruí group, Parque Indígena Aripuanã, Rondônia', *Memórias do Instituto Oswaldo Cruz* 76 (1981): 299–302.

[93] Carvalho-Costa, F.A., Silva, A.G., Souza, A.H., Moreira, C.J.C., Souza, D.L., Valverde, J.G., Jaeger, L.H., Martins, P.P., Meneses, V.F., Araújo, A., Bóia, M.N., 'Pseudoparasitism by *Calodium hepaticum* (syn. *Capillaria hepatica*; *Hepaticola hepatica*) in the Negro River, Brazilian Amazon', *Transactions of the Royal Society of Tropical Medicine and Hygiene* 103 (2009): 1071–3.

Acknowledgements:

In memoriam, Patrick Horne. Research funding provided by CNPq, FAPERJ, PRONEX/FAPERJ, and CAPES/CNPq-Ciência sem Fronteiras

Table 9.1   Intestinal parasites found in coprolites and other human archaeological remains in North America

Parasite Species	Date	Location	Reference
Cestoda			
Diphyllobothrium	1400–1700AD	Aleutian Islands, USA	Bouchet et al. 1999, ref.72
Diphyllobothrium latum	300BC–200AD	Saginaw Valley, Michigan, USA	McClary 1972, ref.94
Diphyllobothrium pacificum	1070–1150AD	Adak Island, Alaska USA	Bouchet et al. 2001, ref.94
	3700–3490BC	Village of Namu, Fitz Hugh Sound, British Columbia, Canada	Bathurst 2005*, ref.94
Hymenolepidid cestode	?	Antelope House, Arizona, USA	Reinhard 1988a, ref.38
	?	Elden Pueblo, Arizona, USA	Hevly et al. 1979, ref.94
	1175–1250AD	Antelope House, Arizona, USA	Reinhard et al. 1987, ref.16
	1070–1250AD	Elden Pueblo, Arizona, USA	Reinhard et al. 1987, ref.16
Other Cestode	5330–250BC	Hogup Cave, Utah, USA	Fry 1977, ref.94
	20AD	Danger Cave, Utah, USA	Fry 1977, ref.94
	1070–1250AD	Elden Pueblo, Arizona, USA	Reinhard et al. 1987, ref.16
	1250–1300AD	Glen Canyon, Utah, USA	Fry 1977, ref.94
	1700–1800AD	Newport, Rhode Island, USA	Reinhard et al. 1986, ref.65
Taeniid cestode	1600–1700AD	Ferryland site Newfoundland, Canada	Horne & Tuck 1996, ref.94
		Elden Pueblo, Arizona, USA	Hevly et al. 1979, ref.94
		Schultz site, Michigan, USA	McClary 1972, ref.94
		Danger Cave, USA	Fry 1977, ref.94
		Rio Zape, Durango, Mexico	New finding
	Middle Holocene	Village of Namu, Fitz Hugh Sound, British Columbia, Canada	Bathurst 2005, ref.94
Trematoda			
Clonorchis sp.	Historical period	Chinese community, Sacramento, California, USA	Hall 1982, ref.94, Reinhard et al. 2008, ref.40

Parasite Species	Date	Location	Reference
Clonorchis sinensis	Historical period	Wong Nim's Property, San Bernardino, California, USA	Reinhard et al. 2008, ref.40
Cryptocotyle lingua	335–475AD	St Lawrence Island, Bering Sea	Zimmerman & Smith 1975, ref.94
Dicrocoelium dendriticum	1600–1700AD	Ferryland Newfoundland, Canada	Horne & Tuck 1996, ref.94
Fasciola spp.	500BC–1150AD	Lovelock Cave, Nevada, USA	Dunn & Watkins 1970, ref.94
Nanophyetus salmincola	Not available	Village of Namu, Fitz Hugh Sound, British Columbia, Canada	Bathurst 2005, ref.94
Opisthorchiformis	1250 AD	Glenn Canyon, Utah, USA	Moore et al. 1974, ref.94
Trematode	500BC–1150AD	Lovelock Cave, Nevada, USA	Dunn & Watkins 1970, ref.94
		Río Zape, Durango, Mexico	New finding
Nematoda			
Ascaridid			New finding
Ascaris lumbricoides	900–1250AD	Antelope House, Arizona, USA	Goncalves et al. 2003, ref.16
	1125–290BC	Upper Salts Cave, Kentucky, USA	Fry 1974, ref.94
	1070–1250AD	Elden Pueblo, Arizona, USA	Hevly et al. 1979, ref.94, Reinhard et al. 1987, ref.16
	372–82BC	Big Bone Cave, Tennessee, USA	Faulkner et al. 1989, ref.94
	405–135BC	Big Bone Cave, Tennessee, USA	Faulkner 1991, ref.94
	1070–1150AD	Adak Island, Alaska, USA	Bouchet et al. 2001, ref.94
	1755–1783AD	Queen Anne Square, Newport, Rhode Island, USA	Reinhard et al. 1986, ref.65
	1720AD	Williamsburg, Virginia, USA	Reinhard 1990, ref.20
	1620AD	Ferryland site, Newfoundland, Canada	Horne & Tuck 1996 **, ref.94
	3050–2050BC	Village of Namu, Fitz Hugh Sound, British Columbia, Canada	Bathurst 2005 *, ref.94

Parasite Species	Date	Location	Reference
Enterobius vermicularis	Colonial Period	Wong Nim's Property, San Bernardino, California, USA	Reinhard et al. 2008, ref.40
	8467–7207BC	Danger Cave, Utah, USA	Fry & Hall 1969, ref.94, Wilke & Hall 1975, ref.94, Fry & Moore 1969, ref.16
	4000BC	Dirty Shame Rockshelter, Oregon, USA	Hall 1976, ref.94
	4010BC–100AD	Hogup Cave, Utah, USA	Fry & Hall 1969, ref.94, Fry & Moore 1969, ref.16
	2100–600BC	Hinds Cave, Texas, USA	Reinhard 1988b, ref.94
	350 BC	Clyde's Cavern, Utah, USA	Hall 1972, ref.94
	372–82BC	Big Bone Cave, Tennessee, USA	Faulkner et al. 1989, ref.94
	405–135BC	Big Bone Cave, Tennessee, USA	Faulkner 1991, ref.94
	350 AD	Turkey Pen Cave, Utah, USA	Reinhard et al. 1987, ref.16
	460–1500AD	Clyde's Cavern, Utah, USA	Hall 1972, ref.94
	505–695AD	Canyon del Muerto, Arizona, USA	El-Najjar et al. 1980, ref.94
	600AD	Río Zape, Durango, Mexico	Reinhard 1990, ref. 20
	?	Río Zape, Durango, Mexico	New finding
	900–1250AD	Hoy House, Mesa Verde, Arizona, USA	Stiger 1977, ref.94
	920–1200AD	Chaco Canyon, New Mexico, USA	Reinhard & Clary 1986, ref.94, Reinhard et al. 1987, ref.16
	950AD	Step House, Mesa Verde, Colorado, USA	Samuels 1965, ref.94
	1070–1250AD	Elden Pueblo, Arizona, USA	Hevly et al. 1979, ref.94, Reinhard et al. 1987, ref.16
	1075–1100AD	Antelope House, Arizona, USA	Fry & Hall 1975, ref.69
	1100–1140AD	Antelope House, Arizona, USA	Fry & Hall 1975, ref.69
	1075–1250AD	Antelope House, Arizona, USA	Reinhard et al. 1987, ref.16

Parasite Species	Date	Location	Reference
	1200–1275AD	Salmon Ruin, New Mexico, USA	Reinhard et al. 1987, ref.16
	1250–1300AD	Inscription House, Arizona, USA	Fry & Hall 1973, ref. 94, Horne 1985, ref.16
	?	Antelope Cave, USA	Fugassa et al. 2011, ref.86
	?	Antelope House, USA	Reinhard 1988a, ref.38
	?	Salmon Ruin,	Reinhard et al. 1985, ref. 94
	?	Antelope House, USA	Fry & Hall 1986, ref.69
	?	Hogup Cave, USA	Fry 1977, ref.94
	?	Danger Cave	Fry 1977, ref.94
	900AD	Antelope House, Arizona, USA	Reinhard 1990, ref.20, Iniguez et al. 2003, ref.19
Hookworm	1700–1300BC	Daws Island, South Carolina, USA	Rathbun et al. 1980 *, ref.67
	372–82BC	Big Bone Cave, Tennessee, USA	Faulkner 1991, ref.94, Faulkner et al. 1989, ref.94
	1125–290BC	Upper Salts Cave, Kentucky, USA	Dusseau & Porter 1974 * in Wilke & Hall 1975, ref.94
	1400–1700AD	Buldir Island, Alaska, USA	Bouchet et al. 1999 **, ref.72
	1700–1800AD	Newport, Rhode Island, USA	Reinhard et al. 1986, ref.65
	??	Río Zape, Mexico	New Finding
	?	Antelope House, USA	Fry & Hall 1986, ref.69
Rhabditiform larvae	405–135BC	Inscription House, Arizona, USA	Fry & Hall 1973, ref.94
	400–1200AD	Big Bone Cave, Tennessee, USA	Faulkner 1991, ref.94
		Clyde's Cavern, Utah, USA	Hall 1972, ref.94
Strongyloides stercoralis	920–1130AD	Chaco Canyon, New Mexico, USA	Reinhard & Clary 1986, ref.94
	1175–1250AD	Antelope House, Arizona, USA	Reinhard et al. 1987*, ref.16
	?	Antelope House, USA	Fry 1980, ref.94, Reinhard 1988a, ref.38
Strongyloides sp.	6800–4800BC	Dust Devil Cave, Utah, USA	Reinhard et al. 1985, ref.94

Parasite Species	Date	Location	Reference
Trichostrongylus spp.	1175–1250AD	Antelope House, Arizona, USA	Reinhard et al. 1987, ref.16
	600AD	Río Zape, Durango, Mexico	Reinhard 1990, ref. 20
		Río Zape, Durango, Mexico	New finding
	1070–1250AD	Elden Pueblo, Arizona, USA	Hevly et al. 1979, ref.94, Reinhard et al. 1987, ref.16
Trichuris trichiura	1070–1250AD	Elden Pueblo, Arizona, USA	
	1700–1800AD	Queen Anne Square, Newport, Rhode Island, USA	Reinhard et al. 1986, ref.65
	1800–1900AD	Greenwich, New York, USA	Reinhard 1990, ref.20
	1720AD	Williamsburg, Virginia, Southwest USA	Reinhard 1990, ref.20
	1600–1700AD	Ferryland, Newfoundland, Canada,	Horne & Tuck 1996, ref.94
	1867–1891AD	Fayette, Michigan, USA	Faulkner et al. 2000, ref.94
	?	Río Zape, Durango, México	New finding
	Colonial Period	Wong Nim's Property, San Bernardino, California, USA	Reinhard et al. 2008, ref.40
Unidentified Nematodes		Inscription House, Arizona, USA	Fry & Hall 1973, ref.94
			Moore et al 1984, ref.94; Reinhard et al. 1987, ref.16
		Salts Cave, Kentucky, USA	Dusseau & Porter 1974 in Wilke & Hall 1975, ref.94
		Salts Cave, Kentucky, USA	Dusseau & Porter 1974 in Wilke & Hall 1975, ref.94
Acanthocephala			
Acanthocephala	8000–2000BC	Hogup Cave, Utah, USA	Fry & Hall 1969, ref.94, Fry 1970, ref.94

Parasite Species	Date	Location	Reference
	4850BC–1550AD	Dirty Shame Rockshelter, Oregon, USA	Hall 1977, ref.94
	9500BC, 8000BC, 2000BC, 20AD	Danger Cave, Utah, USA	Fry & Hall 1969, ref.94, Fry 1980, ref.94
	350BC and 400–1200AD	Clyde's Cavern, Utah, USA	Hall 1972, ref.94
	900–1300AD	Glen Canyon, Utah, USA	Fry & Hall 1969, ref.94, Fry 1977, ref.94
	?	Antelope Cave, USA	Fugassa et al. 2011, ref.86
Macracanthorrynchus sp.	?	Hogup Cave, Utah, USA	Fry 1977, ref.94, Moore et al. 1974, ref.94
Moniliformis clarki	?	Danger Cave, Utah, USA	Fry 1977, ref.94
	?	Glen Canyon, Arizona, USA	Fry 1977, ref.94
	1929–1809BC and 220BC–260AD	Danger Cave, Utah, USA	Moore et al. 1969, ref.94

Key: *uncertain diagnosis; **human origin? BC = Before Christ; AD = Anno Domini/After Christ.

Footnote [94]. McClary, W.H., 'Notes on some Late Middle Woodland coprolites', in J.E. Fitting (ed.), *The Shulz Site at Green Point: A Stratified Occupation Area in the Saginaw Valley of Michigan*, Anthropology Memoir no.4 (Ann Arbor, University of Michigan Museum, 1972), pp. 131–6; Bouchet, F., West, D., Lefèvre, C., Corbett, D., 'Identification of parasitoses in a child burial from Adak Island (Central Aleutian Islands, Alaska)', *Comptes Rendus de l'Académie des sciences* 324 (2001): 123–7; Bathurst, R.R., 'Archaeological evidence of intestinal parasites from coastal shell middens', *Journal of Archaeological Science* 32 (2005): 115–123; Hevly, R.H., Kelly, R.E., Anderson, G.A., Olsen, S.J., 'Comparative effects of climate change, cultural impact, and volcanism in the paleoecology of Flagstaff, Arizona, A.D. 900–1300', in P.D. Sheets and D.K. Grayson (eds), *Volcanic Activity and Human Ecology* (New York: Academic Press, 1979), pp. 487–523; Fry, G.F., *Analysis of Prehistoric Coprolites from Utah*, Anthropology Papers series no. 97 (Salt Lake City: University of Utah Press, 1977); Horne, P.D., Tuck, J.A., 'Archaeoparasitology at a 17th century colonial site in Newfoundland', *Journal of Parasitology* 82 (1996): 512–5; Hall, A., 'Intestinal helminths of man: the interpretation of egg counts', *Parasitology* 85 (1982): 605–613; Zimmerman, M.R., Smith, G.S., 'A probable case of accidental inhumation of 1600 years ago', *Bulletin of the New York Academy of Medicine* 51(1975): 828–837; Dunn, F.L., Watkins, R., 'Parasitological examination of prehistoric human coprolites from Lovelock

Cave, Nevada', in R.F. Heizer and L.K. Napton (eds) *Archaeology and the Prehistoric Great Basin Lacustrine Subsistence Regime as Seen from Lovelock Cave, Nevada*, Archaeological Research Facility Contributions no.10 (Berkeley: University of California, 1970), pp. 178–185; Moore, J.G., Grundmann, A.W., Hall, H.J., Fry, G.F., 'Human fluke infection in Glen Canyon at AD 1250', *American Journal of Physical Anthropology* 41 (1974): 115–7; Fry, G.F., 'Ovum and parasite examination of Salt Cave paleofeces', in P.J. Watson (ed.), *Archaeology of the Mammoth Cave Area* (New York: Academic Press, 1974), p. 61; Faulkner, C.T., Patton, S., Johnson, S.S., 'Prehistoric parasitism in Tennessee: evidence from the analysis of desiccated fecal material collected from Big Bone Cave, Van Buren County, Tennessee', *Journal of Parasitology* 75 (1989): 461–3; Faulkner, C.T., 'Prehistoric diet and parasitic infection in Tennessee: evidence from the analysis of desiccated human paleofeces', *American Antiquity* 56 (1991): 687–700; Fry, G.F., Hall, H.J., 'Parasitological examination of prehistoric human coprolites from Utah', *Proceedings of Utah Academy of Sciences, Arts and Letters* 46 (1969): 102–5; Wilke, P.J., Hall, H.J., *Analysis of Ancient Feces: a Discussion and Annotated Bibliography* (Berkeley: University of California, 1975); Reinhard, K.J., *Diet, Parasitism and Anemia in the Prehistoric Southwest* (College Station, Texas A & M University: PhD Thesis, 1988a); Hall H.J., *Diet and disease at Clyde's Cavern, Utah* (Salt Lake City, University of Utah: PhD Thesis, 1972); El-Najjar, M.Y., Benitez, J., Fry, G., Lynn, G.E., Ortner, D.J., Reyman, T.A., Small, P.A., 'Autopsies on two native American mummies', *American Journal of Physical Anthropology* 53 (1980): 197–202; Stiger, M.A., '*Anasazi Diet: The Coprolite Evidence*' (Boulder: University of Colorado: MA Thesis, 1977); Reinhard, K.J., Clary, K.H., 'Parasite analysis of prehistoric coprolites from Chaco Canyon', in N.J. Akins (ed.), *A Bioarchaeological Approach to Human Burials from Chaco Canyon, New Mexico* (Santa Fe: National Park Service, 1986), pp. 177–86; Samuels, R., 'Parasitological study of long dried fecal samples', *American Antiquity* 31 (1965): 175–9; Fry, G.F., Hall, H.J., *Analysis of Human Coprolites from Inscription House: Preliminary Report* (Tucson: Report to the National Park Service, Arizona Archaeological Center, 1973); Reinhard, K.J., Ambler, J.R., McGuffie, M., 'Diet and parasitism at Dust Devil Cave', *American Antiquity* 50 (1985): 819–824; Fry, G.F., 'Prehistoric diet and parasites in the desert west of North America', in D.L. Browman (ed.), *Early Native Americans* (The Hague: Mouton Press, 1980), pp. 325–339; Faulkner, C.T., Cowie, S.E., Martin, P.E., Martin, S.R., Mayes, C.S., Patton, S., 'Archaeological evidence of parasitic infection from the 19th Century Company Town of Fayette, Michigan', *Journal of Parasitology* 85 (2000): 846–9; Moore, J.G., Krotoskynski, B.K., O'Neill, H.J., 'Fecal odorgrams', *Digestive Disease and Sciences* 29 (1984): 907–911; Fry, G.F., 'Preliminary analysis of the Hogup Cave coprolites', *University of Utah Anthropological Papers* 93 (1970): 247–250; Hall, H.J., 'A paleoscatological study of diet and disease at Dirty Shame Rockshelter, Southeast Oregon', *Tebiwa* 8 (1977): 1–15; Moore, J.G., Fry, G.F., Englert, E., 'Thorny-headed worm infection in North American prehistoric man', *Science* 163 (1969): 1324–5.

Table 9.2   Intestinal parasites found in coprolites and other human archaeological remains in South America

Parasite Species	Date	Location	Reference
Cestoda			
Diphyllobothrium spp.	3000BC	Huaca Prieta, Peru	Callen & Cameron 1960*, ref.3
	3000–1200BC	Huaca Prieta, Peru	Callen & Cameron 1955, ref.3
	2050–3050BC	San Miguel de Azapa, Chile	Reinhard & Urban 2003, ref.95
	Inca Period	Lluta Valley, Chile	Santoro et al. 2003, ref.43
	600–1476AD	Chiribaya Baja, Peru	Holliday et al. 2003, ref.95
	600–1476AD	San Geronimo, Peru	Holliday et al. 2003, ref.95
D. pacificum	1025AD	Osmore, Peru	Martinson et al. 2003, ref.95
	1020–1156AD	Osmore, Peru	Martinson et al. 2003, ref.95
	Chiribaya Alta	Osmore, Peru	Martinson 2002, ref.76
	1025AD	Osmore, Peru	Martinson 2002, ref.76
	2700–2850BC	Huarmey Valley, Peru	Patrucco et al. 1983, ref.81
	50BC	Northern Chile	Reinhard & Aufderheide 1990, ref.95

Parasite Species	Date	Location	Reference
	8050–2050BC	Coastal Peru	Reinhard & Barnum 1991, ref.95
	4110–1950BC	Tiliviche, Iquique, Chile	Ferreira et al. 1984, ref.81
Hymenolepis nana	2050–50BC	Santa Elina, Mato Grosso, Brazil	Gonçalves et al. 2003, ref.16
	6080–5780BC	M22 CCP7, Santa Cruz, Argentina	Fugassa et al. 2007 *, ref.92
	7170–6770BC	CCP7, Santa Cruz, Argentina	Fugassa et al. 2010*, ref.86
	Pre-Inca Period	Lluta Valley, Chile	Santoro et al. 2003, ref.43
Trematoda			
Echinostoma sp.	1350–1430AD	Peruaçu Valley, Minas Gerais, Brazil	Sianto et al. 2005, ref.35
Paragonimus sp.	2500BC–5900BC	Atacama Desert, Chile	Hall 1976, ref.94
Nematoda			
Ancylostomid	5360–5200BC	Pedra Furada, Piauí, Brazil	Ferreira et al. 1987, ref.51
	4100–1950BC	Tiliviche, Iquique, Chile	Gonçalves et al. 2003, ref.16
	3040–2870BC to 565–685AD	Boqueirão Soberbo, Minas Gerais, Brazil	Ferreira et al. 1982, ref.95
	1660–1420BC to 1450–1590AD	Gentio Cave, Minas Gerais, Brazil	Ferreira et al. 1980, ref.6, 1983, ref.16
	550–150BC	Toconao, San Pedro de Atacama, Chile	Gonçalves et al. 2003, ref.16

Parasite Species	Date	Location	Reference
	950–1450AD	Valle Encantado, Neuquén, Argentina	Gonçalves et al. 2003, ref.16
	890–950AD	Tihuanaco, Peru	Allison et al. 1974, ref.70
	Not available	Sítio do Meio, Piauí, Brazil	Gonçalves et al. 2003, ref.16
	7170–6770BC	CCP7, Santa Cruz, Argentina	Fugassa et al. 2010, ref.86
Ascaridid	1770–2028BC	Orejas de Burro, Santa Cruz, Argentina	Fugassa & Barberena 2006, ref.95
Ascaris lumbricoides	6910–6790BC	Sítio do Meio, PI, Brazil	Gonçalves et al. 2003, ref.16, Leles et al. 2008, ref.15
	6050–5050BC	Lapa Pequena, MG, Brazil	Gonçalves et al. 2003, ref.16
	2458–2096BC	Huarmey Valley, Peru	Patrucco et al. 1983, ref.81
	2050–50BC	Santa Elina, Mato Grosso, Brazil	Gonçalves et al. 2003, ref.16
	1660–1420BC to 1450–1590AD	Gruta do Gentio II, Minas Gerais, Brazil	Ferreira et al. 1980, ref.6, 1983, ref.16, Leles et al. 2008, ref.15
	1080–950BC	Tulán, San Pedro de Atacama, Chile	Gonçalves et al. 2003, ref.16, Leles et al. 2008, ref.15
	2458–2096BC	Huarmey Valley, Peru	Patrucco et al. 1983, ref.81

Parasite Species	Date	Location	Reference
	1540±120 BC-1520±70 AD	Gentio Cave, Minas Gerais, Brazil	Gonçalves et al. 2003, ref.16
	1500–1600AD	Nombre de Jesús, Cabo Vírgenes, Argentina	Fugassa et al. 2006, ref.20, Leles et al. 2010, ref.61
Capillarids	Historic	Las Mandíbulas, Tierra del Fuego, Arg	Fugassa et al. 2008c***, ref.95
	ca. 1100 AD	Caleta Falsa, Tierra del Fuego, Arg	Fugassa et al. 2008c***, ref.95
	5930 ± 150 BC	CCP7, Santa Cruz, Argentina	Fugassa et al. 2007*, ref. 92
	1770–2028 cal. BC	Orejas de Burro, Santa Cruz, Argentina	Fugassa & Barberena 2006, ref.95
	6970 ±200 BC	CCP7, Santa Cruz, Argentina	Fugassa et al. 2010, ref.86
	7780 ± 100 BC	CCP7, Santa Cruz, Argentina	Fugassa et al. 2010, ref.86
	4590 ±110 BC	CCP5, PN Perito Moreno, Santa Cruz, Argentina	Fugassa 2006, ref.20
Enterobius vermicularis	4110–1950 BC	Tiliviche, Iquique, Chile	Araújo et al. 1985, ref.44, Gonçalves et al. 2003, ref.16, Iñiguez et al. 2003, ref.19, 2006, ref.46

Parasite Species	Date	Location	Reference
	1080–950 BC	Tulán, San Pedro de Atacama, Chile	Ferreira et al. 1989a, ref.42, Iñiguez et al. 2003, ref.19, 2006, ref.46
	400 BC – 800 AD	Caserones, Tarapacá Valley, Chile	Ferreira et al. 1984, ref.81, Araújo et al. 1985, ref.44, Iñiguez et al. 2003, ref.19, 2006, ref.46
	2277 ± 181 BC	Huarmey Valley, Peru	Patrucco et al. 1983, ref.81
	770–830 BC	Pv35-4, Peru	Patrucco et al 1982, ref.95, 1983, ref.81
	pre-Columbian	Pie de Palo, Argentina	Zimmerman & Morilla 1983, ref.95
	Inca Period	Lluta Valley, Chile	Santoro et al. 2003, ref.43
	4590 ±110 BC	CCP5, PN Perito Moreno, Santa Cruz, Argentina	Fugassa 2007**, ref.95
Metastrongylus sp. or *Physaloptera* sp.	5930 ± 150 BC	CCP7, Santa Cruz, Argentina	Fugassa et al. 2007 *, ref. 92

Parasite Species	Date	Location	Reference
Nematodirus sp.?	5930 ± 150 BC	CCP7, Santa Cruz, Argentina	Fugassa et al. 2007 *, ref.92
	6970 ± 200 BC	CCP7, Santa Cruz, Argentina	Fugassa et al. 2010*, ref.86
	7780 ± 100 BC	CCP7, Santa Cruz, Argentina	Fugassa et al. 2010*, ref.86
	4590 ±110 BC	CCP5, PN Perito Moreno, Santa Cruz, Argentina	Fugassa 2006, ref.20
Rhabditoid larvae	8580 ± 620 BC	CCP7, PN Perito Moreno, Santa Cruz, Argentina	Fugassa 2006, ref.20
Trichostrongylus spp.	1080–950 BC	Tulán, San Pedro de Atacama, Chile	Gonçalves et al. 2003, ref.16
	950–1450 AD	Valle Encantado, Neuquén, Argentina	Gonçalves et al. 2003, ref.16
	1450–1525 AD	Catarpe 2, San Pedro de Atacama, Chile	Gonçalves et al. 2003*, ref.16
	18th century AD	Itacambira, Minas Gerais, Brazil	Araújo et al. 1984, ref.95
Trichuris sp.	19th century AD	Cerro Norte XI, Pali Aike, Santa Cruz, Argentina	Fugassa et al. 2010b**
	4590 ±110 BC	CCP5, PN Perito Moreno, Santa Cruz, Argentina	Fugassa 2007, ref.95
Trichuris trichiura	6050–5050 BP	Lapa Pequena, Minas Gerais, Brazil	Gonçalves et al. 2003, ref.16
	2955±85BC–625±60 AD	Boqueirão Soberbo, Minas Gerais, Brazil	Ferreira et al. 1982, ref.95
	2050–50 BC	Santa Elina, Mato Grosso, Brazil	Gonçalves et al. 2003, ref.16

Parasite Species	Date	Location	Reference
	1540±120BC–1520±70 AD	Gentio Cave, Minas Gerais, Brazil	Ferreira et al. 1980, ref.6, 1983, ref.16
	1080–950 BC	Tulán, San Pedro de Atacama, Chile	Gonçalves et al. 2003, ref.16
	50 BC	Estrago Cave, Pernambuco, Brazil	Ferreira et al. 1989b*, ref.95
	1000 AD	Huarmey Valley, Peru	Patrucco et al. 1983, ref.81
	Pre-Columbian	El Plomo, Santiago, Chile	Pizzi & Schenone 1954, ref.4
	ca. 1500 AD	Inca mummy	Pike 1967**, ref.95
	Colonial Period	Murga culture, Peru	Fouant et al 1982, ref.95
	18th century AD	Itacambira, Minas Gerais, Brazil	Confalonieri et al 1981, ref.95
	Not available	Pedra Furada, Piauí, Brazil	Gonçalves et al. 2003, ref.16
	1000 BC	Tulan, San Pedro de Atacama, Chile	Ferreira et al 1989a, ref.42
	437 ± 48 AD	Parador Nativo, Rio Negro, Argentina	Fugassa & Dubois 2009, ref.95
	1261 ± 44 AD	Centro Minero, Rio Negro, Argentina	Fugassa & Dubois 2009, ref.95
	16th century AD	Nombre de Jesús, Cabo Vírgenes, Argentina	Fugassa et al. 2006, ref.85
	5930 ± 150 BC	CCP7, Santa Cruz, Argentina	Fugassa et al. 2007, ref.92

Parasite Species	Date	Location	Reference
	1770–2028 cal. BC	Orejas de Burro, Santa Cruz, Argentina	Fugassa & Barberena 2006, ref.95
	7780 ± 100 BC	CCP7, Santa Cruz, Argentina	Fugassa et al. 2010, ref.86
	Inca and Pre-Inca Period	Lluta Valley, Chile	Santoro et al. 2003, ref.43
	1020–1156 AD	Osmore, Peru	Martinson et al 2003, ref.95
	770–830 BC	Pv35–4, Peru	Patrucco et al 1982, ref.95, 1983, ref.81
	Historic?	Tierra del Fuego, Argentina	New finding
	Late Holocene	Salitroso, Santa Cruz, Argentina	New finding
Acanthocephala			
Acanthocephala	2955±85BC–625±60 AD	Boqueirão Soberbo, Minas Gerais Brazil	Gonçalves et al. 2003, ref.16
	1540±120BC–1520±70 AD	Gentio Cave, Minas Gerais, Brazil	Gonçalves et al. 2003*, ref.16
	770–830 BC	Pv35–4, Peru	Patrucco et al. 1982, ref.95

Key: *uncertain diagnosis; **human origin? ***pseudo-parasitism? BC = Before Christ; AD = Anno Domini/After Christ

Footnote [95]: Reinhard, K., Urban, O., 'Diagnosing ancient Diphyllobothriasis from Chinchorro mummies', *Memórias do Instituto Oswaldo Cruz* 98 (2003): 191–3; Holiday, D.M., Guillen, S., Richardson, D.J., 'Diphyllobothriasis of the Chiribaya Culture (700–1476 AD) of Southern Peru',

Comparative Parasitology 70 (2003): 171–6; Martinson, E., Reinhard, K.J., Buikstra, J.E., Cruz, K.D., 'Pathoecology of Chiribaya parasitism', *Memórias do Instituto Oswaldo Cruz* 98 (2003): 195–205; Reinhard, K.J., Aufderheide, A.C., 'Diphyllobothriasis in prehistoric Chile and Peru: adaptive radiation of a helminth species to native American populations', *Paleopathology Newsletter* 72 (1990): 18–9; Reinhard, K.J., Barnum, S.V., 'Parasitology as an interpretative tool in archaeology', *American Antiquity* 57 (1991): 231–245; Ferreira, L.F., Araújo, A.J.G., Confalonieri, U.E.C., 'News from the field', *Paleopathology Newsletter* 38 (1982): 5; Fugassa, M., Barberena, R., 'Cuevas y zoonosisantiguas: paleoparasitologíadel sitio Orejas de Burro 1 (Santa Cruz, Argentina)' *Magallania (Punta Arenas)* 34 (2006): 57–62; Patrucco, R., Tello, R., Bonavia, D., '*Homo sapiens sapiens*', in D. Bonavia (ed.), *Los Gavilanes. Mar, Desierto y Oasis en la Historia del Hombre* (Lima: Corporación Peruana de Desarrollo, S.A. – Instituto Arqueológico Alemán, 1982), pp. 226–232; Fugassa, M.H., Taglioretti, V., Gonçalves, M.L.C., Araújo, A., Sardella, N.H., Denegri, G.M., '*Capillaria* spp. findings in Patagonian archaeological sites: statistical analysis of morphometric data', *Memórias do Instituto Oswaldo Cruz* 103 (2008c): 104–5; Zimmerman, M.R., Morilla, R.E., 'Enterobiasis in pre-Columbian America', *Paleopathology Newsletter* 42 (1983): 8; Fugassa, M.H., 'Camélidos, parásitos y ocupaciones humanas: registrospaleoparasitológicos en Cerro Casa de Piedra 7 (Parque Nacional Perito Moreno, Santa Cruz, Argentina)', *Intersecciones en Antropología* 8 (2007): 265–9; Araújo, A.J.G., Confalonieri, U.E.C., Ferreira, L.F., 'Encontro de ovos de Trichostrongylideo e *Trichuris trichiura* em corpo mumificado do período colonial brasileiro', *Revista do Centro de Ciencias Biológicas e da Saúde* (1984): 11–4; Ferreira, L.F., Araújo, A.J.G., Confalonieri, U.E.C., Lima, J.M.D., '*Trichuris trichiura* eggs in human coprolites from the archaeological site of Furna do Estrago, Brejo da Madre de Deus, Pernambuco, Brazil', *Memórias do Instituto Oswaldo Cruz* 84 (1989): 581; Pike, A.W., 'The recovery of parasite eggs from ancient cesspit and latrine deposits: an approach to the study of early parasite infections', in D. Brothwell, A.T. Sandison (eds), *Diseases in Antiquity* (Springfield: CC Thomas, 1967), pp. 184–8; Fouant, M.M., Allison, M., Gerszten, E., Focacci, G., 'Parasitos intestinales entre los indígenas precolombinos', *Revista Chungará* 9 (1982): 285–299; Confalonieri, U.E.C., Araújo, A.J.G., Ferreira, L.F., '*Trichuris trichiura* infection in colonial Brazil', *Paleopathology Newsletter* 35 (1981); Fugassa, M.H., Favier Dubois, C.M., 'Primer registro paleoparasitológico de *Trichuris* SP (Nematoda, Capilariidae) en muestras asociadas a restos humanos del Holoceno tardío de Patagonia septentrional', *Revista Argentina de Antropología Biológica* 1 (2009): 61–72.

Chapter 10

Parasites in European Populations from Prehistory to the Industrial Revolution

Evilena Anastasiou

Introduction

The aim of this paper is to compile the evidence for intestinal parasites in Europe over the centuries[1] and then to discuss its significance for reconstructing aspects of daily life in people who lived there. Paleoparasitology has a long tradition in Europe. By the first half of the twentieth century samples from latrines, cesspools, and bog bodies were being analysed for the remains of both helminths and protozoa. These studies from Europe have revealed a variety of different species infecting the past populations of the continent. This not only helps us to understand health in past communities, but also provides important insights into the social and cultural factors that promoted parasite transmission in the past.

Paleolithic Period

The parasitic environment of Europe prior to the introduction of agriculture is virtually unknown, as the vast majority of evidence for parasites retrieved from European archaeological sites is dated to the Neolithic and subsequent time periods. The only evidence for parasitism in Paleolithic Europe comes from the Upper Paleolithic site (30,000–24,000 years BP) of Arcy-sur-Cure in Yonne, France, where eggs of roundworm (*Ascaris* sp.) were identified in 1996.[2] Based on the archaeological evidence excavated from the cave, Bouchet et al. suggested a human origin for the eggs and proposed that the findings were of the *Ascaris*

---

[1] It must be borne in mind that not all published claims for the presence of a particular parasite are necessarily correct. Where a diagnosis has been made but no illustrations are included in the publication, or where the species identification is questionable, I refer to the findings as 'reported' or 'described' instead of 'identified', so that readers can look up the source for themselves and make up their own minds.

[2] Bouchet, F., Baffier, D., Girard, M., Morel, P., Paicheler, J.C., David, F., 'Paléoparasitologie en contexte pléistocène: premières observations à la Grande Grotte d'Arcy-sur-Cure (Yonne), France', *Comptes Rendus de l'Académie des sciences* 319 (1996): 147–51.

lumbricoides species (human roundworm). Since both the domestication of pigs (9,000 years ago) and the earliest archaeological evidence for hunting wild pigs (cave and rock paintings dated 25,000 years ago) post-dates the parasitological evidence from Arcy-sur-Cure, it has ben argued that hominins were the original hosts of *Ascaris* and that they later infected their domesticated pigs, and not vice versa as was previously thought.[3]

Neolithic Period[4] (4,000–1,700BC)

The paleoparasitological evidence for Neolithic Europe derives from archaeological sites (sediments and coprolites) from France, Germany, Switzerland, Greece and the Netherlands (Table 1). In France, the pile-dwelling Neolithic settlements of Clairvaux (3,600BC) and Chalain (2,700–2,400BC), in the lake area of Jura, provided a rich source of information for the parasitic environment of the region during the Neolithic. Eggs of roundworm (*Ascaris lumbricoides*), hookworm (Ancylostomids), fish tapeworm (*Diphyllobothrium* sp.), liver fluke (*Fasciola hepatica*), beef/pork tapeworm (*Taenia* sp.) and whipworm (*Trichuris trichiura*) have all been identified from these sites.[5] In Germany, the Neolithic sites of the Horgen culture Sipplingen (3,317–3,306BC) and Seekirch-Stockwiesen (3,000–2,900BC) were positive for the presence of the lancet liver fluke (*Dicrocoelium* sp.), while *Dicrocoelium* eggs were also retrieved from the Neolithic sites of Hornstaad-Hornle (3,917–3,905BC) and Alleshausen-Taschenwiesen (2,900–2,600BC).[6]

---

[3]   Loreille, O., Bouchet, F., 'Evolution of ascariasis in humans and pigs: a multi-disciplinary approach', *Memórias do Instituto Oswaldo Cruz* 98 (Suppl. 1) (2003): 39–46.

[4]   Due to the variation in the absolute chronology of the time periods for different parts of Europe, the time limits presented here give the upper and lower limits of each period for central and northwest Europe, but it must be kept in mind that different areas have different absolute chronologies for each time period.

[5]   Bouchet, F., Petrequin, P., Paicheler, J.C., Dommelier, S., 'First palaeoparasitological approach of the Neolithic site in Chalain (Jura, France)', *Bulletin de la Société de Pathologie Exotique* 88 (1995): 265–68; Dommelier-Espejo, S., Bentrad, S.S., Paicheler, J.C., Petrequin, P., Bouchet, F., 'Parasitoses liées à l' alimentation chez les populations néolithiques du lac de Chalain (Jura, France)', *Anthropozoologica* 27 (1998): 41–49; Bouchet, F., 'Intestinal capillariasis in Neolithic inhabitants of Chalain (Jura, France)', *The Lancet* 349 (1997): 256.

[6]   Le Bailly, M., *Evolution de la Relation Hôte/Parasite dans les Systèmes Lacustres Nord Alpins au Néolithique (3900–2900 BC), et Nouvelles Données dans la Détection des Paléoantigènes de Protozoa* (Université de Reims Champagne-Ardenne: PhD Thesis, 2005); Le Bailly, M., Bouchet, F., 'Ancient Dicrocoeliosis: occurrence, distribution and migration', *Acta Tropica* 115 (2010): 175–80.

In the Netherlands, *Fasciola* sp. was reported from the site of Swifterbant (3400–3230BC), along with eggs of whipworm and *Opistochiformes* (bile duct fluke).[7]

In Switzerland, the parasitic environment of the Neolithic has been reconstructed using a number of different species identified from the site of Arbon (3304–3370BC) in the Canton of Thurgau. Roundworm, giant kidney worm (*Dioctophymidae*), fish tapeworm, lancet liver fluke (*Dicrocoelium* sp.), dysentery (*Entamoeba histolytica*), two liver flukes *(Fasciola* sp. and *Opisthorchis* sp.), beef/pork tapeworm, and whipworm have all been identified from Arbon, while eggs of *Dicrocoelium* sp. were also identified from the Neolithic site of Concise.[8] Interestingly, eggs of whipworm were also recovered from the famous Ice Man, or Otzi, whose mummified remains from the Alps were examined for parasitic remains.[9]

Finally, in Greece the only parasite species so far identified derives from the site of Kouphovouno (5000–2000BC), where *Entamoeba histolytica* (dysentery) has been identified with the use of immunological tools (ELISA).[10]

---

[7]   Jansen, J., Boersema, J.H., 'Helminth eggs from the latrines of the Olofskapel Gatehouse, Amsterdam', *Paleopathology Newsletter* 2 (1972): 7–8; Roever-Bonnet, H., Rijpstra, C., Van Renesse, M.A., Peen, C.H., 'Helminth eggs and gregarines from coprolites from the excavations at Swifterbant', *Helinium* 19 (1979): 7–12.

[8]   Le Bailly and Bouchet 2010; Le Bailly, M., Leuzinger, U., Bouchet, F., 'Dioctophymidae eggs in coprolites from Neolithic site of Arbon-Bleiche 3 (Switzerland)', *Journal of Parasitology* 89 (2003): 1073–76; Le Bailly 2005.

[9]   Aspöck, H., Auer, H., Picher, O., '*Trichuris trichiura* eggs in the Neolithic glacier mummy from the Alps', *Parasitology Today* 12 (1996): 255–56.

[10]   Le Bailly, M., Bouchet, F., 'Paléoparasitologie et immunologie: l' example d'Entamoeba histolytica', *ArcheoSciences Revue d'Archaeometrie* 30 (2006): 129–35.

Table 10.1 The earliest evidence for human parasites in Europe currently known

Species	Country	Date	Source
Ancylostomatidae (hookworm)	France	3600BC	Dommelier-Espejo 2001 ref.73
Ascaris lumbricoides (roundworm)	France Switzerland Britain	30–24,000BC 3384–3370BC 2100–600BC	Bouchet et al. 1996, ref.2 Dommelier-Espejo 2001 ref.73 Jones and Nicholson 1988 ref.12
Capillaria sp.	Switzerland France	3900–2900BC 3200–2980BC	Le Bailly 2005 ref.6 Bouchet 1997 ref.5
Dicrocoelium sp.	Germany Austria Switzerland	6000–5000BC Bronze Age 3384–3370BC	Le Bailly 2005 ref.6 Bouchet et al. 2003 ref.11 Dommelier-Espejo 2001 ref.73
Dioctophymatidae (giant kidney worm)	Switzerland	3384–3370BC	Le Bailly et al. 2003 ref.6
Diphyllobothrium latum (fish tapeworm)	France Switzerland	3600BC 3,900–2,900BC	Dommelier-Espejo 2001 ref.73 Le Bailly 2005 ref.6
Entamoeba histolytica (dysentery)	Greece Switzerland	5000–2000BC 3300BC	Le Bailly and Bouchet 2006 ref.10 Goncalves et al. 2004 ref.14
Fasciola hepatica (liver fluke)	Switzerland Netherlands	3900–2900BC 3400–3230BC	Le Bailly 2005 ref.6 Roever-Bonnet et al. 1979 ref.7
Opisthorchiformes (bile duct flukes)	Netherlands Switzerland	3400–3230BC 3384–3370BC	Roever-Bonnet et al. 1979 ref.7 Dommelier-Espejo et al. 1998 ref.5
Taenia sp. (beef/pork tapeworm)	France Switzerland Austria	3900–2900BC 3384–3370BC 0BC/AD	Dommelier-Espejo et al. 1998 ref.5 Le Bailly et al. 2003 ref.8 Aspöck et al. 1999 ref.18
Trichuris trichiura (whipworm)	France Netherlands Switzerland Austria	3600–3500BC 3400–3230BC 3384–3370BC 3300–3200BC	Dommelier-Espejo, 2001 ref.73 Jansen and Boersema, 1972 ref.7 Dommelier-Espejo, 2001 ref.73 Aspöck et al. 1996 ref.9

Bronze Age (2,800–500BC)

Our knowledge of the parasitic environment of Bronze Age Europe is much more restricted than our understanding of the preceding period, as far fewer sites have been analysed. Eggs of *Dicrocoelium* sp. have been identified from the Austrian site of Hallstatt and the French site of Gresine.[11] In Britain, paleoparasitological studies in the county of Somerset (2100–600BC) revealed the presence of roundworm and whipworm.[12] Roundworm and whipworm were also identified from the site of Hulin (1600–1500BC) in the Czech Republic,[13] while the only protozoon to be identified in Bronze Age Europe is *Entamoeba histolytica* (dysentery) from Gresine in France.[14]

Iron Age (8th BC–2nd BC)

During the Iron Age three different species have been identified from Austria, from the site of Hallstatt (500–200BC); these are roundworm, whipworm, and *Dicrocoelium* sp.[15] Whipworm eggs were also reported from Vilshofen in Germany (150–140BC).[16] In Denmark two of the most famous bog bodies, Tollund Man and Grauballe Man, dated to the 4th and 3rd century BC respectively, were described as infected with the human whipworm. Human whipworms and roundworms were also reported from the mummified intestines of the Drobintz Girl (600BC) excavated at the province of Warmia-Masuria in Poland.[17]

---

[11] Bouchet, F., Harter, S., Le Bailly, M., 'The state of the art of paleoparasitological research in the Old World', *Memórias do Instituto Oswaldo Cruz* 98 (Suppl. 1) (2003): 92–102.; Le Bailly and Bouchet 2010.

[12] Jones, A.K.G., Nicholson, C., 'Recent finds of Trichuris and Ascaris ova from Britain', *Paleopathology Newsletter* 62 (1988): 5–6.

[13] Bartošová, L., Ditrich, O., Beneš, J., Frolík, J., Musil, J., 'Paleoparasitological findings in medieval and early modern archaeological deposits from Hradební Street, Chrudim, Czech Republic', *Interdisciplinaria Archaeologica* 2 (2011): 27–38.

[14] Goncalves, C.L.M., da Silva, V.L., de Andrade, C.M., Reinhard, K., da Rocha, G.C., Le Bailly, M., Bouchet, F., Ferreira, L.F., Araújo, A., 'Amoebiasis distribution in the past: first steps using an immunoassay technique', *Transactions of the Royal Society of Tropical Medicine and Hygiene* 98 (2004): 88–91.

[15] Aspöck, H., Flamm, H., and Picher, O., 'Darmparasiten in men-schlichen exkrementen aus prähistorischen salzbergwerken der Hallstatt-Kultur (800–350 v. Chr)', *Zentrallblatt für Bakteriologic und Hygiene Abt Originale A* 223 (1973): 549–58.

[16] Specht, K.W., 'Eine interessante erdprobe aus einer abortgrube im Römerkastell Künzing', *Saalburg-Jahrbuch* 21 (1963): 90–94.

[17] Szidat, L., 'Über die erhaltungsfähigkeit von helmintheneiern in vor- und frühgeschichtlichen moorleichen', *Zeitschrift für Parasitenkunde* 13 (1944): 265–74.

Roman Period (2nd BC–4th AD)

The paleoparasitological record of the Roman Period is quite extensive, with many different species being identified from Austria, Britain, France, Germany, Italy and Poland.

The human roundworm and whipworm have been identified from the site of Hallein (1st century AD) in Austria,[18] from Roman London, York and Carlisle in Britain,[19] from deposits dated between 100BC–500AD from Bremerhaven, Germany,[20] from 1st century AD archaeological sediments in Valkenburg in the Netherlands,[21] and in the intestines of the Karwinden Man (500AD), from Poland. Whipworm has also been identified from Roman Winchester in Britain,[22] Bobigny (2nd AD) in France[23] and Pompeii in Italy.[24]

Besides roundworms and whipworms, which are the most commonly identified species from Roman contexts in Europe, *Dicrocoelium* sp. has been identified from Hallein (1st century AD) in Austria,[25] Winchester in Britain[26] and Reims and Troyes (1st century BC–1st century AD) in France.[27] Fish tapeworm has been reported from Roman contexts in Austria,[28] in London,[29] in Bremerhaven,

---

[18] Aspöck, H., Auer, H., Picher, O., 'Parasites and parasitic diseases in prehistoric human populations in central Europe', *Helminthologia* 36 (1999): 139–45.

[19] Jones, A.K.G., Hutchinson, A.R., 'The Parasitological Evidence', in M.R. McCarthy, *The Structural Sequence and Environmental Remains from Castle Street, Carlisle: Excavations 1981–2* (Cumberland and Westmorland Antiquarian and Archaeological Society, 1991); Wilson, A., Rackham, D.J., 'Parasite eggs', in P.C. Buckland, *The Environmental Evidence from the Church Street Roman Sewer System*, The Archaeology of York series no.14 (1) (York: York Archaeological Trust, 1976), pp. 32–33.

[20] Jansen, J., Over, H.J., 'Het voorkomen van parasieten in terpmateriaal uit Noordwest Duitsland'., *Tijdschr Diergeneesk* 87 (1962): 1377–79.

[21] Jansen, J., Over, H.J., 'Observations on helminth infections in a Roman army camp', in A. Corradetti (ed.), *Proceedings of the First International Congress of Parasitology, Roma Italy, 1964* (Oxford: Pergamon, 1966), p. 791.

[22] Pike, A.W., 'Recovery of helminth eggs from archaeological excavations, and their possible usefulness in providing evidence for the purpose of an occupation', *Nature* 219 (1968): 303–04.

[23] Rousset, J.J., Heron, C., Metrot, P., 'Human helminthiasis at the Gauls', *Histoire Des Sciences Medicales* 30 (1996): 41–46.

[24] Heirbaut, E., Jones, A.K.G., Wheeler, W., 'Archaeometry: methods and analysis', in G.C.M. Jansen, A.O. Koloski-Ostrow and E.M. Moormann (eds), *Roman Toilets: Their Archaeology and Cultural History* (Leuven: Peeters, 2011).

[25] Aspöck et al. 1999.

[26] Pike 1968.

[27] Le Bailly and Bouchet 2010.

[28] Szidat 1944.

[29] De Rouffignac, C., 'Parasite egg survival and identification from Hibernia Wharf, Southwark', *London Archaeologist* 5 (1985): 103–05.

Germany (1100BC–500AD),[30] and from the mummified remains of Karwinden Man (500AD).[31] Beef/pork tapeworm has also been described as present in London[32] and Bremerhaven.[33]

Medieval Period (5th–15th AD)

Of all the time periods for which we have evidence of parasites in Europe, the medieval period is perhaps the best understood and most extensively studied. The available material for analysis increases dramatically at this time, as so many medieval archaeological sites have been excavated across Europe. Furthermore, since the 1980s European paleoparasitologists in Britain and Germany have become increasingly interested in the epidemiology of helminth infections, as well as in the depositional processes that created the archaeological strata of different medieval sites.[34] As a result, many studies have identified a wide variety of different species that parasitised Europeans during the Middle Ages.

While in Austria the only medieval finding is described by Szidat[35] as eggs of fish tapeworm, in Belgium not only fish tapeworm (11th–15th AD), but also *Entamoeba* dysentery, liver fluke (*Fasciola hepatica*) (11th–12th AD), beef/pork tapeworm (11th–13th AD) and whipworm (from the 9th century AD) were identified from the Place d'Armes in Namur.[36] In Denmark at the site of Ribe, eggs of roundworm, *Fasciola* liver fluke, beef/pork tapeworm, and whipworm were reported by Nansen and Jorgensen[37] from strata dated between 750–800AD. Weiss and Moller-Christensen have identified calcified cysts of the

30   Jansen and Over 1962.

31   Szidat 1944.

32   Rouffignac 1985.

33   Jansen and Over 1962.

34   Jones, A.K.G., 'Human parasite remains: prospects for a quantitative approach', in R.A. Hall and K.H. Kenward (eds), *Environmental Archaeology in the Urban Context* (London: The Council for British Archaeology, 1982); Herrmann, B., 'Parasitologisch-epidemiologische auswertungen mittelalterlicher kloaken', *Zeitschrift für Archäologie des Mittelaltes* 13 (1985): 131–61; Herrmann, B., Schulz, U., 'Parasitologische untersuchungen eines spätmittelalterlich-frühneuzeitlichen kloakeninhaltes aus der fronerei auf dem schrangen in Lübeck', *Lübecker Schri Archäol Kultur* 12 (1986): 167–72.

35   Szidat 1944.

36   Goncalves et al. 2004; da Rocha, G.C., Harter, S., Le Bailly, M., Araújo, A., Ferreira, L.F., Serra-Freire, M., Bouchet, F., 'Paleoparasitological remains revealed by seven historic contexts from "Place d'Armes", Namur, Belgium', *Memórias do Instituto Oswaldo Cruz* 101 (Suppl. 2) (2006): 43–52.

37   Nansen, P., Jorgensen, R.J., 'Fund af parasitæg i arkæologisk materiale fra det vikingetidige Ribe', *Nordisk Veterinaer Medicin* 29 (1977): 263–66.

dog tapeworm (*Echinococcus granulosus*) in humans from Naestved (1450AD),[38] while Hansen details the identification of pinworm (*Enterobius vermicularis*) from Greenland (1475AD).[39]

In medieval Britain, human roundworms and whipworms (Figure 10.1, 10.2) have been extracted from Winchester (11th AD),[40] York (9th–16th AD),[41] Southampton (13th–14th AD),[42] Leicester (15th AD),[43] Worcester (15thAD),[44] and Wales (15th AD).[45] During the Middle Ages, hookworm (*Ancylostoma*),[46] *Dicrocoelium dendriticum*,[47] fish tapeworm,[48] *Echinococcus granulosus*,[49] *Fasciola* liver fluke,[50] and beef/pork tapeworm[51] are also reported from British samples.

[38]   Weiss, D.L., Moller-Christensen, V., 'Leprosy, echinococcosis and amulets: a study of a medieval Danish inhumation', *Medical History* 15 (1971): 260–67.

[39]   Hansen, J., 'Les momies du Groenland', *La Recherche* 183 (1986): 1490–98.

[40]   Pike, A.W., Biddle, M., 'Parasite eggs in medieval Winchester', *Antiquity* 40 (1966): 293–97.

[41]   Jones, A.K.G., 'A coprolite from 6–8 Pavement', in A.R. Hall, H.K. Kenward, D. Williams, and R.A. Greig (eds), *Environment and Living Conditions at Two Anglo Scandinavian Sites*, The Archaeology of York series no. 14(4) (York: Council for British Archaeology, 1983); Jones and Nicholson 1988.

[42]   Pike, A.W., 'Parasite eggs: the organic contents of cesspit soil from Southampton, and their significance for the archaeologist and biologist', in C. Platt and R. Coleman-Smith (eds), *Excavations in Medieval Southampton 1953–1969*, (Leicester: Leicester University Press, 1975), pp. 347–48.

[43]   Mitchell, P.D., Yeh, H.-Y., Appleby, J., Buckley, R., 'The intestinal parasites of King Richard III', *The Lancet* 382 (2013): 888.

[44]   Moore, P.D., 'Life seen from a medieval latrine', *Nature* 294 (1981): 614.

[45]   Jones, A.K.G., 'Parasitological investigation', *The Bulletin of the Board of Celtic Studies, Archaeolog a Chelfyddyd* 36 (1989): 258–62.

[46]   Tibesky, K., Sidell, J., 'The parasite remains', in G. Malcolm, D. Bowsher and R. Cowie, *Middle Saxon London, Excavations at the Royal Opera House, 1989–99* (London: Museum of London Archaeology Service, 2003), pp. 333–37.

[47]   Pike, A.W., 'The recovery of parasite eggs from ancient cesspit and latrine deposits: an approach to the study of early parasite infections', in D. Brothwell and A.T. Sandison (eds), *Diseases in Antiquity* (Springfield: C.C. Thomas, 1967), pp. 184–88.

[48]   Rouffignac 1985.

[49]   Wells, C., Dallas, C., 'Romano-British Pathology', *Antiquity* 50 (1976): 53–55; Brothwell, D.R., 'On the complex nature of man-animal relationships from the pleistocene to early agricultural societies', in J.G. Hawkes (ed.), *Conservation and Agriculture* (London: Duckworth, 1978).

[50]   Rouffignac 1985.

[51]   Rouffignac 1985.

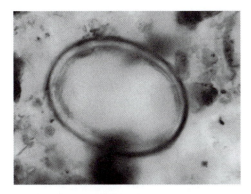

Figure 10.1.
Roundworm egg (*Ascaris lumbricoides*) from the pelvic soil of King Richard III of England (1483–85), Leicester, UK (Image: Piers Mitchell)

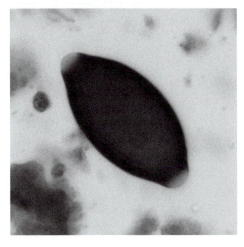

Figure 10.2.
Whipworm egg (*Trichuris trichiura*) from human coprolite from Viking Period York, UK (Image: Evilena Anastasiou).

In France, roundworm and whipworm eggs were extracted from medieval Paris (11th–16th AD)[52] and Montbeliard (15th–16th AD),[53] while eggs of fish tapeworm, bilharzia (*Schistosoma haematobium* and *Schistosoma mansoni*) and *Dicrocoelium* sp. were also extracted from Montbeliard (15th–16th AD).[54] *Dicrocoelium* sp. has been identified from medieval Paris (11th–16th AD), Epinal (13th AD), Villiers-

---

[52] Bouchet, F., 'Recovery of helminth eggs from archaeological excavation of the Grand Louvre (Paris, France)', *Journal of Parasitology* 81 (1995): 785–87.

[53] Goncalves, C.L.M., Araújo, A., Ferreira, L.F., 'Human intestinal parasites in the past: new findings and a review', *Memórias do Instituto Oswaldo Cruz* 98 (Suppl. 1) (2003): 103–18.

[54] Le Bailly and Bouchet 2010; Bouchet, F., Harter, S., Paicheler, J.C., Araújo, A., Ferreira, L.F., 'First recovery of Schistosoma mansoni eggs from a latrine in Europe (15–16th Centuries)', *Journal of Parasitology* 88 (2002): 404–05; Bouchet, F., Paicheler, J.C., 'Paleoparasitologie: présomption d'un cas de bilharziose au XVe siècle à Montbéliard (Doubs, France)', *Comptes Rendu de l'Academie des Sciences Paris* 318 (1995): 811–14.

le-Bel (14th AD) and Rigny (15th–16th AD).[55] Furthermore, in 11th–13th century Pineuilh two different causes of dysentery, *Entamoeba histolytica* and *Giardia duodenalis*, have also been identified.[56]

The bulk of information about the parasitic past of Germany comes from the medieval period, when human roundworms and whipworms are reported from archaeological levels in many different sites, including Lübeck, Schleswig, Berlin, Braunschweig, Hameln, Gottingen, Marburgh, Freiburg, Breisach, Regensburg and Landshut.[57] Fish tapeworm is reported from medieval Hameln, Freiburg, Schleswig and Regensburg, while pinworm (*Enterobius vermicularis*) and beef/ pork tapeworm are described from medieval strata in Gottingen. Finally, *Fasciola* liver fluke is described from medieval Hameln, Freiburg and Braunschweig.[58]

In Riga, Latvia on the Baltic coast a medieval wooden latrine dating from the 14th century was found to contain large numbers of eggs of whipworm, roundworm and fish tapeworm. As far as we are aware, this appears to be the highest concentration of fish tapeworm eggs ever found in an archaeological latrine. The bones of a broad range of fish species were also recovered during the excavation.[59]

Medieval Utrecht (13th–14th AD) and Amsterdam (14th–15th AD) in the Netherlands are described as infected with whipworm and roundworm,[60] demonstrating the wide distribution of these two species in medieval Europe.

The paleoparasitological record from Norway consists only of medieval findings from Oslo, which are dated to the 11th and 15th century AD. These are roundworm, whipworm and fish tapeworm.[61]

In medieval Switzerland, *Echinococcus granulosus*, *Giardia duodenalis* and *Entamoeba histolytica* dysentery have been identified from 7th–9th century levels in Chevenez.[62]

---

[55]   Le Bailly and Bouchet 2010.

[56]   Le Bailly and Bouchet 2006; Le Bailly, M., Goncalves, C.L.M., Harter, S., Prodeo, F., Araújo, A., Bouchet, F., 'New finding of Giardia intestinalis (Eukaryote, Metamonad) in Old World Archaeological site using immunofluorescence and enzyme-linked immunosorbent assays', *Memórias do Instituto Oswaldo Cruz* 103 (2008): 298–300.

[57]   Herrmann 1985.

[58]   Herrmann 1985.

[59]   Yeh, H.-Y., Pluskowski, A., Kalējs, U., Mitchell, P.D. 'Intestinal parasites in a mid-14th century latrine from Riga, Latvia: fish tapeworm and the consumption of uncooked fish in the medieval eastern Baltic region.' *Journal of Archaeological Science* 49 (2014): 83–89.

[60]   Jansen and Boersema 1972; Boersema, J.H., Jansen, J., 'Helminth infections in medieval Utrecht', *Tropical and Geographical Medicine* 27 (1975): 441.

[61]   Jones, A.K.G., 'Parasitological investigations', in E. Schia and K. Griffin (eds), *De Arkeologiske Utgravninger I Gamlegyen, Oslo.* Series no. 5 (Oslo: Alheim and Eide, 1988), pp. 134–37.

[62]   Le Bailly 2005; Le Bailly and Bouchet 2006.

Early Modern (16th–18th AD) and Modern Period (18th–20th AD)

The evidence from the Early Modern and Modern Period is quite restricted to a few findings from Belgium, the Czech Republic, France, England and Spain. In Belgium, whipworm and beef/pork tapeworm were identified from 15th–19th century strata from the Place d'Armes in Namur,[63] while Fernandes et al.[64] identified whipworm and roundworm eggs from 16th century Raversijde.

In the Czech Republic from 14th–18th century archaeological levels at the site of Chrudim, Bartosova et al.[65] have reported eggs of roundworm, hookworm (*Ancylostoma*), fish tapeworm, pinworm (*Enterobius vermicularis*), *Fasciola* liver fluke, Giardia dysentery, dwarf tapeworm *(Hymenolepis nana), Toxocara* sp. and whipworm. However, some of these identifications are open to debate (such as the hookworm).

In France, the early modern paleoparasitological findings come from the site of Marly-le-Roy (17th–18th century AD), where eggs of roundworm, whipworm, beef/pork tapeworm and *Fasciola* liver fluke have been identified.[66]

In England, the early modern parasitic evidence derives from two coprolites excavated from a cesspool in Spitalfields in London[67]. Eggs of roundworm and whipworm were identified in the coprolites, which were dated to the 17th to 18th century AD, thus providing evidence of the hygiene conditions prevalent in early modern London.

Finally, the paleoparasitological record from Spain revealed the presence of roundworm in 18th century Canary Islands[68] and the presence of *Trichinella spiralis* (trichinosis) in 19th century Toledo.[69]

---

[63] Da Rocha et al. 2006.

[64] Fernandes, A., Ferreira, L.F., Goncalves, M.L.C., Bouchet, F., Klein, C.H., Iguchi, T., Sianto, L., Araújo, A., 'Intestinal parasite analysis in organic sediments collected from a 16th-century Belgian archaeological site', *Cadernos de Saúde Pública* 21 (2005): 329–32.

[65] Bartosova et al. 2011.

[66] Bouchet, F., Bentrad, S., Paicheler, J.C., 'Enquête 'Epi-démiologique sur les Helminthiases à la Cour de Louis XIV', *Mini-Synthese Medicine Science* 14 (1998): 463–66.

[67] Anastasiou, E., Mitchell, P.D., Jeffries, N. 'The paleoparasitology of 17th-18th century Spitalfields in London', in P.D. Mitchell and J. Buckberry (eds), *Proceedings of the 12th Annual Conference of the British Association for Biological Anthropology and Osteoarchaeology* (Oxford: Archaeopress, 2012), pp. 53–61.

[68] Botella, H.G., Vargas, J.A., De La Rosa, M.A., Leles, D., Reimers, E.G., Vicente, A., Iñiguez, A., 'Paleoparasitologic, paleogenetic and paleobotanic analysis of XVIII century coprolites from the church La Concepcion in Santa Cruz de Tenerife, Canary Islands, Spain', *Memórias do Instituto Oswaldo Cruz* 105 (2010): 1054–56.

[69] Bellard, F.G., Cortes, A., 'Trichinosis in the mummy of a young girl (Toledo, Spain)', in E. Cockburn and T.A. Reyman (eds), Papers on Paleopathology Presented at the *8th European Members Meeting, Cambridge, England* (Detroit: Paleopathology Association, 1991), p. 11.

Discussion

The evidence presented in this chapter illustrates the extensive research into ancient parasites that has been conducted in Europe. Based on the available evidence, whipworms and roundworms were the most widely distributed species in Europe, both in time and space. This comes as no surprise, since these soil-transmitted helminths are two of the most common parasites with a cosmopolitan distribution today and they have also been identified paleoparasitologically in a multitude of different archaeological contexts from all over the world.[70] There is also good evidence to suggest these two species have been present in humans throughout our evolution.[71] Besides roundworms and whipworms, other commonly identified species from ancient Europe include the tapeworms (*Taenia* sp. and *Diphyllobothrium* sp.) and the liver flukes (*Dicrocoelium* sp. and *Fasciola* sp.).

In contrast to roundworms and whipworms, *Enterobius vermicularis* (pinworm) and *Ancylostoma* sp. (hookworm) are among the least commonly identified species from European sites. Nevertheless, their infrequent identification should not necessarily be interpreted as evidence for their rarity in antiquity, but should rather be linked to the fragile nature of their egg walls and the poor preservation conditions that most European archaeological sites face. The decomposition of organic remains in archaeological samples from Europe rarely allows the identification of species with thin-walled eggs, like those of the pinworms and hookworms. In the Americas the better preservation of the paleoparasitological material in mummies or dried coprolites means that *Enterobius vermicularis* and *Ancylostoma* sp. are among the most commonly identified species.[72] So far *Enterobius vermicularis* has been reported as present only in contexts from Germany, Czech Republic, and Greenland and *Ancylostoma* sp. has been reported as present in archaeological remains from the Czech Republic[73] and France[74].

The *Opisthorchis* liver fluke and *Dioctophymidae* giant kidney worm identified during the Neolithic Period are among the less commonly identified species in European archaeological contexts. While they usually infect animals, they are both known to occasionally infect humans today. The identification of these rare human parasites provides important insights into the great diversity of

---

[70]   Anastasiou, E., 'The Paleoparasitology of the Eastern Mediterranean and Adjacent Regions: Understanding Intestinal Diseases throughout Time', (University of Cambridge: Unpublished PhD Thesis, 2013).

[71]   Mitchell, P.D., 'The origins of human parasites: exploring the evidence for endoparasitism throughout human evolution', *International Journal of Paleopathology* 3 (2013): 191–98.

[72]   Araújo et al., this volume, Ch. 9, p. 174.

[73]   Bartosova et al. 2011. However, some of the diagnoses, such as that of hookworm, are questionable.

[74]   Dommelier-Espejo, S., *Contribution à l'Etude Paléoparasitologique des Sites Néolithiques en Environnement Lacustre dans les Domaines Jurassien et Péri-Alpin* (PhD Thesis Reims: Université de Reims, 2001).

parasite species that infected the populations of Europe throughout antiquity and allow us to hypothesise that the parasitic environment of ancient Europe must have encompassed a plethora of different species, infective to both humans and animals (zoonoses).

From the identified species, those with faecal-oral transmission such as *Trichuris trichiura, Ascaris lumbricoides, Entamoeba histolytica* and *Giardia duodenalis*, as well as parasites like *Fasciola*, which is transmitted through the consumption of unwashed vegetation, or *Strongyloides stercoralis*, which is transmitted when humans come into contact with contaminated water or soil, are generally associated with poor levels of hygiene and inadequate sanitation. This is so because their transmission is increased in populations that do not properly dispose of their faecal waste, that use faeces as fertiliser, that do not properly wash vegetables before consuming them or do not wash their hands before preparing and eating food. Consequently, the widespread identification of these species from different archaeological contexts throughout Europe, as well as their identification in all of the studied time periods, from the Neolithic up to the modern period, indicates a similar level of hygiene throughout antiquity and across different populations. This interpretation is of course not surprising if we consider that the modern perception of cleanliness and the adherence to hygiene practices that today are social norms for most middle class Europeans are ideas originating in the twentieth century.

In contrast, the presence of pork, beef and fish tapeworms (*Taenia* sp. and *Diphyllobothrium* sp.), as well as the presence of the nematode *Trichinella spiralis,* in different parts of Europe as early as the Neolithic, provides important information regarding the dietary habits of the populations that flourished on the continent throughout antiquity. Since these species are transmitted with the consumption of poorly cooked, raw, smoked or salted meat and fish, their identification in different populations of ancient Europe allows us to reconstruct some of the food preparation methods followed in different parts of Europe. More specifically, the frequent identification of these species in the past allows the hypothesis that the consumption of salted, raw, pickled, smoked or poorly cooked fish and meat was widespread throughout Europe in the past. If we consider that salting and smoking were some of the most important and universal practices for the preservation of food prior to the invention of refrigerators, the identification of parasite species associated with salted or smoked meat and fish should follow as a consequence of this practice.

Furthermore, the identification of two different *Schistosoma* species (bilharzia) from France[75] is very interesting, since neither species is endemic in Europe. *Schistosoma mansoni* is a flatworm that lives in the blood vessels of the intestines, while *Schistosoma haematobium* lives in the blood vessels of the kidneys and bladder. Both species require warm, still, fresh water that contains particular types of snails in order to complete their life cycle, and hence the cool winters of Europe

---

[75] Bouchet et al. 2002; Bouchet and Paicheler 1995.

mean that these diseases cannot become endemic there. The presence of these two species in France during the 15th–16th centuries AD must therefore indicate either that infected people from endemic areas such as Africa and the Middle East travelled to Europe, or that Europeans travelled abroad and contracted these parasites before returning home again. Consequently, these findings provide an excellent example of the importance of paleoparasitology for reconstructing migration events and long-distance travelling, as well as for providing insights into the impact that these events had on the transmission of parasitic diseases into new geographical regions.

Additionally, species like *Dicrocoelium* sp. and *Echinococcus granulosus* that employ animals as their normal definitive host (poultry, swine, cats, cattle and dogs) demonstrate both the close relationship that past populations had with their livestock, as well as the constant danger for contracting zoonotic diseases to which past communities were exposed.

In view of the abundance of parasitic diseases identified from ancient European sites, it is not unreasonable to argue that the lifestyle of past European populations would have exposed them to a variety of different infectious diseases, not only parasitic but also viral and bacterial, associated with their cooking practices, their levels of hygiene and their close proximity to animals.

Before concluding this chapter, I would like to highlight that there is still a long way to go in order to comprehensively reconstruct the parasitic past of the Europe. Although paleoparasitology has provided valuable information for the parasitic environment of Britain, Switzerland and France, there is very little evidence for southern and eastern Europe, or for Scandinavia. Therefore, due to our sparse understanding of the parasitic environment of Europe as a whole, any conclusions regarding the directionality and mode of the introduction of different parasite species in the continent, as well as any discussion on changes in species richness through time and space is necessarily limited. For example, although Neolithic Switzerland and France were infected by a wide range of different parasite species, it is not possible based on the current evidence to postulate as to whether this is something specific to the cultural and ecological characteristics of the Neolithic populations of western Europe, or whether other European populations were equally infected by different parasite species.

Similarly, despite reasonable evidence for parasites in the Neolithic, Roman and Medieval periods, little is known about parasite species in the Paleolithic, Mesolithic, Bronze Age, and Iron Age. This lack of evidence restricts our ability to compare the epidemiology over time. Furthermore, our current understanding of the paleoparasitology in Europe allows only brief glimpses into the influence that important events of our cultural evolution had upon the parasitic environment of past civilisations. Therefore, although the available evidence allows us to reconstruct many different aspects of the daily life of past Europeans, such as their hygiene conditions and their dietary habits, at the same time it is insufficient for comparative analyses of parasitism in different cultural and ecological settings. It is therefore necessary to carry out more paleoparasitological studies on material from less studied geographical regions and chronological periods, in order to eventually address larger questions, such as the impact that the introduction of agriculture and the transition to industrialisation had on the transmission of infectious parasitic diseases in Europe.

Conclusion

This paper has reviewed the available evidence for the parasitic environment of ancient Europe and provided an interpretation of its significance for reconstructing aspects of health and the daily life of past European populations. Based upon our current understanding of parasitism in ancient Europe, it is possible to formulate hypotheses about the distribution of different parasite species across time and space, and argue that whipworms, roundworms and tapeworms were among the most widely distributed species infecting past European communities. The identification of parasite species with different life-cycle constraints from archaeological sites across Europe has also allowed inferences about the hygiene conditions and the dietary habits of the civilisations that flourished in the continent. The identification of non-endemic species in European contexts has been utilised to trace migration events and long-distance journeys and to demonstrate the significance of these movements for introducing new diseases into the continent. Consequently, paleoparasitology has succeeded in enriching our knowledge of the lifestyle choices of past European populations and has provided the means to address questions about the inter-relationship between parasitism, cultural behaviour and cultural change.

Chapter 11

A First Attempt to Retrace the History of Dysentery Caused by *Entamoeba histolytica*

Matthieu Le Bailly and Françoise Bouchet

Introduction

Since 1910 following the work of Sir Marc Ruffer, paleoparasitologists and other scientists interested in disease evolution have collected data on ancient parasites from the study of samples taken from archaeological excavations.[1] In the last century, materials thought worthy of study have broadened, extraction methods have standardised[2], and identification techniques have become more precise and advanced. This progress has led to our ability to detect a large range of pathogens including protozoa, and to identify parasites in a variety of organs and tissues such as skin, blood and intestines. Although species determination is sometimes problematic using microscopy, these technical advances may offer new perspectives, especially regarding parasite characterisation.

Much data has now been collected on ancient parasites, and it is possible to begin to retrace parasite history. This is already the case for some human parasites such as pinworms[3] and hookworms,[4] and also helminths normally found in animals

---

[1] Bouchet, F., Harter, S., Le Bailly, M., 'The state of the art of paleoparasitological research in the Old World', *Memórias do Instituto Oswaldo Cruz* 98 (Suppl. 1) (2003): 95–101; Gonçalves, C.L.M., Araújo, A. and Ferreira, L.F., 'Human intestinal parasites in the past: new findings and a review', *Memórias do Instituto Oswaldo Cruz* 98 (Suppl. 1) (2003): 103–118; Horne, P.D.,'A Review of the evidence of human endoparasitism in the pre-Columbian New World through the study of coprolites', *Journal of Archaeological Science* 12 (1985): 299–310 ; Reinhard, K.J., 'Parasitology as an interpretative tool in Archaeology', *American Antiquity* 57 (1992): 231–245; Sianto, L., Chame, M., Silva, C.S.P., Gonçalves, C.L.M., Reinhard, K., Fugassa, M., Araújo, A., 'Animal helminths in human archaeological remains: a review of zoonoses in the past', *Revista do Instituto de Medicina Tropical de São Paulo* 51 (2009): 119–30.

[2] Dufour, B., Le Bailly, M., 'Testing new parasite egg extraction methods in paleoparasitology and an attempt at quantification', *International Journal of Paleopathology* 3 (2013): 199–203.

[3] Araújo, A., Ferreira, L.F., 'Oxyuriasis and prehistoric migrations', *Manguinhos* 2 (1995): 99–109.

[4] Araújo, A., Ferreira, L.F., Confalonieri, U., Chame, M., 'Hookworms and the peopling of America', *Cadernos de Saúde Pública* 2 (1988): 226–233; Ferreira, L.F.,

such as the lancet liver fluke.[5] Here we provide a review of the past occurrences of a human pathogenic amoeba that causes dysentery, *Entamoeba histolytica*. We are including the previously published data and integrate this with new results from the Reims paleoparasitology lab.

Amoebiasis

Entamoeba histolytica is an invasive intestinal pathogenic protozoa (Eukaryota, Amoebozoa, Archamoeba). It is a parasite of humans, but may also infect animals such as primates, cats, dogs and some rodents.[6] By infecting five hundred million people and killing around one hundred thousand humans per year, this parasite is one of the most important causes of morbidity and mortality from parasites in the world.[7]

The organism has a simple life cycle, with two different stages. In the vegetative stage, named the trophozoite, it develops and multiplies on the mucosal surface of intestines. The cyst stage is the form that can be spread to other people in the faeces, especially when diarrhoea is present. In the environment, cysts can remain viable for as little as a few hours to as long as several days, depending upon the conditions. Transition from the trophozoite to cyst stage is still not well understood.[8]

Human infection occurs with the ingestion of cysts in food or water that have been contaminated by human faeces. When localised to the intestines, symptoms include abdominal pain and bloody diarrhoea. However, when parasites reach the general circulation, they can cause fever and may multiply in the liver and some other organs.[9] The diagnosis of amoebiasis in modern hospitals can be made from analysis of faeces or blood with light microscopy, but more commonly

---

Araújo, A., 'On hookworms in the Americas and trans-pacific contact', *Parasitology Today* 12 (1996): 454–454; Montenegro, A., Araújo, A., Eby, M., Ferreira, L.F., Hetherington, R., Weaver, A.J., 'Parasites, paleoclimate, and the peopling of the Americas', *Current Anthropology* 47 (2006): 193–200.

[5]   Le Bailly, M., Bouchet, F., 'Ancient Dicrocoeliosis: occurrence, distribution and migration', *Acta Tropica* 115 (2010): 175–80.

[6]   Acha, P.N., Szyfres, B., *Zoonoses et Maladies Transmissibles Communes aux Hommes et aux Animaux* (Paris: World Organisation for Animal Health, 2005), vol. 3, p. 399; Singh, A., Houpt, E., Petri, W.A., 'Rapid diagnosis of intestinal protozoa, with focus on *Entamoeba histolytica*', *Interdisciplinary Perspectives on Infectious Diseases* (2009): article 547090: 8 pages.

[7]   Baxt, L.A., Singh, U., 'New insights into *Entamoeba histolytica* pathogenesis', *Current Opinion in Infectious Diseases* 21 (2008): 489–494.

[8]   Stanley, S.L., 'Amoebiasis', *The Lancet* 361 (2003): 1025–1034.

[9]   Gentilini, M., *Médecine Tropicale* (Paris: Flammarion, 2001), p. 929; Mehlhorn, H., *Encyclopedic Reference of Parasitology* (Berlin: Springer, 2001), p. 678.

immunological[10] or molecular biology techniques[11] are used due to their ability to differentiate pathogenic forms of Entamoeba from harmless species that appear similar on microscopy.

Amoebiasis in Archaeology

Detection of *Entamoeba histolytica* in archaeological samples is also based upon the recovery of parasite markers. Light microscopy can be employed to try to detect preserved cysts in coprolites or sediment samples taken from the pelvic region of skeletons, cesspits, latrines and all contexts potentially containing human faeces. However, preservation of the cysts is rare in ancient samples as their walls are thin and fragile, and their survival often requires extreme conditions such as a very humid, frozen or extremely dry climate.

As a consequence of this fragility, other biomolecular tools have been used to detect traces of amoeba in ancient samples. In particular, Enzyme Linked ImmunoSorbent Assays (ELISA) have given key positive results during the last ten years, and allowed us to identify many ancient outbreaks of dysentery. Analyses carried out in the Reims laboratory used the 'Entamoeba histolytica II' test,[12] as has been the case for the majority of the research performed on ancient *E. histolytica* by other units. This ELISA test allows the detection of an adhesin produced specifically by *E. histolytica*, as it bonds to it via monoclonal antibodies targeted to this protein alone.[13] The test has good sensitivity and specificity, and moreover no cross-reactivity with other related microorganisms such as the non-pathogenic amoebas *E. dispar* or *E. moshkovskii*.

---

[10]   Haque, R., Neville, L.M., Hahn, P., Petri, W.A., 'Rapid diagnosis of *Entamoeba* infection by using *Entamoeba* and *Entamoeba histolytica* stool antigen detection kits', *Journal of Clinical Microbiology* 33 (1995): 2558–2561; Haque, R., Ali, K.M., Akther, S., Petri, W.A., 'Comparison of PCR, isoenzyme analysis, and antigen detection for diagnosis of *Entamoeba histolytica* infection', *Journal of Clinical Microbiology* 36 (1998): 449–452.

[11]   Beck, D.L., Tanyuksel, M., Mackey, A.J., Haque, R., Trapaidze, N., Pearson, W.R., Loftus, B., Petri, W.A., '*Entamoeba histolytica*: sequence conservation of the Gal/GalNAc lectin from clinical isolates', *Experimental Parasitology* 101 (2002): 157–163; Roy, S., Kabir, M., Mondal, D., Ali, I.K.M., Petri, W.A., Haque, R., 'Real-time-PCR assay for diagnosis of *Entamoeba histolytica* infection', *Journal of Clinical Microbiology* 43 (2005): 2168–2172.

[12]   *Entamoeba histolytica* II ELISA test is manufactured by TECHLAB®.

[13]   Haque, R., Mollah, N.U., Ali, K.M., Alam, K., Eubanks, A., Lyerly, D., Petri, W.A., 'Diagnosis of amebic liver abscess and intestinal infection with the TechLab *Entamoeba histolytica* II antigen detection and antibody tests', *Journal of Clinical Microbiology* 38 (2000): 3235–3239; Mirelman, D., Nuchamowitz, Y., Stoblarsky, T., 'Comparison of use of enzyme-linked immunosorbent assay-based kits and PCR amplification of rRNA genes for simultaneous detection of *Entamoeba histolytica* and *E. dispar*', *Journal of Clinical Microbiology* 35 (1997): 2405–2407.

Review of Past Evidence for *E. Histolytica*

Published discoveries of amoeba from archaeological contexts are quite rare. Only five articles are known to date describing the discovery of *Entamoeba histolytica* or *Entamoeba* sp. traces using microscopy or immunology (See Table 11.1). In this paragraph, we give a synthesis of these occurrences classified in their discovery order.

The first remains of *Entamoeba* sp. from archaeological samples were described by Witenberg in 1961.[14] Using light microscopy, cysts identified as *E. histolytica* were found in two coprolites from a Judean Desert cave in Nahal Mishmar, dated from the Bar-Kochba period (132–135 AD). However, no images were reproduced in the paper to confirm this diagnosis. It should also be remembered that the pathogenic *E. histolytica* and the commensal, harmless *E. dispar* and *E. moshkovskii* appear identical under the microscope.

In 1982, Fouant et al. analysed 80 coprolite samples from pre-Columbian mummies from Peru and Chile.[15] Authors identified cysts of *Entamoeba* sp. in 10 samples using microscopy. In a second step, authors used *E. histolytica* specific ELISA tests to confirm the amoeba species. However, immunological tests were all negative for the *E. histolytica* specific antigens. According to the author two explanations could be raised. One possibility was that the cysts were not the *E. histolytica* species, but *E. coli* species[16]. A second possibility was that the cysts has lost their antigenicity over time, so no longer triggered a positive test.

In 2004, Gonçalves et al. published the first collective work on *Entamoeba histolytica*.[17] ELISA tests specific for the human pathogenic amoeba were applied to 90 samples originating from the three major paleoparasitology labs in the world at that time (Brazil, USA and France), and covering a broad range of dates and geographic locations. Among these samples, 20 were positive for *E. histolytica* antigen. The most ancient positive results were in samples recovered in Switzerland dating to around 3,400 BC.

In 2005, during his thesis research, Le Bailly tested 102 samples collected from 19 archaeological sites of different dates and geographic locations.[18] Among

---

[14]   Witenberg, G., 'Human parasites in archaeological findings', *Bulletin of the Israel Exploration Society* 25 (1961): 86.

[15]   Fouant, M.M., Allison, M., Gerszten, E., Focacci, G., 'Parasitos intestinales entre los indigenas precolombinos', *Revista Chungará* 9 (1982): 285–299.

[16]   Authors did not indicate that, in fact, cysts of *E. histolytica* are different in size to the cysts of *E. coli*.

[17]   Gonçalves, C.L.M., da Silva, V.L., de Andrade, C.M., Reinhard, K., da Rocha, G.C., Le Bailly, M., Bouchet, F., Ferreira, L.F., Araújo, A., 'Amoebiasis distribution in the past: first steps using an immunoassay technique', *Transactions of the Royal Society of Tropical Medicine and Hygiene* 98 (2004): 88–91.

[18]   Le Bailly, M., *Les Parasites dans les Lacs Nord Alpins au Néolithique (3900–2900 BC), et Nouvelles Données dans la Détection des Paléoantigènes de Protozoa* (Sarrebruck: Editions Universitaires Européennes, 2011), p. 291; Le Bailly, M., Bouchet, F., 'Paléoparasitologie et immunologie : l'exemple d'*Entamoeba histolytica*', *Archéosciences* 30 (2006): 129–135 ;

Table 11.1 Synthesis of published data (grey rows) and new Reims laboratory data (white rows) for *Entamoeba histolytica*. Type of sample: C = coprolite, S = sediment

Site names	Country	Date	Sample nature	Origin structure	Positive samples	Data origin (Thesis/lab analysis/ article)	Species	Employed method
Fortin Minana	Argentina	19th c. AD	S	Cesspits	9	Gonçalves et al., 2004, ref.17	*Entamoeba histolytica*	ELISA
Mageroy	Belgium	Roman period	S	Latrines	3	Lab analyses	*Entamoeba histolytica*	ELISA
Namur	Belgium	14th-18th c. AD	S	Cesspits	2	Gonçalves et al., 2004, ref.17	*Entamoeba histolytica*	ELISA
-	Chile	Pre-Columbian	C	Mummies	8	Fouant et al., 1982, ref.15	*Entamoeba* sp.	Microscopy
Gresine	France	500 BC	S	Occupation layers	1	Gonçalves et al., 2004, ref.17	*Entamoeba histolytica*	ELISA
Troyes	France	1st c. BC-1st c. AD	S	Latrines/Cesspits	3	Lab analyses	*Entamoeba histolytica*	ELISA
Lattes	France	1st-2nd c. AD	S	Cesspits	2	Le Bailly & Bouchet, 2006, ref.18	*Entamoeba histolytica*	ELISA
Lisses	France	Roman period	S	Pit	1	Lab analyses	*Entamoeba histolytica*	ELISA
Castillon-du-Gard	France	3rd c. AD	S	Cesspits	2	Gonçalves et al., 2004, ref.17	*Entamoeba histolytica*	ELISA
Pineuilh	France	11th-13th c. AD	S	Occupation layers	2	Le Bailly & Bouchet, 2006, ref.18	*Entamoeba histolytica*	ELISA
Villiers-le-Bel	France	14th c. AD	S	Multiple tomb	2	Lab analyses	*Entamoeba histolytica*	ELISA

Site names	Country	Date	Sample nature	Origin structure	Positive samples	Data origin (Thesis/lab analysis/ article)	Species	Employed method
Brouage	France	17th c. AD	S	Latrines/Barrels	3	Lab analyses	*Entamoeba histolytica*	ELISA
Kouphovouno	Greece	5000-2000 BC	S	Burial	5	Le Bailly & Bouchet, 2006, ref.18	*Entamoeba histolytica*	ELISA
Nahal Mishmar	Israel	132-135 AD	C	-	2	Witenberg, 1961, ref.14	*Entamoeba histolytica*	Microscopy
Acre	Israel	13th c. AD	S	Latrines/ Cesspool	6	Mitchell et al., 2008, ref.19	*Entamoeba histolytica*	ELISA
Roma	Italy	Roman period	S	Sediment core	2	Lab analyses	*Entamoeba histolytica*	ELISA
-	Peru	Pre-Columbian	C	Mummies	2	Fouant et al., 1982, ref.15	*Entamoeba* sp.	Microscopy
Concise	Switzerland	3700 BC	S	Occupation layers	1	Lab analyses	*Entamoeba histolytica*	ELISA
Arbon-Bleiche 3	Switzerland	3384-3370 BC	S	Occupation layers	3	Gonçalves et al., 2004, ref.17	*Entamoeba histolytica*	ELISA
Chevenez	Switzerland	7th-9th c. AD	S	Human skeleton	5	Le Bailly & Bouchet, 2006, ref.18	*Entamoeba histolytica*	ELISA
Canyon de Chelly	USA	12th-13th c. AD	S	Cesspits	3	Gonçalves et al., 2004, ref.17	*Entamoeba histolytica*	ELISA
Meadowlark cemetery	USA	19th c. AD	S	Burial	3	Le Bailly & Bouchet, 2006, ref.18	*Entamoeba histolytica*	ELISA

these samples, ELISA specific tests revealed the presence of amoeba antigens in 17 samples. The most ancient positive results were in samples recovered from a Greek site dating from between 5,000 and 2,000 BC.

Finally, in 2008 Mitchell et al. identified *E. histolytica* using ELISA on soil sediments from a large communal latrine in the crusader period city of Acre, in Israel.[19] The latrines were in the headquarters of the military order of St John (the Knights Hospitaller), and the contents were radiocarbon-dated to the 13th century AD. This discovery was the first to show the presence of dysentery in the Middle East using immunological techniques, although it is presumed that the latrines were primarily for the use of European crusaders who had travelled to the east.

New Data

New data were obtained from research undertaken at the Reims paleoparasitology lab over the last 20 years. Among these analyses, 15 samples of coprolites and sediments were positive for *E. histolytica*. These came from seven different archaeological sites, and were all identified using ELISA tests. To reduce the risk of possible antibody/antigen complex alteration during the ELISA analysis, archaeological samples were rehydrated for one week in ultrapure water (Direct Q-5 system, Millipore®), and stored at 2–4°C. Samples were then roughly filtered by using microsieves to discard the largest soil elements. ELISA tests were then performed following the manufacturer recommendations.

An interesting pattern in the results was noted: positive new results appear exclusively in Western Europe. However, analyses were performed on samples from many other countries such as Lithuania, Kazakhstan, China, Cyprus, Israel, Lebanon, Egypt, Sudan, Samoa and Chile. During these analyses, no other evidence for human dysentery was found.

New cases were discovered in samples from France, Italy, and Belgium for the Roman and medieval periods. But the most remarkable is the Swiss sample from the Neolithic lakeside settlement of Concise, dated to around 3,700 years BC. This site is actually the oldest one in which *Entamoeba histolytica* has ever been found. It confirmed the presence of the parasite in Western Europe during the Neolithic Period, as was previously demonstrated by Gonçalves et al. in 2004.[20]

---

[19]   Mitchell, P.D., Stern, E., Tepper, Y., 'Dysentery in the crusader kingdom of Jerusalem: an ELISA analysis of two medieval latrines in the city of Acre (Israel)', *Journal of Archaeological Science* 35 (2008): 1849–53.

[20]   Gonçalves et al. 2004.

The Significance of Positive and Negative ELISA Tests

The use of ELISA for the detection of pathogens in archaeological samples raises a number of questions due to the fact that results of these tests are colorimetric reactions in a test plate, and not directly visible indicators of parasites such as their eggs or cysts. The *Entamoeba histolytica* II test from TechLab has been developed to enable hospital microbiology labs to accurately detect *Entamoeba histolytica*, with good sensitivity and specificity. The test offers clear differentiation between *E. histolytica* and *E. dispar* or *E. moshkovskii*. These are two harmless, non-pathogenic amoebas, identical in form and size to the pathogenic species.[21] No cross-reactions have been observed in clinical laboratory tests with other intestinal pathogens such as *Giardia intestinalis* or *Entamoeba coli* either.[22]

Following the detection of a human-specific amoeba antigen, positive samples can be automatically classified as of human or human-mixed origin, even when no selection is performed prior to testing the samples. This property makes it possible to characterise some archaeological structures such as latrines, or demonstrates the presence of human faecal matter in different contexts.

How to interpret negative results in samples may also be problematic. Several explanations can be put forward, including, of course, the absence of amoeba. However, the parasite may be present but not in high enough concentrations to trigger a positive result in the ELISA test kit. Many parasite cysts are required in any one test well to trigger the required colour change indicating a positive test. Other explanations for a negative test in a sample that does contain amoeba include poor preservation conditions before excavation, the presence of natural inhibitors in the soil samples, the funerary treatments performed on cadavers, or possible variations of parasite strain with a change in epitope morphology. We have to remember that thousands of years ago the adhesin produced by the parasite may have been slightly different to the form produced today due to evolution of the Entamoeba organism, and so very old samples may theoretically be less likely to trigger a positive test when the organism is nevertheless present in the sample. All these points highlight how a positive ELISA result is very likely to be a true indicator of the presence of *Entamoeba histolytica* in the sample, while a negative

---

[21]   Pillai, D.R., Keystone, J.S., Sheppard, D.C., MacLean, J.D., MacPherson, D.W., Kain, K.C., '*Entamoeba histolytica* and *Entamoeba dispar*: epidemiology and comparison of diagnostic methods in a setting of nonendemicity', *Clinical Infectious Diseases* 29 (1999): 320–321; Visser, L.G., Verweij, J.J., Van Esbroeck, M., Edeling, W.M., Clerinx, J., Polderman, A.M., 'Diagnostic methods for differentiation of *Entamoeba histolytica* and *Entamoeba dispar* in carriers: performance and clinical implications in a non-endemic setting', *International Journal of Medical Microbiology* 296 (2006): 397–403.

[22]   Furrows, S.J., Moody, A.H., Chiodini, P.L., 'Comparison of PCR and antigen detection methods for the diagnosis of *Entamoeba histolytica* infection', *Journal of Clinical Pathology* 57 (2004): 1264–1266.

result may indicate absence of the parasite, or just that the test is unable to detect its presence.

Data Synthesis: An Attempt to Retrace Amoeba History

In light of all these results, it is interesting to note the presence of dysentery from *E. histolytica* in the Old World in prehistoric Europe. The parasite has been detected twice in Neolithic Switzerland, and also in Greece during the pre-Hellenic period. In France, the first evidence dates from around 500BC, in the Bronze Age. The Roman period is quite well represented with occurrences in Western Europe, in France, Belgium, and Italy. The parasite was also described in Israel during the first century AD, but this identification was made using microscopy, and no photo was published. In the medieval period, evidence for dysentery was recovered in Europe from France, Belgium, Switzerland, and in the Middle East from Israel, during the crusades.

If we argue that Witenberg's 1961 paper[23] was correct, the medieval traces from Acre could be just a continuum of the presence of the pathology in this region. However, if the first century occurrence is considered unreliable, it is more reasonable to assume that the parasite was transported to the Middle East by the crusaders from Europe, where it had been present since the Neolithic. However, it is important to remember that the parasite has also been identified in samples from prehistoric Greece.

Concerning the Americas, pre-Columbian amoebas noted on microscopy by Fouant et al. in 1982 were not confirmed when using immunological tests specific for *E. histolytica*.[24] It is quite likely that the cysts observed down the microscope were a different species of amoeba, which may or may not have caused any symptoms. The first reliable evidence for *E. histolytica* so far identified in the New World is from North America in the 12th century AD. Other positive results have been found even later, in 19th century sites in the USA and Argentina. Despite analyses performed by American paleoparasitologists on pre-Columbian and post-colonial sites, no other examples have been found in South America prior to the 19th century.[25]

In the light of these results, and the worldwide current distribution of the human pathogenic amoeba,[26] it appears that the current strain of *E. histolytica* could be of Old World origin. It may have then been transported to the Americas around the 12th century AD or before, by the way of past human migrations, for example via Greenland or Aleutian's. It is always possible that other strains of *E. histolytica* could have been present in the Americas before this date, but the ELISA test we

---

[23]　Witenberg 1961.
[24]　Fouant et al. 1982.
[25]　Gonçalves et al. 2004.
[26]　Mehlhorn 2001.

use today may be unable to detect them if they were sufficiently different to those strains found worldwide today.

Conclusion

Integration of modern tools in paleoparasitological research has become crucial for the future development of this research field. The use of advanced biomolecular techniques such as ELISA allows a diagnosis down to species level, a degree of resolution that is rarely possible for amoebic parasites using microscopy and current morphometric data banks. However, even if the utilisation of immunology and molecular biology is to be developed further, the use of microscopy must also be improved. This is because microscopy is still the lone tool that provides clear observational evidence for ancient parasites.

Data collected here on *Entamoeba histolytica* suggests an Old World origin for the current strain of the parasite, with a possible diffusion to the Americas around a thousand years ago. This work demonstrates once again the role of human migrations in the diffusion of pathogens, and in the current worldwide distribution of these diseases. This has already been observed for other parasites including schistosomiasis and dicrocoeliasis.[27] Finally, it is always important to bear in mind the potential for the evolution of human infectious diseases over time, as this could make the biomolecular detection of ancient organisms much more challenging.

Acknowledgements

This work was supported by the CNRS (Program on 'Infectious Diseases and Environment 2010'), TechLab®, Millipore®, the University of Reims and the University of Franche-Comté. The authors thank our colleagues, both archaeologists and anthropologists, for their precious samples and their confidence in us.

---

[27]	Araújo, A., Ferreira, L.F., 'Paleoparasitology of schistosomiasis', *Memórias do Instituto Oswaldo Cruz* 92 (1997): 717; Le Bailly and Bouchet 2010.

Chapter 12

A Better Understanding of Sanitation and Health in the Past

Piers D. Mitchell

At the start of this book we proposed that perhaps the most important questions we have regarding sanitation in the past are how did sanitation change as early populations changed their lifestyles from hunter-gatherers to city dwellers, and what impact did their sanitation technologies have upon their health?[1] This volume has brought together the latest evidence from many different geographical regions and time periods in order to provide a body of information to help us start to frame our answers. While there is little or no evidence available for many parts of the world and many time periods, we can use what data there is to draw some conclusions. Clearly these will need to be reconsidered in the future once a more complete archaeological assessment of sanitation technologies across the world has been made, and once a comprehensive study of ancient intestinal diseases has been made for these civilisations.

Early hunter-gatherers have left little evidence for how they approached the disposal of human waste, but using modern knowledge of how sanitation affects our risk of contracting infectious diseases we can create a theoretical model of past health scenarios.[2] These suggest that in small groups who moved on regularly, the risk of diarrhoeal illnesses and faecal oral parasites would have been much lower than for later time periods when humans began to settle, build towns, farm crops and fertilise them with human faeces. However, early hunter-gatherers would still have been at risk of contracting those parasites endemic in the wild animals they hunted unless the food was thoroughly cooked to kill off the intermediate forms of the parasites.

Archaeological study of the early civilisations of the Middle East region has shown how sanitation technologies developed there.[3] In the towns of ancient Mesopotamia we find that early rulers invested in state projects such as palaces, fortifications and irrigation canals, but not latrines, drains or sewers. However, individuals did often develop their own sanitation solutions. From the late 4th and early 3rd millennium BC, deep-pit and sloped-drain toilets were being used within houses, often in a small room that appears to have been dedicated to this purpose

---

[1]   Mitchell, this volume, Ch. 1, p. 4.
[2]   Mitchell, this volume, Ch. 2, p. 14.
[3]   McMahon, this volume, Ch. 3, p. 19.

alone. By the 3rd millennium BC baked-brick toilet seats started to appear, and by the 2nd millennium BC the design started to allow flushing with water. However, toilets at this time were by no means universal, and most people did not have one. It is likely that those without a toilet took their waste out to the town rubbish tip each day. However, it is also clear that human waste had a value, as it was often used as fertiliser to improve crop yields via manuring.

In ancient Greece the earliest sanitation dates from 2100–1600BC in the Minoan civilisations on Crete.[4] The presence of toilet seats, sewerage systems and flushing capabilities using rainwater is broadly comparable with that found in Asia Minor and Mesopotamia at that time. In consequence it is quite likely that the concept of the toilet spread to Crete from mainland Asia Minor and Mesopotamia. By the 4th century BC toilets started to be seen across Greece, with anatomically shaped seats and latrines in both public and private buildings. As towns increased in size, larger public latrines were built with a rectangular design having rows of toilet seats facing each other, and also washing facilities. The Romans spread this concept across their empire with sophisticated public latrines with running water, sponges and ventilation. Once Christianity was adopted in the eastern Roman Empire (Byzantine Empire) there appears to have been modification to the design of public latrines that gave more privacy and sex segregation.

Rome itself faced a sanitation challenge of an entirely different scale to most other cities in the Mediterranean region on account of its huge population by ancient standards. We have seen that despite its multi-seat public lavatories, sanitation in residential quarters was not given the same emphasis in urban planning as were the grand public buildings of the time. Many drains and sewers were not covered so that people might fall in and flies could breed easily. Many multi-storey tenement blocks had little or no sanitation facilities. When the Tiber flooded in the winter human waste was often washed back up drains into the streets. However, there were regulations in force that helped to improve sanitation by removing human waste from the streets and from blocked sewers, and that forbad the throwing of waste from windows above into streets, where people would be walking.[5]

We might have expected medieval London to be in a rather different sanitary situation to ancient Rome. Medieval London was smaller than ancient Rome, it was not the centre of a huge empire, and it did not have a tradition of large state sponsored engineering projects or grand public buildings. However, comparison with ancient Rome found that medieval London had broadly comparable facilities and regulations in place to address sanitation problems. The areas in which Rome did well, medieval London also managed quite well. Similarly, the aspects of sanitation that London found challenging were just as troublesome for those in ancient Rome.[6]

---

[4]   Antoniou and Angelaki, this volume, Ch. 4, p. 41.
[5]   Taylor, this volume, Ch. 5, p. 69.
[6]   Taylor, this volume, Ch. 5, p. 94.

In York we have seen how sanitation evolved in the same town over nearly two thousand years as shown from excavation of Roman, Viking, medieval and Victorian latrines and rubbish tips.[7] The Roman fortress in York had a stone-lined sewer, there were deep wells providing clean drinking water, and the city seems to have had effective waste collection systems as very little human waste has been detected during excavations. In the Viking age there was no use of a sewerage system, and while cess pits were common, human waste was frequently detected across the town. The parasites whipworm and roundworm were common, and these are spread by the faecal contamination of food crops and the preparation of meals with dirty hands. The remains of many flies, dung-eating beetles and other insects were recovered. At this time the ground level of the town appears to have raised significantly, suggesting that waste was not removed from the town but allowed to accumulate. In medieval York sanitation appeared at a similar level with the presence of wicker or barrel-lined latrines with seats, but no evidence for a more co-ordinated approach to keeping the town clean. Between the 14th and 17th centuries, brick-lined latrines appeared, and by the 19th century Victorian communal latrines were found outside rows of cheaper terraced housing. In all time periods from Roman onwards, large numbers of human fleas and lice were recovered, showing that this aspect of bodily cleanliness and sanitation did not change dramatically over time. All this evidence would suggest for Britain that away from the capital city of London, the sanitation provided by the Romans was of a much better standard than was the case in the Viking period or in medieval times after the Norman conquest.

Intestinal diseases such as parasites have been explored here in detail to help understand this aspect of health in the past. Some parasites are spread directly as a result of poor sanitation, and these are often termed the faecal oral parasites due to their transfer in faecal material. Roundworm and whipworm are the most common parasites of this type. Past research has shown that these parasites have been infecting humans throughout our evolution and originated with us in Africa.[8] However, a number of studies have shown that these parasites only started to become widespread and common in populations who had settled in towns and started to farm crops.[9] This shows that increasing human population size coupled with using human faeces as crop fertiliser has contributed in a significant way to the success of these parasites in humans.

Another intestinal parasite that seemed to become much more common when hunter-gatherers changed lifestyle to settled farmers is the pinworm. The evidence for this comes from the Americas, where the fragile eggs are fairly well preserved

---

[7]   Hall and Kenward, this volume, Ch. 6, p. 99.

[8]   Mitchell, P.D., 'The origins of human parasites: exploring the evidence for endoparasitism throughout human evolution', *International Journal of Paleopathology* 3 (2013): 191–98.

[9]   Seo and Shin, this volume, Ch. 8, p. 158; Anastasiou and Mitchell, this volume, Ch. 7, p. 141.

in desiccated coprolites. This parasite causes anal itching at night and is typically spread by hands that have been scratching at night time. It seems that increased population density and the continuous use of houses over the generations led to more effective transmission of this parasite than was the case for smaller hunter-gatherer bands without permanent housing or a sedentary lifestyle.[10]

Other species of parasite that humans suffered with throughout our evolution were contracted in different ways. Some were by eating specific foods such as the beef tapeworm, pork tapeworm and fish tapeworm, others were by wading in warm fresh water such as schistosomiasis and dracunculiasis, and others still from insect bites such as leishmaniasis and filariasis. A proportion of these species were brought to other parts of the world as humans migrated out of Africa, but some found their life cycle could not be sustained outside Africa and so could not be spread by migrations.[11]

As humans migrated to Europe, Asia and the Americas they were exposed to new species of parasite normally infecting the animals there, and some of these were spread to humans. In Asia these included the Chinese liver fluke, oriental schistosomiasis, the Gymnophalloides intestinal fluke, the Metagonimus intestinal fluke and the Paragonimus lung fluke. A good many of these Asian parasites were contracted by the consumption of raw fish, or wading in water where these fish lived. Hence the East Asian habit of eating raw fish (such as sushi) has led to a huge illness burden over the centuries.[12] The remains of some people have been found with these parasites in areas where they are no longer endemic (e.g. *Gymnophalloides seoi* in Hadong, Korea).[13] This may mean that the person moved to the area after contracting the parasite elsewhere, or may indicate that the past distribution of certain parasites species was different to that found today.

In Europe we find a species of fish tapeworm (*Diphyllobothrium latum*) in northern regions that is different to African, Asian or South American species and would have been new to early migrants.[14] Finding this parasite in the Middle East, outside its endemic region, has demonstrated how crusaders from northern Europe migrated on military expeditions in the medieval period taking their parasites in their intestines.[15] Worldwide testing for Entamoeba dysentery has found that all early archaeological cases have come from Europe.[16] While the genus may have

---

[10]   Araújo et al., this volume, Ch. 9, p. 174.

[11]   Mitchell 2013.

[12]   Seo and Shin, this volume, Ch. 8, p. 154.

[13]   Seo, M., Shin, D.H., Guk, S.M., Oh, C.S., Lee, E.J., Shin, M.H., Kim, M.J., Lee, S.D., Kim, Y.S., Yi, Y.S., Spigelman, M., Chai, J.Y., '*Gymnophalloides seoi* eggs from the stool of a 17th century female mummy found in Hadong, Republic of Korea', *Journal for Parasitology* 94 (2008): 467–472.

[14]   Anastasiou, this volume, Ch. 10, pp. 143.

[15]   Mitchell, P.D., Anastasiou, E., Syon, D., 'Human intestinal parasites in crusader Acre: evidence for migration with disease in the medieval period', *International Journal of Paleopathology* 1 (2011): 132–37.

[16]   Le Bailly and Bouchet, this volume, Ch. 11, p. 227.

originated in Africa since it is found in apes there,[17] it may be that the species *Entamoeba histolytica* that infects modern humans originated in Europe.

In the Americas there were further new parasite species that migrating humans contracted, such as the Pacific fish tapeworm, dwarf tapeworm and Chagas disease. However, it seems that many of the parasites present in humans in Asia were not transmitted to the Americas when early humans made the first migrations. It has been argued that the tough, cold conditions associated with crossing the Bering land bridge cleansed migrants of many of their parasites, such as hookworm, threadworm, whipworm and roundworms. This is because the journey would have taken many years longer than the lifespan of these parasites, and the environment did not support the re-infection of the population with their own parasites as lifecycles required a period of maturation in warm moist conditions outside the human body. The parasites that did make it to the Americas with early settlers did not have this requirement in their life cycles. The later appearance of those parasites that could not survive the Bering land crossing would be compatible with introduction by later waves of settlement groups making the faster sea crossing.[18]

The wide-ranging evidence presented in this volume has allowed comparisons to be made between different continents, time periods, and cultures with very different lifestyles. We have seen how intestinal disease changed as early humans changed from hunter-gatherer lifestyles to become herders, agriculturalists, and industrialists. Once they developed towns they gradually realised that sanitation mattered, and over the millennia past civilisations invented the toilet, focussed on maintaining cleaner water, introduced waste collection and also sanitation legislation. It was only by the industrial period that people began to realise that intestinal disease could be caused by infectious organisms such as bacteria, viruses and parasites. Ever since that time, one key aim of medicine has been to determine how to minimise the risk of diarrhoeal illness and parasites. Although the developed world has acquired sanitation technology and social hygiene practices that make such diseases rare in these regions, large parts of the world where the poorest people live still struggle on with sanitation at the level of those early civilisations from thousands of years ago. It is only when all people across the planet have access to effective toilets, clean water and soap, and when human faeces are no longer required as crop fertiliser that we can finally break the cycle of re-infection that causes so much illness and death around the world. Clearly the effect of disease caused by poor sanitation is not a topic restricted to our history, but we can certainly learn much from what archaeology and history can tell us about this aspect of our past.

---

[17] Mitchell 2013.

[18] Araújo et al., this volume, Ch. 9, pp. 175–6.

Bibliography

Acha, P.N., Szyfres, B., *Zoonoses et Maladies Transmissibles Communes aux Hommes et aux Animaux* (Paris, World Organisation for Animal Health, 2005).

Addyman, P.V., 'The archaeology of public health at York, England', *World Archaeology* 21(1989): 244–64.

Aelian, *De Natura Animalium*, trans. A.F. Scholfield, volume III (Cambridge: Loeb, 1959).

Agatsuma, T., Iwagami, M., Liu, C.X., Rajapakse, R.P.V., Mondal, M.M.H., Kitikoons, V., Ambus, S., Agatsuma, Y., Blair, D., Higuchi, T., 'Affinities between Asian non-human Schistosoma species, the S. indicum group, and the African human Schistosomes', *Journal of Helminthology* 76 (2002): 7–19.

Allison, E.P., Hall, A.R., Jones, A.K.G., Kenward, H.K., Robertson, A., 'Report on plant and invertebrate remains', in R.L. Kemp (ed.), *Anglian Settlement at 46–54 Fishergate*. The Archaeology of York series 7(1) (York: Council for British Archaeology, 1996), p. 85–105.

Allison, M.J., Bergman, T., Gerszten, E., 'Further studies on fecal parasites in antiquity', *American Journal of Clinical Pathology* 112 (1999): 605–09.

Allison, M.J., Pezzia, A., Hasegawa, I., Gerszten, E., 'A case of hookworm infestation in a pre-Columbian American', *American Journal of Physical Anthropology* 41 (1974): 103–6.

Amulree, Lord, 'Hygienic conditions in ancient Rome and modern England', *Medical History* 17 (1973): 244–255.

Anastasiou, E., *The Paleoparasitology of the Eastern Mediterranean and Adjacent Regions: Understanding Intestinal Diseases throughout Time* (Cambridge, University of Cambridge: PhD Thesis, 2014).

Anastasiou. E., 'Parasites in European populations from prehistory to the industrial revolution', in P.D. Mitchell (ed.), *Sanitation, Latrines and Intestinal Parasites in Past Populations* (Farnham: Ashgate, 2014), pp. 203–17.

Anastasiou, E., Lorentz, K.O., Stein, G.J., Mitchell, P.D. 'Prehistoric schistosomiasis parasite found in the Middle East'. *Lancet Infectious Diseases* 14 (2014): 553-4.

Anastasiou, E., Mitchell, P.D., 'Paleopathology and genes: investigating the genetics of infectious diseases in excavated human skeletal remains and mummies from past populations', *Gene* 828 (2013): 33–40.

Anastasiou, E., Mitchell, P.D., 'Human intestinal parasites from a latrine in the 12th century Frankish castle of Saranda Kolones in Cyprus', *International Journal of Paleopathology* 3 (2013): 218–23.

Anastasiou, E., Mitchell, P.D., 'Human intestinal parasites and dysentery in Africa and the Middle East prior to 1500', in P.D. Mitchell (ed.), *Sanitation, Latrines and Intestinal Parasites in Past Populations* (Farnham: Ashgate, 2014), pp. 121–47.

Anastasiou, E., Mitchell, P.D., Jeffries, N., 'The paleoparasitology of 17th–18th century Spitalfields in London', in P.D. Mitchell and J. Buckberry (eds), *Proceedings of the 12th Conference of the British Association for Biological Anthropology and Osteoarchaeology* (Oxford: Archaeopress, 2012), p. 53–61.

Angelakis, A.N., Koutsoyiannis, D., 'Urban water resources management in ancient Greek times', in B.A. Stewart and T. Howell (eds), *The Encyclopedia of Water Sciences* (New York: Markel Dekker, 2003), pp. 999–1008.

Angelakis, A.N., Koutsoyiannis, D., Papanikolaou, P., 'On the geometry of the Minoan water conduits', in I. Koyuncu, Z. Sen, S. Ozturk, M. Altinbas, and I. Ozturk (eds), *Proceedings of the 3rd IWA International Symposium on Water and Wastewater Technologies in Ancient Civilizations* (Istanbul: Istanbul Technical University, 2012), pp. 172–177.

Angelakis, A.N., Koutsoyiannis, D., Tchobanoglous, G., 'Urban wastewater and stormwater technologies in the ancient Greece', *Water Research* 39 (2005): 210–220.

Angelakis, A.N., Lyrintzis, A.G., Spyridakis, S.V., 'A brief history of water and wastewater technologies in Minoan Crete, Greece', in I. Koyuncu, Z. Sen, S. Ozturk, M. Altinbas, and I. Ozturk (eds), *Proceedings of the 3rd IWA International Symposium on Water and Wastewater Technologies in Ancient Civilizations* (Istanbul: Istanbul Technical University, 2012), pp. 208–216.

Angelakis, A.N., Spyridakis, S.V., 'The status of water resources in Minoan times: a preliminary study', in A.N. Angelakis and A.S. Issar (eds), *Diachronic Climatic Impacts on Water Resources with Emphasis on Mediterranean Region* (Heidelberg: Springer-Verlag, 1996), pp. 161–191.

Angelakis, A.N., Spyridakis, S.V., 'Wastewater management in Minoan times', in E. Diamadopoulos and G.P. Korfiatis (eds), *Proceedings of the Meeting on Protection and Restoration of Environment* (Chania: Technical University of Crete, 1996) pp. 549–558.

Antoniou, G.P., 'Lavatories in ancient Greece', *Water Science and Technology: Water Supply* 7 (2007): 155–164.

Antoniou, G.P., 'Ancient Greek lavatories: operation with reused water', in L.W. Mays (ed.), *Ancient Water Technologies* (Dordrecht: Springer, 2010), pp. 67–86.

Antoniou, G.P., Angelakis, A.N., 'Latrines and wastewater sanitation technologies in ancient Greece', in P.D. Mitchell (ed.), *Sanitation, Latrines and Intestinal Parasites in Past Populations* (Farnham: Ashgate, 2014), pp. 41–68.

Araújo, A., Confalonieri, U., Ferreira, L.F., 'Oxyurid (Nematoda) eggs from coprolites from Brazil', *Journal of Parasitology* 68 (1982): 511–12.

Araújo, A.J.G., Confalonieri, U.E.C., Ferreira, L.F., 'Encontro de ovos de Trichostrongylideo e *Trichuris trichiura* em corpo mumificado do período colonial brasileiro', *Revista do Centro de Ciencias Biológicas e da Saúde* (1984): 11–4.

Araújo, A., Ferreira, L.F., 'Oxyuriasis and prehistoric migrations', *Manguinhos* 2 (1995): 99–109.

Araújo, A., Ferreira, L.F., 'Paleoparasitology of schistosomiasis', *Memórias do Instituto Oswaldo Cruz* 92 (1997): 717.

Araújo, A., Ferreira, L.F., 'Paleoparasitology and the antiquity of human host-parasite relationships', *Memórias do Instituto Oswaldo Cruz* 98 (Suppl. 1) (2000): 89–93.

Araújo, A., Ferreira, L.F., Confalonieri, U., 'A contribution to the study of helminth findings in archaeological material in Brazil', *Revista Brasileira de Biologia* 41 (1981): 873–81.

Araújo, A., Ferreira, L.F., Confalonieri, U., Chame, M., 'Hookworms and the peopling of America', *Cadernos de Saúde Pública* 2 (1988): 226–233.

Araújo, A., Ferreira, L.F., Confalonieri, U., Nunez, L., Ribeiro Filho, B.M., 'The finding of Enterobius vermicularis eggs in pre-Columbian human coprolites', *Memórias do Instituto Oswaldo Cruz* 80 (1985): 141–43.

Araújo, A., Ferreira, L.F., Fugassa, M., Leles, D., Sianto, L., de Souza, S.M.M., Dutra, J., Iñiguez, A., Reinhard, K., 'New World paleoparasitology', in P.D. Mitchell (ed.), *Sanitation, Latrines and Intestinal Parasites in Past Populations* (Farnham: Ashgate, 2014), pp. 165–202.

Araújo, A., Jansen, A.M., Bouchet, F., Reinhard, K., Ferreira, L.F., 'Parasitism, the diversity of life, and paleoparasitology', *Memórias do Instituto Oswaldo Cruz* 98 (Suppl. 1) (2003): 5–11.

Araújo, A., Jansen, A.M., Reinhard, K., Fereira, L.F., 'Paleoparasitology of Chagas disease: a review', *Memórias do Instituto Oswaldo Cruz* 104 (2009): 9–16.

Araújo, A., Reinhard, K., Bastos, O.M., Costa, L.C., Pirmez, C., Iniquez, A., Vicente, A.C., Morel, C.M., Ferreira, L.F., 'Paleoparasitology: perspectives with new techniques', *Revista do Instituto de Medicina Tropical de São Paulo* 40 (1998): 371–76.

Araújo, A., Reinhard, K., Ferreira, L.F., 'Parasite findings in archaeological remains: diagnosis and interpretation', *Quaternary International* 180 (2008): 1–4.

Araújo, A., Reinhard, K., Ferreira, L.F., Gardner, S.L., 'Parasites as probes for prehistoric human migrations?', *Trends in Parasitology* 24 (2008): 112–15.

Armelagos, G.J., Brown, P.J., Turner, B., 'Evolutionary, historical and political economic perspectives on health and disease', *Social Science and Medicine* 61 (2005): 755–65.

Arriaza, B., *Beyond Death: the Chinchorro Mummies of Ancient Chile* (Washington, DC: 1995).

Arriaza, B., Standen V.G., Cassman, V., Santoro, C.M., 'Chinchorro culture: pioneers of the coast of the Atacama Desert' in H. Silverman and W.H. Isbell (eds), *Handbook of South American Archaeology* (New York: Springer, 2008), pp. 45–58.

Arriaza, B., Reinhard, K., Araújo, A., Orellana, N.C., Standen, V.G., 'Possible influence of the ENSO phenomenon on the pathoecology of diphyllobothriasis and anisakiasis in ancient Chinchorro populations', *Memórias do Instituto Oswaldo Cruz* 105 (2010): 66–72.

Aspöck, H., Auer, H., Picher, O., '*Trichuris trichiura* eggs in the neolithic glacier mummy from the Alps', *Parasitology Today* 12 (1996): 255–56.

Aspöck, H., Auer, H., Picher, O., 'Parasites and parasitic diseases in prehistoric human populations in central Europe', *Helminthologia* 36 (1999): 139–45.

Aspöck, H., Flamm, H., Picher, O., 'Darmparasiten in men-schlichen exkrementen aus prähistorischen salzbergwerken der Hallstatt-Kultur (800–350 v. Chr)', *Zentrallblatt für Bakteriologic und Hygiene Abt Originale A* 223 (1973): 549–58.

Aufderheide, A.C., *The Scientific Study of Mummies* (Cambridge: Cambridge University Press, 2003).

Aufderheide, A.C., Salo, W., Madden, M., Streitz, J., Buikstra, J., Guhl, F., Arriaza, B., Renier, C., Wittmers, L.E., Fornaciari, G., Allison, M., 'A 9,000-year record of Chagas' disease', *Proceedings of the National Academy of Sciences of the United States of America* 101 (2004): 2034–2039.

Baeten, J., Marinova, E., De Laet, V., Degryse, P., de Vos, D., Waelkens., M., 'Faecal biomarker and archaeobotanical analyses in sediments from a public latrine shed new light on ruralisation in Sagalassos, Turkey', *Journal of Archaeological Science* 39 (2012) : 1143–1159.

Baqir, T., 'Iraq Government Excavations at 'Aqar Quf Third Interim Report, 1944–5', *Iraq* 8 (1946): 73–93.

Barnes, E., *Diseases and Human Evolution* (Albuquerque: University of New Mexico Press, 2005).

Barron, C.M., *London in the Later Middle Ages: Government and People, 1200–1500* (Oxford: Oxford University Press, 2004).

Bartošová, L., Ditrich, O., Beneš, J., Frolík, J., Musil, J., 'Paleoparasitological findings in medieval and early modern archaeological deposits from Hradební Street, Chrudim, Czech Republic', *Interdisciplinaria Archaeologica* 2 (2011): 27–38.

Bateman, O. M., Smith, S., *A Comparison of the Health Effects of Water Supply and Sanitation in Urban and Rural Guatemala*. WASH Field Report No. 352 (Washington, DC: US Agency for International Development, 1991).

Bateman, O. M., Smith, S., Roark, P., *A Comparison of the Health Effects of Water Supply and Sanitation in Urban and Rural Areas of Five African Countries.* WASH Report No. 398 (Washington, DC: US Agency for International Development, 1993).

Bathurst, R.R., 'Archaeological evidence of intestinal parasites from coastal shell middens', *Journal of Archaeological Science* 32 (2005): 115–123.

Battini-Villard, L., *L'Espace Domestique en Mésopotamie de la IIIe Dynastie d'Ur à l'*Époque *Paléo-Babylonienne*. BAR International Series 767 (Oxford: Archaeopress, 1999).

Baxt, L.A., Singh, U., 'New insights into *Entamoeba histolytica* pathogenesis', *Current Opinion in Infectious Diseases* 21 (2008): 489–494.

Beck, D.L., Tanyuksel, M., Mackey, A.J., Haque, R., Trapaidze, N., Pearson, W.R., Loftus, B., Petri, W.A., '*Entamoeba histolytica*: sequence conservation of the Gal/GalNAc lectin from clinical isolates', *Experimental Parasitology* 101 (2002): 157–163.

Bellard, F.G., Cortes, A., 'Trichinosis in the mummy of a young girl (Toledo, Spain)', in E. Cockburn and T.A. Reyman (eds), Papers on Paleopathology Presented at the *8th European Members Meeting, Cambridge, England* (Detroit: Paleopathology Association, 1991), p. 11.

Belshaw, R., 'A note on the recovery of *Thoracochaeta zosterae* (Haliday) (Diptera: Sphaeroceridae) from archaeological deposits', *Circaea* 6 (1989): 39–41.

Bengtson, H., *Griechische Geschichte*, 9th edition (Munich: Beck, 2002), pp. 8–15.

Bethell, P.H., Goad, L.J., Evershed, R.P., 'The study of biomarkers of human activity: the use of coprostanol in the soil as an indicator of human faecal material', *Journal of Archaeological Science* 21 (1994): 619–32.

Bianucci, R., Mattutino, G., Lallo, R., Charlier, P., Jouin-Spriet, H., Peluso, A., Higham, T., Torre, C., Rabino Massa, E., 'Immunological evidence of *Plasmodium falciparum* infection in a child mummy from the Early Dynastic Period', *Journal of Archaeological Science* 35 (2008): 1880–1885.

Biggs, R., 'Medicine, surgery, and public health in ancient Mesopotamia', *Journal of Assyrian Academic Studies* 19 (2005): 1–19.

Biggs, R., Brinkman, J., Civil, M., Farber, W., Gelb, I., Oppenheim, A.L., Reiner, E., Roth, M., Stolper, M. (eds), *The Assyrian Dictionary, Volume 18, T* (Chicago: Oriental Institute, 2006).

Board of Education, Fukuoka City, *Kouro-kan III, Fukuoka City Archaeological Site Report No. 355 (Fukuokashi, Kouro-kan Ato III, Fukuoka-shi Maizo-Bunkazai Chosa houkokusho)* (Fukuoka City, Japan: Board of Education, 1993).

Boersema, J.H., Jansen, J., 'Helminth infections in medieval Utrecht', *Tropical and Geographical Medicine* 27 (1975): 441.

Bond, J.M., O'Connor, T.P., *Bones from Medieval Deposits at 16–22 Coppergate and other Sites in York*. The Archaeology of York series 15(5) (York: Council for British Archaeology, 1999).

Borrero, L.A., 'Human dispersal and climatic conditions during Late Pleistocene times in Fuego-Patagonia', *Quaternary International* 53–53 (1999): 93–99.

Botella, H.G., Vargas, J.A., De La Rosa, M.A., Leles, D., Reimers, E.G., Vicente, A., Iñiguez, A., 'Paleoparasitologic, paleogenetic and paleobotanic analysis of XVIII century coprolites from the church La Concepcion in Santa Cruz de Tenerife, Canary Islands, Spain', *Memórias do Instituto Oswaldo Cruz* 105 (2010): 1054–56.

Bouchet, F., 'Recovery of helminth eggs from archaeological excavation of the Grand Louvre (Paris, France)', *Journal of Parasitology* 81 (1995): 785–87.

Bouchet, F., 'Intestinal capillariasis in Neolithic inhabitants of Chalain (Jura, France)', *The Lancet* 349 (1997): 256.

Bouchet, F., Baffier, D., Girard, M., Morel, P., Paicheler, J.C., David, F., 'Paléoparasitologie en contexte pléistocène: premières observations à la Grande Grotte d'Arcy-sur-Cure (Yonne), France', *Comptes Rendus de l Académie des sciences* 319 (1996): 147–51.

Bouchet, F., Bentrad, S., Paicheler, J.C., 'Enquête Epidémiologique sur les Helminthiases à la Cour de Louis XIV', *Mini-Synthese Medicine Science* 14 (1998): 463–66.

Bouchet, F., Guidon, N., Dittmar, K., Harter, S., Ferreira, L.F., Chaves, M.S., Reinhard, K., Araújo, A., 'Parasite remains in archaeological sites', *Memórias do Instituto Oswaldo Cruz* 98 (Suppl. 1) (2003): 47–52.

Bouchet, F., Harter, S., Le Bailly, M., 'The state of the art of paleoparasitological research in the Old World', *Memórias do Instituto Oswaldo Cruz* 98 (Suppl. 1) (2003): 95–101.

Bouchet, F., Harter, S., Paicheler, J. C., Araújo, A., Ferreira, L. F., 'First recovery of Schistosoma mansoni eggs from a latrine in Europe (15–16th centuries)', *Journal of Parasitology* 88 (2002): 404–05.

Bouchet, F., Lefèvre, C., West, D., Corbett, D., 'First paleoparasitological analysis of a midden in the Aleutian Island (Alaska): results and limits', *Journal of Parasitology* 85 (1999): 369–72.

Bouchet, F., Paicheler, J.C., 'Paleoparasitologie: présomption d'un cas de bilharziose au XVe siècle à Montbéliard (Doubs, France)', *Comptes Rendus de l'Académie des Sciences* 318 (1995): 811–14.

Bouchet, F., Petrequin, P., Paicheler, J.C., Dommelier, S., 'First palaeoparasitological approach of the Neolithic site in Chalain (Jura, France)', *Bulletin de la Société de Pathologie Exotique* 88 (1995): 265–68.

Bouchet, F., West, D., Lefèvre, C., Corbett, D., 'Identification of parasitoses in a child burial from Adak Island (Central Aleutian Islands, Alaska)', *Comptes Rendus de l'Académie des sciences* 324 (2001): 123–7.

Boyd, R., Silk, J.B., *How Humans Evolved*, 3rd edition (New York: WW Norton, 2003).

Breeze, D.J., 'The Roman Fort on the Antonine Wall at Bearsden', in D.J. Breeze (ed.), *Studies in Scottish Antiquity* (Edinburgh: Donald, 1984), pp. 32–68.

Brothwell, D.R., 'On the complex nature of man-animal relationships from the pleistocene to early agricultural societies', in J.G. Hawkes (ed.), *Conservation and Agriculture* (London: Duckworth, 1978).

Bruce-Chwatt, L.J., 'Paleogenesis and paleo-epidemiology of primate malaria', *Bulletin of World Health Organization* 32 (1965): 363–87.

Bruschi, F., Maseti, M., Locci, M.T., Ciranni, R., Fornaciari, G., 'Cystercercosis in an Egyptian mummy of the late Ptolemaic Period', *American Journal of Tropical Medicine and Hygiene* 74 (2006): 598–599.

Buccellati, G., Kelly-Buccellati, M., 'The royal palace at Urkesh and the daughter of Naram-Sin', *Annales Archeologiques Arabes Syriennes* 44 (2001): 63–69.

Buckland, P.C., *The Environmental Evidence from the Church Street Roman Sewer System*. The Archaeology of York series 14(1) (York: York Archaeological Trust, 1976).

Buikstra, J., Cook, D., 'Paleopathology: an American account', *Annual Review of Anthropology* 9 (1980): 433–70.

Buxton, M., Walker, H., 'Fish-eating in medieval England', in H. Walker (ed.), *Food and Cookery: Fish Food from the Waters* (Totnes: Prospect Books, 1998) pp. 51–59.

Buyeo National Research Institute of Cultural Heritage, *The Achievement and Significance of Excavation on the Wanggungri Site in Iksan* (Buyeo: Buyeo National Research Institute of Cultural Heritage, 2009).

Cahill, J., Reinhard, K., Tarler, D., Warnock, P., 'It had to happen: scientists examine remains of ancient bathroom', *Biblical Archaeological Review* 17 (1991): 64–9.

Cairncross, S., Hunt, C., Boisson, S., Bostoen, K., Curtis, V., Fung, I.C., Schmidt, W.P., 'Water, sanitation and hygiene for the prevention of diarrhoea', *International Journal of Epidemiology* 39 Suppl. 1 (2010): i193–205.

Calagero, S., Reinhard, K., Vinton, S.D., 'Inca expansion and parasitism in the Lluta Valley: preliminary data', *Memórias do Instituto Oswaldo Cruz* 98 (Suppl. 1) (2003): 161–63.

Callen, E.O., Cameron, T.W.M., 'The diet and parasites of pre-historic Huaca Prieta Indians as determined by dried coprolites', *Proceedings of the Royal Society of Canada* 7 (1955): 51–2.

Callen, E.O., Cameron, T.W.M., 'A prehistoric diet revealed in coprolites', *New Scientist* 8 (1960): 35–40.

Cameron, T.W.M., *Parasites and Parasitism* (New York: John Wiley and Sons, 1956).

Camillo-Coura, L., 'Control of soil-transmitted helminthiasis: co-ordinated control projects' in D.W.T. Compton, M.C. Nesheim and Z.S. Pawlowski (eds), *Ascariasis and its Public Health Significance* (London: Taylor and Francis, 1985), pp. 253–63.

Capuno, J.J., Tan, C.A., Fabella, V.M., 'Do piped water and flush toilets prevent child diarrhoea in rural Philippines?', *Asia Pacific Journal of Public Health* 11 (2011): doi: 10.1177/1010539511430996.

Carrott, J., Kenward, H., 'Species associations among insect remains from urban archaeological deposits and their significance in reconstructing the past human environment', *Journal of Archaeological Science* 28 (2001): 887–905.

Carvalho-Costa, F.A., Silva, A.G., Souza, A.H., Moreira, C.J.C., Souza, D.L., Valverde, J.G., Jaeger, L.H., Martins, P.P., Meneses, V.F., Araújo, A., Bóia, M.N., 'Pseudoparasitism by *Calodium hepaticum* (syn. *Capillaria hepatica*; *Hepaticola hepatica*) in the Negro River, Brazilian Amazon', *Transactions of the Royal Society of Tropical Medicine and Hygiene* 103 (2009): 1071–3.

Carver, M.O.H., Donaghey, S., Sumpter, A.B., *Riverside Structures and a Well in Skeldergate and Buildings in Bishophill*. The Archaeology of York series 4(1) (London: Council for British Archaeology, 1978).

Cassius Dio, *Roman History*, Trans. E. Cary, vols. V & VII (Cambridge: Loeb, 1914).

Cassius Dio, *The Roman History: the Reign of Augustus*, trans. I. Scott-Kilvert (Harmondsworth: Penguin, 1987).

Castleden, R., *Minoans: Life in Bronze Age Crete* (London: Routledge, 1993).

Cato, *Cato and Varro: On Agriculture*, trans. W.D. Hooper & H.B. Ash (Loeb: Cambridge, 1999).

Celsus, *De Medicina*, trans. W.G. Spencer (Cambridge: Loeb, 1935).

Chai, J.Y., Park, J.H., Han, E.T., Shin, E.H., Kim, J.L., Hong, K.S., Rim, H.J., Lee, S.H., 'A nationwide survey of the prevalence of human Gymnophalloides seoi infection on western and southern coastal islands in the Republic of Korea', *Korean Journal of Parasitology* 39 (2001): 23–30.

Chamonard, J., *Le Quartier du Theatre*, Collection Exploration Archéologique de Délos no.8, 3 vols (Paris: Boccard, 1922–1924).

Chang, K.H., *Gyeongju Weolseong eui josayeonguwa yeoksajeok euieui. Symposium of Gyeongju National Research Institute of Cultural Heritage. Gyeongju Weolseong eui eojewa oneul, gurigo mirae* (Gyeongju: Gyeongju National Research Institute of Cultural Heritage, 2007).

Chavasse, D.C., Shier, R.P., Murphy, O.A., Huttly, S.R., Cousens, S.N., Akhtar, T., 'Impact of fly control on childhood diarrhoea in Pakistan: community-randomised trial', *Lancet* 353/9146 (1999): 22–5.

Cheng, T.O., 'Glimpses of the past from the recently unearthed ancient corpses in China', *Annals of Internal Medicine* 101 (1984): 714–5.

Chew, H.M., Kellaway, W. (eds), *London Assize of Nuisance* 1301–1431 (London: London Record Society, 1973).

Cicero, *On Old Age, On Friendship, On Divination*, trans. W.A. Falconer (Cambridge: Loeb, 2001).

Cicero, *De Re Publica, De Legibus*, trans. C.W. Keyes (Cambridge: Loeb, 1928).

CIL = *Corpus Inscriptionum Latinarum*

Cilliers, L., Retief, F.P., 'City planning in Graeco-Roman times with emphasis on health facilities' *Akroterian* 51 (2006): 43–56.

Classen, C., Howes, D., Synnott, A., *Aroma: the Cultural History of Smell* (London: Routledge, 1994).

Cockayne, E., *Hubbub: Filth, Noise and Stench in England* (New Haven: Yale University Press, 2007).

Cockburn, A., Cockburn, E., Reyman, T.A., *Mummies, Disease and Ancient Cultures*, 2nd edition (Cambridge: Cambridge University Press, 1998).

Cohen, M.N., Crane-Kramer, G., 'The state and future of paleoepidemiology', in C. Greenblatt and M. Spigelman (eds), *Emerging Pathogens* (Oxford: Oxford University Press, 2003), pp. 79–91.

Cohen, D., Green, M., Block, C., Slepon, R., Ambar, R., Wasserman, S.S., Levine, M.M., 'Reduction of transmission of shigellosis by control of houseflies (*Musca domestica*)', *Lancet* 337/8748 (1991): 993–7.

Coimbra Jr, C.E.A., Mello, D.A., 'Enteroparasites and *Capillaria* sp. found in Indians of the Suruí group, Parque Indígena Aripuanã, Rondônia', *Memórias do Instituto Oswaldo Cruz* 76 (1981): 299–302.

Combes, C., 'Where do human Schistosomes come from? An evolutionary approach', *Trends in Ecology and Evolution* 5 (1990): 334–37.

Confalonieri, U.E.C., Araújo, A.J.G., Ferreira, L.F., '*Trichuris trichiura* infection in colonial Brazil', *Paleopathology Newsletter* 35 (1981).

Conference Working Group, 'Re-use policies and research needs', in A. Pacey (ed.), *Sanitation in Developing Countries* (Chichester: Wiley 1978a), pp. 201–5.

Conference Working Group, 'Composting as a treatment process', in A. Pacey (ed.), *Sanitation in Developing Countries* (Chichester: Wiley 1978b), pp. 205–7.

Conway, D.J., 'Tracing the dawn of Plasmodium falciparum with mitochondrial genome sequences', *Trends in Genetics* 19 (2003): 671–74.

Cooper, T.P., 'The medieval highways, streets, open ditches and sanitary conditions of the City of York', *Yorkshire Archaeological Journal* 22 (1913): 270–86.

Corpus Inscriptionum Latinarum.I.2 = Lommatzsch, E., and Mommsen, T., *Inscriptiones Latinae antiquissimae ad C. Caesaris mortem. cura Ernesti Lommatzsch ; consilio et auctoritate Academiae litterarum regiae Borussicae a Theodoro Mommsen editae. Pars posterior, Fasciculus I* (Berolini: G. Reimerum, 1918).

Corpus Inscriptionum Latinarum.VI = Henzen, W. and Rossi, G.B., *Inscriptiones urbis Romae latinae. consilio et auctoritate Academiae litterarum regiae Borussicae collegerunt Guilelmus Henzen et Iohannes Baptista de Rossi ; ediderunt Eugenius Bormann, Guilelmus Henzen. Pars prima* (Berolini: G. Reimerum, 1876).

Cox, F.E.G., 'History of human parasitology', *Clinical Microbiology Reviews* 15 (2002): 595–612.

Crane, B.D., 'Filth, garbage and rubbish: refuse disposal, sanitary reform, and nineteenth-century yard deposits in Washington, DC', *Historical Archaeology* 34 (2000): 20–38.

Cros, G., Heuzey, L., Thureau-Dangin, F., *Nouvelles Fouilles de Tello* (Paris: Ernest Leroux, 1910).

Cummings, L.S., Nepstad-Thornberry, C., Puseman, K., *Paleofeces from the Ramaditas Site in Northern Chile: Addressing Middle to Late Formative Period Diet and Health* (1999). Unpublished manuscript on file with Paleo Research Institute and Beloit College, Beloit, Wisconsin Stable. URL: http://core.tdar.org/document/378500, DOI: doi:10.6067/XCV8TQ60WS

D'Anastasio, R., Staniscia, T., Milia, M.L., Manzoli, L., Capasso, L., 'Origin, evolution and paleoepidemiology of brucellosis', *Epidemiology and Infection* 7 (2010): 1–8.

Da Rocha, G.C., Harter, S., Le Bailly, M., Araújo, A., Ferreira, L.F., Serra-Freire, M., Bouchet, F., 'Paleoparasitological remains revealed by seven historic contexts from "Place d'Armes", Namur, Belgium', *Memórias do Instituto Oswaldo Cruz* 101 (Suppl. 2) (2006): 43–52.

Darling, S.T., 'Observations on the geographical and ethnological distribution of hookworms', *Parasitology* 12 (1921): 217–233.

Darwin, C., *On the Origin of Species by Means of Natural Selection, or the Preservation of Favoured Races in the Struggle for Life* (London: John Murray, 1859).

Deelder, A.M., Miller, R.L., de Jonge, N., Krijger, F.W., 'Detection of schistosome antigen in mummies', *The Lancet* 335 (1990): 724–5.

De Feo, G., Mays, L.W., Angelakis, A.N., 'Water and wastewater management technologies in ancient Greek and Roman civilizations', in P. Wilderer (ed.), *Treatise on Water Science*, vol. 1 (Oxford: Academic Press, 2011), pp. 3–22.

Delougaz, P.P., *The Temple Oval at Khafajah*. Publication 53 (Chicago: Oriental Institute, 1940).

Delougaz, P.P., Hall, H., Lloyd, S., *Private Houses and Graves in the Diyala Region*. Publication 88 (Chicago: Oriental Institute, 1967).

Delougaz, P.P., Lloyd, S., *Pre-Sargonid Temples in the Diyala Region*. Publication 58 (Chicago: Oriental Institute, 1942).

De Meyer, L. (ed.), *Tell ed-Der IV, Progress Reports (First Series)* (Leuven: Peeters, 1978).

De Meyer, L. (ed.), *Tell ed-Der II, Progress Reports (Second Series)* (Leuven: Peeters, 1984).

De Rouffignac, C., 'Parasite egg survival and identification from Hibernia Wharf, Southwark', *London Archaeologist* 5 (1985): 103–05.

De Souza, S.M., de Carvalho, D.M., Lessa, A., 'Paleoepidemiology: is there a case to answer?', *Memórias do Instituto Oswaldo Cruz* 98 (Suppl. 1) (2003): 21–7.

De Souza, S.M.M., 'Millenary Egyptian mummies – non invasive excursions', in H. Werner Jr. and J. Lopes (eds), *3D Technologies – Palaeontology, Archaeology, Fetology* (Rio de Janeiro: Livraria & Editora Revinter LTDA, 2009), pp. 77–104.

Despres, L., Imbert-Establet, D., Combes, C., Bonhomme, F., 'Molecular evidence linking hominid evolution to recent radiation of Schistosomes (Platyhelminthes: Trematoda)', *Molecular Phylogenetics and Evolution* 1 (1992): 295–304.

Dickson, J. H., Brough, D.W., 'Biological studies of a Pictish midden', in U. Körber-Grohne and H. Küster (eds), *Archäobotanik*. Dissertationes Botanicae series no. 133 (Berlin: J. Cramer, 1989), pp. 155–66.

Dillehay, T., 'Probing deeper into first American studies', *Proceedings of the National Academy of Science of the United States of America* 106 (2009): 971–78.

Dittmar, K., Steyn, M., 'Paleoparasitological analysis of coprolites from K2, an iron age archaeological site in South Africa: the first finding of Dicrocoelium sp. eggs', *Journal of Parasitology* 90 (2004): 171–73.

Dobney, K., Hall, A., Kenward, H., 'It's all garbage … A review of bioarchaeology in the four English Colonia towns', in H. Hurst (ed.), *The Coloniae of Roman Britain: New studies and a review*. Journal of Roman Archaeology Supplementary Series 36 (Gloucester: Journal of Roman Archaeology, 1999), pp. 15–35.

Dodge, H., 'Greater than the pyramids: the water supply of Ancient Rome', in J. Coulston and H. Dodge (eds), *Ancient Rome: The Archaeology of the Eternal City* (Oxford: Oxford University School of Archaeology, 2000) pp. 166–209.

Dommelier-Espejo, S., *Contribution à l'Etude Paléoparasitologique des Sites Néolithiques en Environnement Lacustre dans les Domaines Jurassien et Péri-Alpin* (PhD Thesis Reims: Université de Reims, 2001).

Dommelier-Espejo, S., Bentrad, S.S., Paicheler, J.C., Petrequin, P., Bouchet, F., 'Parasitoses liées à l'alimentation chez les populations néolithiques du lac de Chalain (Jura, France)', *Anthropozoologica* 27 (1998): 41–49.

Douglas, M., *Purity and Danger: an Analysis of Concepts of Pollution and Taboo* (London: Routledge, 2005).

Dufour, B., Le Bailly, M., 'Testing new parasite egg extraction methods in paleoparasitology and an attempt at quantification', *International Journal of Paleopathology* 3 (2013): 199–203.

Dunn, F.L., Watkins, R., 'Parasitological examination of prehistoric human coprolites from Lovelock Cave, Nevada', in R.F. Heizer and L.K. Napton (eds), *Archaeology and the Prehistoric Great Basin Lacustrine Subsistence Regime as Seen from Lovelock Cave, Nevada,* Archaeological Research Facility Contributions no.10 (Berkeley: University of California, 1970), pp. 178–185.

El-Najjar, M.Y., Benitez, J., Fry, G., Lynn, G.E., Ortner, D.J., Reyman, T.A., Small, P.A., 'Autopsies on two native American mummies', *American Journal of Physical Anthropology* 53 (1980): 197–202.

El-Najjar, M.Y., Lozof, B., Ryan, D.J. 'The paleoepidemiology of porotic hyperostosis in the American Southwest: radiographical and ecological considerations', *American Journal of Roentgenology Radium Therapy Nuclear Medicine* 125 (1975): 918–25.

Emerson, P.M., Lindsay, S.W., Walraven, G.E., Faal, H., Bøgh, C., Lowe, K., Bailey, R.L., 'Effect of fly control on trachoma and diarrhoea', *Lancet* 353/9162 (1999): 1401–3.

Eshed, V., Gopher, A., Gage, T.B., Hershkovitz, I., 'Has the transition to agriculture reshaped the demographic structure of prehistoric populations? New evidence from the Levant', *American Journal of Physical Anthropology* 124 (2004): 315–29.

Esry, S.A., Potash, J.B., Roberts, L., Shiff, C., 'Effects of improved water supply and sanitation on ascariasis, diarrhoea, dracunculiasis, hookworm infection, schistosomiasis, and trachoma', *Bulletin of the World Health Organization* 69 (1991): 609–21.

Evans, S.A., *The Palace of Minos at Knossos: a Comparative Account of the Successive Stages of the Early Cretan Civilization as Illustrated by the Discoveries* (New York: Hafner, 1964).

Evans, A.C., Markus, M.B., Mason, R.J., Steel, R., 'Late stone-age coprolite reveals evidence of prehistoric parasitism', *South African Medical Journal* 86 (1996): 274–75.

Faulkner, C.T., 'Prehistoric diet and parasitic infection in Tennessee: evidence from the analysis of desiccated human paleofeces', *American Antiquity* 56 (1991): 687–700.

Faulkner, C.T., Cowie, S.E., Martin, P.E., Martin, S.R., Mayes, C.S., Patton, S., 'Archaeological evidence of parasitic infection from the 19th Century Company Town of Fayette, Michigan', *Journal of Parasitology* 85 (2000): 846–9.

Faulkner, C.T., Patton, S., Johnson, S.S., 'Prehistoric parasitism in Tennessee: evidence from the analysis of desiccated fecal material collected from Big Bone Cave, Van Buren County, Tennessee', *Journal of Parasitology* 75 (1989): 461–3.

Fernandes, A., Ferreira, L.F., Gonçalves, M.L.C., Bouchet, F., Klein, C.H., Iguchi, T., Sianto, L., Araújo, A., 'Intestinal parasite analysis in organic sediments collected from a 16th-century Belgian archaeological site', *Cadernos de Saúde Pública* 21 (2005): 329–32.

Fernandes, A., Iñiguez, A.M., Lima, V.S., Souza, S.M., Ferreira, L.F., Vicente, A.C., Jansen, A.M., 'Pre-Columbian Chagas disease in Brazil: *Trypanosoma cruzi* I in the archaeological remains of a human in Peruaçu Valley, Minas Gerais, Brazil', *Memórias do Instituto Oswaldo Cruz* 103 (2008): 514–16.

Ferreira, L.F., 'O fenômeno parasitismo', *Revista da Sociedade Brasileira de Medicina Tropical* 4 (1973): 261–77.

Ferreira, L.F., Araújo, A., 'On hookworms in the Americas and trans-pacific contact', *Parasitology Today* 12 (1996): 454–454

Ferreira, L.F., Araújo, A., Confalonieri, U., 'Subsídios para a paleoparasitologia do Brasil 1. Parasitos encontrados em coprólitos no município de Unaí, Minas Gerais', Abstracts, IV Congresso Brasileiro de Parasitologia, Campinas (São Paulo, 1979), p. 56.

Ferreira, L.F., Araújo, A., Confalonieri, U., 'Finding of helminth eggs in human coprolites from Unai, Minas Gerais, Brazil', *Transactions of the Royal Society of Tropical Medicine and Hygiene* 76 (1980): 798–800.

Ferreira, L.F., Araújo, A.J.G., Confalonieri, U.E.C., 'News from the field', *Paleopathology Newsletter* 38 (1982): 5.

Ferreira, L.F., Araújo, A., Confalonieri, U., 'The finding of helminth eggs in a Brazilian mummy', *Transactions of the Royal Society of Tropical Medicine and Hygiene* 77 (1983): 65–7.

Ferreira, L.F., Araújo, A., Confalonieri, U., Chame, M., Ribeiro, B.M., 'Encontro de ovos de ancilostomídeos em coprólitos humanos datados de 7.230 +/- 80 anos, Piauí, Brasil' *Anais da Academia Brasileira de Ciencias* 59 (1987): 280–81.

Ferreira, L.F., Araújo, A.J.G., Confalonieri, U.E.C., Lima, J.M.D., '*Trichuris trichiura* eggs in human coprolites from the archaeological site of Furna do Estrago, Brejo da Madre de Deus, Pernambuco, Brazil', *Memórias do Instituto Oswaldo Cruz* 84 (1989): 581.

Ferreira, L.F., Araújo, A., Confalonieri, U., Nuñez, L., 'The finding of *Diphyllobothrium pacificum* in human coprolites (4100–1950 BC) from Northern Chile', *Memórias do Instituto Oswaldo Cruz* 79 (1984): 175–80.

Ferreira, L.F., Araújo, A., Confalonieri, U., Nuñez, L., 'Infecção por *Enterobius vermicularis* em populações agro-pastoris pré-colombianas de San Pedro de Atacama, Chile', *Memórias do Instituto Oswaldo Cruz* 84 (suppl. 4) (1989): 197–99.

Ferreira, L.F., Britto, C., Cardoso, M.A., Fernandez, O., Reinhard, K., Araújo, A., 'Paleoparasitology of Chagas disease revealed by infected tissues from Chilean mummies', *Acta Tropica* 75 (2000): 79–84.

Ferreira, L.F., Reinhard, K.J., Araújo, A. (eds), *Fundamentos da Paleoparasitologia* (Rio de Janeiro: Editora Fiocruz, 2011).

Fonseca Filho, O., *Parasitismo e Migrações Pré-Históricas* (Rio de Janeiro: Mauro Familiar Editora, 1972).

Filimonos (Φιλήμονος), Μ., 'Τα αστικά απορρίμματα στην αγροτική παραγωγή. Η μαρτυρία της αρχαίας Ρόδου', in *Ι. Λυριτζής και Α. Σάμψων* (eds), Αρχαιολογία και Περιβάλλον στα Δωδεκάνησα. Έρευνα και Πολιτισμικός Τουρισμός. *Διεθνές Συνέδριο, Τμήμα Μεσογειακών Σπουδών, Εργαστήριο Αρχαιομετρίας,. Έκδοση Πρακτικών* (Ροδος, 2000) (in Greek).

Fink, A., 'Levantine standardized luxury in the late Bronze Age: waste management at Tell Atchana (Alalakh)', in A. Fantalkin and A. Yasur-Landau (eds), *Bene Israel: Studies in the Archaeology of Israel and the Levant during the Bronze and Iron Ages in Honour of Israel Finkelstein*. Culture and History of the Ancient Near East 31 (Leiden: Brill, 2008), pp.165–96.

Fink, G., Günther, I., Hill, K., 'The effect of water and sanitation on child health: evidence from the demographic and health surveys 1986–2007', *International Journal of Epidemiology* 40 (2011): 1196–204.

Fletcher, H.A., Donoghue, H.D., Holton, J., Pap, I., Spigelman, M., 'Widespread occurrence of Mycobacterium tuberculosis DNA from 18th–19th century Hungarians', *American Journal of Physical Anthropology* 201 (2003): 144–52.

Flower, C.T. (ed.), *Public Works in Mediaeval Law*, vol. II (London: Quaritch, 1923).

Fonseca Filho, O., 'Parasitological and clinical relationship between Asiatic and Oceanian tokelau and Brazilian chimbere of some Mato Grosso Indians' *Boletim do Museu Nacional* 6 (1930): 201–21.

Fonseca Filho, O., *Parasitismo e Migrações Pré-Históricas* (Rio de Janeiro: Mauro Familiar Editora, 1972).

Foster, S., Duke, J.A., *A Field Guide to Medicinal Plants and Herbs of Eastern and Central North America*. 2nd edition (Boston: Houghton Mifflin, 1999).

Fotedar, R., 'Vector potential of houseflies (*Musca domestica*) in the transmission of *Vibrio cholerae* in India', *Acta Tropica* 78 (2001): 31–4.

Fouant, M.M., Allison, M., Gerszten, E., Focacci, G., 'Parasitos intestinales entre los indigenas precolombinos', *Revista Chungará* 9 (1982): 285–299.

Freitas, O., '*Doenças Africanas no Brasil*', Bibliotheca Pedagogica Brasileira, Brasiliana volume 51, série V (São Paulo: Cia Editora Nacional, 1935), p. 21–30.

Frontinus, *Strategems and Aqueducts of Rome*, trans. C.E. Bennett (Cambridge: Loeb, 2003).

Fry, G.F., 'Preliminary analysis of the Hogup Cave coprolites', *University of Utah Anthropological Papers* 93 (1970): 247–250.

Fry, G.F., 'Ovum and parasite examination of Salt Cave paleofeces', in P.J. Watson (ed.), *Archaeology of the Mammoth Cave Area* (New York: Academic Press, 1974), p. 61.

Fry, G.F., *Analysis of Prehistoric Coprolites from Utah*, Anthropology Papers series no. 97 (Salt Lake City: University of Utah Press, 1977).

Fry, G.F., 'Prehistoric diet and parasites in the desert west of North America', in D.L. Browman (ed.), *Early Native Americans* (The Hague: Mouton Press, 1980), pp. 325–339.

Fry, G.F., Hall, H.J., 'Parasitological examination of prehistoric human coprolites from Utah', *Proceedings of Utah Academy of Sciences, Arts and Letters* 46 (1969): 102–5.

Fry, G.F., Hall, H.J., *Analysis of Human Coprolites from Inscription House: Preliminary Report* (Tucson: Report to the National Park Service, Arizona Archaeological Center, 1973).

Fry, G., Hall, H.J., 'Human coprolites from Antelope House: preliminary analysis', *Kiva* 41 (1975): 87–96.

Fry, G.F., Hall, H.J., 'Human coprolites', in D.P. Morris (ed.), *Archaeological Investigations at Antelope House* (Washington, DC: National Park Service, 1986), pp. 165–88.

Fry, G.F., Moore, J.G., '*Enterobius vermicularis*: 10,000-year-old human infection', *Science* 166 (1969): 1620.

Fry, L.M., Cowden, J.R., Watkins, D.W., Clasen, T., Mihelcic, J.R., 'Quantifying health improvements from water quantity enhancement: an engineering perspective applied to rainwater harvesting in West Africa', *Environmental Science and Technology* 44 (2010): 9535–41.

Fugassa, M.H., *Enteroparasitosis en Poblaciones Cazadoras-Recolectoras de Patagonia Austral* (PhD Thesis, Universidad Nacional de Mar del Plata, Argentina, 2006).

Fugassa, M.H., 'Camélidos, parásitos y ocupaciones humanas: registrospaleoparasitológicos en Cerro Casa de Piedra 7 (Parque Nacional Perito Moreno, Santa Cruz, Argentina)', *Intersecciones en Antropología* 8 (2007): 265–9.

Fugassa, M.H., Araújo, A., Guichón, R.A., 'Quantitative paleoparasitology applied to archaeological sediments', *Memórias do Instituto Oswaldo Cruz* 101 (suppl. 2) (2006): 29–33.

Fugassa, M.H., Araújo, A., Sardella, N., Denegri, G.M., 'New paleoparasitological finding in caves from Patagonia, Argentina', *Paleopathology Newsletter* 137 (2007): 17–21.

Fugassa, M., Barberena, R., 'Cuevas y zoonosisantiguas: paleoparasitologíadel sitio Orejas de Burro 1 (Santa Cruz, Argentina)' *Magallania (Punta Arenas)* 34 (2006): 57–62.

Fugassa, M.H., Beltrame, M.O., Sardella, N.H., Civalero, M.T., Aschero, C., 'Paleoparasitological results from coprolites dated at the Pleistocene-Holocene transition as source of paleoecological evidences in Patagonia', *Journal of Archaeological Science* 37 (2010a): 880–4.

Fugassa, M.H., Favier Dubois, C.M., 'Primer registro paleoparasitológico de *Trichuris* SP (Nematoda, Capilariidae) en muestras asociadas a restos humanos del Holoceno tardío de Patagonia septentrional', *Revista Argentina de Antropología Biológica* 1 (2009): 61–72.

Fugassa, M., Guichón, R.A., 'Modelos paleoepidemiológicos para el Holoceno patagónico', *7th Jornadas de Arqueología de la Patagonia*. 21–25 April 2008, Conference Proceedings Abstracts (Ushuaia, 2008), p. 30.

Fugassa, M.H., Reinhard, K.J., Johnson, K.L., Gardner, S.L., Vieira, M., Araújo, A., 'Parasitism of prehistoric humans and companion animals from Antelope Cave, Mojave County, Northwest Arizona', *Journal of Parasitology* 97 (2011): 862–867.

Fugassa, M.H., Sardella, N.H., Guichón, R.A., Denegri, G.M., Araújo, A., 'Paleoparasitological analysis applied to skeletal sediments of meridional Patagonian collections', *Journal of Archaeological Science* 35 (2008a): 1408–11.

Fugassa, M.H., Sardella, N.H., Taglioretti, V., Reinhard, K., Araújo, A., 'Morphometric variability in oocysts of *Eimeria macusaniensis* (Guerrero et al. 1967) in archaeological samples from the Holocene of Patagonia, Argentina', *Journal of Parasitology* 94 (2008b): 1418–20.

Fugassa, M., Taglioretti, V., Gonçalves, M.L.C., Araújo, A., Sardella, N.H., Denegri, G.M., '*Capillaria* spp. findings in Patagonian archaeological sites: statistical analysis of morphometric data', *Memórias do Instituto Oswaldo Cruz* 103 (2008c): 104–5.

Fuller, K., 'Hookworm: not a pre-Columbian pathogen', *Medical Anthropology* 17 (1997): 297–308.

Furrows, S.J., Moody, A.H., Chiodini, P.L., 'Comparison of PCR and antigen detection methods for the diagnosis of *Entamoeba histolytica* infection', *Journal of Clinical Pathology* 57 (2004): 1264–1266.

Gaertringen, J.F.W.R.A.H., *Thera 3* (Berlin, 1899).

Gale, E.A.M., 'A missing link in the hygiene hypothesis?', *Diabetologia* 45 (2002): 588–94.

Galen, *On the Properties of Foodstuffs*, trans. O. Powell (Cambridge: Cambridge University Press, 2003).

Garcia, L.S., *Practical Guide to Diagnostic Parasitology*, 2nd edition. (Washington: ASM Press, 2009).

Gaspar, M.D., Deblasis, P., Fish, S.K., Fish, P.R., 'Sambaqui (shell mound) societies of coastal Brazil', in H. Silverman and W.H. Isbell (eds), *Handbook of South American Archaeology* (New York: Springer, 2008), pp. 319–35.

Gentilini, M., *Médecine Tropicale* (Paris, Flammarion, 2001).

Gibson, M., 'Umm el-Jir, A Town in Akkad', *Journal of Near Eastern Studies* 31 (1972): 237–294.

Gibson, M., al-Azm,A., Reichel,C., Quntar,S., Franke, J., Khalidi, L., Hritz, C., Altaweel, M., Coyle, C., Colantoni, C., Tenney, J., Abdul Aziz, G., Hartnell, T., 'Hamoukar: a summary of three seasons of excavation', *Akkadica* 123 (2002): 11–34.

Gifford, C., *Food and Cooking in Viking Times* (London: Wayland, 2009).

Glen, D.R., Brooks, D.R., 'Parasitological evidence pertaining to the phylogeny of the hominoid primates', *Biological Journal of the Linnean Society* 27 (2008): 331–54.

Gonçalves, M.L.C., Araújo, A., Duarte, R., Pereira da Silva, J., Reinhard, K., Bouchet, F., Ferreira, L.F., 'Detection of *Giardia duodenalis* antigen in coprolites using a commercially available enzyme-linked immonosorbent assay', *Transaction of the Royal Society of Tropical Medicine and Hygiene* 96 (2002): 640–43.

Gonçalves, C.L.M., Araújo, A., Ferreira, L.F., 'Human intestinal parasites in the past: new findings and a review', *Memórias do Instituto Oswaldo Cruz* 98 (Suppl. 1) (2003): 103–118.

Gonçalves, C.L.M., da Silva, V.L., de Andrade, C.M., Reinhard, K., da Rocha, G.C., Le Bailly, M., Bouchet, F., Ferreira, L.F., Araújo, A., 'Amoebiasis distribution in the past: first steps using an immunoassay technique', *Transactions of the Royal Society of Tropical Medicine and Hygiene* 98 (2004): 88–91.

Gowers, E., 'The Anatomy of Rome from Capitol to Cloaca', *Journal of Roman Studies* 85 (1995): 23–52.

Graham, J.W., *The Palaces of Crete* (Princeton: Princeton University Press, 1987).

Gray, H.F., 'Sewerage in ancient and medieval times', *Sewage Works Journal* 12 (1940): 939–946.

Grauer, A. (ed.), *A Companion to Paleopathology* (Chichester: Wiley-Blackwell, 2012).

Green, A. (ed.), *Abu Salabikh Excavations Volume 4; The 6G Ash Tip and Its Contents: Cultic and Administrative Discard from the Temple?* (London: British School of Archaeology in Iraq, 1993).

Greig, J., 'Plant Resources', in G.G. Astill and A. Grant (eds), *The Countryside of Medieval England* (Oxford: Blackwell, 1992), pp.108–27.

Guhl, F., Jaramillo, C., Vallejo, G.A., Yockteng, R., Cárdenas-Arroyo, F., Fornaciari, G., Arriaza, B., Aufderheide, A.C., 'Isolation of Trypanosoma cruzi DNA in 4,000-year-old mummified human tissue from northern Chile', *American Journal of Physical Anthropology* 108 (1999): 401–407.

Guichón, R.A., Suby, J.A., Casali, R., Fugassa, M.H., 'Health at the time of Native-European contact in Southern Patagonia: first steps, results, and prospects', *Memórias do Instituto Oswaldo Cruz* 101 (Suppl. 2) (2006): 97–05.

Guidon, N., Pessis, A.M., 'Serra da Capivara National Park, Brazil: cultural heritage and society', *World Archaeology* 39 (2007): 406–16.

Guilaine, J., Le Brun, A., Mort, F.L., Vigne, J.D., Bouchet, F., Harter, S., 'Premières données parasitologiques sur les populations humaines précéramiques Chypriotes (VIIIe et VIIe millénaires av. J.-C.)', *Paléorient* 31 (2005): 43–54.

Gummerman, G.J., Westfall, D.A., Weed, C.S., *Archaeological Investigations on Black Mesa: The 1969–1970 Seasons* (Arizona: Prescott College Pr., 1972).

Gunn, A., Pitt, S.J., *Parasitology: An Integrated Approach* (Chichester: Wiley-Blackwell, 2012)

Hagen, A., *Anglo-Saxon Food and Drink: Production, Processing, Distribution and Consumption* (Hockwold cum Wilton: Anglo Saxon Books, 2006).

Hall, A., 'Intestinal helminths of man: the interpretation of egg counts', *Parasitology* 85 (1982): 605–613.

Hall, A.R., '…The cockle of rebellion, insolence, sedition…', *Interim: Bulletin of the York Archaeological Trust* 8 (1981): 5–8.

Hall, A.R., Jones, A.K.G. and Kenward, H.K. 'Cereal bran and human faecal remains from archaeological deposits – some preliminary observations', in B. Proudfoot (ed.), *Site, Environment and Economy*. Symposia of the Association for Environmental Archaeology 3. British Archaeological Reports (International Series) 173 (Oxford: Archaeopress, 1983), pp. 85–104.

Hall, A.R., Kenward, H.K., *Environmental Evidence from the Colonia: General Accident and Rougier Street*. The Archaeology of York series 14(6) (London: Council for British Archaeology, 1990).

Hall, A.R., Kenward, H., 'Disentangling dung: pathways to stable manure', *Environmental Archaeology* 1 (1998): 123–6.

Hall, A.R., Kenward, H. (2000), 'Technical Report: Plant and invertebrate remains from Anglo-Scandinavian deposits at 4–7 Parliament Street (Littlewoods Store), York (site code 99.946)', *Reports from the EAU, York* 2000/22.

Hall, A.R., Kenward, H. 'Can we identify biological indicator groups for craft, industry and other activities?', in P. Murphy and P.E.J. Wiltshire (eds), *The Environmental Archaeology of Industry*. Symposia of the Association for Environmental Archaeology 20 (Oxford: Oxbow, 2003), pp. 114–30.

Hall, A.R., Kenward, H.K. 'Setting people in their environment: plant and animal remains from Anglo-Scandinavian York', in R.A. Hall, D.W. Rollason, M. Blackburn, D.N. Parsons, G. Fellows-Jensen, A.R. Hall, H.K. Kenward, T.P. O'Connor, D. Tweddle, A.J. Mainman and N.S.H. Rogers, *Aspects of Anglo-Scandinavian York*. The Archaeology of York series 8(4) (York: Council for British Archaeology, 2004), pp. 372–426 and references pp. 507–21.

Hall, A.R., Kenward, H.K., 'Development-driven archaeology: bane or boon for bioarchaeology?', *Oxford Journal of Archaeology* 25 (2006): 213–24.

Hall, A.R., Kenward, H.K., 'Plant and invertebrate indicators of leather production: from fresh skin to leather offcuts', in R. Thomson and Q. Mould (eds), *Leather Tanneries: The Archaeological Evidence* (London: Archetype, 2011), pp. 9–32.

Hall, A.R., Kenward, H.K., 'Sewers, cesspits and middens: a survey of the evidence for 2,000 years of waste disposal in York, UK', in P.D. Mitchell (ed.), *Sanitation, Latrines and Intestinal Parasites in Past Populations* (Farnham: Ashgate, 2014), pp. 99–119.

Hall, A.R., Kenward, H., Girvan, L., McKenna, R. (2007), 'Investigations of plant and invertebrate macrofossil remains from excavations in 2004 at 62–8 Low Petergate, York (site code 2002.421)', *Reports from the Centre for Human Palaeoecology, University of York* 2007/06.

Hall, A.R., Kenward, H., Jaques, D., Carrott, J. (2000), 'Technical Report: Environment and industry at Layerthorpe Bridge, York (site code YORYM 1996.345)', *Reports from the Environmental Archaeology Unit, York* 2000/64.

Hall, A.R., Kenward, H.K., Robertson, A. (1993a), 'Investigation of medieval and post-medieval plant and invertebrate remains from Area X of the excavations in The Bedern (south-west), York (YAT/Yorkshire Museum sitecode 1973–81.13 X): Technical report', *Ancient Monuments Laboratory Report* 56/93.

Hall, A.R., Kenward, H.K., Robertson, A. (1993b), 'Investigation of medieval and post-medieval plant and invertebrate remains from Area IV of the excavations in The Bedern (north-east), York (YAT/Yorkshire Museum sitecode 1976–81.14 IV): Technical report', *Ancient Monuments Laboratory Report* 57/93.

Hall, A.R., Kenward, H.K., Robertson, A. (1993c), 'Investigation of medieval and post-medieval plant and invertebrate remains from Area II of the excavations in The Bedern (north-east), York (YAT/Yorkshire Museum sitecode 1976–81.14 II): Technical report', *Ancient Monuments Laboratory Report* 58/93.

Hall, A.R., Kenward, H.K., Williams, D., *Environmental Evidence from Roman Deposits at Skeldergate*. The Archaeology of York series 14(3) (London: Council for British Archaeology, 1980).

Hall, A.R., Kenward, H.K., Williams, D., Greig, J.R.A., *Environment and Living Conditions at Two Anglo-Scandinavian Sites*. The Archaeology of York series 14(4) (London: Council for British Archaeology, 1983).

Hall, H.J., *Diet and disease at Clyde's Cavern, Utah* (Salt Lake City, University of Utah: PhD Thesis, 1972).

Hall, H.J., 'A paleoscatological study of diet and disease at Dirty Shame Rockshelter, Southeast Oregon', *Tebiwa* 8 (1977): 1–15.

Hall, H.R., *A Season's Work at Ur, al-Ubaid, Abu Shahrain (Eridu) and Elsewhere, Being an Official Account of the British Archaeological Mission to Babylonia 1919* (London: Methuen, 1930).

Halliday, S., *The Great Stink of London* (Stroud: Sutton, 2001).

Halpenny, C.M., Kosi, K.G., Valdés, V.E., Scott, M.E., 'Prediction of child health by household density and asset-based indices in impoverished indigenous villages in rural Panama', *American Journal of Tropical Medicine and Hygiene* 86 (2012): 280–91.

Han, E.T., Guk, S.M., Kim, J.L., Jeong H.J., Kim, S.N., Chai, J.Y., 'Detection of parasite eggs from archaeological excavations in the Republic of Korea', *Memórias do Instituto Oswaldo Cruz* 98 (2003): 123–126.

Hansen, J., 'Les momies du Groenland', *La Recherche* 183 (1986): 1490–98.

Haque, R., Neville, L.M., Hahn, P., Petri, W.A., 'Rapid diagnosis of *Entamoeba* infection by using *Entamoeba* and *Entamoeba histolytica* stool antigen detection kits', *Journal of Clinical Microbiology* 33 (1995): 2558–2561.

Haque, R., Ali, K.M., Akther, S., Petri, W.A., 'Comparison of PCR, isoenzyme analysis, and antigen detection for diagnosis of *Entamoeba histolytica* infection', *Journal of Clinical Microbiology* 36 (1998): 449–452.

Haque, R., Mollah, N.U., Ali, K.M., Alam, K., Eubanks, A., Lyerly, D., Petri, W.A., 'Diagnosis of amebic liver abscess and intestinal infection with the TechLab *Entamoeba histolytica* II antigen detection and antibody tests', *Journal of Clinical Microbiology* 38 (2000): 3235–3239.

Harris, H.D., *The Origins and Spread of Agriculture and Pastoralism in Eurasia: Crops, Felds, Flocks and Herds* (London: UCL Press, 1996).

Harrison, M., *London Beneath the Pavement* (London: Peter Davies, 1961).

Hart, G.D., Millet, N.B., Rideout, D.F., Scott, J.W., Lynn, G.E., Reyman, T.A., Boni, U.D., Barraco, R.A., Zimmerman, M.R., Lewin, P.K., Horne, P.D, 'Autopsy of an Egyptian mummy (Nakht-R.O.M.-1)', *Canadian Medical Association Journal* 117 (1977): 461–76.

Harter, S., *Implication de la Paléoparasitologie dans l'Etude des Populations Anciennes de la Vallée du Nil et du Proche-Orient: Etudes de Cas* (PhD Thesis: Université de Reims Champagne-Ardenne, 2003).

Harter, S., Le Bailly, M., Janot, F., Bouchet, F., 'First paleoparasitological study of embalming rejects jar found in Saqqara, Egypt', *Memórias do Instituto Oswaldo Cruz* 98 (Suppl. 1) (2003): 119–21.

Harter, S., Bouchet, F., Mumcuoglu, K.Y., Zias, J., 'Toilet practices among members of the Dead Sea Scroll sect at Qumran (100BC–68AD)', *Revue de Qumran* 21 (2004): 579–84.

Harter, S., Le Bailly, M., Janot, F., Bouchet, F., 'First paleoparasitological study of an embalming rejects jar found in Saqqara, Egypt', *Memórias do Instituto Oswaldo Cruz* 98 (Suppl. 1) (2003): 119–21.

Harris, D.R. (ed.), *The Origins and Spread of Agriculture and Pastoralism in Eurasia: Crops, Fields, Flocks and Herds* (London: UCL Press, 1996).

Hawass, Z., Gad, Y., Ismail, S., Khairat, R., Fathalla, D., Hasan, N., Ahmed, A., Elleithy, H., Ball, M., Gaballah, F., Wasef, S., Fateen, M., Amer, H., Gostner, P., Selim, A., Zink, A., Pusch, C.M., 'Ancestry and pathology in King Tutankhamun's family', *Journal of the American Medical Association (JAMA)* 303 (2010): 638–647.

Heinonen-Tanski, H., van Wijk-Sibesma, C., 'Human excreta for plant production', *Bioresource Technology* 96 (2005): 403–11.

Heirbaut, E., Jones, A.K.G., Wheeler, W., 'Archaeometry: methods and analysis', in G.C.M. Jansen, A.O. Koloski-Ostrow and E.M. Moormann (eds), *Roman Toilets: Their Archaeology and Cultural History* (Leuven: Peeters, 2011).

Helbaek, H. 'Samarran irrigation agriculture at Choga Mami in Iraq', *Iraq* (1972): 25-48.

Heller, L., 'Who really benefits from environmental sanitation services in the cities? An intra-urban analysis in Betim, Brazil', *Environment and Urbanization* 11 (1999): 133–144.

Hemker, C., *Altorientalische Kanalisation; Untersuchungen zu Be-und Entwässerungsanlagen im Mesopotamisch, Syrisch, Anatolischen Raum.* Gesellscahft 22 (Munster: Abhandlung der Deutschen Orient, 1993).

Heo, J., *Donguibogam* (Seoul, 1613).

Herrmann, B., 'Parasitologisch-epidemiologische auswertungen mittelalterlicher kloaken', *Zeitschrift für Archäologie des Mittelaltes* 13 (1985): 131–61.

Herrmann, B., Schulz, U., 'Parasitologische untersuchungen eines spätmittelalterlich-frühneuzeitlichen kloakeninhaltes aus der fronerei auf dem schrangen in Lübeck', *Lübecker Schri Archäol Kultur* 12 (1986): 167–72

Herrmann, B., 'Parasite remains from medieval latrine deposits: an epidemiologic and ecologic approach', *Actes des Troisiemes Journees Anthropologiques, Notes et Monographies Techniques* 24 (1988): 135–42.

Hevly, R.H., Kelly, R.E., Anderson, G.A., Olsen, S.J., 'Comparative effects of climate change, cultural impact, and volcanism in the paleoecology of Flagstaff, Arizona, A.D. 900–1300', in P.D. Sheets and D.K. Grayson (eds), *Volcanic Activity and Human Ecology* (New York: Academic Press, 1979), pp. 487–523.

Hibbs, A.C., Secor, W.E., Gerven, D.V., Armelagos, G.J., 'Irrigation and infection: the immunoepidemiology of schistosomiasis in Ancient Nubia', *American Journal of Physical Anthropology* 145 (2011): 290–98.

Hippocrates 'Περί άερων ύδάτων τοπων (On airs, waters, places)', in T.E. Page (ed.) and W.H.S. Jones (trans.), *The Loeb Classical Library* 147, vol. 1 (London, 1962).

Hoberg, E.P., 'Phylogeny of Taenia: species definitions and origins of human parasites', *Parasitology International* 55 (2006): S23–S30.

Hoberg, E.P., Alkire, N.L., Queiroz, A., Jones, A., 'Out of Africa: origins of the Taenia tapeworms in humans', *Proceedings of the Royal Society B: Biological Sciences* 268 (2001): 781–87.

Hodge, A.T., *Roman Aqueducts and Water Supply* (London: Duckworth, 1995).

Hoepfner, W. (ed.), *Geschichte des Wohnens*, vol. 1 (Stuttgart: Deutsche Verlags-Anstalt, 1999).

Hoeppli, R., 'Some early views on parasites and parasitic infections shared by the people of Borneo, Malaya and China', *Proceedings of the Alumni Association of Malaya* 7 (1954): 3–17.

Hoeppli, R., 'The knowledge of parasites and parasitic infections from ancient times to the 17th century', *Experimental Parasitology* 5 (1956): 398–419.

Hoeppli, R., *Parasites and Parasitic Infection in Early Medicine and Science* (Singapore: University of Malaya Press, 1959).

Hoffman, M.A., 'The social context of trash disposal in an early dynastic Egyptian town', *American Antiquity* 39 (1974): 35–50.

Hofreiter, M., Serre, D., Poinar, H.N., Kuch, M., Pääbo, S., 'Ancient DNA', *Nature Reviews Genetics* 2 (2001): 353–359.

Hogrewe, W., Joyce, S., Perez, E., *The Unique Challenges of Improving Peri-Urban Sanitation* WASH Technical Report 86. (Washington, DC: US Agency for International Development, 1993).

Holiday, D.M., Guillen, S., Richardson, D.J., 'Diphyllobothriasis of the Chiribaya Culture (700–1476 AD) of Southern Peru', *Comparative Parasitology* 70 (2003): 171–6.

Holmes, T., *Early Humans: the Pleistocene and Holocene Epochs* (New York: Chelsea House, 2009).

Home, G., *Roman London AD 43–457* (London: Eyre and Spottiswoode, 1948).

Horne, P.D., 'A review of the evidence of human endoparasitism in the pre-Columbian New World through the study of coprolites', *Journal of Archaeological Science* 12 (1985): 299–310.

Horne, P.D., 'First evidence of Enterobiasis in ancient Egypt', *Journal of Parasitology* 88 (2002): 1019–21.

Horne, P., Redford, S., 'Aspergillosis and dracunculiasis in mummies from the tomb of Parannefer', *Paleopathology Newsletter* 92 (1995): 10–12.

Horne, P.D., Tuck, J.A., 'Archaeoparasitology at a 17th century colonial site in Newfoundland', *Journal of Parasitology* 82 (1996): 512–5.

Hu, S.Y., 'Study on the parasite eggs in an ancient corpse from Zhangguo Chu Tomb No. 1 in Mashan brick-field of Jiangling County, Hubei', *Chinese Journal of Parasitology and Parasitic Disease* 2 (1984): 8.

Hubbe, M., Neves, W.A., Amaral, H.L., Guidon, N., '"Zuzu" strikes again: morphological affinities of the early Holocene human skeleton from Toca dos Coqueiros, Piaui, Brazil', *American Journal of Physical Anthropology* 134 (2007): 285–91.

Hudson, E.H., 'Treponematosis and pilgrimage', *American Journal of Medical Science* 246 (1963): 645–56.

Hugot, J.P., Reinhard, K., Gardner, S.L., 'Human enterobiasis in evolution: origin, specificity and transmission', *Parasite* 6 (1999): 201–08.

Hume, J.C.C., Lyons, E.J., Day, K.P., 'Human migration, mosquitoes and the evolution of Plasmodium falciparum', *Trends in Parasitology* 19 (2003): 144–49.

Hunter-Mann, K., 'Scratching the surface of Early Modern York: the Block E excavation, Hungate', *Yorkshire Archaeology Today* 12 (2007): 12–14.

ILS = *Inscriptiones Latinae Selectae,* 3 vols (1892–1916): Herman Dessau (ed.), Berlin.

Iñiguez, A.M., Reinhard, K.J., Araújo, A., Ferreira, L.F., Vicente, A.C.P., 'Enterobius vermicularis: ancient DNA from North and South American human coprolites', *Memórias do Instituto Oswaldo Cruz* 98 (2003): 67–69.

Iñiguez, A.M., Reinhard, K.J., Gonçalves, M.L.C., Ferreira, L.F., Araújo, A., Paulo Vicente, A.C., 'SL1 RNA gene recovery from Enterobius vermicularis ancient DNA in pre-Columbian human coprolites', *International Journal of Parasitology* 36 (2006): 1419–1425.

Ingemark, C.A., 'The octopus in the sewers: an ancient legend analogue', *Journal of Folklore Research* 45 (2008): 145–170.

Isherwood, I., Jarvis, H., Fawcitt, R.A., 'Radiology of the Manchester mummies', in A.R. David and E. Tapp (eds), *Evidence Embalmed: Modern Medicine and the Mummies of Ancient Egypt* (Manchester: Manchester University Press, 1984) pp. 25–64.

Jackson, R., *Doctors and Diseases in the Roman Empire* (London: British Museum Publications, 1988).

James P., Thorpe N., *Ancient Inventions* (New York: Ballantine Books, 1995).

Jansen, J., Boersema, J.H., 'Helminth eggs from the latrines of the Olofskapel Gatehouse, Amsterdam', *Paleopathology Newsletter* 2 (1972): 7–8.

Jansen, M., 'Water supply and sewage disposal at Mohenjo-Daro', *World Archaeology* 21 (1989): 177–192.

Jansen, G.C.M., 'Private toilets at Pompeii: appearance and operation', in S.E. Bon and R. Jones (eds), *Sequence and Space in Pompeii* (Oxford: Oxbow, 1997), pp. 121–34.

Jansen, G.C.M., 'Systems for the disposal of waste and excreta in Roman cities: the situation in Pompeii, Herculaneum and Ostia', in X.D. Raventós and J-A. Remolà (eds), *Sordes Urbis: La Elimanación de Residuos en la Ciudad Romana. Actes de La Reunión de Roma* (15–16 de noviembre de 1996) (Roma: L'Erma di Bretschneider, 2000), pp. 37–49.

Jansen, G.C.M., Koloski-Ostrow, A.O., Moormann, E.M. (eds), *Roman Toilets: Their Archaeology and Cultural History* (Leuven: Peeters, 2011).

Jansen, J., Over, H.J., 'Het voorkomen van parasieten in terpmateriaal uit Noordwest Duitsland'., *Tijdschr Diergeneesk* 87 (1962): 1377–79.

Jansen, J., Over, H.J., 'Observations on helminth infections in a Roman army camp', in A. Corradetti (ed.), *Proceedings of the First International Congress of Parasitology, Roma Italy, 1964* (Oxford: Pergamon, 1966): p. 791.

Jarcho, S., 'Some observations on diseases in prehistoric North America', *Bulletin of the History of Medicine* 38 (1964): 1–19.

Jashemski, W.F., 'The Excavation of a shop-house garden at Pompeii (I.xx.5)', *American Journal of Archaeology* 81 (1977): 217–227.

Jasim, S.A., 'Structure and Function in an Ubaid Village', in E. Henrickson and I. Thuesen (eds), *Upon This Foundation – The Ubaid Reconsidered* (Copenhagen: Carsten Niehbuhr Institute, 1989), pp. 79–88.

Jensen, P.K., Phuc, P.D., Knudsen, L.G., Dalsgaard, A., Konradsen, F., 'Hygiene versus fertiliser: the use of human excreta in agriculture – a Vietnamese example', *International Journal of Hygiene and Environmental Health* 211 (2008): 432–9.

Johannessen, S., Hastorf, C.A. (eds), *Corn and Culture in the Prehistoric New World* (Boulder, Colorado: Westview Press, 1994).

Johnson, K.L., Reinhard, K., Sianto, L., Araújo, A., Gardner, S.L., Janovy Jr, J., 'A tick from a prehistoric Arizona coprolite', *Journal of Parasitology* 94 (2008): 296–98.

Jones, A.K.G., 'Human parasite remains: prospects for a quantitative approach', in A.R. Hall and H.K Kenward (eds), *Environmental Archaeology in the Urban Context* (London: Council for British Archaeology, 1982), pp. 66–70.

Jones, A.K.G., 'A coprolite from 6–8 Pavement', in A.R. Hall, H.K. Kenward, D. Williams and J.R.A. Greig, *Environment and Living Conditions at Two Anglo-Scandinavian Sites*. The Archaeology of York series 14(4) (London: Council for British Archaeology, 1983), pp. 225–9.

Jones, A.K.G., 'Parasitological investigations', in E. Schia and K. Griffin (eds), *De Arkeologiske Utgravninger I Gamlegyen, Oslo*. Series no. 5 (Oslo: Alheim and Eide, 1988), pp. 134–37.

Jones, A.K.G., 'Parasitological investigation', *The Bulletin of the Board of Celtic Studies, Archaeolog a Chelfyddyd* 36 (1989): 258–62.

Jones, A.K.G., Hutchinson, A.R., 'The Parasitological Evidence', in M.R. McCarthy, *The Structural Sequence and Environmental Remains from Castle Street, Carlisle: Excavations 1981–2* (Cumberland and Westmorland Antiquarian and Archaeological Society, 1991).

Jones, A.K.G., Nicholson, C., 'Recent finds of Trichuris and Ascaris ova from Britain', *Paleopathology Newsletter* 62 (1988): 5–6.

Jones, R., 'Why manure matters', in R. Jones (ed.), *Manure Matters: Historical, Archaeological and Ethnographic Perspectives* (Farnham: Ashgate, 2012) pp. 1–11.

Jørgensen, D., 'Cooperative sanitation: managing streets and gutters in late medieval England and Scandinavia', *Technology and Culture* 49 (2008): 547–567.

Juvenal, *Juvenal and Persius*, trans. S.M. Braund (Cambridge: Loeb, 2004).

Kanazawa, I., Miyakake, Y., 'Insect remains', in *The Preliminary Report of the Excavations of Ikegami-Sone Site* (Osaka: Board of Education, Asaka Prefectural Government, 1990), pp. 107–16.

Kamash, Z., 'Interpreting the archaeological evidence: latrines and the senses' in G.C.M. Jansen, A.O. Koloski-Ostrow and E.M. Moormann (eds), *Roman Toilets, Their Archaeology and Cultural History* (Leuven: Peeters Press, 2011), pp. 181–83.

Kariuki, J.G., Magambo, K.J., Njeruh, M.F., Muchiri, E.M., Nzioka, S.M., Kariuki, S., 'Effects of hygiene and sanitation interventions on reducing diarrhoea prevalence among children in resource constrained communities: case study of Turkana District, Kenya', *Journal of Community Health* 37 (2012): 1178–84.

Keene, D., 'Rubbish in medieval towns', in A.R. Hall and H.K. Kenward (eds), *Environmental Archaeology in the Urban Context* (London: Council for British Archaeology, 1982), pp. 26–30.

Kenward, H. (2009), 'Invertebrates in archaeology in the north of England' (*English Heritage) Research Department Report Series* 12/2009.(availableonlineathttp:// services.english-heritage.org.uk/ResearchReportsPdfs/012_2009WEB.pdf)

Kenward, H., Carrott, J., 'Insect species associations characterise past occupation sites', *Journal of Archaeological Science* 33 (2006): 1452–73.

Kenward, H.K., Hall, A.R., *Biological Evidence from Anglo-Scandinavian Deposits at 16–22 Coppergate. The Archaeology of York* series 14(7) (York: Council for British Archaeology, 1995).

Kenward, H., Hall, A., 'Enhancing bioarchaeological interpretation using indicator groups: stable manure as a paradigm', *Journal of Archaeological Science* 24 (1997): 663–73.

Kenward, H., Hall, A., 'Decay of delicate organic remains in shallow urban deposits: are we at a watershed?', *Antiquity* 74 (2000): 519–25.

Kenward, H.K., Hall, A.R., 'Easily decayed organic remains in urban archaeological deposits: value, threats, research directions and conservation', in O. Brinkkemper, J. Deeben, J. van Doesburg, D. Hallewas, E.M. Theunissen and A.D. Verlinde (eds), *Vakken in Vlakken. Archeologische Kennis in Lagen.* Nederlandse Archeologische Rapporten 32 (Amersfoort: Rijksdienst voor het Oudheikundig, 2006), pp. 183–98.

Kenward, H., Hall, A., 'Urban organic archaeology: an irreplaceable palaeoecological archive at risk', *World Archaeology* 40 (2008): 584–96.

Kenward, H., Hall, A., 'Dung and stable manure on waterlogged archaeological occupation sites: some ruminations on the evidence from plant and invertebrate remains', in R.L.C. Jones (ed.), *Manure Matters* (Farnham: Ashgate, 2012), pp. 79–95.

Kenward, H., Hall, A., Jaques, D., Carrott, J., Cousins, S. (2003), 'Assessment of biological remains from excavations at Waterstones bookshop, 28–29 High Ousegate, York (site code: 2002.475)', *Palaeoecology Research Services Report* 2003/50.

Kenward, H.K., Hall, A.R., Jones, A.K.G., *Environmental evidence from a Roman well and Anglian pits in the Legionary Fortress. The Archaeology of York* series 14(5) (London: Council for British Archaeology, 1986).

Kenward, H., Large, F., 'Insects in urban waste pits in Viking York: another kind of seasonality', *Environmental Archaeology* 3 (1998): 35–53.

Khairat, R., Ball, M., Chang, C.-C.H., Bianucci, R., Nerlich, A.G., Trautmann, M., Ismail, S., Shanab, B.M.L., Karim, A.M., Gad, Y.Z., Pusch, C.M., 'First insights into the metagenome of Egyptian mummies using next-generation sequencing', *Journal of Applied Genetics* (2013): doi.org/10.1007/s13353–013–0145–1.

King, W., 'How high is too high? Disposing of dung in seventeenth-century Prescot', *The Sixteenth Century Journal* 23 (1992): 443–57.

Kinnier-Wilson, J., Reynolds, E., 'On Stroke and Facial Palsy in Babylonian Texts', in I. Finkel and M. Geller (eds), *Disease in Babylonia* (Leiden: Brill, 2007). pp. 67–99.

Kliks, M.M., 'Paleoparasitology: on the origins and impact of human-helminth relationships', in N.A. Croll and J.H. Cross (eds), *Human Ecology and Infectious Disease* (New York: Academic Press, 1983), pp. 291–313.

Kliks, M.M., 'Helminths as heirlooms and souvenirs: a review of New World paleoparasitology', *Parasitology Today* 6 (1990): 93–100.

Kline, A.S. (ed.), *Suetonius: the Lives of the Twelve Caesars*. VIII, Vespasian XXIII (2010) http://www.poetryintranslation.com/PITBR/Latin/Suethome. htm. [Accessed 1 May 2014].

Knights, B.A., Dickson, C.A., Dickson, J.H., 'Evidence concerning the Roman military diet at Bearsden, Scotland, in the 2nd century AD', *Journal of Archaeological Science* 10 (1983): 139–52.

Koloski-Ostrow, A.O., 'Finding social meaning in the public latrines of Pompeii', in N. de Haan and G.C.M. Jansen (eds), *Cura Aquarum in Campania* (Leiden: PVBA, 1996), pp. 79–86.

Koloski-Ostrow, A.O., 'Cacator cave malum: the subject and object of Roman public latrines in Italy during the first centuries BC and AD', in G.C.M. Jansen (ed.), *Cura Aquarum in Sicilia* (Leiden: Peeters, 2000), pp. 289–95.

Koloski-Ostrow, A.O., 'Location and Context of Toilets', in G.C.M. Jansen, A.O. Koloski-Ostrow and E.M. Moormann (eds), *Roman Toilets, Their Archaeology and Cultural History* (Leuven: Peeters, 2011), pp. 113–14.

Koutsoyiannis, D., Angelakis, A.N., 'Hydrologic and hydraulic sciences and technologies in ancient Greek times', in B.A. Stewart and T. Howell (eds), *The Encyclopedia of Water Sciences* (New York: Markel Dekker, 2003), pp. 415–417.

Koutsoyiannis, D., Zarkadoulas, N., Angelakis, A.N., Tchobanoglous, G., 'Urban water management in ancient Greece: legacies and lessons', *ASCE, Journal of Water Resources Planning & Management* 134 (2008): 45–54.

Kumar, S., Vollmer, S., 'Does access to improved sanitation reduce childhood diarrhoea in rural India?', *Health Economics* 22 (2013): 410–27.

Kurosaki, S., *The Toilet Features of the Fujiwara Palace Site* (Nara: Nabunken, 1992).

Kwangju National Museum (KNM), 'Shinchang-dong wetland site I: report on the research of antiquities of the Kwangju National Museum', *Kwangju National Museum* 33 (1997): 159–166.

Lawrence, D.N., Neel, J.V., Abadie, S.H., Moore, L.L., Adams, L.J., Healy, G.R., Kagan, I.G., 'Epidemiologic studies among Amerindian populations of Amazonia III. Intestinal parasitoses in newly contacted and acculturating villages', *American Journal of Tropical Medicine and Hygiene* 29 (1908): 530–7.

Le, T.H., Blair, D., McManus, D.P., 'Mitochondrial genomes of human helminths and their use as markers in population genetics and phylogeny', *Acta Tropica* 77 (2000): 243–56.

Le Bailly, M., *Evolution de la Relation Hôte/Parasite dans les Systèmes Lacustres Nord Alpins au Néolithique (3900–2900 BC), et Nouvelles Données dans la Détection des Paléoantigènes de Protozoa* (Université de Reims Champagne-Ardenne: Unpublished PhD Thesis, 2005).

Le Bailly, M., *Les Parasites dans les Lacs Nord Alpins au Néolithique (3900–2900 BC), et Nouvelles Données dans la Détection des Paléoantigènes de Protozoa.* (Sarrebruck : Editions Universitaires Européennes, 2011).

Le Bailly, M., Bouchet, F., 'Paléoparasitologie et immunologie : l'exemple d'*Entamoeba histolytica*', *Archéosciences Revue d'Archaeometrie* 30 (2006): 129–135.

Le Bailly, M., Bouchet, F., 'Ancient Dicrocoeliosis: occurrence, distribution and migration', *Acta Tropica* 115 (2010): 175–80.

Le Bailly, M., Bouchet, F., 'A first attempt to retrace the history of dysentery caused by *Entamoeba histolytica*', in P.D. Mitchell (ed.), *Sanitation, Latrines and Intestinal Parasites in Past Populations* (Farnham: Ashgate, 2014), pp. 219–228.

Le Bailly, M., Gonçalves, C.L.M., Harter, S., Prodeo, F., Araújo, A., Bouchet, F., 'New finding of Giardia intestinalis (Eukaryote, Metamonad) in Old World Archaeological site using immunofluorescence and enzyme-linked immunosorbent assays', *Memórias do Instituto Oswaldo Cruz* 103 (2008): 298–300.

Le Bailly, M., Leuzinger, U., Bouchet, F., 'Dioctophymidae eggs in coprolites from Neolithic site of Arbon-Bleiche 3 (Switzerland)', *Journal of Parasitology* 89 (2003): 1073–76.

Le Bailly, M., Mouze, S., Rocha, G.C.D., Heim, J.-L., Lichtenberg, R., Dunand, F., Bouchet, F. 'Identification of *Taenia* sp. in a mummy from a Christian necropolis in El-Deir, oasis of Kharga, ancient Egypt', *Journal of Parasitology* 96 (2010): 213–215.

Le Brun, A., 'At the other end of the sequence; the Cypriot Aceramic Neolithic as seen from Khirokitia', in S. Swiny (ed.), *The Earliest Prehistory of Cyprus: From Colonization to Exploitation* (Boston: American School of Oriental Research, 2001), pp. 109–18.

Lee, I.S., Lee, E.J., Park, J.B., Baek, S.H., Oh, C.S., Lee, S.D., Kim, Y.S., Bok, G.D., Hong, J.W., Lim, D.S., Shin, M.H., Seo, M., Shin, D.H., 'Acute traumatic death of a 17th century general based on examination of mummified remains found in Korea', *Annals of Anatomy* 191 (2009): 309–320.

Lee, S.-H., 'Transition of parasitic diseases in Korea', *Journal of Korean Medical Association* 50 (2007): 937–945.

Leles, D., Araújo, A., Ferreira, L.F., Vicente, A.C.P., Iñiguez, A.M., 'Molecular paleoparasitological diagnosis of *Ascaris* sp. from coprolites: new scenery of ascariasis in pre-Columbian South America times', *Memórias do Instituto Oswaldo Cruz* 103 (2008): 106–108.

Leles, D., Gardner, S.L., Reinhard, K., Iñiguez, A.M., Araújo, A., 'Are Ascaris lumbricoides and Ascaris suum a single species?' *Parasites & Vectors* 5 (2012): 42.

Leles, D., Reinhard, K., Fugassa, M., Ferreira, L.F., Iñiguez, A.M., Araújo, A., 'A parasitological paradox: why is ascarid infection so rare in the prehistoric Americas?', *Journal of Archaeological Sciences* 37 (2010): 1510–20.

Lemerle, P., 'Palestre romaine à Philippes', *Bulletin de Correspondance Hellénique* 61 (1937): 86–102.

Lenzen, H., *XXI Vorläufiger Bericht über die von dem Deutschen Archäologischen Institut und der Deutschen Orient-Gesellschaft aus Mitteln der Deutschen Forschungsgemeinschaft Unternommenen Ausgrabungen in Uruk-Warka, Winter 1962/63* (Berlin: Gebr. Mann., 1965).

Lenzen, H., *XXII Vorläufiger Bericht über die von dem Deutschen Archäologischen Institut und der Deutschen Orient-Gesellschaft aus Mitteln der Deutschen Forschungsgemeinschaft Unternommenen Ausgrabungen in Uruk-Warka, Winter 1963/64* (Berlin: Gebr. Mann., 1966).

Levine, O.S., Levine, M.M., 'Houseflies (*Musca domestica*) as mechanical vectors of shigellosis', *Reviews of Infectious Diseases* 13 (1991): 688–96.

Lewin, R., Foley, R., *Principles of Human Evolution* (Oxford: Blackwell, 2003);

Leyerle, B., 'Refuse, filth, and excrement in the homilies of John Chrysostom', *Journal of Late Antiquity* 2 (2009): 337–356.

Liangbiao, C., Tao, H., 'Scanning electron microscopic view of parasites worm ova in an ancient corpse', *Acta Academica Sinicae* 3 (1981): 64–5.

Libanius, *Opera*, vol.III, Orationes XXVI-L (Hildesheim: G. Olm, 1963).

Liebeschuetz, W., 'Rubbish disposal in Greek and Roman cities' in X.D. Raventós and J-A. Remolà (eds), *Sordes Urbis: La Elimanación de Residuos en la Ciudad Romana* (Roma: L'Erma di Bretschneider, 2000), pp. 51–61.

Lima, V.S., Iñiguez, A.M., Otsuki, K., Ferreira, L.F., Araújo, A., Vicente, A.C.P., Jansen, A.M., 'Chagas disease by *Trypanosoma cruzi* lineage I in a hunter-gatherer ancient population in Brazil', *Emerging Infectious Diseases* 14 (2008): 1001–2.

Liu, W.-Q., Liu, J., Zhang, J.-H., Long, X.-C., Lei, J.-H., Li, Y.-L., 'Comparison of ancient and modern *Clonorchis sinensis* based on ITS1 and ITS2 sequences', *Acta Tropica* 101 (2007): 91–94.

Livy, *History of Rome*, Books 35–37, trans. E.T. Sage (Cambridge: Loeb, 1997).

Long, H.C., *Plants Poisonous to Livestock* (Cambridge: Cambridge University Press, 1917).

Loreille, O., Bouchet, F., 'Evolution of ascariasis in humans and pigs: a multi-disciplinary approach', *Memórias do Instituto Oswaldo Cruz* 98 (Suppl. 1) (2003): 39–46.

Loreille, O., Roumat, E., Verneau, O., Bouchet, F., Hänni, C., 'Ancient DNA from *Ascaris*: extraction amplification and sequences from eggs collected in coprolites', *International Journal for Parasitology* 31 (2001): 1101–1106.

Lyrintzis, A., Angelakis, A.N., 'Is the "Labyrinth" a water catchment technology? A preliminary approach', in A.N. Angelakis and D. Koutsoyannis (eds), *IWA Specialty Conference: 1st International Symposium on Water and Wastewater Technologies in Ancient Civilizations* (Iraklion: Institute of Iraklion, 2006), pp. 163–174.

MacDonald, C.F., Driessen, J.M., 'The drainage system of the domestic quarter in the palace at Knossos', *Annual of the British School at Athens* 83 (1988): 235–258.

MacDonald C. F., Driessen, J.M., 'The storm drains of the east wing at Knossos', *Bulletin de Correspondance Hellénique*, Suppl. 19 (1990): 141–146.

Magnusson, R., *Water Technology in the Middle Ages: Cities, Monasteries, and Waterworks After the Roman Empire* (Baltimore: Johns Hopkins University Press, 2001).

Manter, H.W., 'Some aspects of the geographical distribution of parasites', *Journal of Parasitology* 53 (1967): 2–9.

Martial, *Epigrams*, 3 vols. trans. D.R. Shackleton Bailey (Cambridge: Loeb, 2002–6).

Martin, H., *Fara: A Reconstruction of the Ancient Mesopotamian City of Shuruppak* (Birmingham: Chris Martin, 1988).

Martinson, E., *Assessing the Etiology of Cribra Orbitalia and Porotic Hyperostosis: A Case Study of the Chiribaya of the Osmore Drainage, Peru* (University of New Mexico: PhD Thesis, 2002).

Martinson, E., Reinhard, K.J., Buikstra, J.E., Cruz, K.D., 'Pathoecology of Chiribaya parasitism', *Memórias do Instituto Oswaldo Cruz* 98 (2003): 195–205.

Matsui, A., Kanehara, M., Kanehara, M., 'Palaeoparasitology in Japan - discovery of toilet features', *Memórias do Instituto Oswaldo Cruz* 98 (Suppl. 1) (2003): 127–136.

Maurizio, A., *Die Geschichte unserer Pflanzennahrung von den Urzeiten bis zur Gegenwart* (Berlin: P. Parey, 1927).

McClary, W.H., 'Notes on some Late Middle Woodland coprolites', in J.E. Fitting (ed.), *The Shulz Site at Green Point: A Stratified Occupation Area in the Saginaw Valley of Michigan*, Anthropology Memoire no. 4 (Ann Arbor, University of Michigan Museum, 1972), pp. 131–6.

McCobb, L.M.E., Briggs, D.E.G., Evershed, R.P., Hall, A.R., Hall, R.A., 'Preservation of fossil seeds from a 10th century AD cess pit at Coppergate, York', *Journal of Archaeological Science* 28 (2001): 929–40.

McCobb, L.M.E., Briggs, D.E.G., Hall, A.R., Kenward, H.K., 'Preservation of invertebrates in 16th century cesspits at St Saviourgate, York', *Archaeometry* 46 (2004): 157–69.

McCown, D., Haines. R., *Nippur I: Temple of Enlil, Scribal Quarter, and Soundings*, Publication 78 (Chicago: Oriental Institute, 1967).

McMahon, A., *Nippur V: The Early Dynastic to Akkadian Transition; The WF Sounding at Nippur*. Publication 129 (Chicago: Oriental Institute, 2006).

McMahon, A., 'Waste management in early urban southern Mesopotamia', in P.D. Mitchell (ed.), *Sanitation, Latrines and Intestinal Parasites in Past Populations* (Farnham: Ashgate, 2014), pp. 19–39.

McMahon, A., Weber, J., Soltysiak, A., 'Late Chalcolithic mass graves at Tell Brak, Syria, and violent conflict during the growth of early city-states', *Journal of Field Archaeology* 36 (2011): 201–220.

McVaugh, M.R., 'Arnald of Villanova's Regimen Almarie (Regimen Castra Sequentium) and medieval military medicine', *Viator* 23 (1992): 201–13.

Medeiros, R.P., 'Povos indígenas do sertão nordestino no período colonial: descobrimento, alianças, resistência e encobrimento', *FUMDHAmentos* 2 (2002): 7–52.

Melhorn, H., *Encyclopedic Reference of Parasitology* (Berlin: Springer, 2001).

Meltzer, D.J., 'Peopling of North America', *Development in Quaternary Science* 1 (2003): 539–63.

Merrifield, R., *London: City of Romans* (London: Batsford, 1983).

Miller, R.L., Armelagos, G.J., Ikram, S., Jonge, D.N., Krijger, F.W., Deelder, A.M., 'Paleoepidemiology of Schistosoma infection in mummies', *British Medical Journal* 304 (1992): 555–556.

Milner, G.R., Boldsen, J.L., 'Estimating age and sex from the skeleton, a paleopathological perspective', in A. Grauer (ed.), *A Companion to Paleopathology*. (Chichester: Wiley-Blackwell, 2012) pp. 268–84.

Mirelman, D., Nuchamowitz, Y., Stoblarsky, T., 'Comparison of use of enzyme-linked immunosorbent assay-based kits and PCR amplification of rRNA genes for simultaneous detection of *Entamoeba histolytica* and *E. dispar*', *Journal of Clinical Microbiology* 35 (1997): 2405–2407.

Mitchell, P.D., 'The myth of the spread of leprosy with the crusades', in C. Roberts, K. Manchester, M. Lewis (eds), *The Past and Present of Leprosy* (Oxford: Archaeopress, 2002) pp. 175–81.

Mitchell, P.D., *Medicine in the Crusades: Warfare, Wounds and the Medieval Surgeon* (Cambridge: Cambridge University Press, 2004).

Mitchell, P.D., 'Retrospective diagnosis, and the use of historical texts for investigating disease in the past', *International Journal of Paleopathology* 1 (2011): 81–88.

Mitchell, P.D., 'The spread of disease with the crusades', in B. Nance and E.F. Glaze (eds), *Between Text and Patient: The Medical Enterprise in Medieval and Early Modern Europe* (Florence: Sismel, 2011), pp. 309–330.

Mitchell, P.D., 'The origins of human parasites: exploring the evidence for endoparasitism throughout human evolution', *International Journal of Paleopathology* 3 (2013): 191–98.

Mitchell, P.D., 'Assessing the impact of sanitation upon health in early human populations from hunter-gatherers to ancient civilisations, using theoretical modelling', in P.D. Mitchell (ed.), *Sanitation, Latrines and Intestinal Parasites in Past Populations* (Farnham: Ashgate, 2014), pp. 5–17.

Mitchell, P.D., Anastasiou, E., Syon, D., 'Human intestinal parasites in crusader Acre: evidence for migration with disease in the medieval period', *International Journal of Paleopathology* 1 (2011): 132–137.

Mitchell, P.D., Huntley, J., Sterns, E., 'Bioarchaeological analysis of the 13th century latrines of the crusader hospital of St. John at Acre, Israel', in V. Mallia-Milanes (ed.), *The Military Orders: volume 3. Their History and Heritage* (Aldershot: Ashgate, 2008), p. 213–23.

Mitchell, P.D., Stern, E., 'Parasitic intestinal helminth ova from the latrines of the 13th century crusader hospital of St. John in Acre, Israel', in M. La Verghetta and L. Capasso (eds), *Proceedings of the XIIIth European Meeting of the Paleopathology Association, Chieti, Italy* (Teramo: Edigrafital, 2001), pp. 207–13.

Mitchell, P.D., Stern, E., Tepper, Y., 'Dysentery in the crusader kingdom of Jerusalem: an ELISA analysis of two medieval latrines in the city of Acre (Israel)', *Journal of Archaeological Science* 35 (2008): 1849–53.

Mitchell, P.D., Tepper, Y., 'Intestinal parasitic worm eggs from a crusader period cesspool in the city of Acre (Israel)', *Levant* 39 (2007): 91–5.

Mitchell, P.D., Yeh, H.-Y., Appleby, J., Buckley, R., 'The intestinal parasites of King Richard III', *The Lancet* 382 (2013): 888.

Moore, J.G., Fry, G.F., Englert, E., 'Thorny-headed worm infection in North American prehistoric man', *Science* 163 (1969): 1324–5.

Moore, J.G., Grundmann, A.W., Hall, H.J., Fry, G.F., 'Human fluke infection in Glen Canyon at AD 1250', *American Journal of Physical Anthropology* 41 (1974): 115–7.

Moore, J.G., Krotoskynski, B.K., O'Neill, H.J., 'Fecal odorgrams. A method for partial reconstructions of ancient and modern diets', *Digestive Disease and Sciences* 29 (1984): 907–911.

Moore, P.D., 'Life seen from a medieval latrine', *Nature* 294 (1981): 614.

Montenegro, A., Araújo, A., Eby, M., Ferreira, L.F., Hetherington, R., Weaver, J.A., 'Parasites, paleoclimate, and the peopling of the Americas: Using the hookworm to time the Clovis migration', *Current Anthropology* 47 (2006): 193–200.

Morgan, J.A.T., Dejong, R.J., Kazibwe, F., Mkoji, G.M., Loker, E.S., 'A newly-identified lineage of Schistosoma', *International Journal of Parasitology* 33 (2003): 977–85.

Morgan, J.A.T., Dejong, R.J., Snyder, S.D., Mkoji, G.M., Loker, E.S, 'Schistosoma mansoni and Biomphalaria: past history and future trends', *Parasitology* 123 (2001): 211–28.

Morrison, S.S., *Excrement in the Late Middle Ages: Sacred Filth and Chaucer's Fecopoetics* (New York: Palgrave Macmillan, 2008).

Mosso, A., *Escursioni nel Mediterraneo e gli Scavi di Creta* (Milan: Fratelli Treves, 1907).

Mumcuoglu, K.Y., Zias, J., 'Head lice, Pediculus humanus capitis (Anoplura:Pediculidae) from hair combs excavated in Israel and dated from the first century BC to the eighth century AD', *Journal of Medical Entomology* 25 (1988): 545–47.

Mumcuoglu, K.Y., Zias, J., 'Pre-Pottery Neolithic B head lice found in Nahal Hemar Cave and dated 6900–6300 BCE (uncalibrated)', *Atikot* 20 (1991): 167–168.

Mumcuoglu, K.Y., Zias, J., Tarshis, M., Lavi, M., Stiebe, G.D., 'Body louse remains in textiles excavated at Masada, Israel', *Journal of Medical Entomology* 40 (2003): 585–87

Murray, H., *Where to go in York: The History of the Public Conveniences in the City of York* (York: Voyager, 2000).

Myriantheos, M. (1987) 'The bastion at the SE side of the Sinai monastery wall', in *Proceedings of the 7th Symposium of Byzantine Archaeology and Art* (Athens: XAE, 1987), p. 55 (in Greek).

Nansen, P., Jorgensen, R.J., 'Fund af parasitæg i arkæologisk materiale fra det vikingetidige Ribe', *Nordisk Veterinaer Medicin* 29 (1977): 263–66.

Needham, S., Spence, T., 'Refuse and the formation of middens', *Antiquity* 71 (1997): 77–90.

Neudecker, R., *Die Pracht der Latrine: zum Wandel Öffentlicher Bedürfnisanstalten in der Kaiserzeitlichen Stadt München* (Munich: Pfeil, 1994).

Neves, W.A., Hubbe, M., Pilo, L.B., 'Early Holocene human skeletal remains from Sumidouro Cave, Lagoa Santa, Brazil: history of discoveries, geological and chronological context, and comparative cranial morphology', *Journal of Human Evolution* 52 (2007): 16–30

Nezamabadi, M., Aali, A., Stöllner, Th., Mashkour, M., Le Bailly, M., 'Paleoparasitological analysis of samples from Chehrabad salt mine (Northwestern Iran)', *International Journal of Paleopathology* 3 (2013): 229–233.

Nimpuno, K., 'Criteria for evaluating excreta disposal techniques', in A. Pacey (ed.), *Sanitation in Developing Countries* (Chichester: Wiley, 1978), pp. 43–48.

Ngui, R., Ishak, S., Chuen, C.S., Mahmud, R., Lim, Y.A., 'Prevalence and risk factors of intestinal parasitism in rural and remote West Malaysia', *PLoS Neglected Tropical Diseases* 5 (2011): e974.

Ngui, R., Lim, Y.A., Chong Kin, L., Sek Chuen, C., Jaffar, S., 'Association between anaemia, iron deficiency anaemia, neglected parasitic infections and socioeconomic factors in rural children of West Malaysia', *PLoS Neglected Tropical Diseases* 6 (2012): e1550.

Norman, G., Pedley, S., Takkouche, B., 'Effects of sewerage on diarrhoea and enteric infections: a systematic review and meta-analysis', *Lancet Infectious Diseases* 10 (2010): 536–44.

Nozais, J.P., 'The origin and dispersion of human parasitic disease in the Old World (Africa, Europe and Madagascar)', *Memórias do Instituto Oswaldo Cruz* 98 (Suppl. 1) (2003): 13–19.

O'Connor, T.P., *Bones from the General Accident Site, Tanner Row*. The Archaeology of York series 15(2) (London: Council for British Archaeology, 1988).

O'Connor, T.P., *Bones from Anglo-Scandinavian levels at 16–22 Coppergate*. The Archaeology of York series 15(3) (London: Council for British Archaeology, 1989).

O'Connor, T.P., *Bones from 46–54 Fishergate*. The Archaeology of York series 15(4) (London: Council for British Archaeology, 1991).

Oh, C.S., Seo, M., Chai, J.Y., Lee, S.J., Kim, M.J., Park, J.B., Shin, D.H., 'Amplification and sequencing of *Trichuris trichiura* ancient DNA extracted from archaeological sediments', *Journal of Archaeological Science* 37 (2010a): 1269–1273.

Oh, C.S., Seo, M., Lim, N.J., Lee, S.J., Lee, E.J., Lee, S.D., Shin, D.H., 'Paleoparasitological report on *Ascaris* aDNA from an ancient East Asian sample', *Memórias do Instituto Oswaldo Cruz* 105 (2010b): 225–228.

Osborne, P.J., 'An insect fauna from a modern cesspit and its comparison with probable cesspit assemblages from archaeological sites', *Journal of Archaeological Science* 10 (1983): 453–63.

Orlandos, A., 'The role of the Roman building located north of the clock of Andronikos Kiristos', *Proceedings of the Athens Academy* (1940): 251–260 (in Greek).

Ortega, Y.R., Bonavia, D., '*Cryptosporidium, Giardia*, and *Cyclospora* in ancient Peruvians', *Journal of Parasitology* 89 (2003): 635–36.

Pääbo, S., Poinar, H., Serre, D., Jaenicke-Després,V., Hebler, J., Rohland, N., Kuch, M., Krause, J., Vigilant, L., Hofreiter, M., 'Genetic analyses from ancient DNA', *Annual Review of Genetics* 38 (2004): 645–79.

Palliser, D.M., 'Epidemics in Tudor York', *Northern History* 8 (1973): 45–63.

Palliser, D.M., 'Civic mentality and the environment in Tudor York', *Northern History* 18 (1982): 78–115.

Palma, R.L., 'Ancient head lice on a wooden comb from Antinoe, Egypt', *Journal of Egyptian Archaeology* 77 (1991): 194.

Palmer, R.R., Colton, J., *A History of the Modern World* (New York: Alfred A. Knopf, 1971).

Palyvou, C., *Akrotiri Thera: an Architecture of Affluence 3500 years old* (Philadelphia: INSTAP, 2005), pp. 41–42, 51–53.

Pasternak, C. (ed.), *What Makes Us Human?* (Oxford: Oneworld, 2007).

Patrucco, R., Tello, R., Bonavia, D., '*Homo sapiens sapiens*', in D. Bonavia (ed.), *Los Gavilanes. Mar, Desierto y Oasis en la Historia del Hombre* (Lima: Corporación Peruana de Desarrollo, S.A. – Instituto Arqueológico Alemán, 1982), pp. 226–232.

Patrucco, R., Tello, R., Bonavia, D., 'Parasitological studies of coprolites of pre-Hispanic Peruvian populations', *Current Anthropology* 24 (1983): 393–94.

Pearce-Duvet, J.M.C., 'The origin of human pathogens: evaluating the role of agriculture and domestic animals in the evolution of human disease', *Biological Reviews* 81 (2006): 369–82.

Petronius, *Petronius: Satyricon and Seneca: Apocolocyntosis*, trans. M. Heseltine and W.H.D. Rouse (Cambridge: Loeb, 2005).

Phuc, P.D., Konradsen, F., Phuong, P.T., Cam, P.D., Dalsgaard, A., 'Practice of using human excreta as fertilizer and implications for health in Nghean Province, Vietnam', *Southeast Asian Journal of Tropical Medicine and Public Health* 37 (2006): 222–9.

Pike, A.W., 'The recovery of parasite eggs from ancient cesspit and latrine deposits: an approach to the study of early parasite infections', in D. Brothwell and A.T. Sandison (eds), *Diseases in Antiquity* (Springfield: C.C. Thomas, 1967), pp. 184–88.

Pike, A.W., 'Recovery of helminth eggs from archaeological excavations, and their possible usefulness in providing evidence for the purpose of an occupation', *Nature* 219 (1968): 303–04.

Pike, A.W., 'Parasite eggs: the organic contents of cesspit soil from Southampton, and their significance for the archaeologist and biologist', in C. Platt and R. Coleman-Smith (eds), *Excavations in Medieval Southampton 1953–1969* (Leicester: Leicester University Press, 1975), pp. 347–48.

Pike, A.W., Biddle, M., 'Parasite eggs in medieval Winchester', *Antiquity* 40 (1966): 293–97.

Pillai, D.R., Keystone, J.S., Sheppard, D.C., MacLean, J.D., MacPherson, D.W., Kain, K.C., '*Entamoeba histolytica* and *Entamoeba dispar*: epidemiology and comparison of diagnostic methods in a setting of nonendemicity', *Clinical Infectious Diseases* 29 (1999): 320–321.

Pizzi, T., Schenone, H., 'Hallazgo de huevos de *Trichuris trichiura* en contenido intestinal de un cuerpo arqueológico incaico' *Boletin Chileno de Parasitologia* 9 (1954): 73–5.

Platon, M., 'New indications for the problems of purgatory cisterns and bathrooms in Minoan World', in *Proceedings of the 6th International Cretologic Congress* (Chania: Literary Association Chrysostomos, 1990), A2:141–155 (in Greek).

Pliny the Elder, *Naturalis Historia*, trans. W.H.S. Jones (Cambridge: Loeb, 1956).

Pliny the Elder, *Histoire Naturelle*, Livre XXXV, trans. R. Bloch (Paris: Les Belles Lettres, 1981).

Pliny the Younger, *The Letters of the Younger Pliny*, trans. B. Radice (London: Heinemann, 1969).

Postgate, J.N., 'Excavations at Abu Salabikh, 1978–79', *Iraq* 42 (1980): 87–104.

Postgate, J.N., 'How many Sumerians per Hectare? Probing the anatomy of an early city', *Cambridge Archaeological Journal* 4 (1994): 47–65.

Preusser, C., *Die Wohnhäuser in Assur*. Gesellschaft 64 (Berlin: Wissenschaftliche Veröffentlichung der Deutschen Orient, 1954).

Prati, J.G., Souza, S.M.M., 'Prehistoric tuberculosis in America: adding comments in a literature review', *Memórias do Instituto Oswaldo Cruz* 98(Suppl. 1) (2003): 151–9.

Pruthi, R.K., *Prehistory and Harappan Civilization* (Delhi: APH, 2004).

Pucciarelli, H.M., González-José, R., Neves, W.A., Sardi, M.L., Rozzi, F.R., 'East-West cranial differentiation in pre-Columbian populations from Central and North America', *Journal of Human Evolution* 54 (2008): 296–30.

Rathbun, T.A., Sexton, J., Michie, J., 'Disease patterns in a formative period South Carolina coastal population', in P. Willey and F.H. Smith (eds), *The Skeletal Biology of Aboriginal Populations in the Southeastern United States* (Knoxville: Tennessee Anthropological Association, 1980), pp. 53–74.

Rawcliffe, C., *Urban Bodies: Communal Health in Late Medieval English Towns and Cities* (Woodbridge: The Boydell Press, 2013).

Reinhard, K.J., *Diet, Parasitism and Anemia in the Prehistoric Southwest* (College Station, Texas A & M University: PhD Thesis, 1988).

Reinhard, K.J., 'Cultural ecology of prehistoric parasitism on the Colorado Plateau as evidenced by coprology', *American Journal of Physical Anthropology* 77 (1988): 355–66.

Reinhard, K.J., 'Archaeoparasitology in North America', *American Journal of Physical Anthropology* 82 (1990): 145–63.

Reinhard, K.J., 'Parasitology as an interpretative tool in archaeology', *American Antiquity* 57 (1992): 231–245.

Reinhard, K.J., 'Effects of parasitism on Ancestral Pueblo maternal and infant health', *American Journal of Physical Anthropology* Suppl. 40 (2004): 179.

Reinhard, K.J., Ambler, J.R., McGuffie, M., 'Diet and parasitism at Dust Devil Cave', *American Antiquity* 50 (1985): 819–824.

Reinhard, K.J., Anderson, G.A.A., Hevly, R.H., 'Helminth remains from prehistoric coprolites on the Colorado Plateau', *Journal of Parasitology* 73 (1987): 630–39.

Reinhard, K., Araújo, A., 'Archaeoparasitology', in D.M. Pearshall (ed.), *Encyclopedia of Archaeology* (New York: Elsevier, 2008), pp. 494–501.

Reinhard, K., Araújo, A., Ferreira, L.F., Coimbra, C.E., 'American hookworm antiquity', *Medical Anthropology* 20 (2001): 96–101.

Reinhard, K., Araújo, A., Sianto, L., Costello, J.G. and Swope, K., 'Chinese liver flukes in latrine sediments from Wong Nim's property, San Bernandino, California: archaeoparasitology of the Caltrans District Headquarters', *Journal of Parasitology* 94 (2008): 300–03.

Reinhard, K.J., Aufderheide, A.C., 'Diphyllobothriasis in prehistoric Chile and Peru: adaptive radiation of a helminth species to native American populations', *Paleopathology Newsletter* 72 (1990): 18–9.

Reinhard, K.J., Barnum, S.V., 'Parasitology as an interpretative tool in archaeology', *American Antiquity* 57 (1991): 231–245.

Reinhard, K.J., Bryant, V.M., 'Pathoecology and the future of coprolite studies', in A.W.M. Stodder (ed.), *Reanalysis and Reinterpretation in Southwestern Bioarchaeology* (Tempe: Arizona State University, 2008), pp. 199–216.

Reinhard, K., Clary, K.H., 'Parasite analysis of prehistoric coprolites from Chaco Canyon', in N.J. Akins (ed.), *A Biocultural Approach to Human Burials from Chaco Canyon, New Mexico* (Santa Fe: National Park Service, 1986), pp. 177–86.

Reinhard, K., Confalonieri, U., Herrmanni, B., Ferreira, L.F., Araújo, A., 'Recovery of parasite remains from coprolites and latrines: aspects of paleoparasitological technique', *Homo* 37 (1986): 217–39

Reinhard, K.J., Geib, P.R., Callahan, M.M., Hevly, R.H., 'Discovery of colon contents in a skeletonized burial: soil sampling for dietary remains', *Journal of Archaeological Science* 19 (1992): 697–705.

Reinhard, K., Hevly, R.H., Anderson, G.A., 'Helminth remains from prehistoric Indian coprolites on the Colorado Plateau', *Journal of Parasitology* 73 (1987): 630–39.

Reinhard, K., Urban, O., 'Diagnosing ancient Diphyllobothriasis from Chinchorro mummies', *Memórias do Instituto Oswaldo Cruz* 98 (2003): 191–3.

Reuther, O., *Die Innenstadt von Babylon (Merkes).* Gesellschaft 47 (Berlin: Wissenschaftliche Veröffentlichung der Deutschen Orient, 1926).

Reyman, T.A., 'Schistosomal cirrhosis in an Egyptian mummy', *Yearbook of Physical Anthropology* 20 (1976): 356–358.

Roberts, C., Manchester, K., *The Archaeology of Disease* (Stroud: Sutton Publishing, 2005).

Robinson, D., *Olynthos VIII (*Baltimore: Johns Hopkins, 1938).

Robinson, O., *Ancient Rome: City Planning and Administration* (London: Routledge, 1992).

Rodda, J.C., Ubertinin, L. (eds), *The Basis of Civilization: Water Science?* (Wallingford: International Association of Hydrological Science, 2004).

Rodríguez-Almedia, E., 'Roma, una città self-cleaning?' in X.D. Raventós and J-A. Remolà (eds), *Sordes Urbis: La Elimanación de Residuos en la Ciudad Romana* (Roma: L'Erma di Bretschneider, 2000), pp. 123–27.

Roever-Bonnet, H., Rijpstra, C., Van Renesse, M.A., Peen, C.H., 'Helminth eggs and gregarines from coprolites from the excavations at Swifterbant', *Helinium* 19 (1979): 7–12.

Rousset, J.J., Heron, C., Metrot, P., 'Human helminthiasis at the Gauls', *Histoire Des Sciences Medicales* 30 (1996): 41–46.

Roy, S., Kabir, M., Mondal, D., Ali, I.K.M., Petri, W.A., Haque, R., 'Real-time-PCR assay for diagnosis of *Entamoeba histolytica* infection', *Journal of Clinical Microbiology* 43 (2005): 2168–2172.

Ruffer, M.A., 'Note on the presence of Bilharzia haematobia in Egyptian mummies of the Twentieth Dynasty', *The British Medical Journal* 1 (1910): 16.

Sabine, E., 'Butchering in mediaeval London', *Speculum* 8 (1933): 335–353.

Sabine, E., 'Latrines and cesspools of mediaeval London' *Speculum* 9 (1934): 303–321.

Sabine, E., 'City cleaning in mediaeval London' *Speculum* 12 (1937): 19–43.

Safar, F., Mustafa, M.-A., Lloyd, S., *Eridu* (Baghdad: State Organization of Antiquities and Heritage, 1981).

Sallares, R., Gomzi, S., 'Biomolecular archaeology of malaria', *Ancient Biomolecules* 3 (2001): 195–213.

Salvato, J.A., *Environmental Sanitation* (New York: Wiley, 1958).

Salvato, J.A., *Environmental Engineering and Sanitation* (New York: Wiley, 1982).

Samuels, R., 'Parasitological study of long dried fecal samples', *American Antiquity* 31 (1965): 175–9.

Santoro, C., Vinton, S.D., Reinhard, K.J., 'Inca expansion and parasitism in the Lluta Valley: preliminary data', *Memórias do Instituto Oswaldo Cruz* 98 (suppl. 1) (2003): 161–3.

Schatzman, P., *Kos (*Berlin: Deutsches Archäologisches Institut, 1932), Tfl 34, pp. 68–69.

Scherrer, P. (ed.), *Ephesus: the New Guide* (Vienna: Ege Yayinlari, 2000), p. 168.

Schiffer, M., *Behavioral Archaeology* (New York: Academic Press, 1976).

Schmidt, G.D., Roberts, L.S., *Foundations of Parasitology*, 7th edn. (New York: McGraw-Hill, 2006).

Scobie, A., 'Slums, sanitation and mortality', *Klio* 68 (1986): 399–433.

Scott, S.P. (ed.), *The Civil Law* (New York: AMS Press, 1973).

Scurlock, J., 'Ancient Mesopotamian house gods', *Journal of Ancient Near Eastern Religions* 3 (2003): 99–106.

Scurlock, J., Andersen, B., *Diagnoses in Assyrian and Babylonian Medicine* (Urbana: University of Illinois, 2005).

Semba, R.D., Kraema, K., Sun, K., de Pee, S., Akhter, N., Moench-Pfanner, R., Rah, J.H., Campbell, A.A., Badham, J., Bloem, M.W., 'Relationship of the presence of a household improved latrine with diarrhea and under-five child mortality in Indonesia', *American Journal of Tropical Medicine and Hygiene* 84 (2011): 443–50.

Seneca, *Epistles 66–92*, trans. R.M. Gummere (Cambridge: Loeb, 2006).

Seo, M., Guk, S.M., Kim, J.L., Chai, J.Y., Bok, G.D., Park, S.S., Oh, C.S., Kim, M.J., Yi, Y.S., Shin, M.H., Kang, I.U., Shin, D.H., 'Paleoparasitological report on the stool from a medieval child mummy in Yangju, Korea', *Journal of Parasitology* 93 (2007): 589–592.

Seo, M., Oh, C.S., Chai, J.Y., Lee, S.J., Park, J.B., Lee, B.H., Park, J.H., Cho, G.H., Hong, D.W., Park, H.U., Shin, D.H., 'The influence of differential burial preservation on the recovery of parasite eggs in soil samples from Korean medieval tombs', *Journal of Parasitology* 96 (2010): 366–370.

Seo, M., Shin, D.H., 'Parasitism, cesspits and sanitation in East Asian countries prior to modernisation', in P.D. Mitchell (ed.), *Sanitation, Latrines and Intestinal Parasites in Past Populations* (Farnham: Ashgate, 2014), pp. 149–64.

Seo, M., Shin, D.H., Guk, S.M., Oh, C.S., Lee, E.J., Shin, M.H., Kim, M.J., Lee, S. D., Kim, Y.S., Yi, Y.S., Spigelman, M., Chai, J.Y. 'Gymnophalloides seoi eggs from the stool of a 17th century female mummy found in Hadong, Republic of Korea', *Journal of Parasitology* 94 (2008): 467–72.

SHA = *Scriptores Historiae Augustae, Scriptores Historiae Augustae, vol. III, trans. D. Magie (Cambridge: Loeb, 1932).*

SHA = *Scriptores Historiae Augustae, The Lives of the Later Caesars*, trans. A. Birley. (Harmondsworth: Penguin, 1976).

Shafer, H.J., Marek, M., Reinhard, K.J., 'Mimbres burial with associated colon remains from the NAN Ranch Ruin, New Mexico', *Journal of Field Archaeology* 16 (1989): 17–30.

Shanks, H., 'The puzzling channels in ancient latrines', *Biblical Archaeology Review* 28 (2002): 49–51.

Shillito, L-M., Bull, I., Matthews, W., Almond, M., Williams, J., Evershed, R., 'Biomolecular and micromorphological analysis of suspected faecal deposits at Neolithic Çatalhöyük, Turkey', *Journal of Archaeological Science* 38 (2011): 1869–1877.

Shillito, L.-M., Matthews, W., Almond, M., Bull, I., 'The microstratigraphy of middens: capturing daily routine in rubbish at Neolithic Çatalhöyük, Turkey', *Antiquity* 85 (2011): 1024–1038.

Shin, D.H., Chai, J.Y., Park, E.A., Lee, W., Lee, H., Lee, J.S., Choi, Y.M., Koh, B.J., Park, J.B., Oh, C.S., Bok, G.D., Kim, W.L., Lee, E., Lee, E.J., Seo, M., 'Finding ancient parasite larvae in a sample from a male living in late 17th century Korea', *Journal of Parasitology* 95 (2009a): 768–771.

Shin, D.H., Lim, D.S., Choi, K.J., Oh, C.S., Kim, M.J., Lee, I.S., Kim, S.B., Shin, J.E., Bok, G.D., Chai, J.Y., Seo, M., 'Scanning electron microscope study of ancient parasite eggs recovered from Korean mummies of the Joseon Dynasty', *Journal of Parasitology* 95 (2009b): 137–145.

Shin, D.H., Oh, S.C., Chung, T., Yi, S.Y., Chai, Y.J., Seo, M., 'Detection of parasite eggs from a moat encircling the royal palace of Silla, the ancient Korean kingdom', *Journal of Archaeological Science* 36 (2009c): 2534–39.

Shuval, H.I., 'Parasitic disease and waste-water irrigation', in A. Pacey (ed.), *Sanitation in Developing Countries* (Chichester: Wiley, 1978), pp. 210–15.

Sianto, L., *'Parasitismo em Populações Pré-Colombianas: Helmintos de Animais em Coprólitos de Origem Humana do Parque Nacional Serra da Capivara, PI, Brasil'* (Escola Nacional de Saúde Pública, Fundação Oswaldo Cruz, Rio de Janeiro: PhD Thesis, 2008).

Sianto, L., Chame, M., Silva, C.S.P., Gonçalves, C.L.M., Reinhard, K., Fugassa, M., Araújo, A., 'Animal helminths in human archaeological remains: a review of zoonoses in the past', *Revista do Instituto de Medicina Tropical de São Paulo* 51 (2009): 119–30.

Sianto, L., Reinhard, K.J., Chame, M., Mendonça, S., Gonçalves, M.L.C., Fernandes, A., Ferreira, L.F., Araújo, A., 'The finding of *Echinostoma* (Trematoda: Digenea) and hookworm eggs in coprolites collected from a Brazilian mummified body dated 600–1,200 years before present', *Journal of Parasitology* 91 (2005): 972–5.

Silva, J.C., Egan, A., Friedman, R., Munro, J.B., Carlton, J.M., Hughes, A.L., 'Genome sequences reveal divergence times of malaria parasite lineages', *Parasitology* 138 (2011): 1737–49.

Silverman, H., Isbell, W.H. (eds), *Handbook of South American Archaeology* (New York: Springer, 2008).

Singh, A., Houpt, E., Petri, W.A., 'Rapid diagnosis of intestinal protozoa, with focus on *Entamoeba histolytica*', *Interdiscipinary Perspectives on Infectious Diseases* (2009): article 547090: 8 pages.

Slaus, M., 'Osteological and dental markers of health in the transition from the Late Antique to the early medieval period in Croatia', *American Journal of Physical Anthropology* 136 (2008): 455–69.

Smith, D., Kenward, H., 'Roman grain pests in Britain: implications for grain supply and agricultural production', *Britannia* 42 (2011): 243–62.

Smith. M., 'The archaeology of South Asian cities', *Journal of Archaeological Research* 14 (2006): 97–142.

Snyder, S., Loker, E.S., 'Evolutionary relationships among the Schistosomatidae (Platyhelminthes: Digenea) and an Asian origin for Schistosoma', *Journal of Parasitology* 86 (2000): 283–88.

Soper, F., 'The report of a nearly pure *Ancylostoma duodenale* infestation in native South American Indians and a discussion of its ethnological significance', *American Journal of Hygiene* 7 (1927): 174–84.

Specht, K.W., 'Eine interessante erdprobe aus einer abortgrube im Römerkastell Künzing', *Saalburg-Jahrbuch* 21 (1963): 90–94.

Sperber, D., *The City in Roman Palestine* (New York: Oxford University Press, 1988).

Sprent, J.F.A., 'Evolutionary aspects of immunity of zooparasitic infections', in G.J. Jackson (ed.), *Immunity to Parasitic Animals* (New York: Appleton, 1969), pp. 3–64.

Stanley, S.L., 'Amoebiasis', *The Lancet* 361 (2003): 1025–1034.

Starr, R., *Nuzi, Report on the Excavations at Yorgan Tepa Near Kirkuk, Iraq* (Cambridge MA: Harvard University Press, 1939).

Steckel, R.H., Rose, J.C., Larsen, C.S., Walker, P.L., 'Skeletal health in the western hemisphere from 4000 B.C. to the present', *Evolutionary Anthropology* 11(4) (2002): 142–55.

Stiger, M.A., *Anasazi Diet: The Coprolite Evidence* (Boulder, University of Colorado: MA Thesis, 1977).

Stone, L., Lurquin, P.F. (eds), *Genes, Culture and Human Evolution: a Synthesis* (Oxford: Blackwell, 2007).

Strommenger, E., *Habuba Kabira, Eine Stadt vor 5000 Jahren* (Mainz: von Zabern, 1980).

Su, T.C., 'A scanning electron microscopic study on the parasite eggs in an ancient corpse from a tomb of Chu Dynasty, the Warring State, in Jiangling County, Hubei Province', *Journal of Tongji Medical University* 7 (1987): 63–64.

Suetonius, *The Twelve Caesars*, trans. R. Graves (London: Penguin, 1989).

Szidat, L., 'Über die erhaltungsfähigkeit von helmintheneiern in vor- und frühgeschichtlichen moorleichen', *Zeitschrift für Parasitenkunde* 13 (1944): 265–74.

Tacitus, *The Annals of Imperial Rome*, trans. M. Grant (London: Penguin, 1989).

Tapp, E., 'Disease and the Manchester mummies – the pathologist's role', in A.R. David and E. Tapp (eds), *Evidence Embalmed: Modern Medicine and the Mummies of Ancient Egypt* (Manchester: Manchester University Press, 1984), pp. 99–101.

Tapp, E., Wildsmith, K., 'The autopsy and endoscopy of the Leeds mummy', in A.R. David and E. Tapp (eds), *The Mummy's Tale: The Scientific and Medical Investigation of Natsef-Amun, Priest in the Temple at Karnack* (London: Michael O'Mara, 1992), pp. 132–153.

Taylor, C., 'The disposal of human waste: a comparison between ancient Rome and medieval London', *Past Imperfect* 11 (2005): 53–72.

Taylor, C., *The Design and Uses of Bath-House Palaestrae Roman North Africa* (University of Alberta: Unpublished PhD Thesis, 2009).

Taylor, C., 'A tale of two cities: the efficacy of ancient and medieval sanitation methods', in P.D. Mitchell (ed.), *Sanitation, Latrines and Intestinal Parasites in Past Populations* (Farnham: Ashgate, 2014), pp. 69–97.

Taylor, J.H., *Egyptian Mummies* (London: British Museum, 2010).

Taylor, T., *The Artificial Ape: How Technology Changed the Course of Human Evolution* (New York: Palgrave Macmillan, 2010).

Tibesky, K., Sidell, J., 'The parasite remains', in G. Malcolm, D. Bowsher and R. Cowie, *Middle Saxon London, Excavations at the Royal Opera House, 1989–99* (London: Museum of London Archaeology Service, 2003), pp. 333–37.

Thiem, V.D., Schmidt, W.P., Suziki, M., Tho, L.H., Yanai, H., Ariyoshi, K., Anh, D.D., Yoshida, L.M., 'Animal livestock and the risk of hospitalised diarrhoea in children under 5 years in Vietnam', *Tropical Medicine and International Health* 17 (2012): 613–21.

Thompson, H., Wycherlay, R., *The Agora of Athens XIV* (Princeton: ASCSA, 1972).

Thureau-Dangin, F., *Til Barsip* (Paris: Geuthner, 1936).

Tobler, A., *Excavations at Tepe Gawra II* (Philadelphia: University Museum, 1950).

Trench R., Hillman, E., *London Under London: a Subterranean Guide* (London: Murray, 1985).

Trümper, M., 'Gender and space, "public" and "private"', in S.L. James and S. Dillon (eds), *A Companion to Women in the Ancient World* (Oxford: Wiley-Blackwell, 2012), pp. 288–303.

Turner, G., 'The state apartments of late Assyrian palaces', *Iraq* 32 (1970): 177–213.

U, K.M., Khin, M., Wai, N.N., Hman, N.W., Myint, T.T., Butler, T., 'Risk factors for the development of persistent diarrhoea and malnutrition in Burmese children', *International Journal of Epidemiology* 21 (1992): 1021–9.

Uga, S., Hoa, N.T., Noda, S., Moji, K., Cong, L., Aoki, Y., Rai, S.K., Fujimaki, Y., 'Parasite egg contamination of vegetables from a suburban market in Hanoi, Vietnam', *Nepal Medical College Journal* 11 (2009): 75–8.

Ur, J., 'CORONA satellite photography and ancient road networks: a northern Mesopotamian case study', *Antiquity* 77 (2003): 102–115.

Van Cleave, H.J. Ross, J.A., 'A method for reclaiming dried zoological specimens', *Science* 105 (1947): 318.

Van Vaerenbergh, J., 'The latrines in and near the Roman baths of Italy: a nice compromise with a bad smell', in G. Wiplinger (ed.), *Cura Aquarum in Ephesos* (Leuven: Peeters, 2006), pp.453–59.

Varisco, D., 'Zibl and Zira'a: coming to terms with manure in Arab agriculture' in R. Jones (ed.), *Manure Matters: Historical, Archaeological and Ethnographic Perspectives* (Ashgate: Farnham, 2012), pp. 129–43.

Varro, *Cato and Varro: On Agriculture*, trans. W.D. Hooper and H.B. Ash (Cambridge: Loeb, 1999).

Varro, *On the Latin Language*, trans. R.G. Kent (Cambridge: Loeb, 1999).

Vatin, C., 'Jardins et services voirie', *Bulletin de Correspondance Hellénique* 100 (1976): 555–64.

Vilaça, A.M.N., 'Relations between funerary cannibalism and warfare cannibalism: the question of predation', *Ethnos* (Stockholm) 65 (2000): 83–106.

Visser, L.G., Verweij, J.J., Van Esbroeck, M., Edeling, W.M., Clerinx, J., Polderman, A.M., 'Diagnostic methods for differentiation of *Entamoeba histolytica* and *Entamoeba dispar* in carriers: performance and clinical implications in a non-endemic setting', *International Journal of Medical Microbiology* 296 (2006): 397–403.

Volkman, S.K., Barry, A.E., Lyons, J.E., Nielsen, K.M., Thomas, M.S., Choi, M., Thakore, S.S., Day, K.P., Wirth, D.F., Hartl, D.L., 'Recent origin of Plasmodium falciparum from a single progenitor', *Science* 293 (2001): 482–84.

Vuorinen, H.S., Juuti, P.S., Katko, T.S., 'History of water and health from ancient civilization to modern times', *Water Science & Technology* 7 (2007): 49–57.

Waldron, T., *Palaeopathology* (Cambridge: Cambridge University Press, 2009).

Walker, P.L., Bathurst, R.R., Richman, R., Gjerdrum, T., Andrushko, V.A., 'The causes of porotic hyperostosis and cribra orbitalia: a reappraisal of the iron-deficiency-anemia hypothesis', *American Journal of Physical Anthropology* 139 (2009): 109–125.

Walton, P., *Textiles, Cordage and Raw Fibre from 16–22 Coppergate.* The Archaeology of York series 17(5) (London: Council for British Archaeology, 1989).

Webb, S.C., Hedges, R.E.M., Robinson, M., 'The seaweed fly *Thoracochaeta zosterae* (Hal.) in inland archaeological contexts: $\partial^{13}C$ and $\partial^{15}N$ solves the problem', *Journal of Archaeological Science* 25 (1998): 1253–57.

Wei, D.X., Yang, W.Y., Huang, S.Q., Lu, Y.F., Su, T.C., Ma, J.H., Hu, W.X., Xie, N.F., 'Parasitological investigation on the ancient corpse of the Western Han Dynasty unearthed from tomb No. 168 on Phoenix Hill in Jiangling County', *Acta Academiae Medicinae Wuhan* 1 (1981): 16–23.

Wei, O., 'Internal organs of a 2100-year-old female corpse', *The Lancet* 302 (1973): 1198.

Weiss, D.L., Moller-Christensen, V., 'Leprosy, echinococcosis and amulets: a study of a medieval Danish inhumation', *Medical History* 15 (1971): 260–67.

Wells, C., Dallas, C., 'Romano-British Pathology', *Antiquity* 50 (1976): 53–55.

Whitwell, J.B., *The Church Street Sewer and an adjacent Building*. The Archaeology of York series 3(1) (London: Council for British Archaeology, 1976).

Wilbur, A.K., Buikstra, J.E., 'Patterns of tuberculosis in the Americas: how can modern biomedicine inform the ancient past?', *Memórias do Instituto Oswaldo Cruz* 101 (Suppl. 2) (2006): 59–66.

Wilke, P.J., Hall, H.J., *Analysis of Ancient Feces: a Discussion and Annotated Bibliography* (Berkeley: University of California, 1975).

Wilkinson, T.J., 'Extensive sherd scatters and land-use intensity: some recent results', *Journal of Field Archaeology* 16 (1989): 31–46.

Wilkinson, T.J., 'Linear hollows in the Jazira, Upper Mesopotamia', *Antiquity* 67 (1993): 548–562.

Wilkinson, T.J., 'The structure and dynamics of dry-farming states in upper Mesopotamia', *Current Anthropology* 35 (1994): 483–520.

Wilson, A., 'Toilets' in G.C.M. Jansen, A.O. Koloski-Ostrow and E.M. Moormann (eds), *Roman Toilets, Their Archaeology and Cultural History* (Leuven: Peeters, 2011), pp.99–105.

Wilson, A., Rackham, D.J., 'Parasite eggs', in P.C. Buckland, *The Environmental Evidence from the Church Street Roman Sewer System*, The Archaeology of York series no.14 (1) (York: York Archaeological Trust, 1976), pp. 32–33.

Witenberg, G., 'Human parasites in archaeological findings', *Bulletin of the Israel Exploration Society* 25 (1961): 86.

Wood, J.W., Milner, G.R., Harpending, H.C., Weiss, K.M., 'The osteological paradox: problems of inferring prehistoric health from skeletal samples', *Current Anthropology* 33 (1992): 343–58.

Woolley, C.L., *The Royal Cemetery, Ur Excavations 2* (London: British Museum, 1934).

Woolley, C.L., *The Early Periods: Ur Excavations 4* (London: British Museum, 1956).

Woolley, C.L., *The Neo-Babylonian and Persian Periods: Ur Excavations 9* (London: British Museum, 1962).

Woolley, C.L., Mallowan, M., *The Old Babylonian Period: Ur Excavations 7* (London: British Museum, 1976).

World Health Organization, WHO, 'Malaria, Fact Sheet', http://www.who.int/mediacentre/factsheets/fs094/en/index.html. [Accessed 1 May 2014].

World Health Organization, WHO, 'The World Health Report', http://www.who.int/whr/2004/en/report04_en.pdf. [Accessed 1 May 2014].

Wright, L., *Clean and Decent: the Fascinating History of the Bathroom and the Water Closet* (London: Routledge and Kegan Paul, 1960).

Wu, Z., Guan, Y., Zhou, Z., 'Study of an ancient corpse of the Warring States period unearthed from Tomb No. 1 at Guo-Jia Gang in Jingmen City (a comprehensive study)', *Journal of Tongji Medical University* 16 (1996): 1–5, 10.

Yang, W.Y., Wei, D.X., Song, G.F., Wu, Z.B., Teng, R.S., 'Parasitologic investigations on the ancient corpse of Chu dynasty the warring states unearthed from the Ma-zhuan tomb No. 1, Jiangling County', *Acta Academiae Medicinae Wuhan* 14 (1984): 43–45.

Yegül, F., *Bathing in the Roman World* (Cambridge: Cambridge University Press, 2010).

Yeh, H.-Y., Pluskowski, A., Kalējs, U., Mitchell, P.D. 'Intestinal parasites in a mid-14th century latrine from Riga, Latvia: fish tapeworm and the consumption of uncooked fish in the medieval eastern Baltic region.' *Journal of Archaeological Science* 49 (1994): 83-89.

Zeigelbauer, K., Speich, B., Mäusezahl, D., Bos, R., Keiser, J., Utzinger, J., 'Effect of sanitation on soil-transmitting helminth infection: systematic review and meta-analysis', *PLoS Medicine* 9 (2012): e1001162.

Zias, J., Tabor, J.D., Harter-Lailheugue, S., 'Toilets at Qumran, the Essenes, and the scrolls, new anthropological data and old theories', *Revue de Qumran* 22 (2006): 631–640.

Zias, J.E., Mumcuoglu, K.Y., 'Case reports on paleopathology: calcified hydatic cysts', *Paleopathology Newsletter* 73 (1991): 7–8.

Zimmerman, M.R., Morilla, R.E., 'Enterobiasis in pre-Columbian America', *Paleopathology Newsletter* 42 (1983): 8.

Zimmerman, M.R., Smith, G.S., 'A probable case of accidental inhumation of 1600 years ago', *Bulletin of the New York Academy of Medicine* 51(1975): 828–837.

Zink, A.R., Grabner, W., Reischl, U., Wolf, H., Nerlich, A.G., 'Molecular study on human tuberculosis in three geographically distinct and time delineated populations from ancient Egypt', *Epidemiology and Infection* 130 (2003): 239–49.

Zink, A., Spigelman, M., Schraut, B., Greenblatt, C.L., Nerlich, A.G., Donoghue, H.D., 'Leishmaniasis in ancient Egypt and upper Nubia', *Emerging Infectious Diseases* 12 (2006): 1616–17.

Zinsser, H., *Rats, Lice and History* (London: MacMillan Press, 1985).

Index